Aho-Girl

\ˈahôˌgərl\ *Japanese, noun.*
A clueless girl.

7 | **Hiroyuki**

AHO-GIRL 7

Ｘ + 🌻 + 🍌 = AHO-GIRL

AHO

CONTENTS

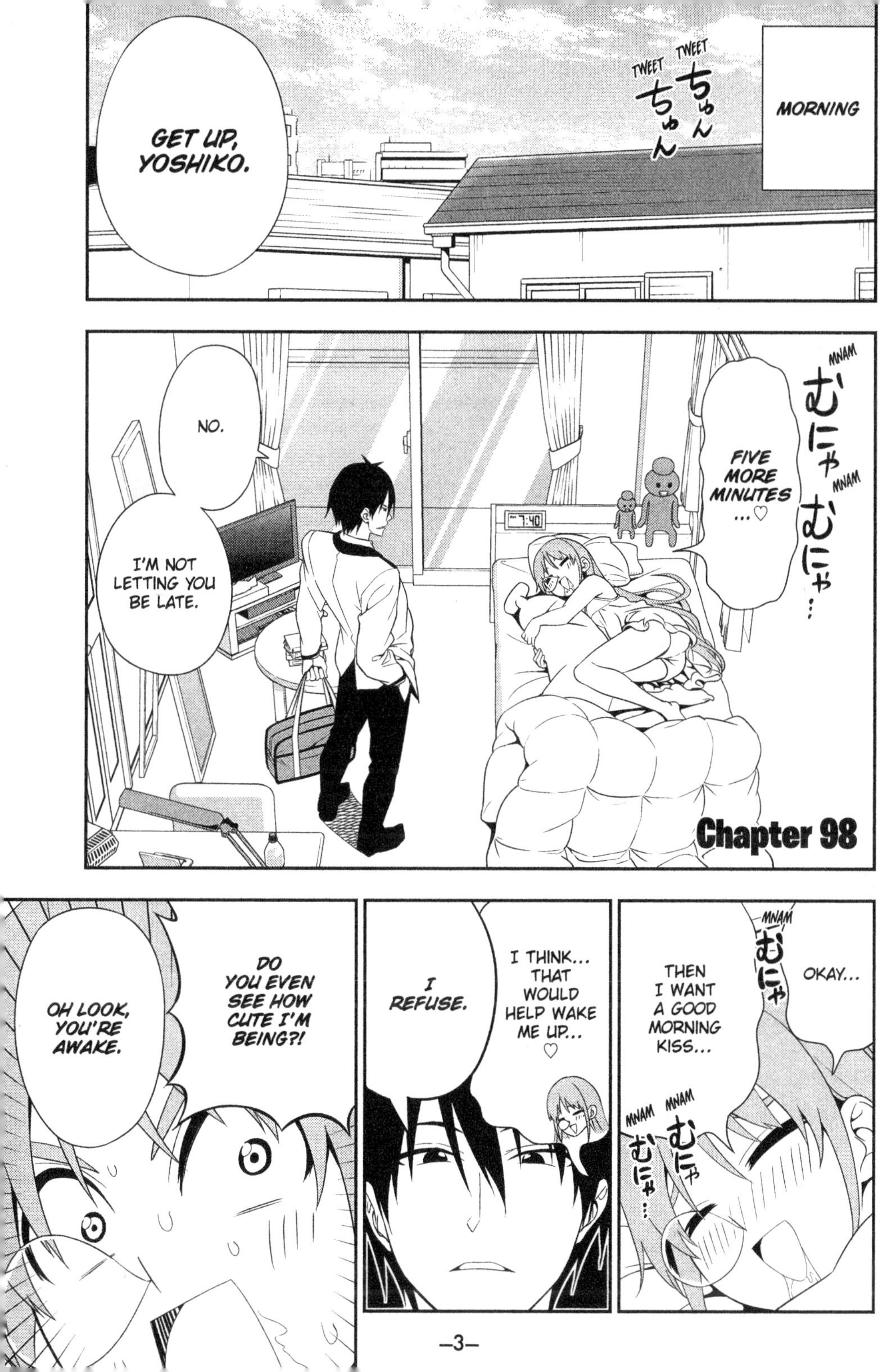
MORNING
ちゅんちゅん
TWEET TWEET
GET UP, YOSHIKO.
むにゃむにゃ…
MNAM MNAM
FIVE MORE MINUTES …♡
NO.
I'M NOT LETTING YOU BE LATE.
Chapter 98
むにゃ
MNAM
OKAY…
THEN I WANT A GOOD MORNING KISS…
むにゃむにゃ…
MNAM MNAM
I THINK… THAT WOULD HELP WAKE ME UP… ♡
I REFUSE.
DO YOU EVEN SEE HOW CUTE I'M BEING?!
OH LOOK, YOU'RE AWAKE.

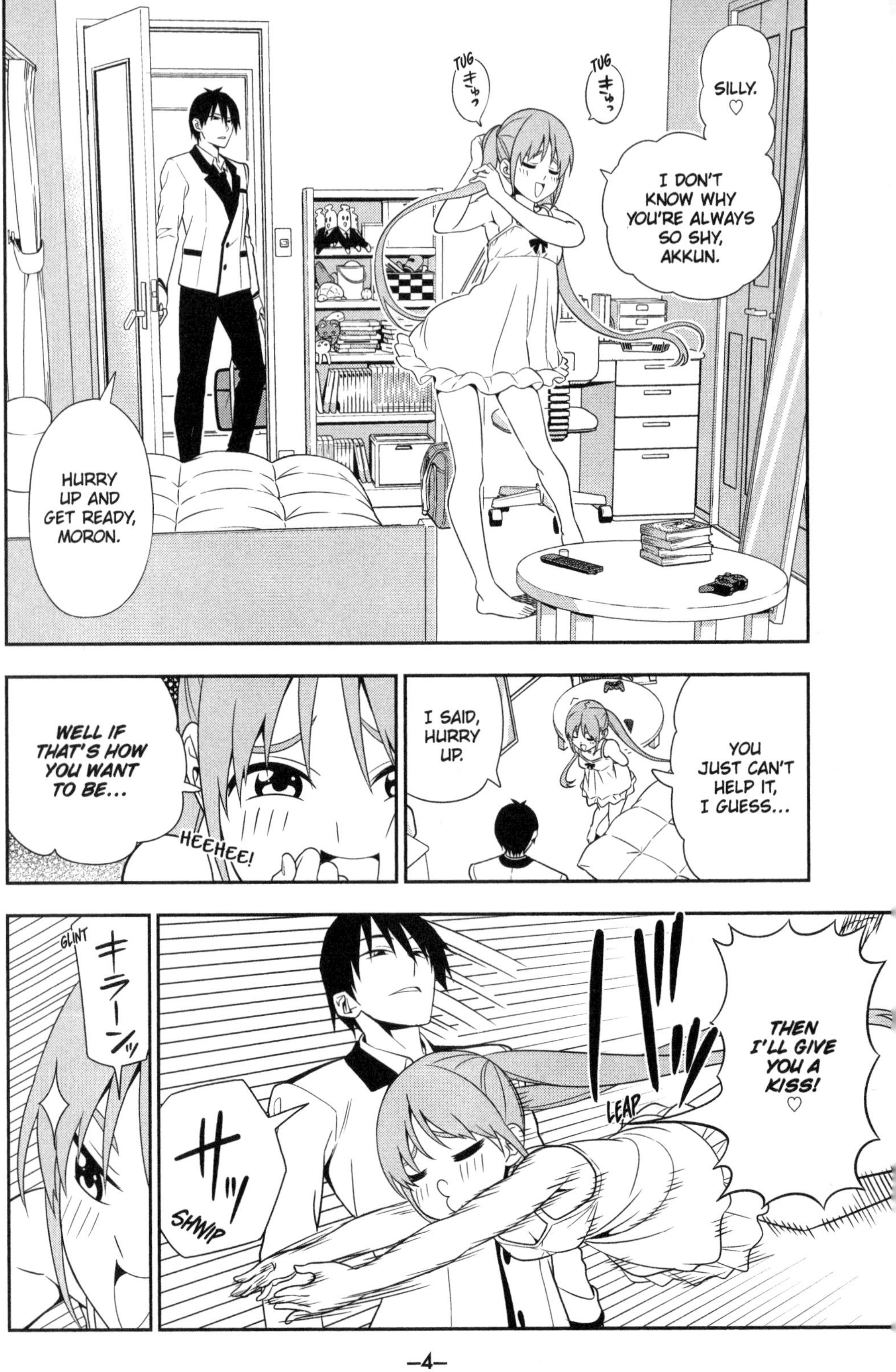

SILLY. ♡
I DON'T KNOW WHY YOU'RE ALWAYS SO SHY, AKKUN.
TUG きゅっ
TUG きゅっ
HURRY UP AND GET READY, MORON.
YOU JUST CAN'T HELP IT, I GUESS...
I SAID, HURRY UP.
WELL IF THAT'S HOW YOU WANT TO BE...
HEEHEE!
THEN I'LL GIVE YOU A KISS! ♡
LEAP
サッ
SHWIP
GLINT
キラーンッ

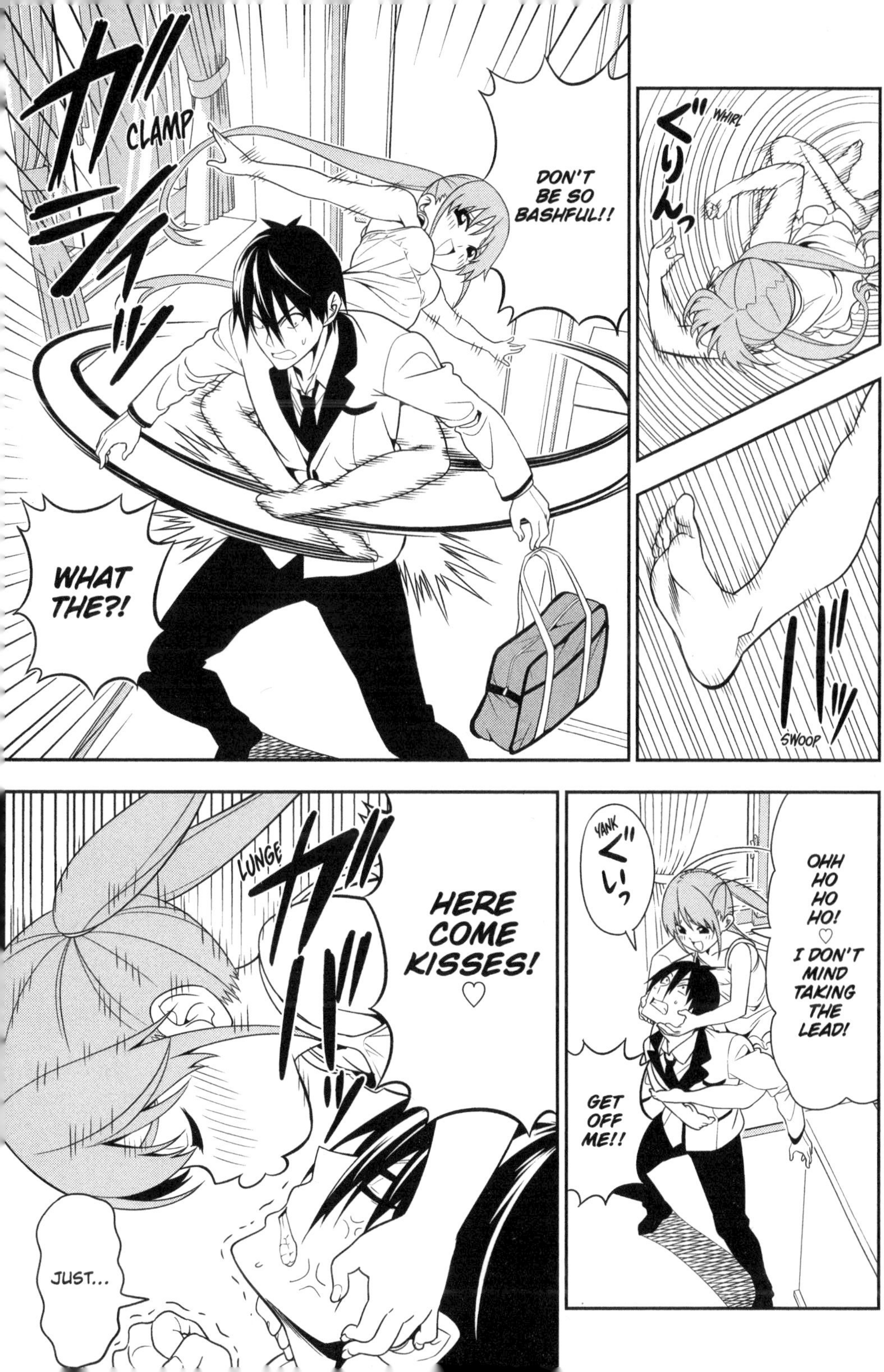
ぐりんっ
WHIRL
バッ
SWOOP
DON'T BE SO BASHFUL!!
ガシィッ
CLAMP
WHAT THE?!
ぐいっ
YANK
OHH HO HO HO! ♡ I DON'T MIND TAKING THE LEAD!
GET OFF ME!!
HERE COME KISSES! ♡
ガバッ
LUNGE
JUST...

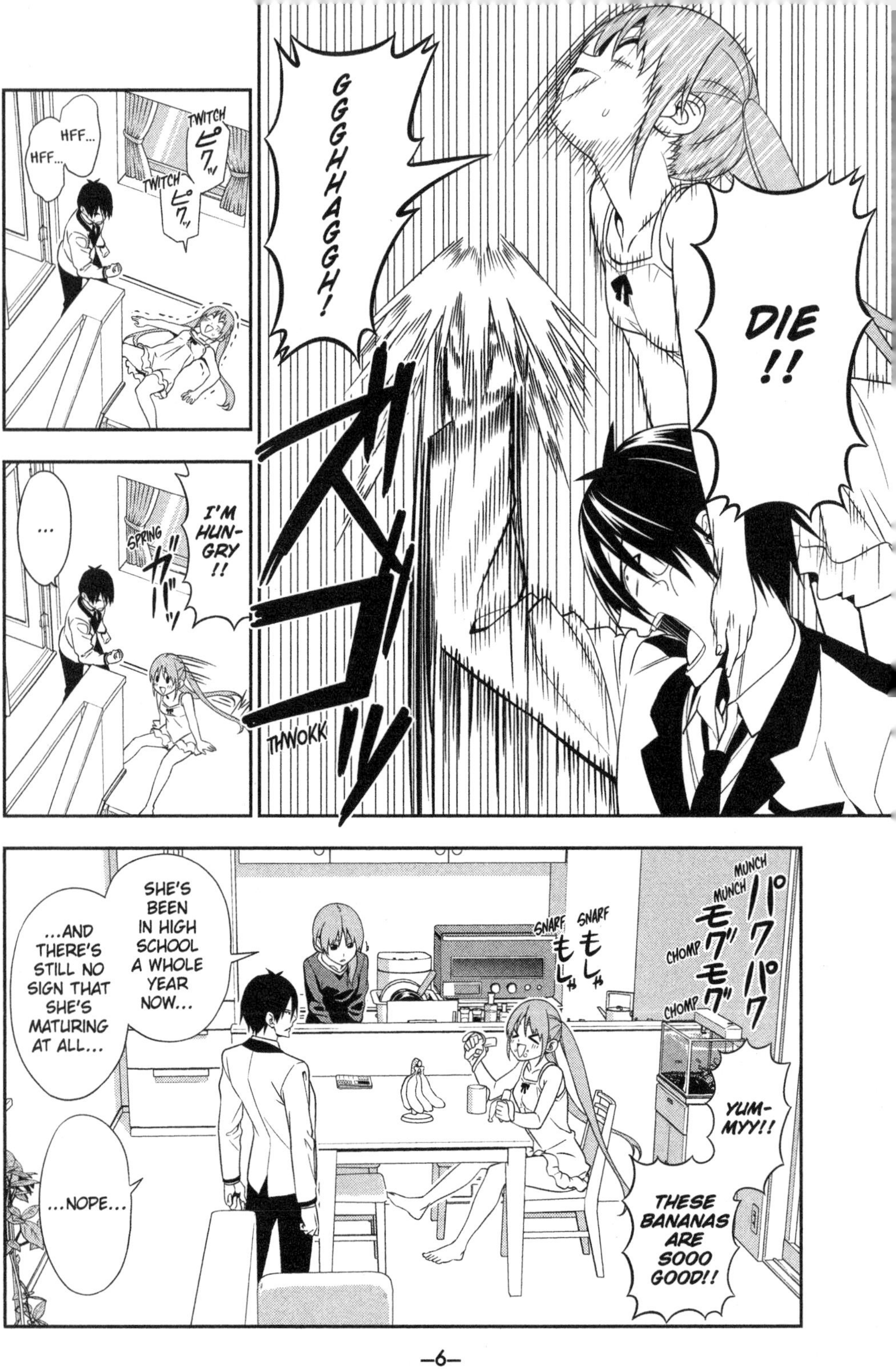
DIE!!
GGGHHAGGGH!
THWOKK
HFF... HFF...
TWITCH ピクッ
TWITCH ピクッ
...
I'M HUN-GRY!!
SPRING ガバッ
MUNCH MUNCH パクパク
CHOMP CHOMP モグモグ
SNARF SNARF もしゃもしゃ
YUM-MYY!!
THESE BANANAS ARE SOOO GOOD!!
SHE'S BEEN IN HIGH SCHOOL A WHOLE YEAR NOW...
...AND THERE'S STILL NO SIGN THAT SHE'S MATURING AT ALL...
...NOPE...

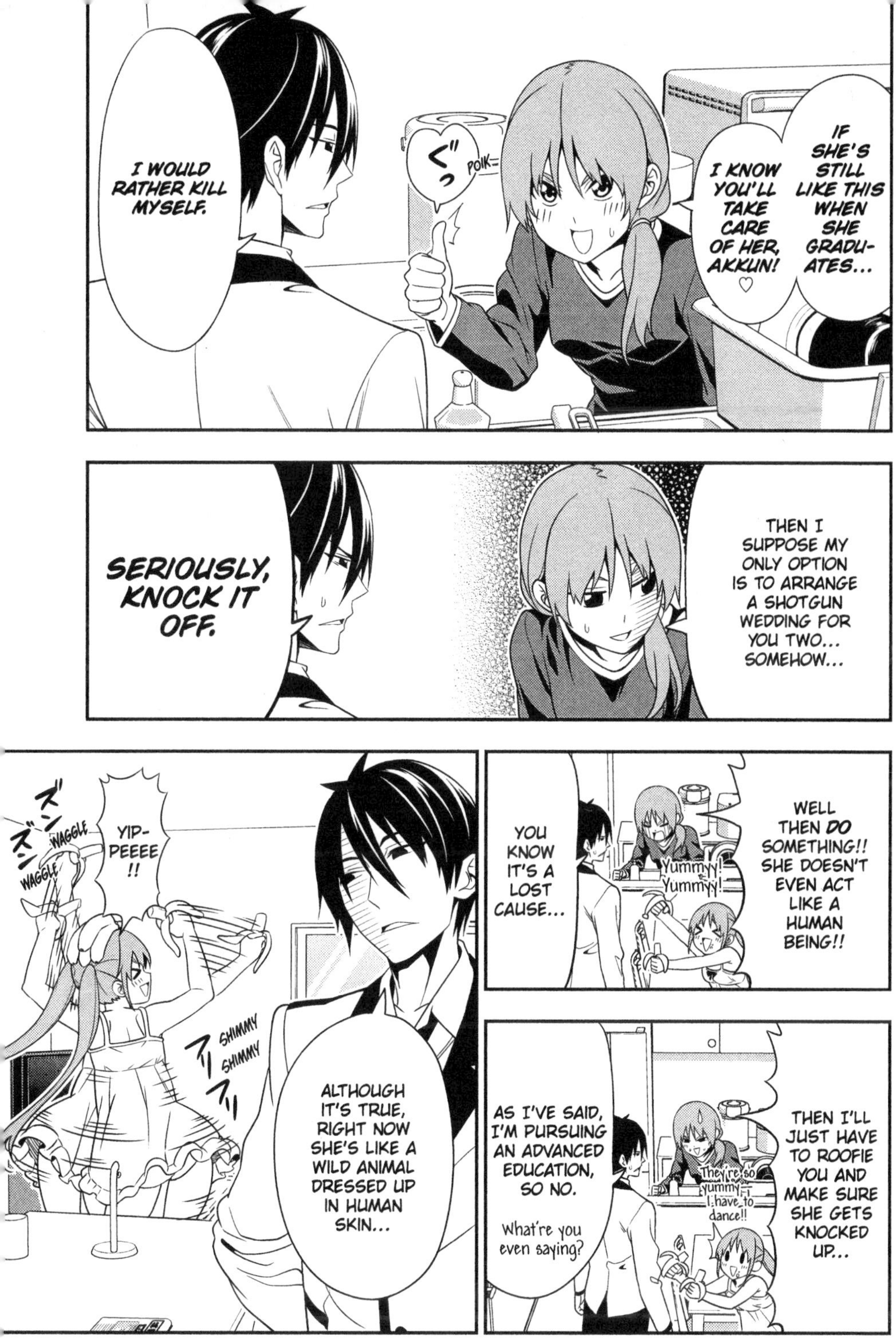
IF SHE'S STILL LIKE THIS WHEN SHE GRADUATES...
I KNOW YOU'LL TAKE CARE OF HER, AKKUN! ♡
ぐっ
POIK
I WOULD RATHER KILL MYSELF.
THEN I SUPPOSE MY ONLY OPTION IS TO ARRANGE A SHOTGUN WEDDING FOR YOU TWO... SOMEHOW...
SERIOUSLY, KNOCK IT OFF.
WELL THEN DO SOMETHING!! SHE DOESN'T EVEN ACT LIKE A HUMAN BEING!!
Yummyy! Yummyy!
YOU KNOW IT'S A LOST CAUSE...
THEN I'LL JUST HAVE TO ROOFIE YOU AND MAKE SURE SHE GETS KNOCKED UP...
They're so yummy I have to dance!!
AS I'VE SAID, I'M PURSUING AN ADVANCED EDUCATION, SO NO.
What're you even saying?
ALTHOUGH IT'S TRUE, RIGHT NOW SHE'S LIKE A WILD ANIMAL DRESSED UP IN HUMAN SKIN...
SHIMMY SHIMMY
YIP-PEEEE!!
WAGGLE WAGGLE
ズンズン

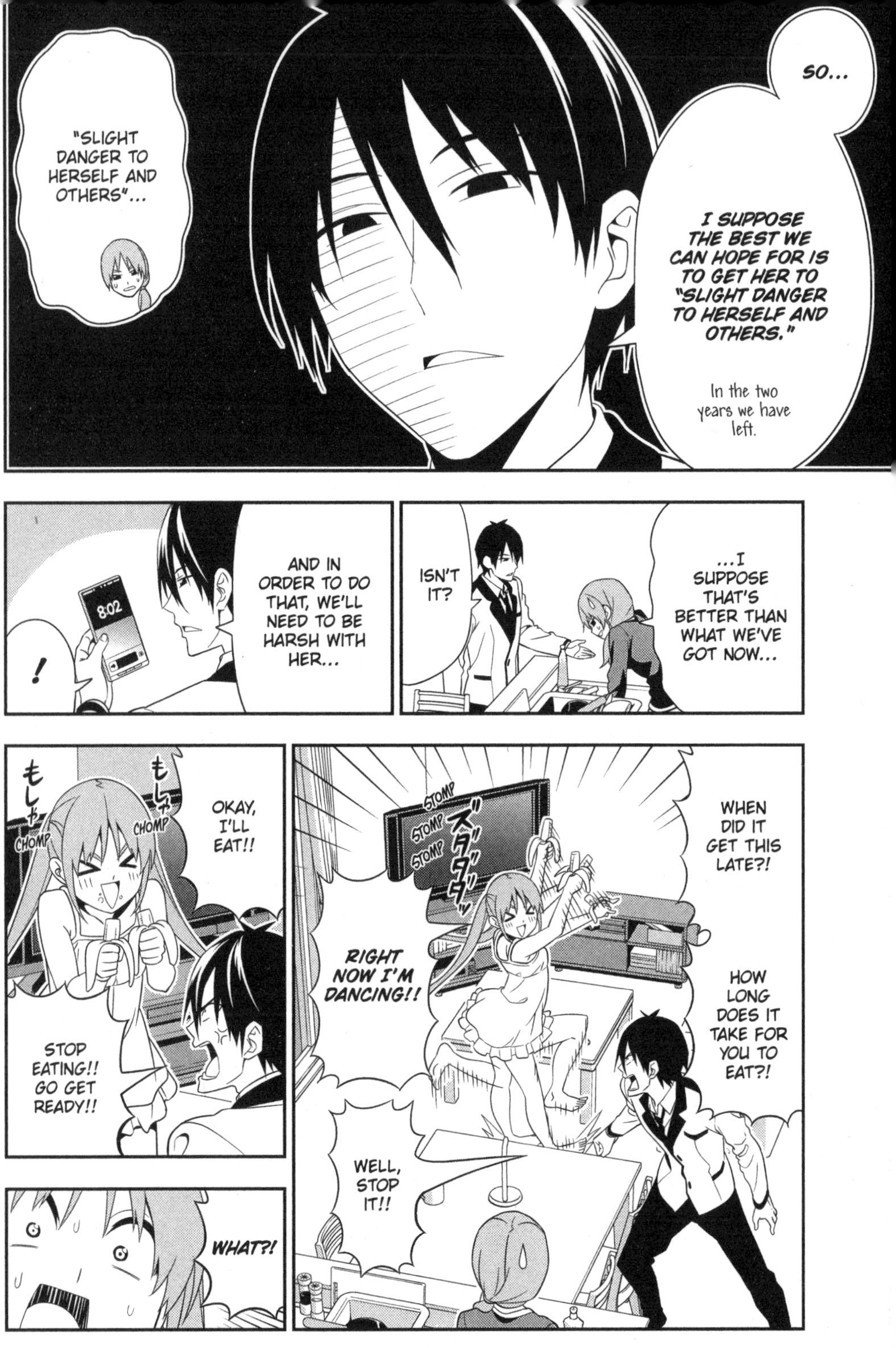
SO...
I SUPPOSE THE BEST WE CAN HOPE FOR IS TO GET HER TO "SLIGHT DANGER TO HERSELF AND OTHERS."
In the two years we have left.
"SLIGHT DANGER TO HERSELF AND OTHERS"...
...I SUPPOSE THAT'S BETTER THAN WHAT WE'VE GOT NOW...
ISN'T IT?
AND IN ORDER TO DO THAT, WE'LL NEED TO BE HARSH WITH HER...
8:02
!
WHEN DID IT GET THIS LATE?!
HOW LONG DOES IT TAKE FOR YOU TO EAT?!
STOMP
STOMP
STOMP
ズダダダッ
RIGHT NOW I'M DANCING!!
WELL, STOP IT!!
もしゃ
CHOMP
もしゃ
CHOMP
OKAY, I'LL EAT!!
STOP EATING!! GO GET READY!!
WHAT?!

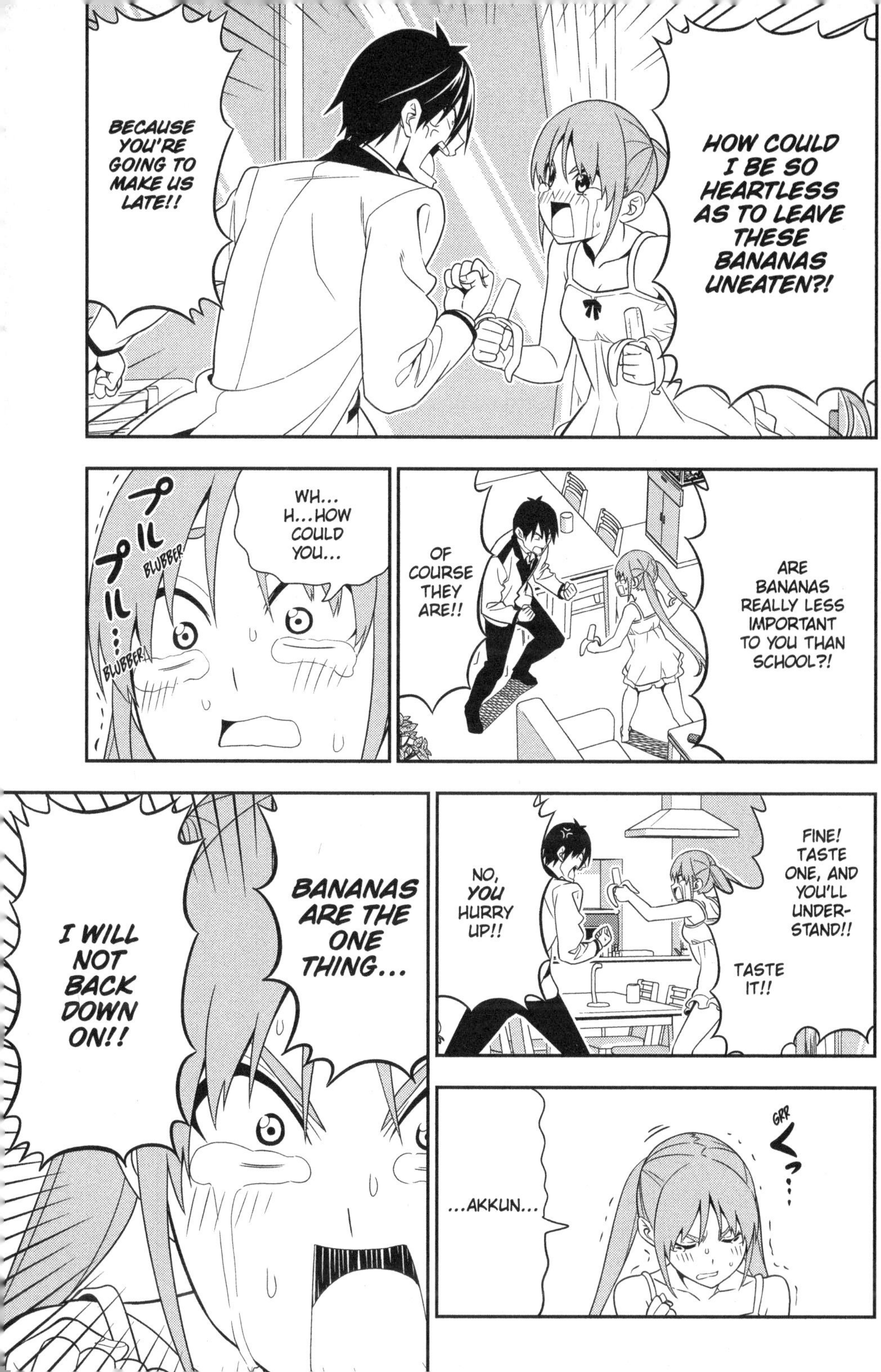
HOW COULD I BE SO HEARTLESS AS TO LEAVE THESE BANANAS UNEATEN?!
BECAUSE YOU'RE GOING TO MAKE US LATE!!
ARE BANANAS REALLY LESS IMPORTANT TO YOU THAN SCHOOL?!
OF COURSE THEY ARE!!
WH... H...HOW COULD YOU...
プルプル…
BLUBBER BLUBBER
FINE! TASTE ONE, AND YOU'LL UNDER-STAND!!
TASTE IT!!
NO, YOU HURRY UP!!
く…
GRR
...AKKUN...
BANANAS ARE THE ONE THING...
I WILL NOT BACK DOWN ON!!

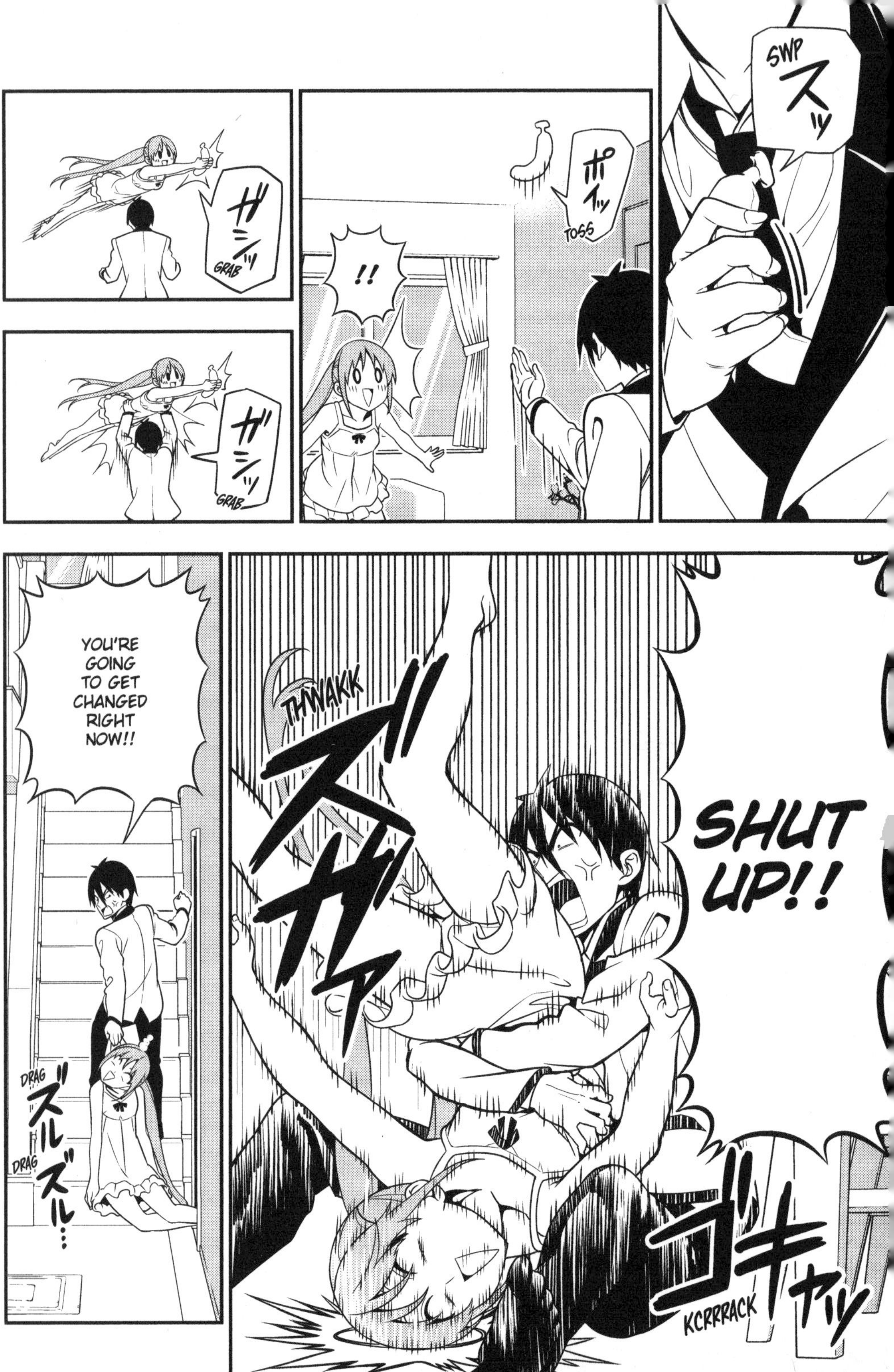
SWP
スッ
ポイッ
TOSS
!!
ガシッ
GRAB
ガシッ
GRAB
THWAKK
ズガァ
SHUT UP!!
ゴキャッ
KCRRACK
YOU'RE GOING TO GET CHANGED RIGHT NOW!!
DRAG
ズルズル…
DRAG

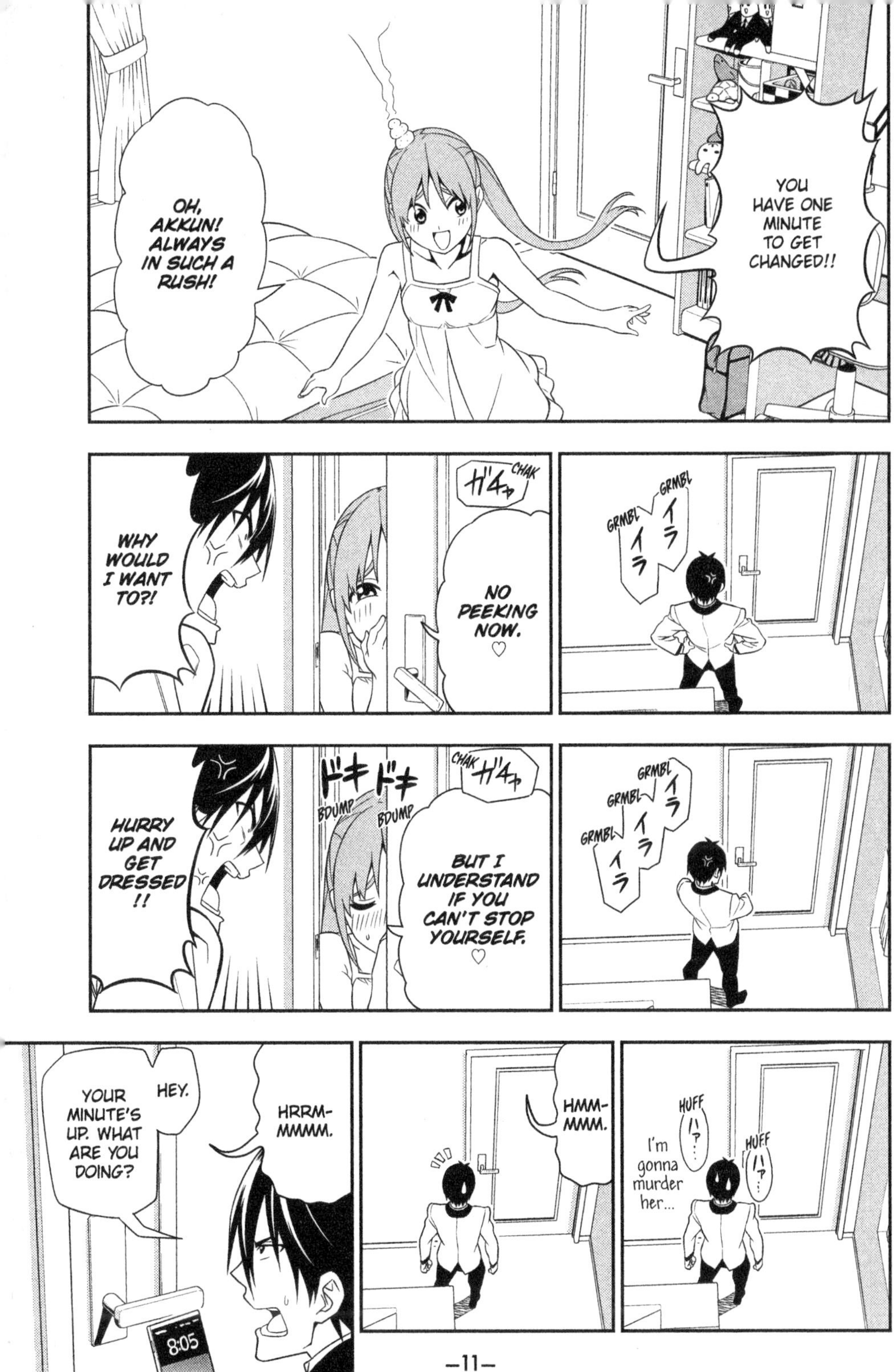
YOU HAVE ONE MINUTE TO GET CHANGED!!
OH, AKKUN! ALWAYS IN SUCH A RUSH!
GRMBL イラ
GRMBL イラ
ガチャ CHAK
NO PEEKING NOW. ♡
WHY WOULD I WANT TO?!
GRMBL イラ
GRMBL イラ
GRMBL イラ
ガチャ CHAK
BUT I UNDERSTAND IF YOU CAN'T STOP YOURSELF. ♡
ドキドキ BDUMP BDUMP
HURRY UP AND GET DRESSED!!
HUFF ハァ…
I'm gonna murder her...
HUFF ハァ…
HMM-MMM.
HRRM-MMMM.
HEY.
YOUR MINUTE'S UP. WHAT ARE YOU DOING?
8:05

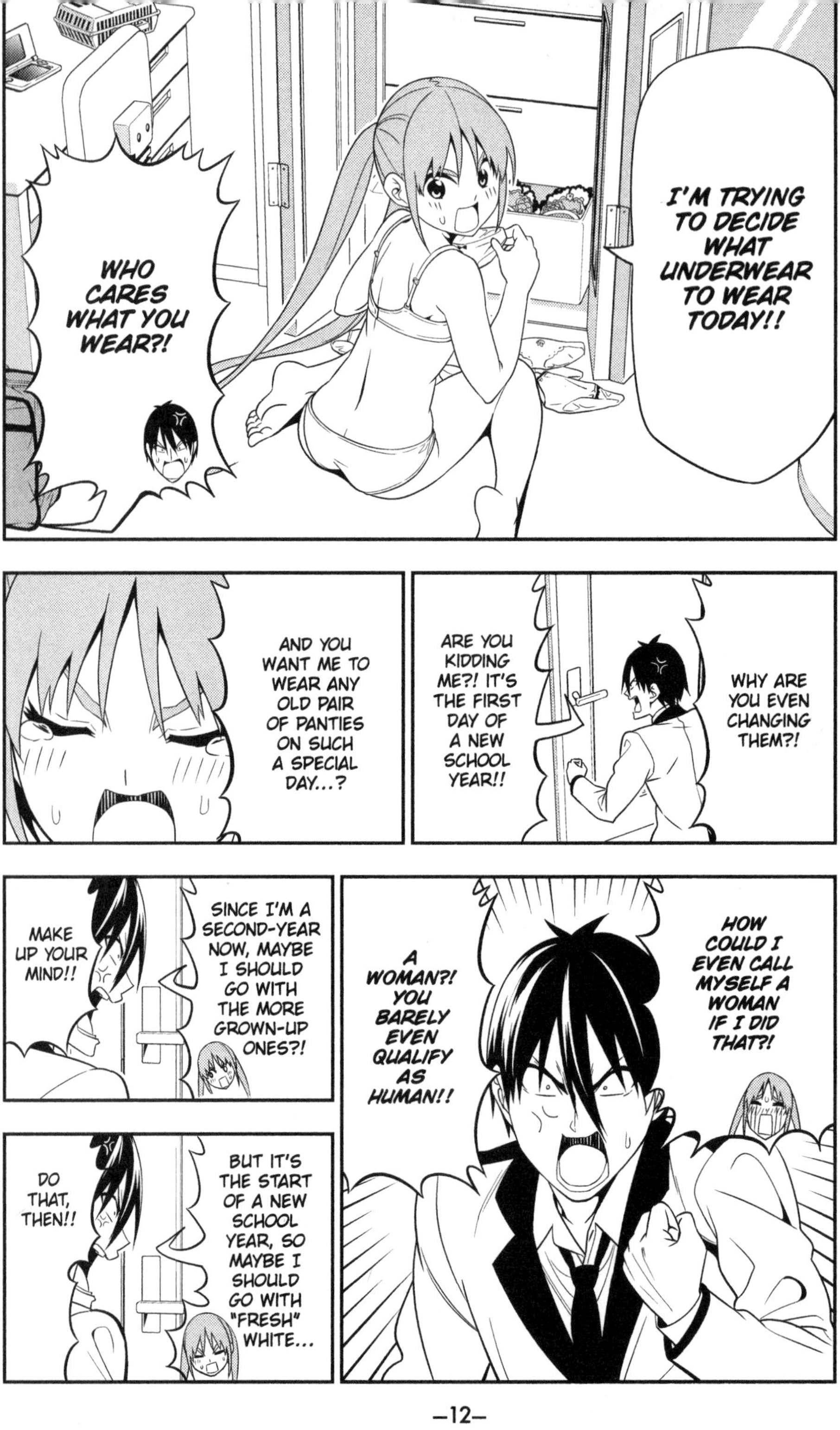
I'M TRYING TO DECIDE WHAT UNDERWEAR TO WEAR TODAY!!
WHO CARES WHAT YOU WEAR?!
WHY ARE YOU EVEN CHANGING THEM?!
ARE YOU KIDDING ME?! IT'S THE FIRST DAY OF A NEW SCHOOL YEAR!!
AND YOU WANT ME TO WEAR ANY OLD PAIR OF PANTIES ON SUCH A SPECIAL DAY...?
HOW COULD I EVEN CALL MYSELF A WOMAN IF I DID THAT?!
A WOMAN?! YOU BARELY EVEN QUALIFY AS HUMAN!!
SINCE I'M A SECOND-YEAR NOW, MAYBE I SHOULD GO WITH THE MORE GROWN-UP ONES?!
MAKE UP YOUR MIND!!
BUT IT'S THE START OF A NEW SCHOOL YEAR, SO MAYBE I SHOULD GO WITH "FRESH" WHITE...
DO THAT, THEN!!

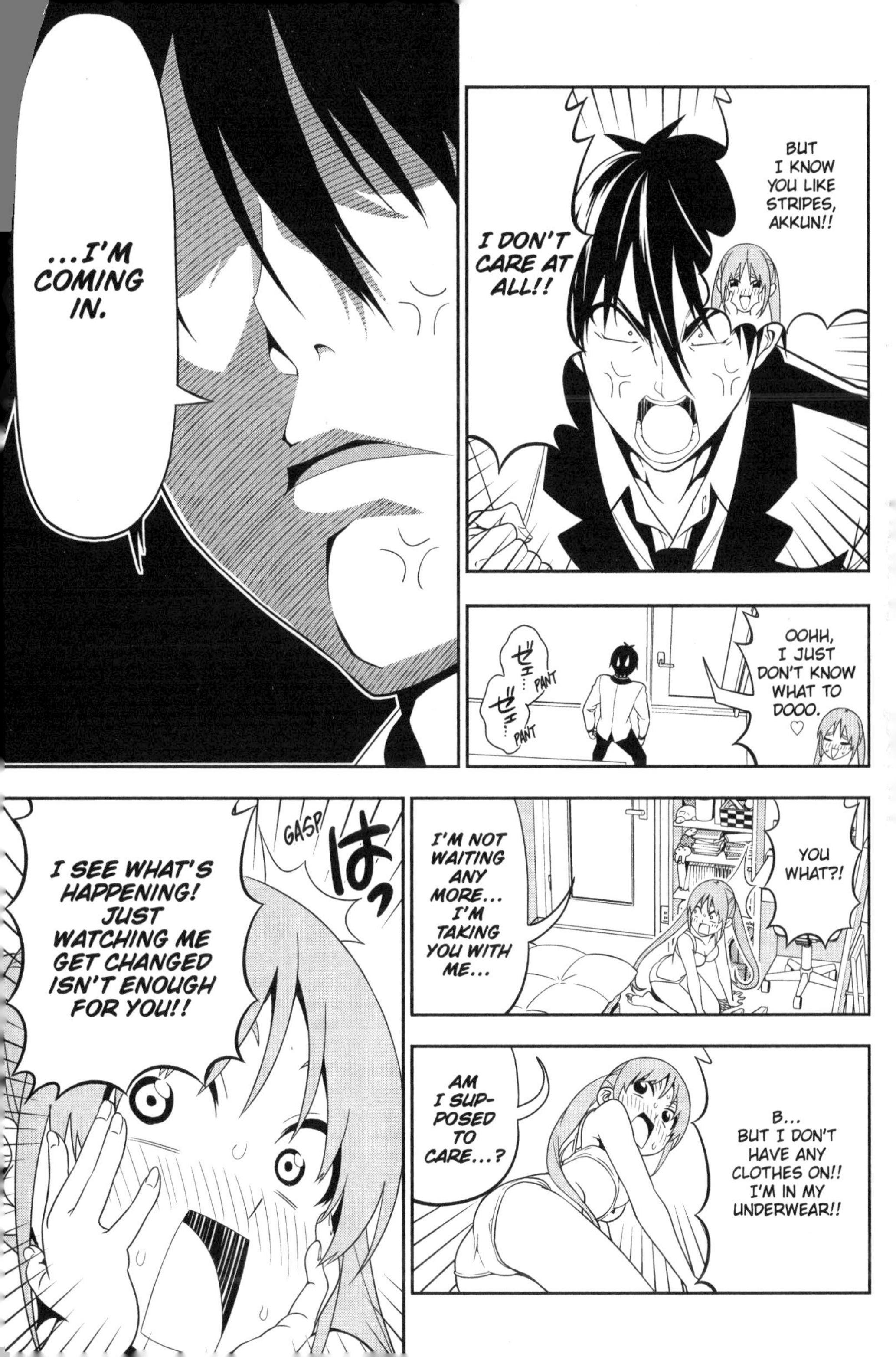
BUT I KNOW YOU LIKE STRIPES, AKKUN!!
I DON'T CARE AT ALL!!
OOHH, I JUST DON'T KNOW WHAT TO DOOO. ♡
ゼェ… PANT
ゼェ… PANT
...I'M COMING IN.
YOU WHAT?!
I'M NOT WAITING ANY MORE... I'M TAKING YOU WITH ME...
B... BUT I DON'T HAVE ANY CLOTHES ON!! I'M IN MY UNDERWEAR!!
AM I SUP-POSED TO CARE...?
はっ GASP
I SEE WHAT'S HAPPENING! JUST WATCHING ME GET CHANGED ISN'T ENOUGH FOR YOU!!

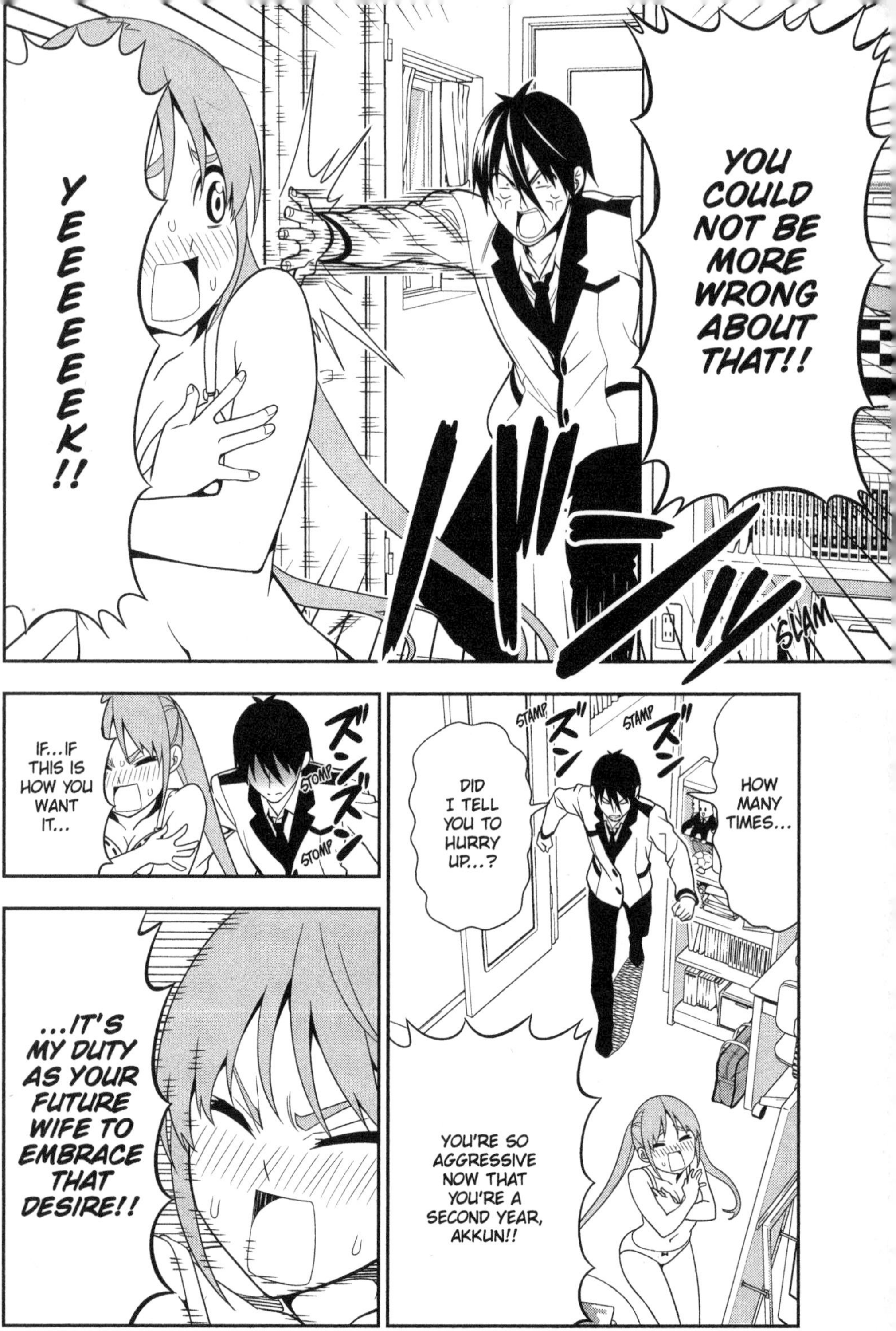

YOU COULD NOT BE MORE WRONG ABOUT THAT!!
SLAM
YEEEEEEK!!
HOW MANY TIMES...
STAMP
ズン
STAMP
ズン
DID I TELL YOU TO HURRY UP...?
YOU'RE SO AGGRESSIVE NOW THAT YOU'RE A SECOND YEAR, AKKUN!!
ズンズン
STOMP
STOMP
IF...IF THIS IS HOW YOU WANT IT...
...IT'S MY DUTY AS YOUR FUTURE WIFE TO EMBRACE THAT DESIRE!!

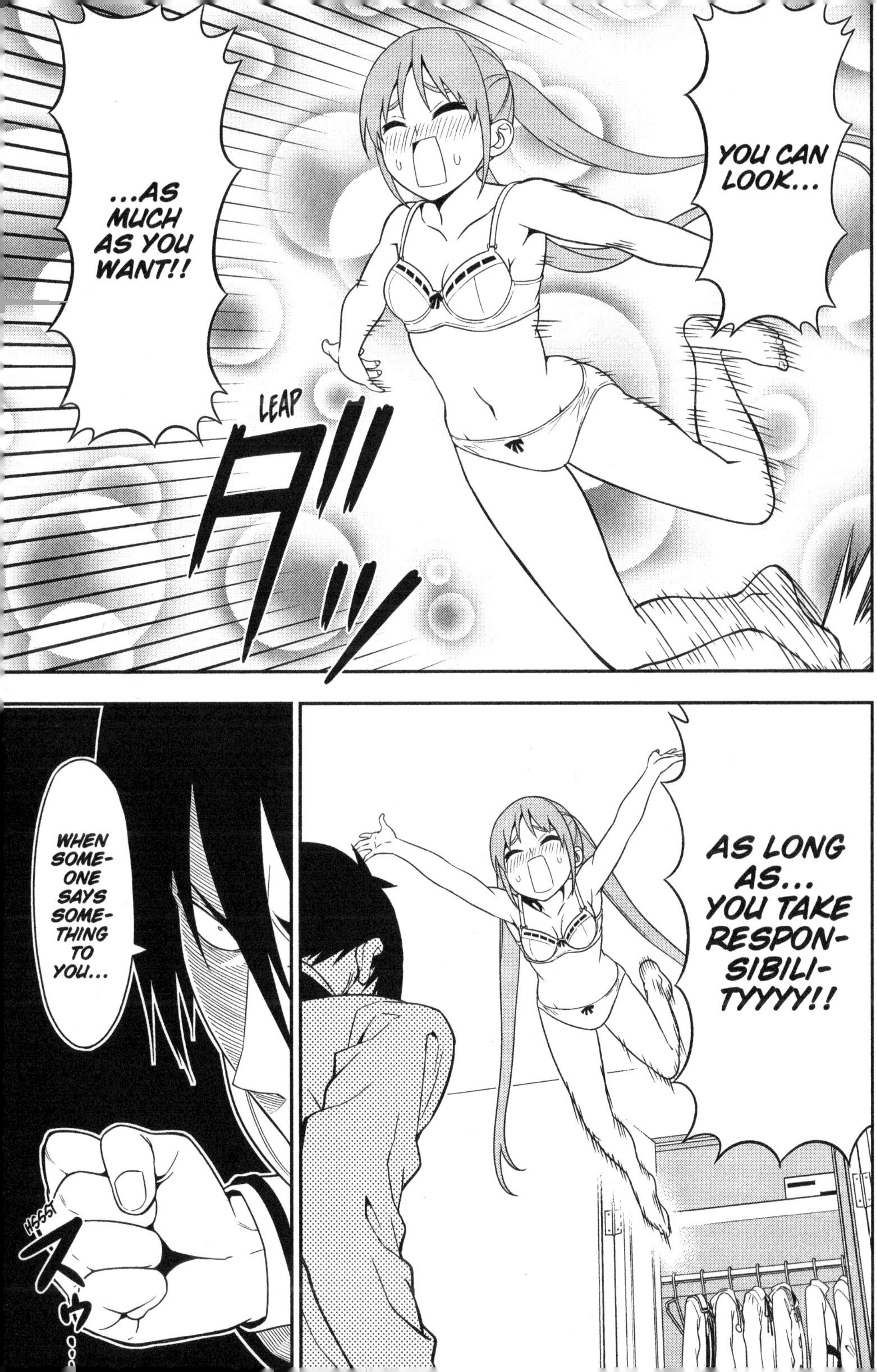
YOU CAN LOOK...
...AS MUCH AS YOU WANT!!
LEAP
AS LONG AS... YOU TAKE RESPON-SIBILI-TYYYY!!
WHEN SOME-ONE SAYS SOME-THING TO YOU...
HSSST

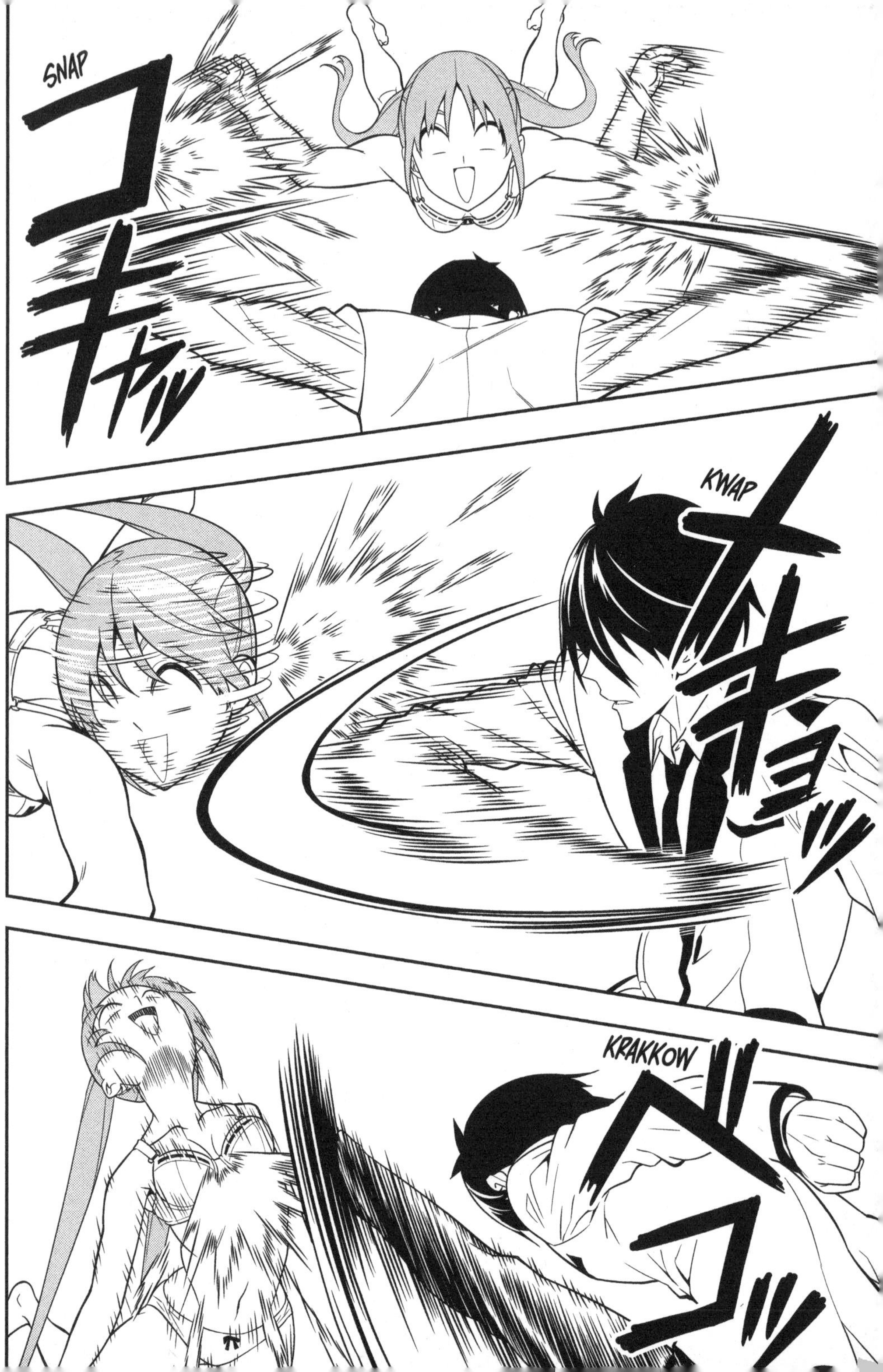
SNAP
コキャッ
KWAP
KRAKKOW

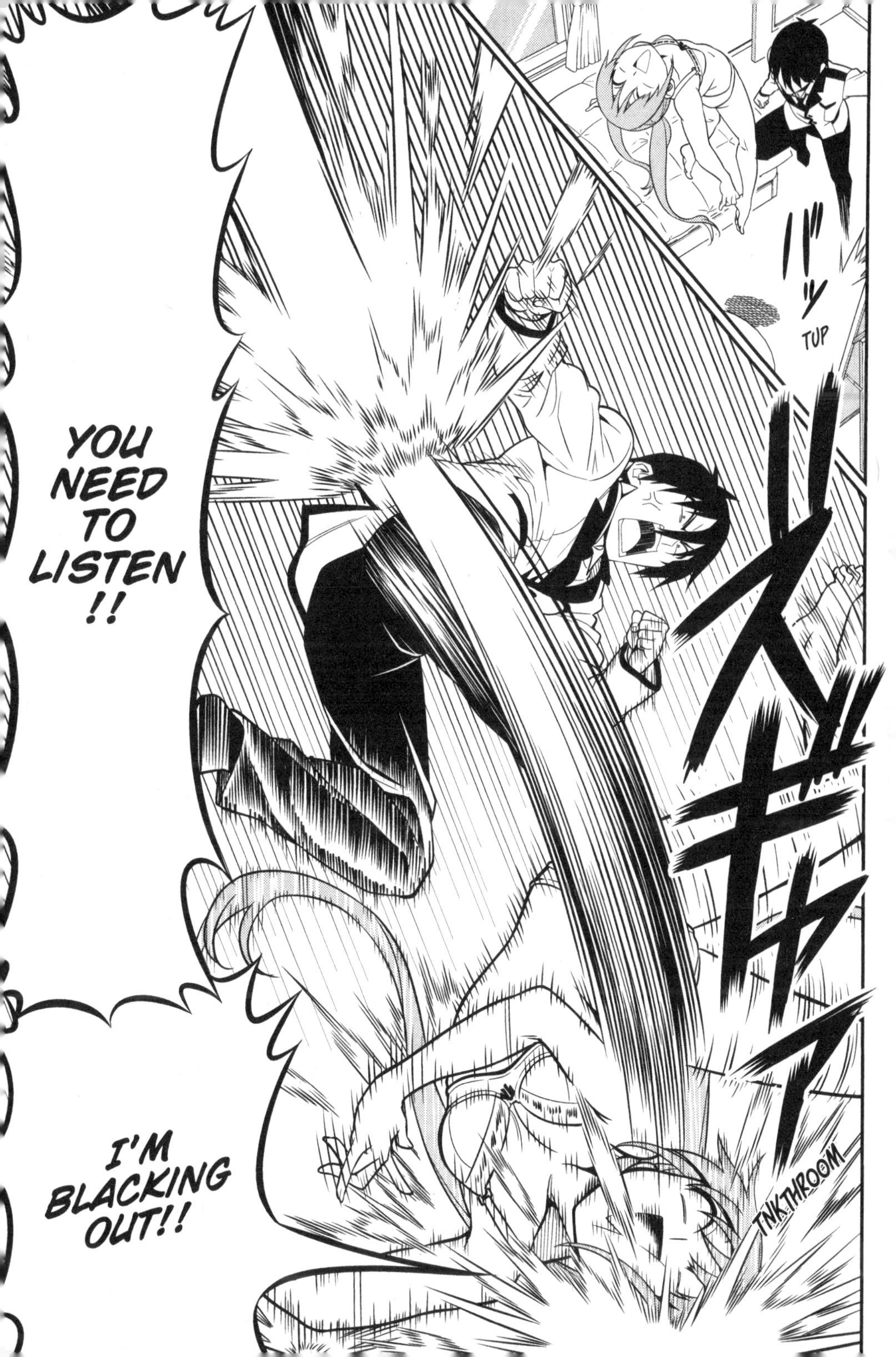
TUP
TNKTHROOM
YOU NEED TO LISTEN!!
I'M BLACKING OUT!!

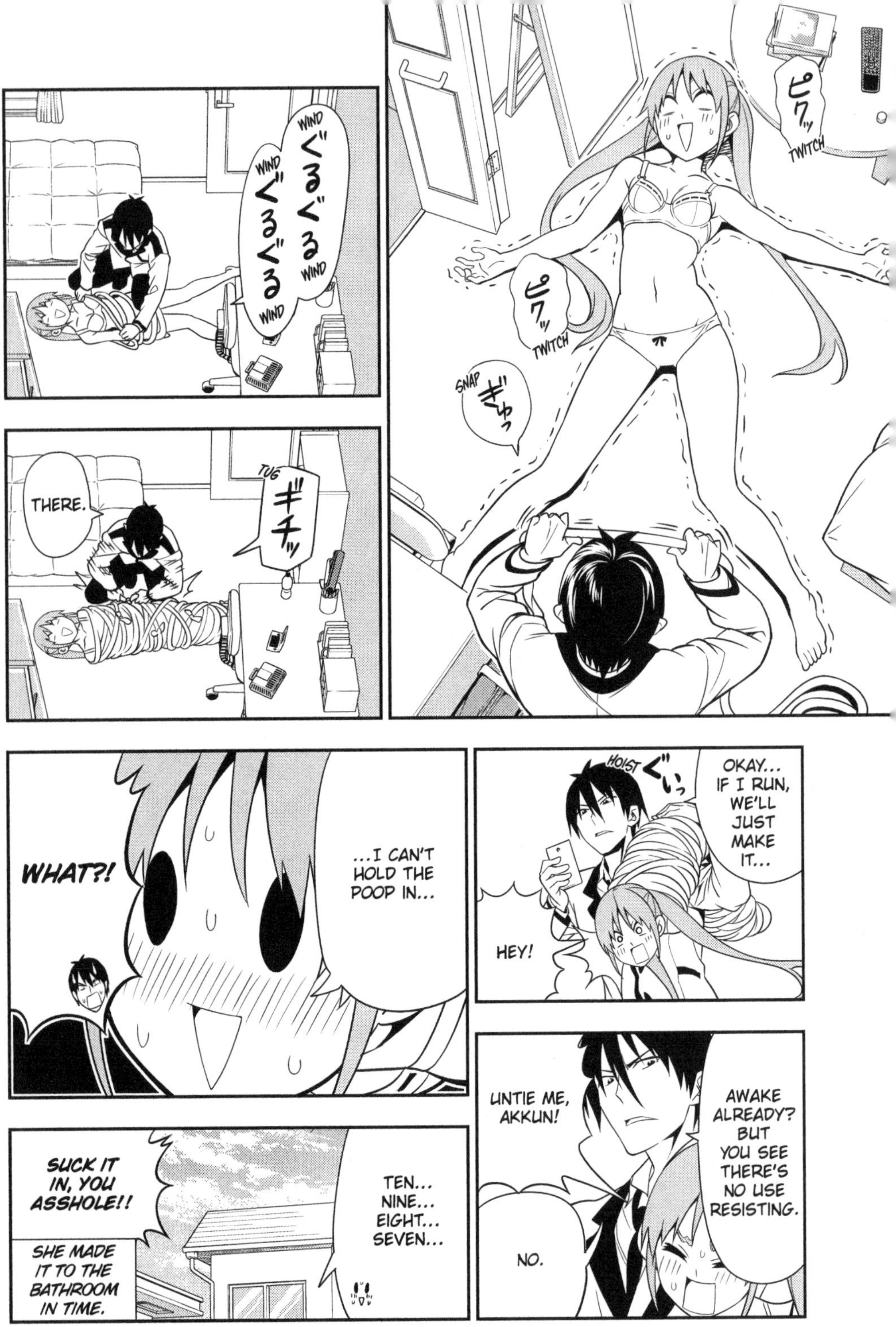
ピクッ TWITCH
ピクッ TWITCH
SNAP ぎゅっ
WIND ぐるぐる WIND
WIND ぐるぐる WIND
TUG ギチッ
THERE.
HOIST ぐいっ
OKAY... IF I RUN, WE'LL JUST MAKE IT...
HEY!
...I CAN'T HOLD THE POOP IN...
WHAT?!
AWAKE ALREADY? BUT YOU SEE THERE'S NO USE RESISTING.
UNTIE ME, AKKUN!
NO.
TEN... NINE... EIGHT... SEVEN...
SUCK IT IN, YOU ASSHOLE!!
SHE MADE IT TO THE BATHROOM IN TIME.

A Maiden's Shame

COME ON!! HURRY UP IN THERE!!
RAGE イラ
RAGE イラ
RAGE イラ
JUST TAKE A SHIT ALREADY!!
I CAN'T BELIEVE YOU WANT TO LISTEN TO ME POOP, AKKUN!!
いや～ん!
NOOOOO!
SHUT UP!!
THEY WERE TARDY.

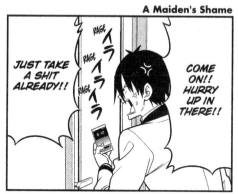

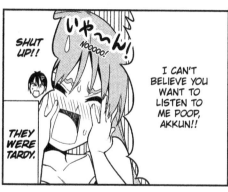

(The battle we refuse to lose is)

Aho-Girl

\'ahô,gərl\ *Japanese, noun*.

A clueless girl.

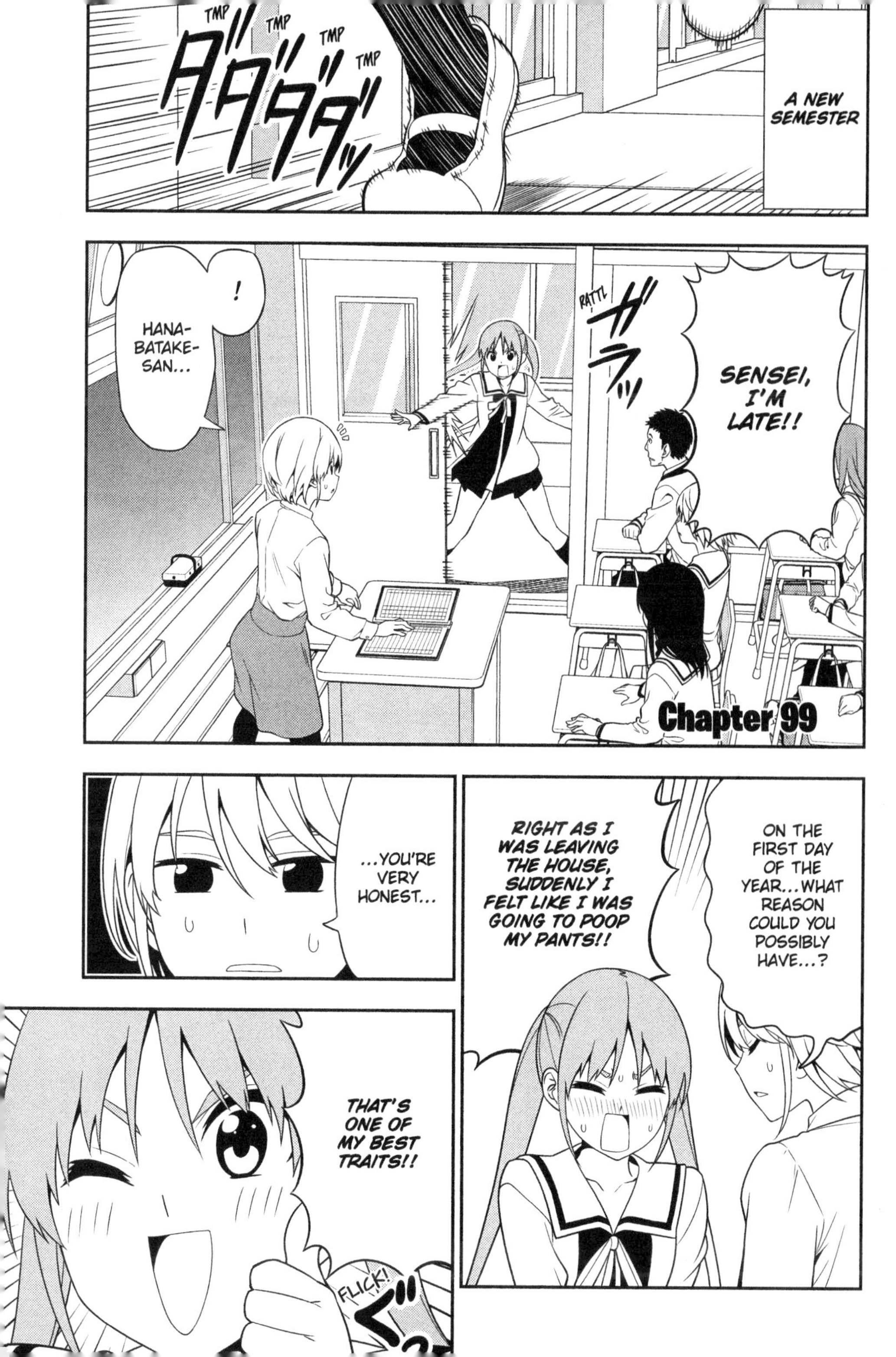
A NEW SEMESTER
TMP TMP TMP TMP
SENSEI, I'M LATE!!
RATTL
!
HANA-BATAKE-SAN...
Chapter 99
ON THE FIRST DAY OF THE YEAR...WHAT REASON COULD YOU POSSIBLY HAVE...?
RIGHT AS I WAS LEAVING THE HOUSE, SUDDENLY I FELT LIKE I WAS GOING TO POOP MY PANTS!!
...YOU'RE VERY HONEST...
THAT'S ONE OF MY BEST TRAITS!!
FLICK!

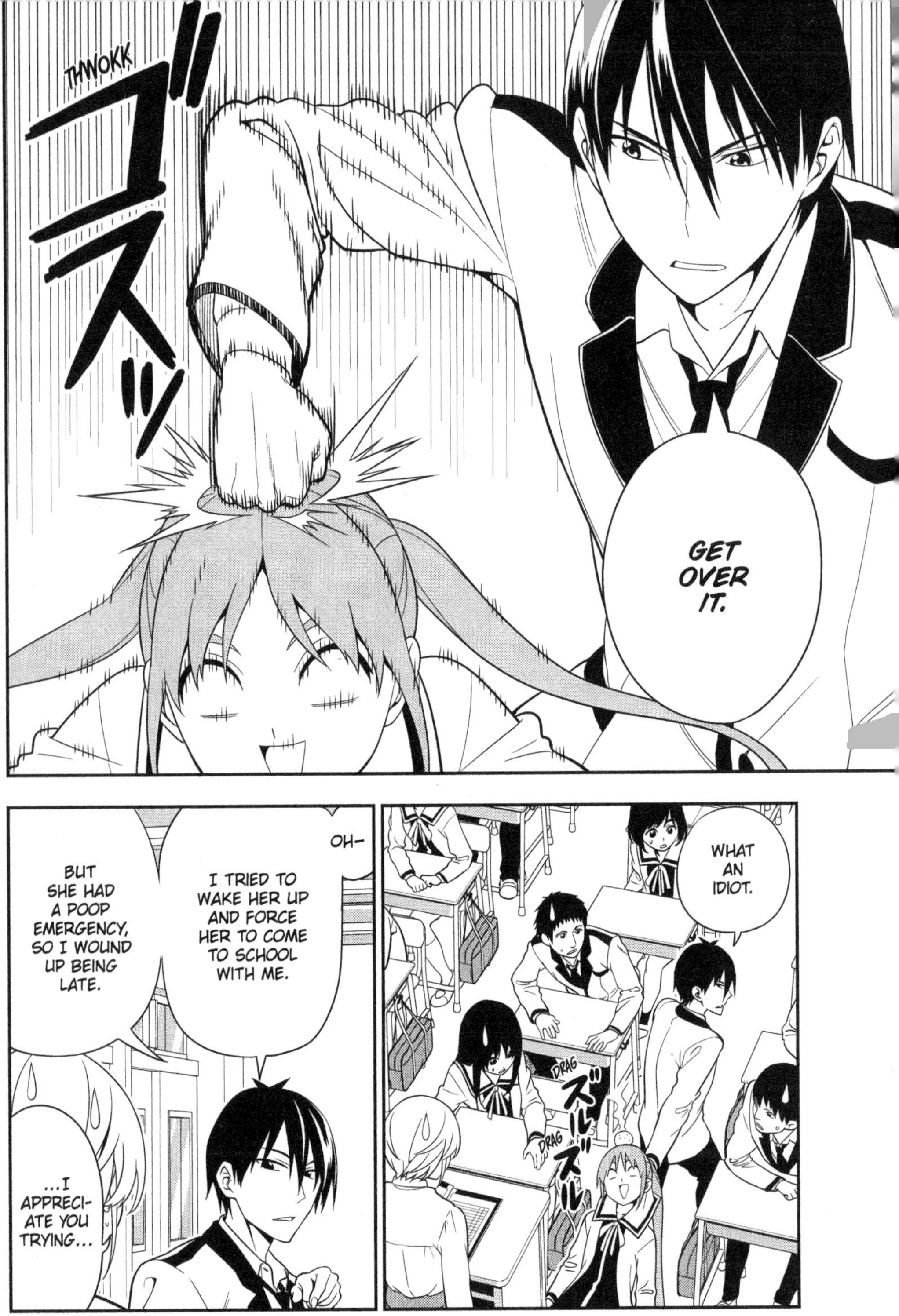
THWOKK
ゴスッ
GET OVER IT.
WHAT AN IDIOT.
DRAG
ズル
DRAG
ズル
OH-
I TRIED TO WAKE HER UP AND FORCE HER TO COME TO SCHOOL WITH ME.
BUT SHE HAD A POOP EMERGENCY, SO I WOUND UP BEING LATE.
...I APPRECI-ATE YOU TRYING...

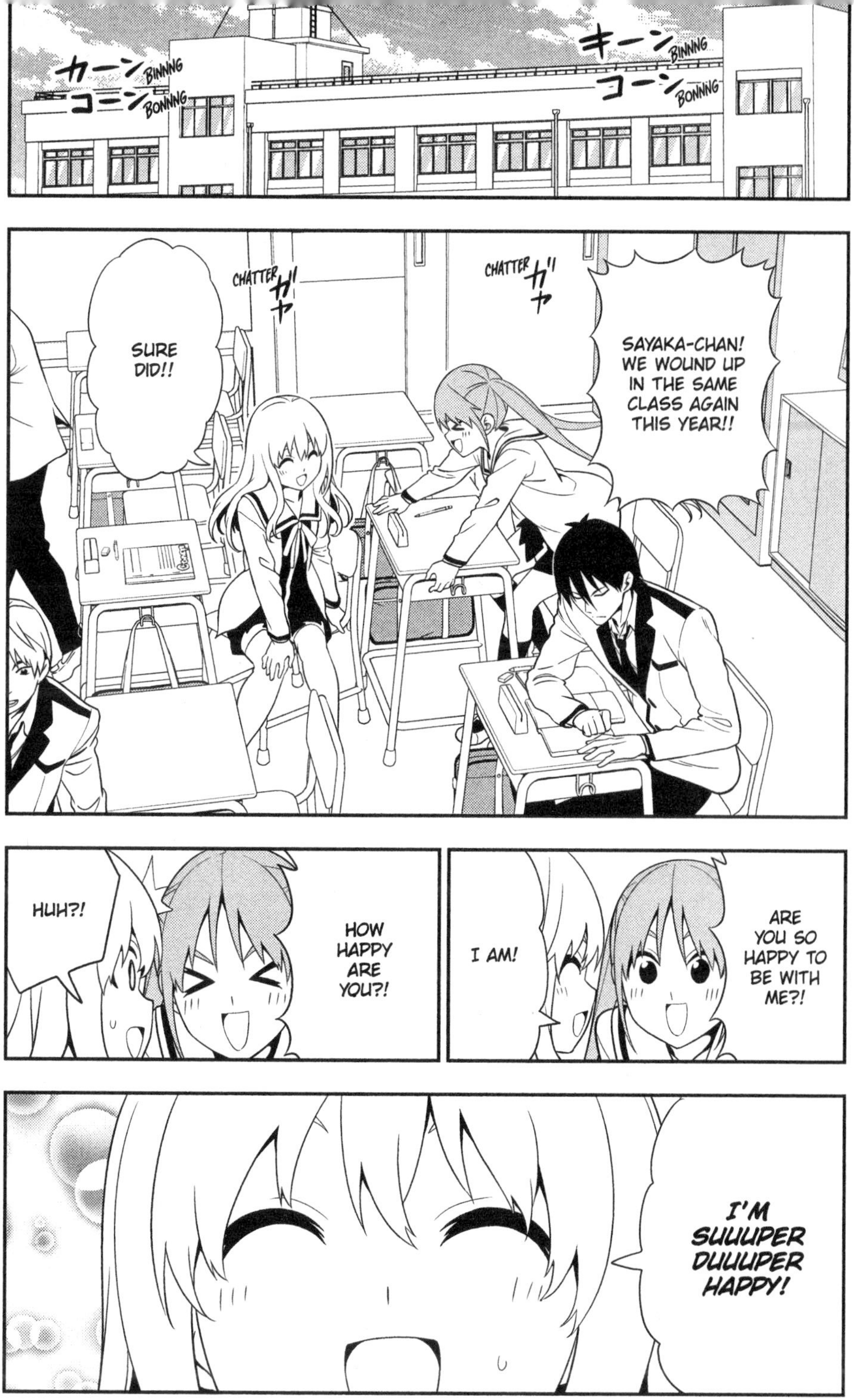
キーン BINNNG
コーン BONNNG
カーン BINNNG
コーン BONNNG
SAYAKA-CHAN! WE WOUND UP IN THE SAME CLASS AGAIN THIS YEAR!!
CHATTER ガヤ
CHATTER ガヤ
SURE DID!!
ARE YOU SO HAPPY TO BE WITH ME?!
I AM!
HOW HAPPY ARE YOU?!
HUH?!
I'M SUUUPER DUUUPER HAPPY!

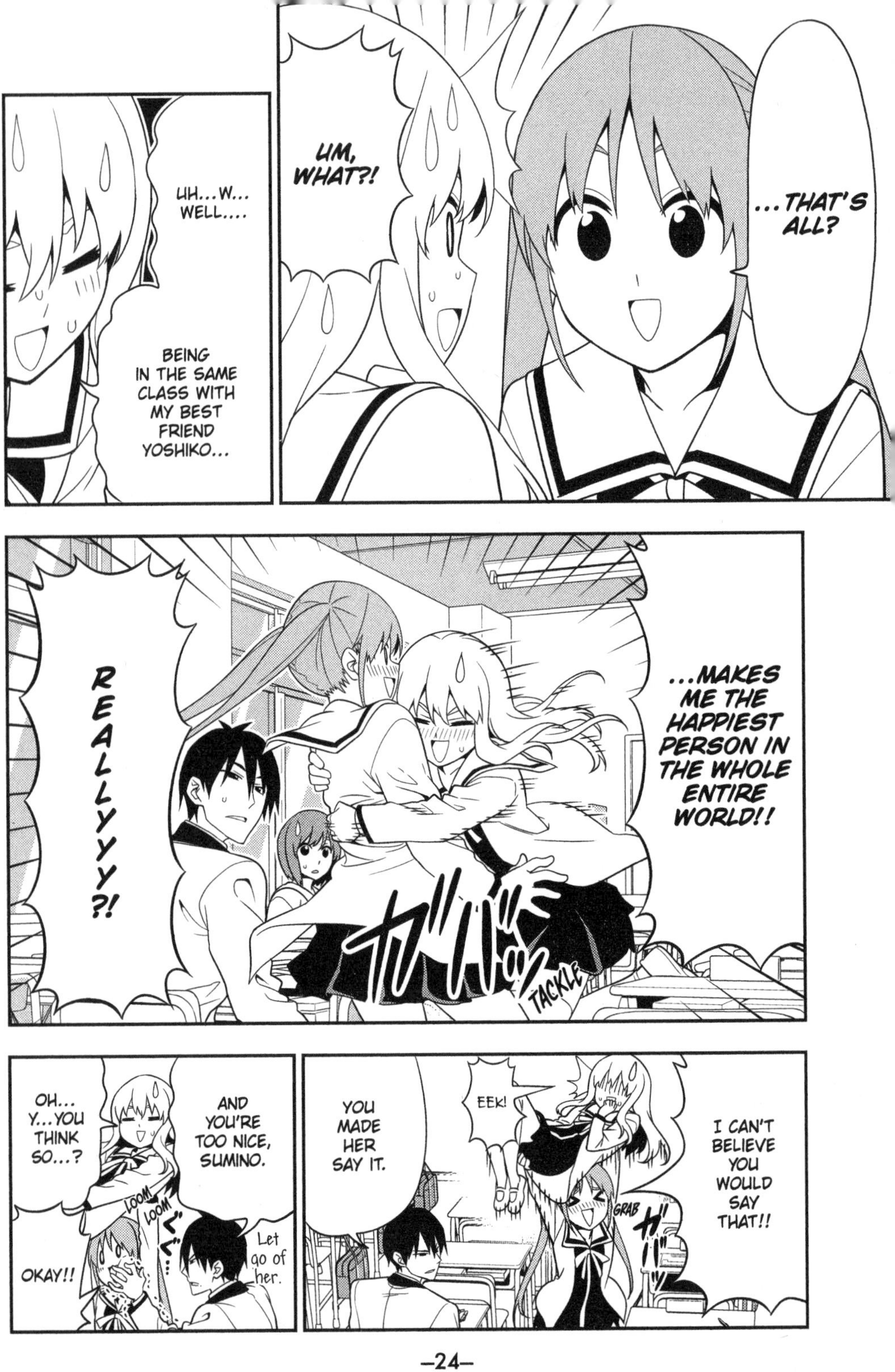
...THAT'S ALL?
UM, WHAT?!
UH...W... WELL....
BEING IN THE SAME CLASS WITH MY BEST FRIEND YOSHIKO...
...MAKES ME THE HAPPIEST PERSON IN THE WHOLE ENTIRE WORLD!!
REALLYYY?!
TACKLE
I CAN'T BELIEVE YOU WOULD SAY THAT!!
GRAB
EEK!
YOU MADE HER SAY IT.
AND YOU'RE TOO NICE, SUMINO.
OH... Y...YOU THINK SO...?
LOOM LOOM
Let go of her.
OKAY!!

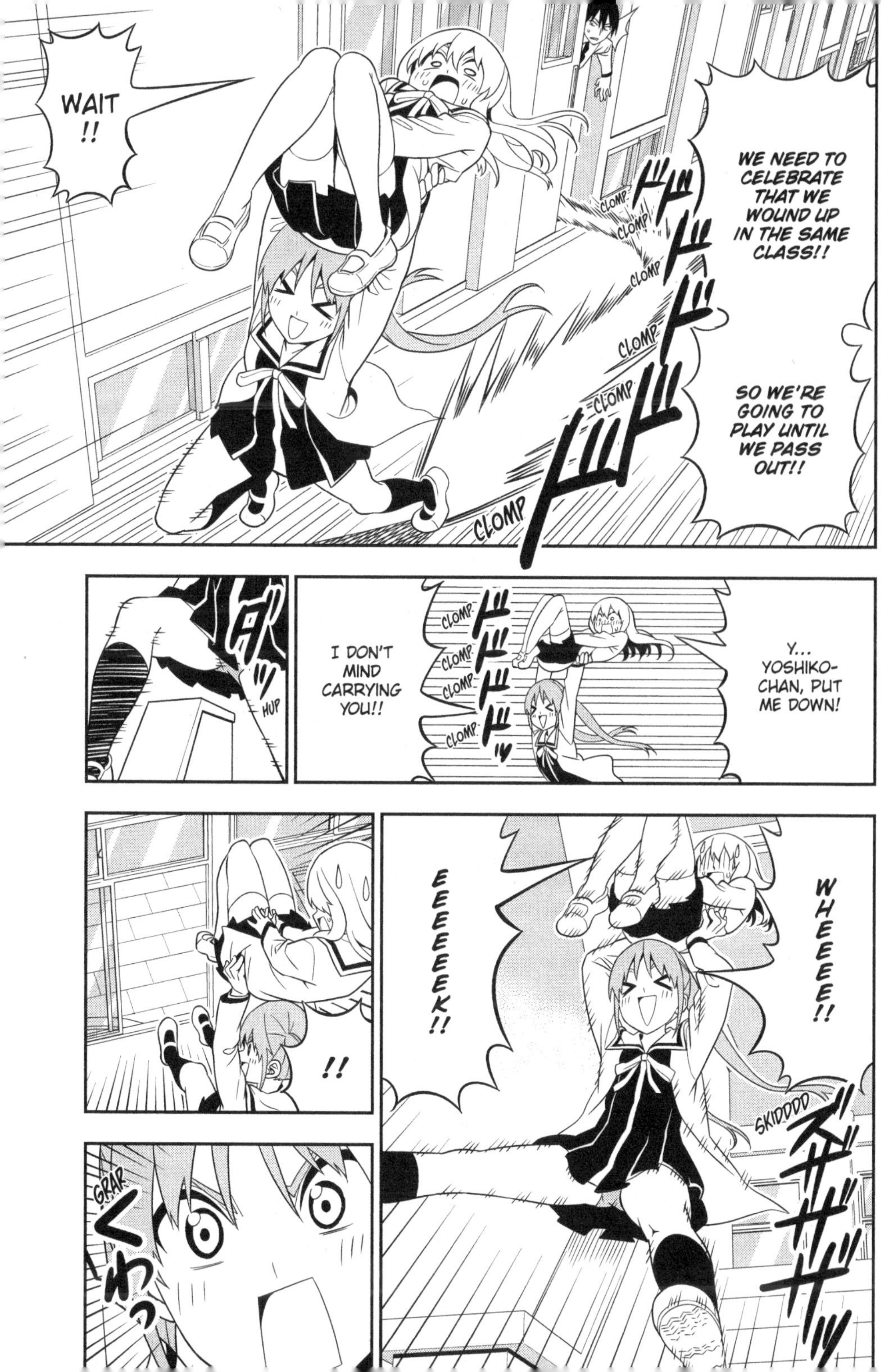
WE NEED TO CELEBRATE THAT WE WOUND UP IN THE SAME CLASS!!
SO WE'RE GOING TO PLAY UNTIL WE PASS OUT!!
CLOMP CLOMP CLOMP CLOMP CLOMP CLOMP
WAIT !!
Y... YOSHIKO-CHAN, PUT ME DOWN!
I DON'T MIND CARRYING YOU!!
CLOMP CLOMP CLOMP CLOMP
HUP
WHEEEEE!!
EEEEEEEK!!
SKIDDDD
!!
GRAR

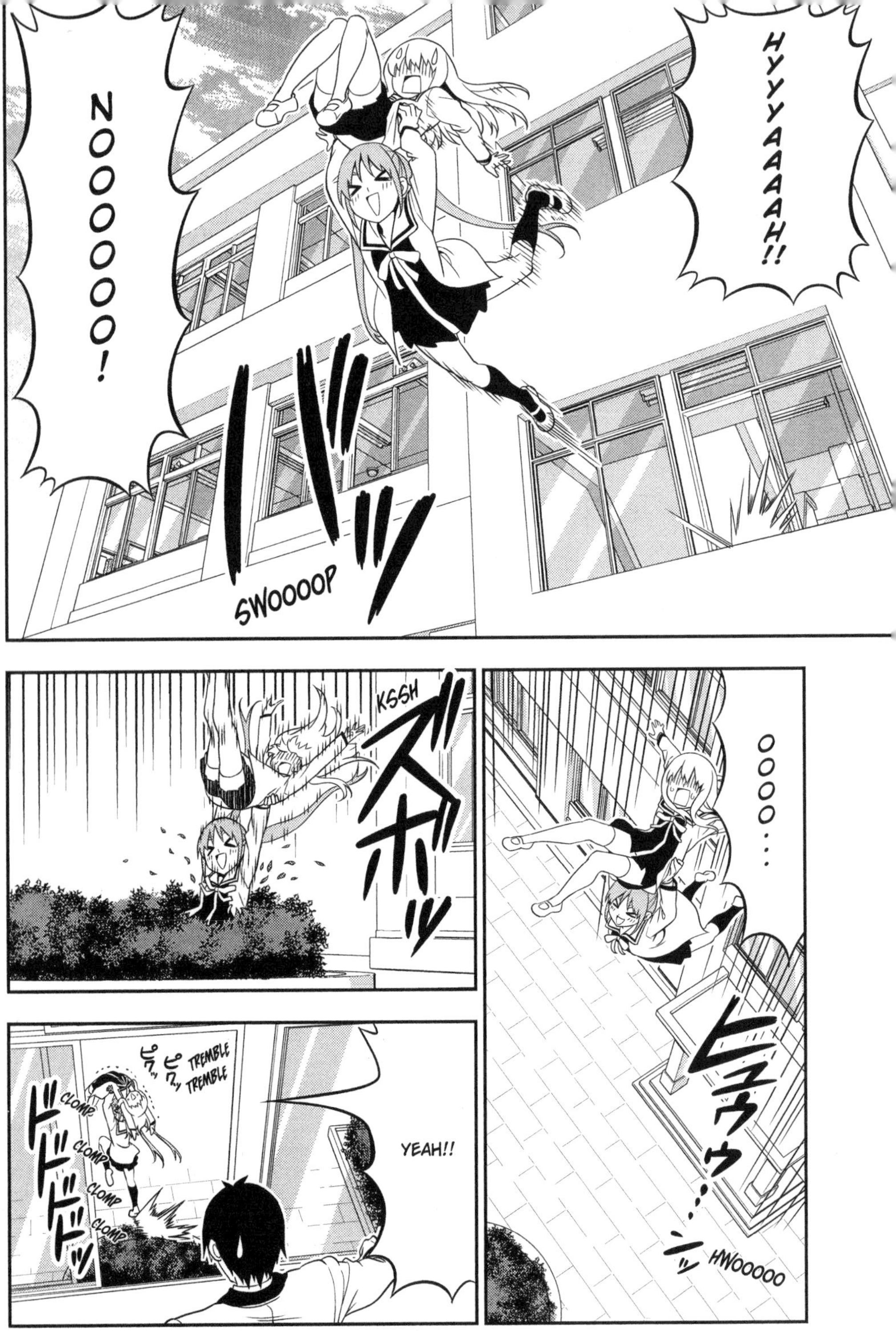
HYYYAAAAAH!!
NOOOOOOOO!
SWOOOOP
OOOO...
ヒュウゥ…ンッ
HWOOOOO
KSSH
ズボッ
YEAH!!
ピクッ ピクッ
TREMBLE TREMBLE
ドドドドッ
CLOMP CLOMP CLOMP CLOMP

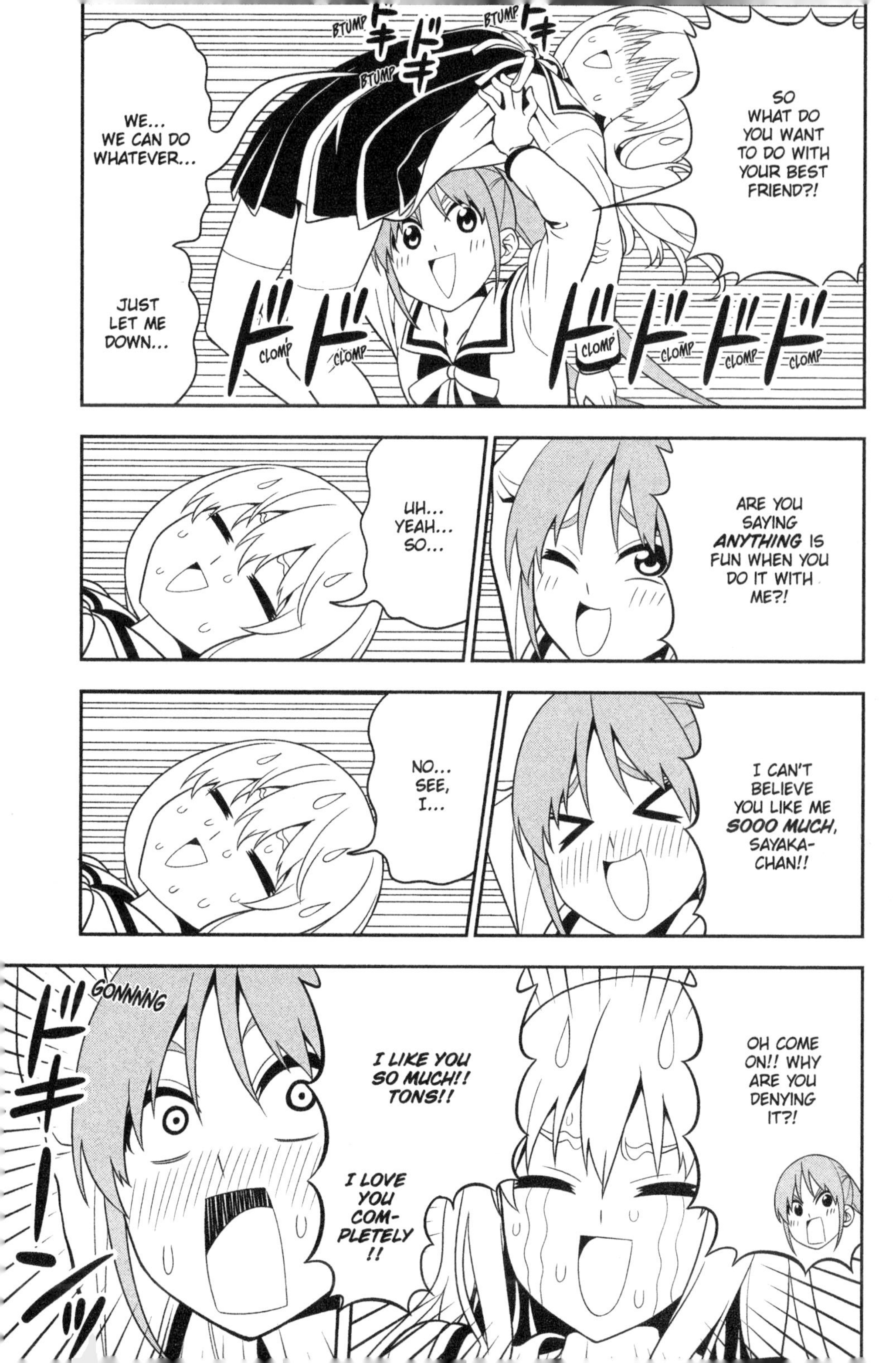
BTUMP
BTUMP
BTUMP
SO WHAT DO YOU WANT TO DO WITH YOUR BEST FRIEND?!
WE... WE CAN DO WHATEVER...
JUST LET ME DOWN...
CLOMP
CLOMP
CLOMP
CLOMP
CLOMP
CLOMP
ARE YOU SAYING *ANYTHING* IS FUN WHEN YOU DO IT WITH ME?!
UH... YEAH... SO...
I CAN'T BELIEVE YOU LIKE ME *SOOO MUCH*, SAYAKA-CHAN!!
NO... SEE, I...
OH COME ON!! WHY ARE YOU DENYING IT?!
I LIKE YOU SO MUCH!! TONS!!
I LOVE YOU COM-PLETELY!!
GONNNNG

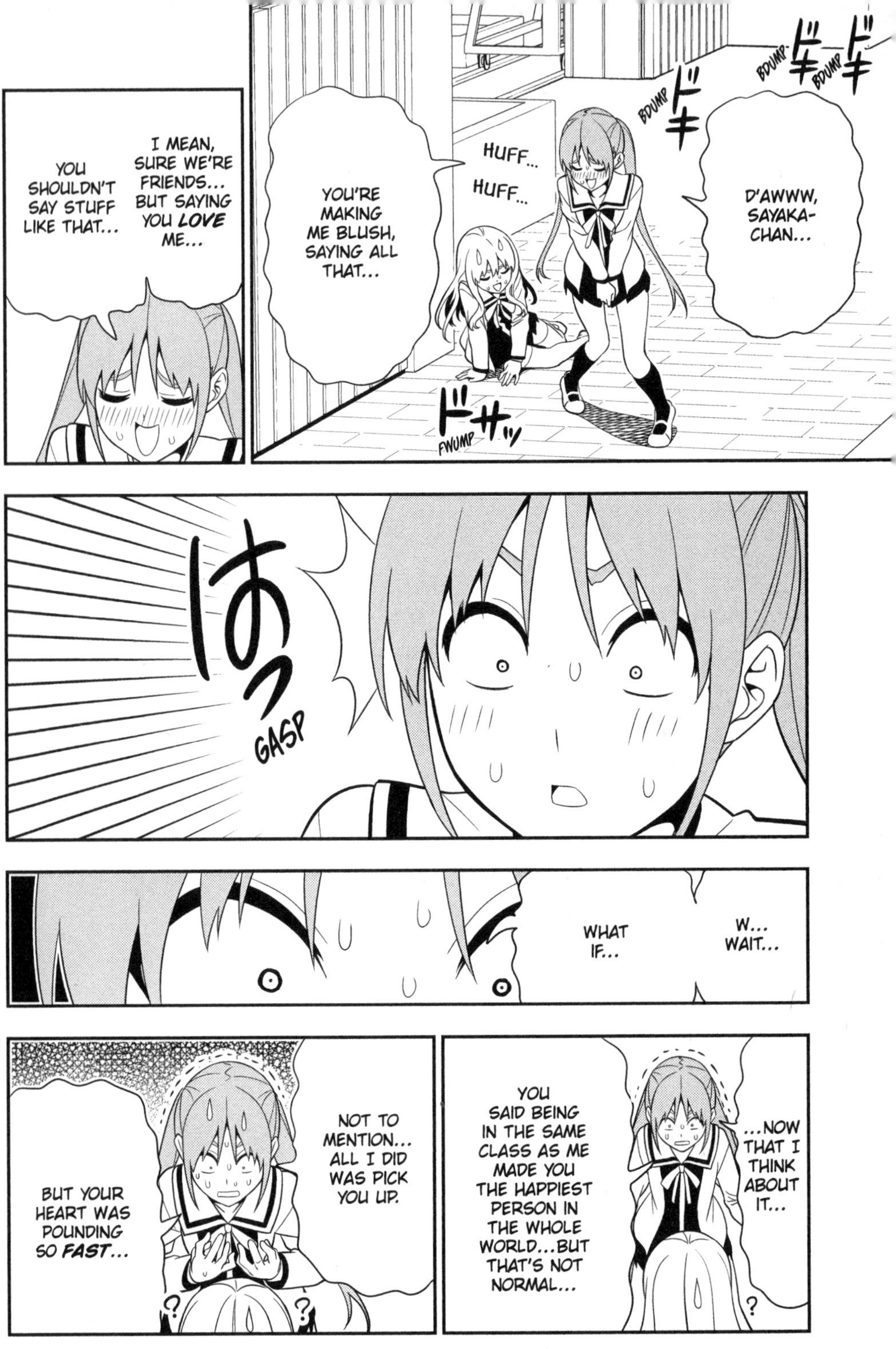
BDUMP ドキ BDUMP ドキ BDUMP ドキ
D'AWWW, SAYAKA-CHAN...
HUFF...
HUFF...
YOU'RE MAKING ME BLUSH, SAYING ALL THAT...
ドサッ FWUMP
I MEAN, SURE WE'RE FRIENDS... BUT SAYING YOU **LOVE** ME...
YOU SHOULDN'T SAY STUFF LIKE THAT...
はっ GASP
W... WAIT...
WHAT IF...
...NOW THAT I THINK ABOUT IT...
YOU SAID BEING IN THE SAME CLASS AS ME MADE YOU THE HAPPIEST PERSON IN THE WHOLE WORLD...BUT THAT'S NOT NORMAL...
?
NOT TO MENTION... ALL I DID WAS PICK YOU UP.
BUT YOUR HEART WAS POUNDING SO **FAST**...
?
?

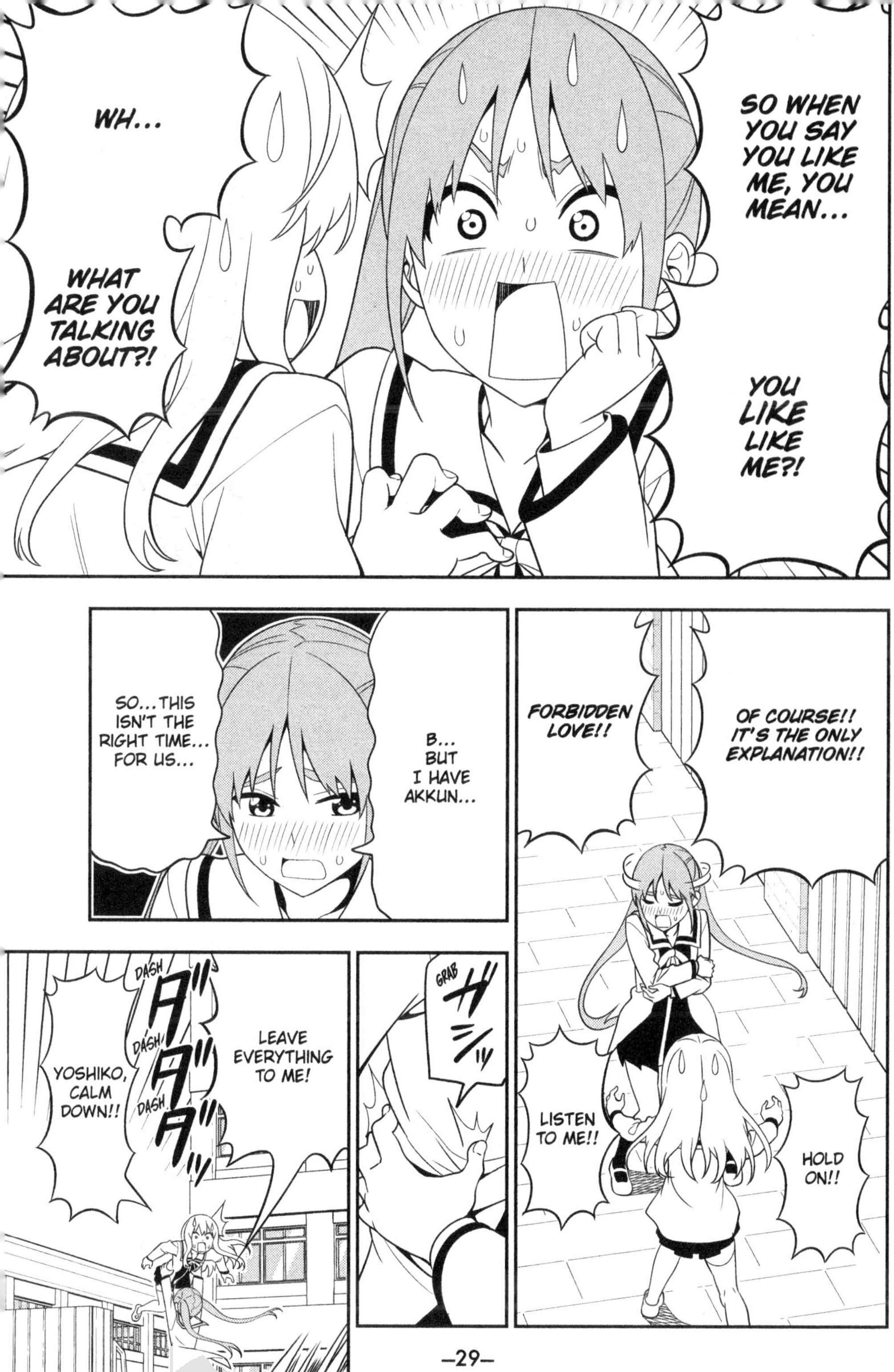
SO WHEN YOU SAY YOU LIKE ME, YOU MEAN...
YOU LIKE LIKE ME?!
WH...
WHAT ARE YOU TALKING ABOUT?!
OF COURSE!! IT'S THE ONLY EXPLANATION!!
FORBIDDEN LOVE!!
HOLD ON!!
LISTEN TO ME!!
B... BUT I HAVE AKKUN...
SO... THIS ISN'T THE RIGHT TIME... FOR US...
GRAB
LEAVE EVERYTHING TO ME!
DASH
DASH
DASH
YOSHIKO, CALM DOWN!!

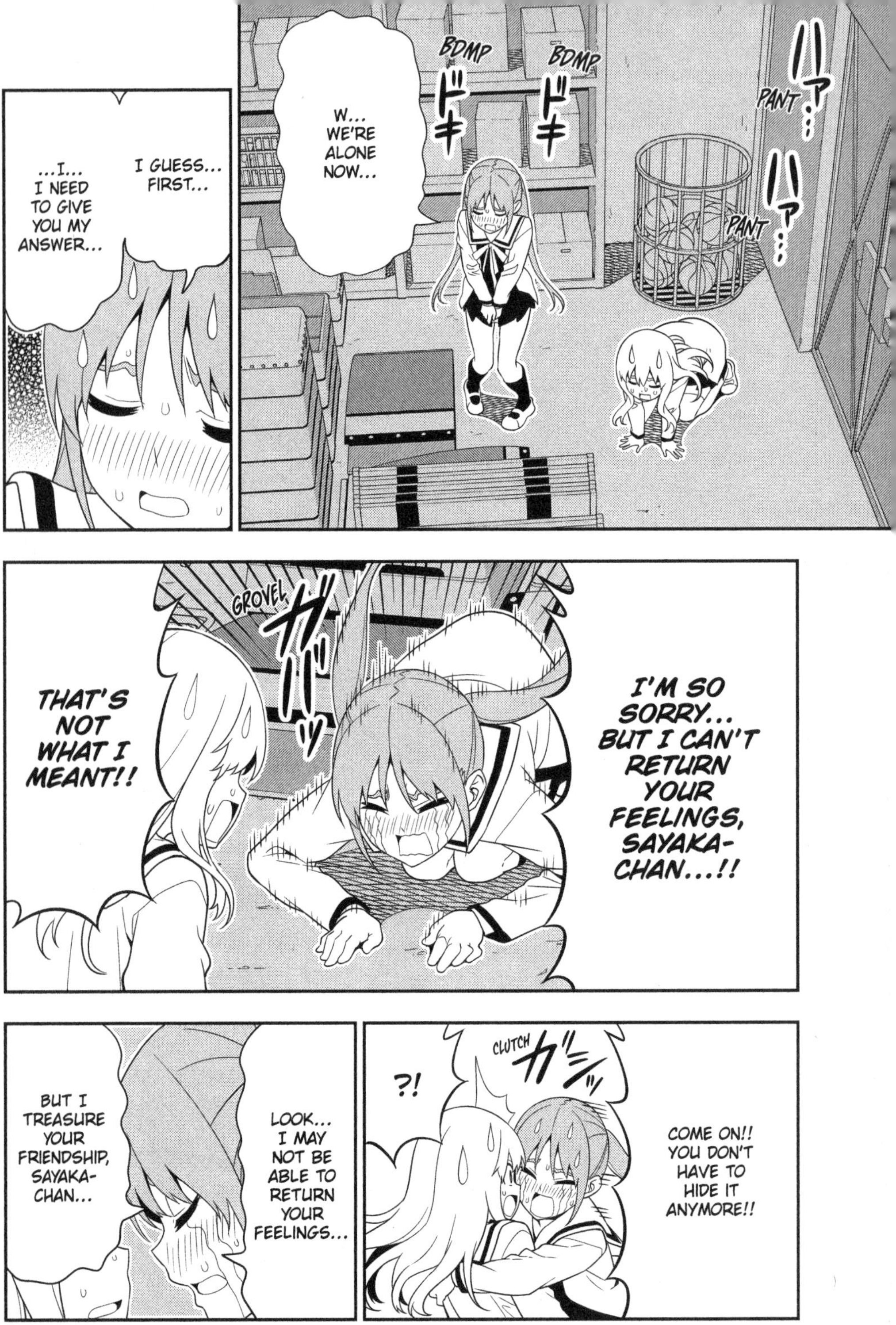
PANT
ハァ…
PANT
ハァ…
BDMP
ドキ
BDMP
ドキ
W... WE'RE ALONE NOW...
I GUESS... FIRST...
...I... I NEED TO GIVE YOU MY ANSWER...
I'M SO SORRY... BUT I CAN'T RETURN YOUR FEELINGS, SAYAKA-CHAN...!!
GROVEL
ガバッ
THAT'S NOT WHAT I MEANT!!
COME ON!! YOU DON'T HAVE TO HIDE IT ANYMORE!!
CLUTCH
ガシッ
?!
LOOK... I MAY NOT BE ABLE TO RETURN YOUR FEELINGS...
BUT I TREASURE YOUR FRIENDSHIP, SAYAKA-CHAN...

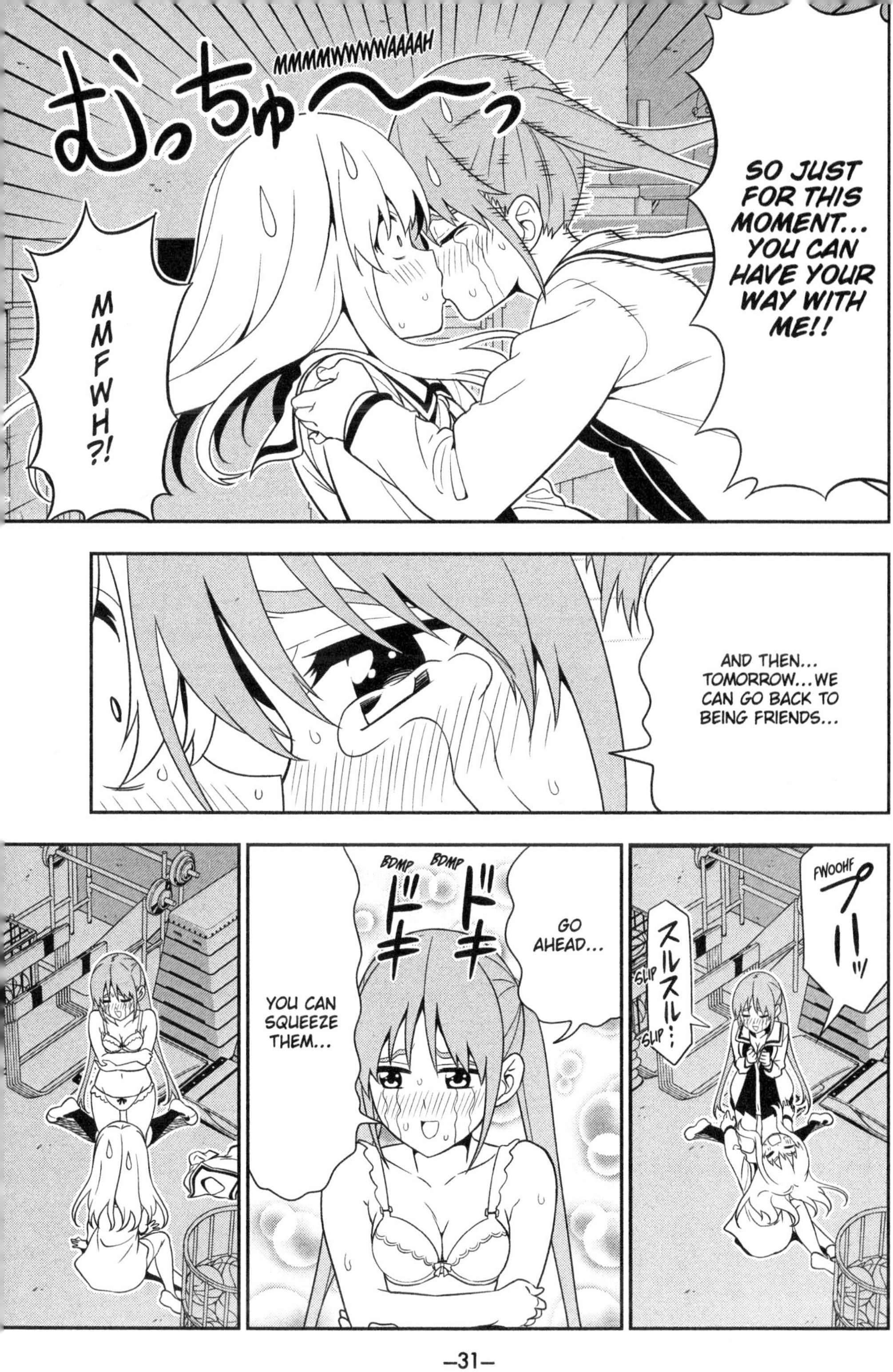
SO JUST FOR THIS MOMENT... YOU CAN HAVE YOUR WAY WITH ME!!
むっちゅ〜〜っ
MMMMWWWWAAAAH
MMFWH?!
AND THEN... TOMORROW... WE CAN GO BACK TO BEING FRIENDS...
FWOOHF
スルスル‥
SLIP SLIP
ドキドキ
BDMP BDMP
GO AHEAD...
YOU CAN SQUEEZE THEM...

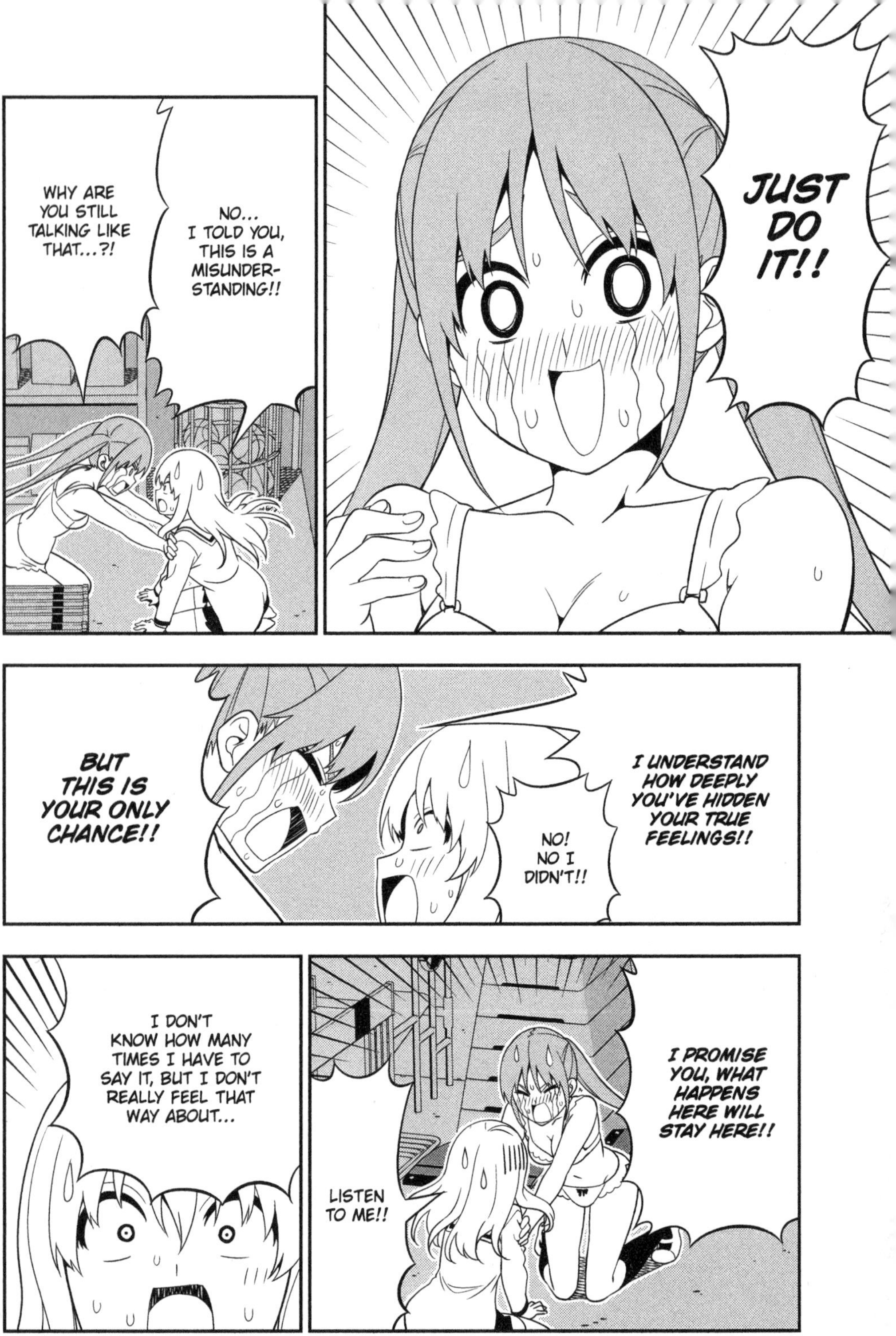
JUST DO IT!!
NO... I TOLD YOU, THIS IS A MISUNDER-STANDING!!
WHY ARE YOU STILL TALKING LIKE THAT...?!
I UNDERSTAND HOW DEEPLY YOU'VE HIDDEN YOUR TRUE FEELINGS!!
NO! NO I DIDN'T!!
BUT THIS IS YOUR ONLY CHANCE!!
I PROMISE YOU, WHAT HAPPENS HERE WILL STAY HERE!!
LISTEN TO ME!!
I DON'T KNOW HOW MANY TIMES I HAVE TO SAY IT, BUT I DON'T REALLY FEEL THAT WAY ABOUT...

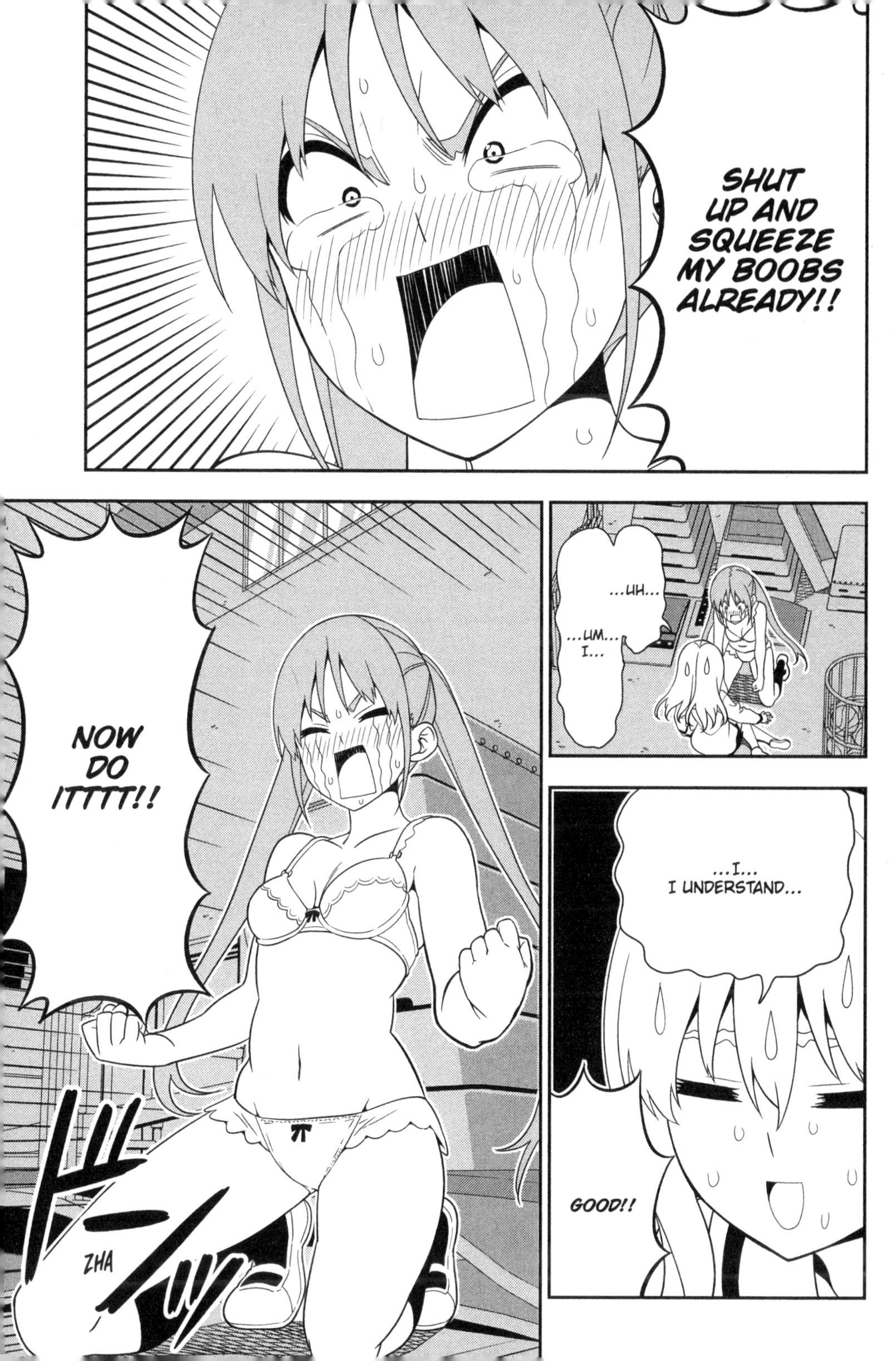
SHUT UP AND SQUEEZE MY BOOBS ALREADY!!
...UH...
...UM... I...
...I... I UNDERSTAND...
GOOD!!
NOW DO ITTTTT!!
ZHA

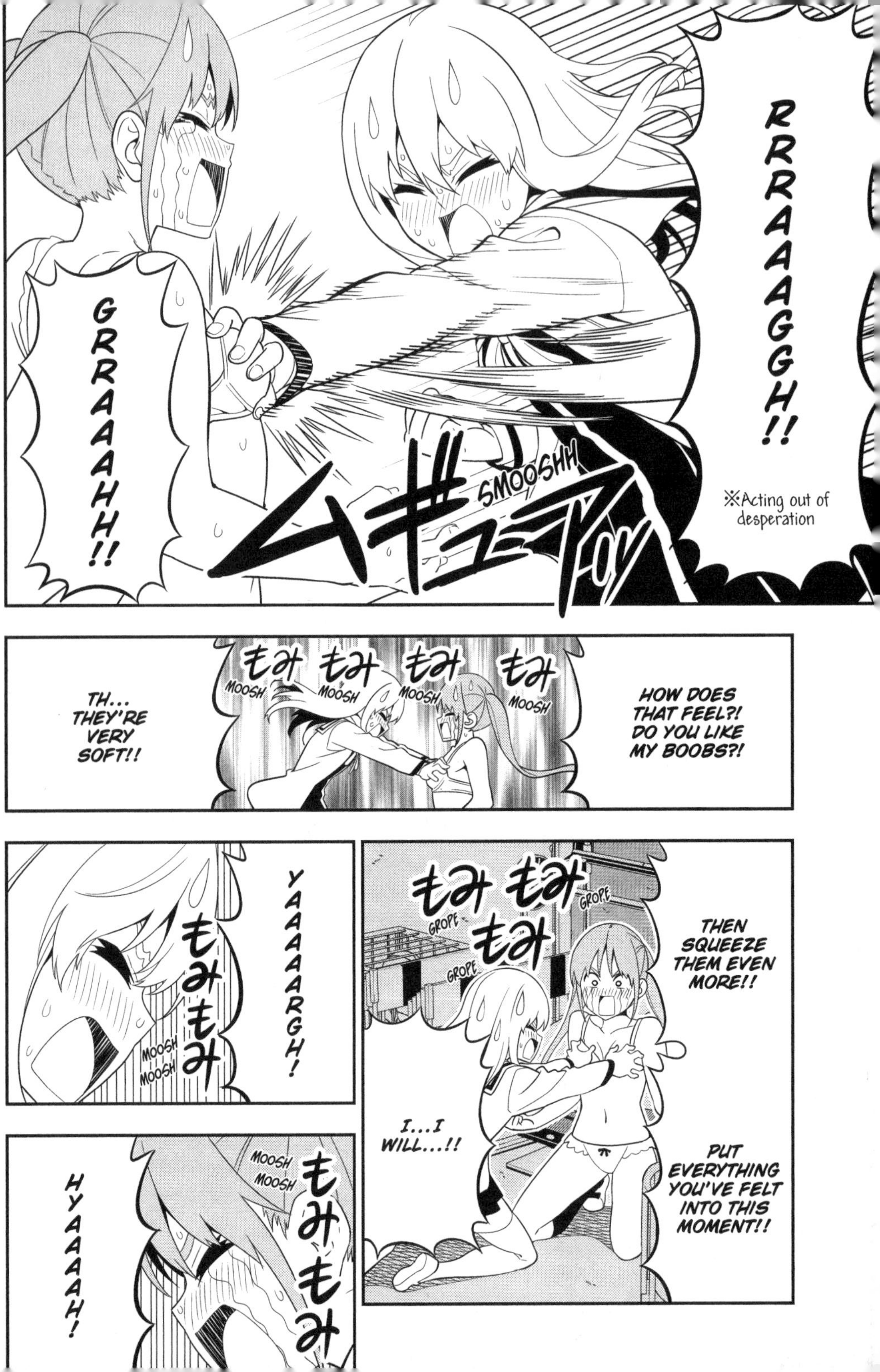
RRRAAAAGGGH!!
※Acting out of desperation
ムギュー
SMOOSHH
GRRAAAAHH!!
HOW DOES THAT FEEL?! DO YOU LIKE MY BOOBS?!
もみ
MOOSH
もみ
MOOSH
もみ
MOOSH
もみ
MOOSH
TH... THEY'RE VERY SOFT!!
THEN SQUEEZE THEM EVEN MORE!!
もみ もみ もみ
GROPE GROPE GROPE
PUT EVERYTHING YOU'VE FELT INTO THIS MOMENT!!
I...I WILL...!!
YAAAAAARGH!
もみもみ
MOOSH MOOSH
もみもみ
MOOSH MOOSH
HYAAAAAH!

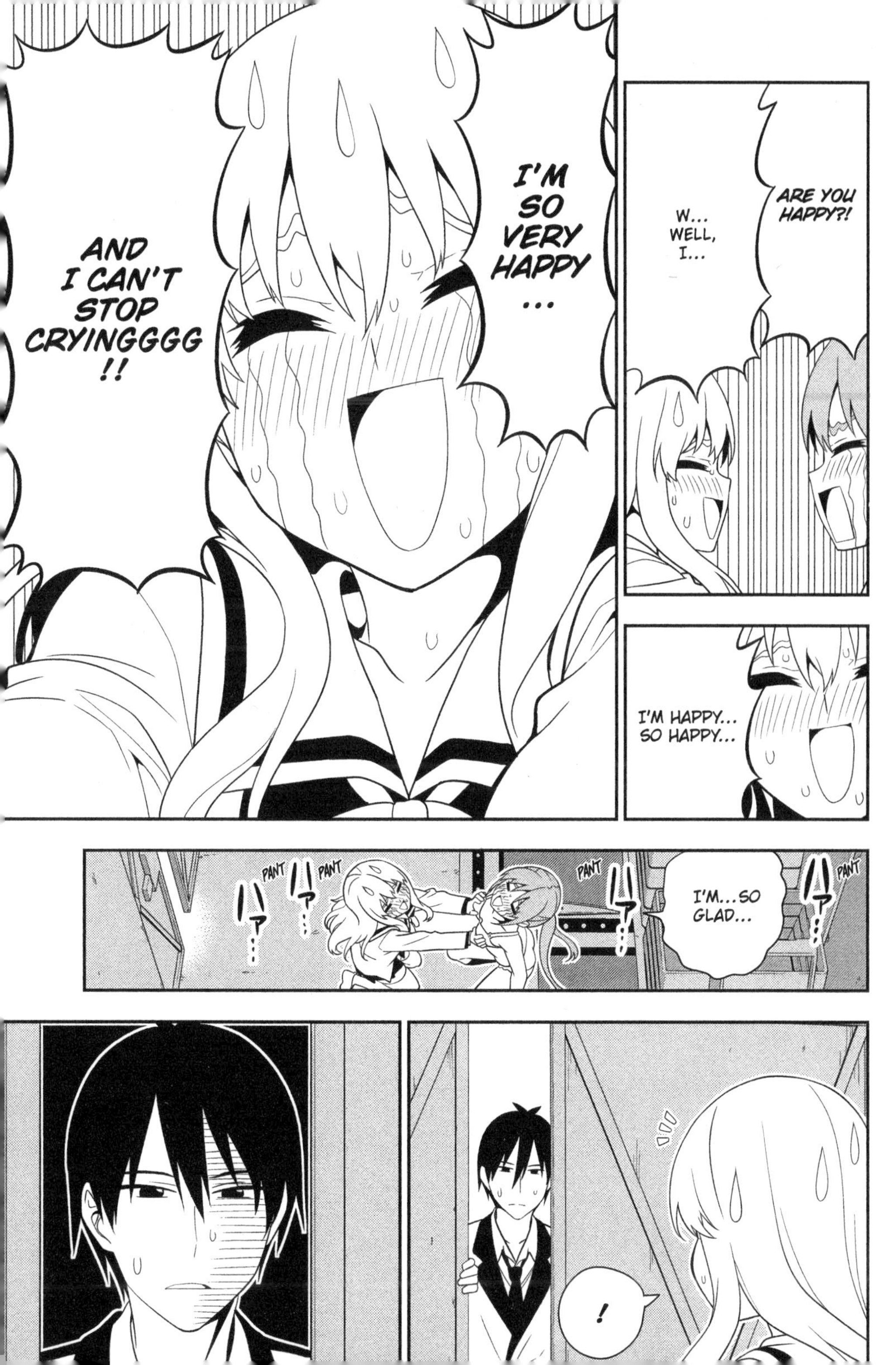

ARE YOU HAPPY?!
W... WELL, I...
I'M HAPPY... SO HAPPY...
I'M SO VERY HAPPY ...
AND I CAN'T STOP CRYINGGGG !!
PANT
I'M...SO GLAD...
PANT
PANT
PANT
!

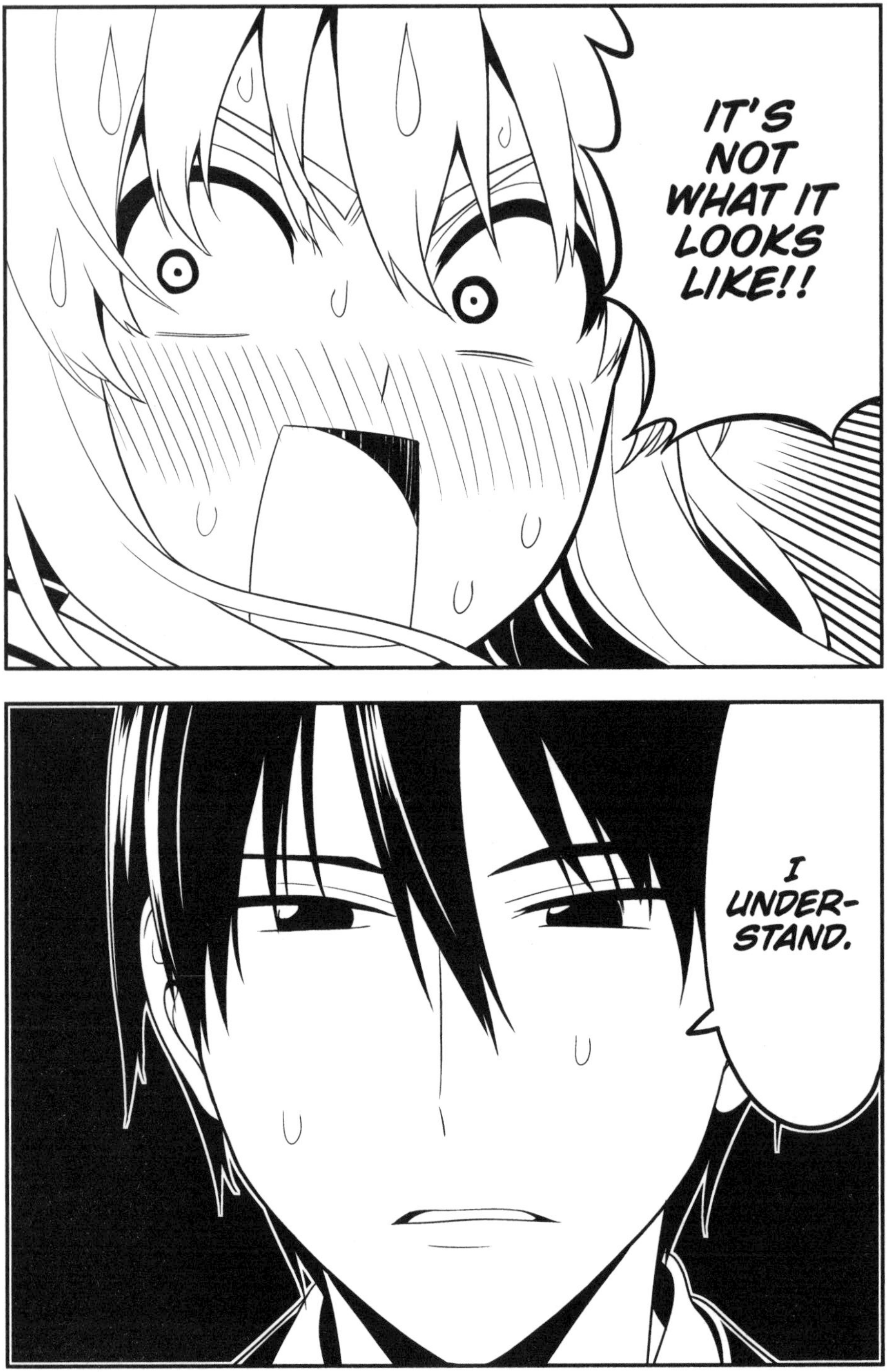
IT'S NOT WHAT IT LOOKS LIKE!!
I UNDER-STAND.

Say How You Really Feel

I THINK YOU'D DO WELL TO BE A LITTLE MORE HONEST, SUMINO...
...IN WHAT WAY...?
YOU ACTUALLY HATE YOSHIKO, DON'T YOU?
THAT'S NOT TRUE! REALLY!!

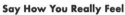

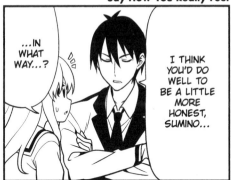

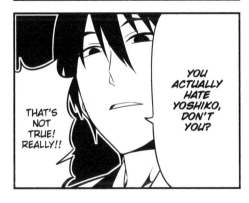

(Look, there—it's)

Aho-Girl

\\'ahô͵gərl\\ *Japanese, noun.*
A clueless girl.

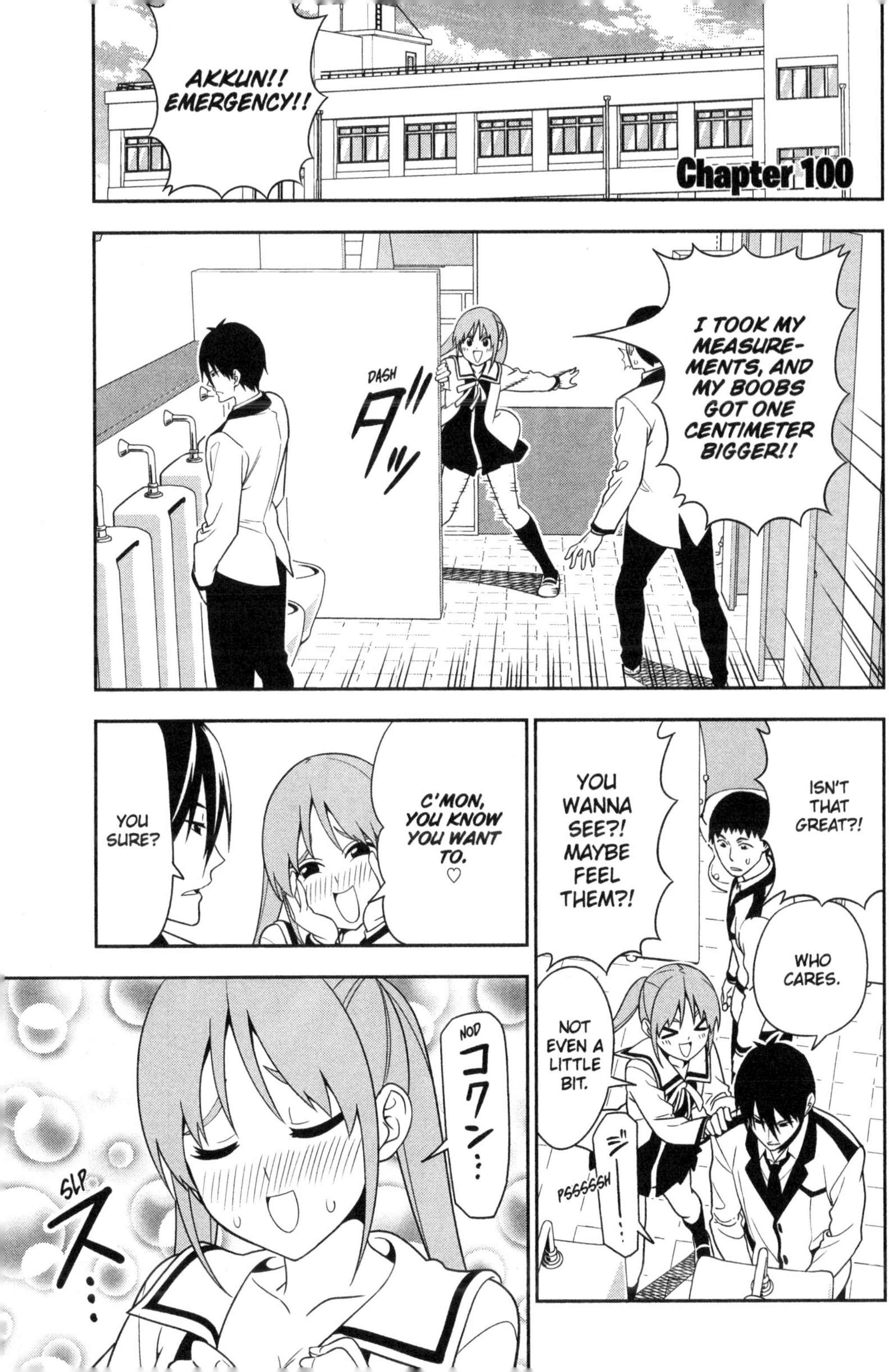
AKKUN!! EMERGENCY!!
Chapter 100
I TOOK MY MEASUREMENTS, AND MY BOOBS GOT ONE CENTIMETER BIGGER!!
DASH
ISN'T THAT GREAT?!
YOU WANNA SEE?! MAYBE FEEL THEM?!
WHO CARES.
NOT EVEN A LITTLE BIT.
PSSSSSH
C'MON, YOU KNOW YOU WANT TO. ♡
YOU SURE?
NOD
SLP

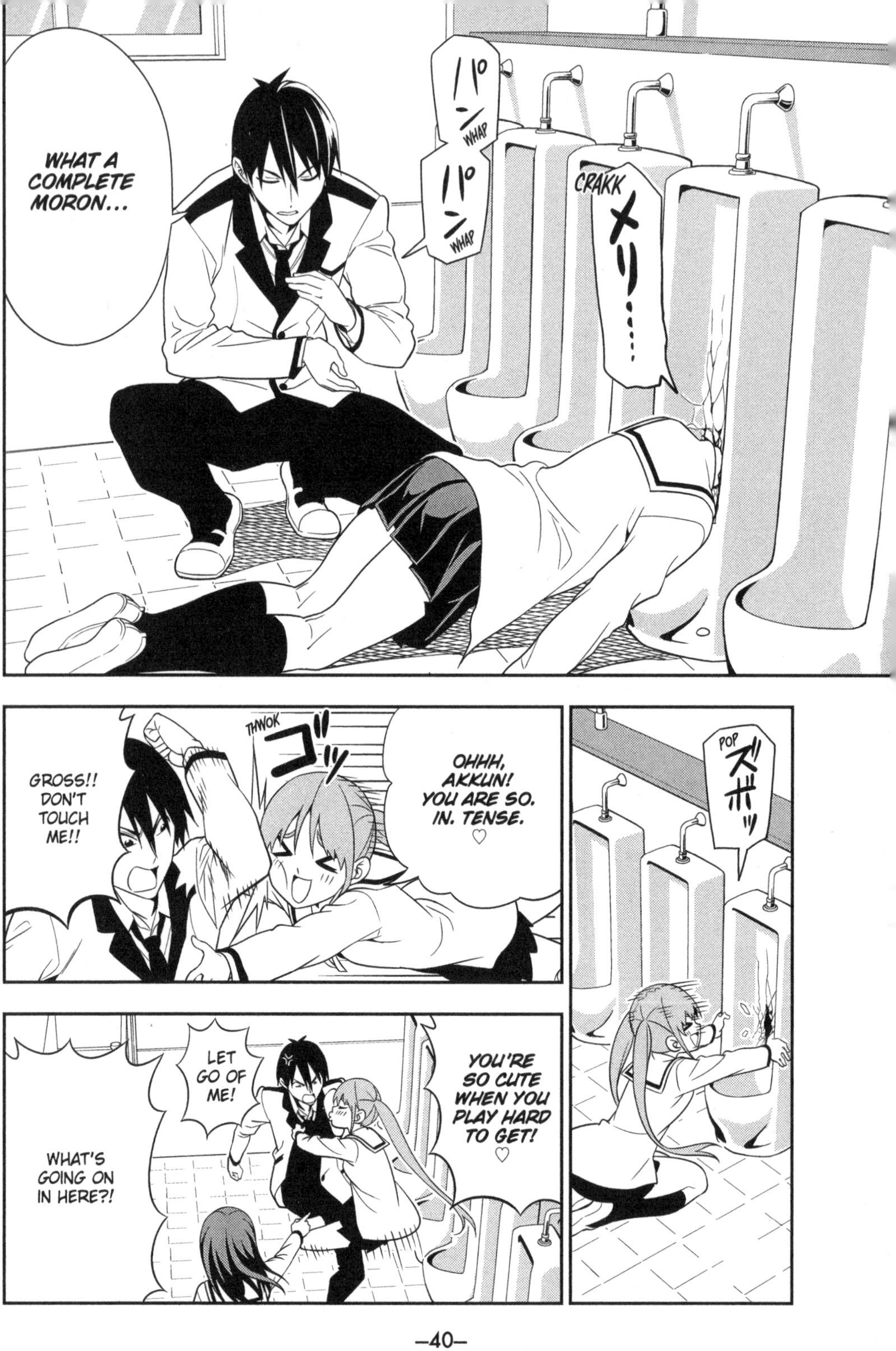
CRAKK
メリ……
パン
WHAP
パン
WHAP
WHAT A COMPLETE MORON...
POP
ズボッ
OHHH, AKKUN! YOU ARE SO. IN. TENSE. ♡
THWOK
ゴッ
GROSS!! DON'T TOUCH ME!!
YOU'RE SO CUTE WHEN YOU PLAY HARD TO GET! ♡
LET GO OF ME!
WHAT'S GOING ON IN HERE?!

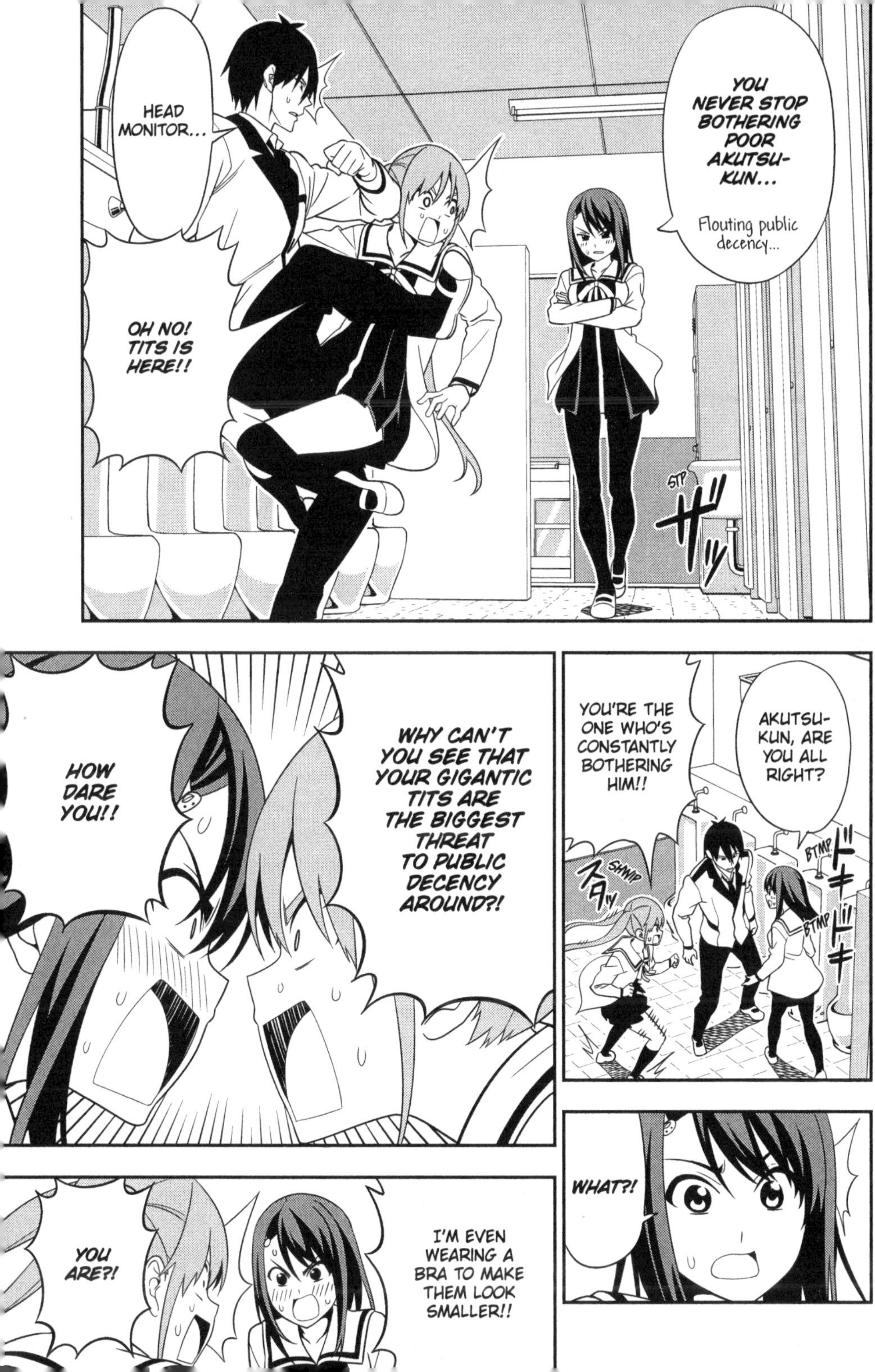
YOU NEVER STOP BOTHERING POOR AKUTSU-KUN...
Flouting public decency...
STP
HEAD MONITOR...
OH NO! TITS IS HERE!!
AKUTSU-KUN, ARE YOU ALL RIGHT?
BTMP
BTMP
YOU'RE THE ONE WHO'S CONSTANTLY BOTHERING HIM!!
SHWIP
WHY CAN'T YOU SEE THAT YOUR GIGANTIC TITS ARE THE BIGGEST THREAT TO PUBLIC DECENCY AROUND?!
HOW DARE YOU!!
WHAT?!
I'M EVEN WEARING A BRA TO MAKE THEM LOOK SMALLER!!
YOU ARE?!

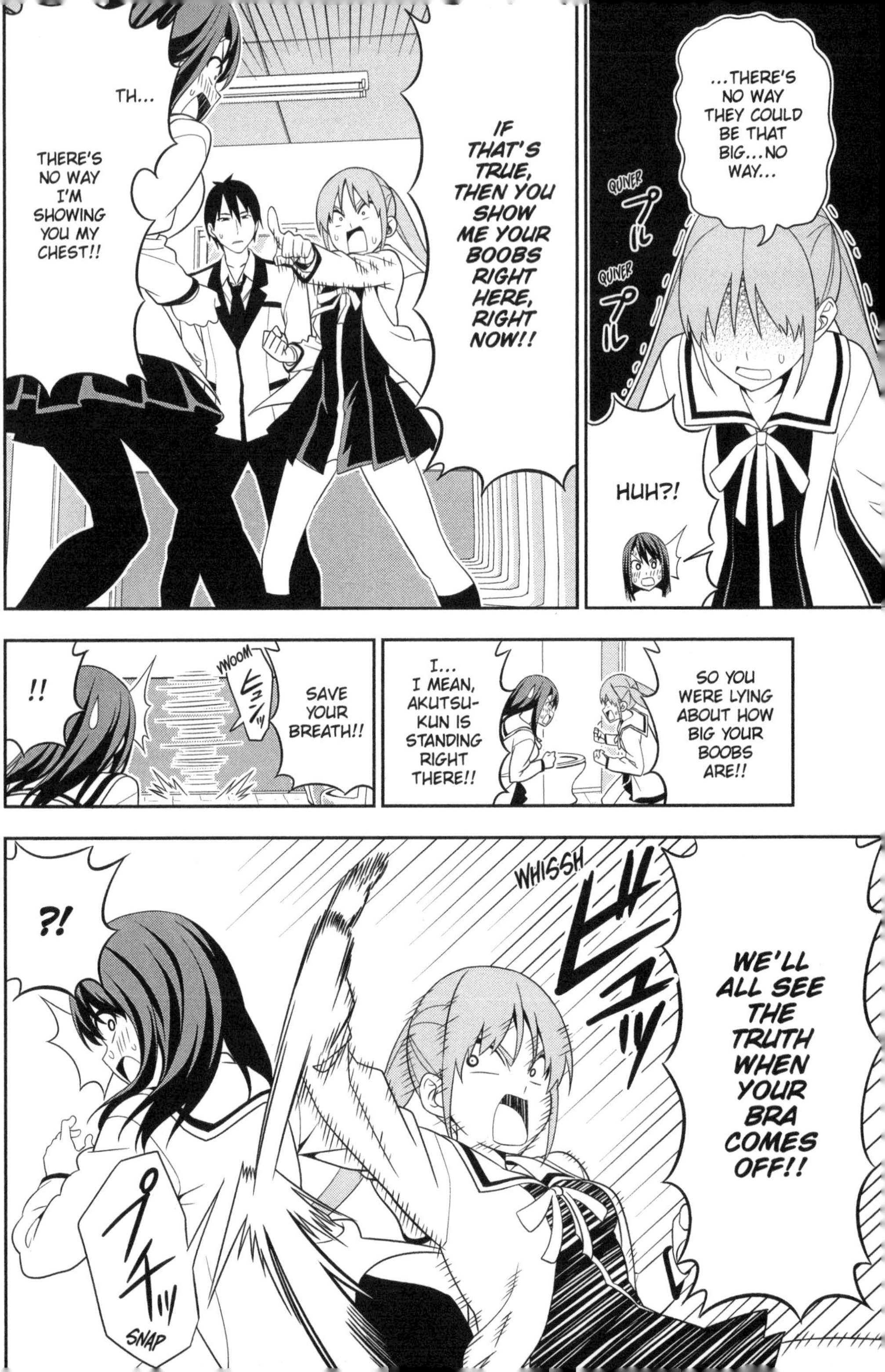
...THERE'S NO WAY THEY COULD BE THAT BIG...NO WAY...
QUIVER プル
QUIVER プル
HUH?!
IF THAT'S TRUE, THEN YOU SHOW ME YOUR BOOBS RIGHT HERE, RIGHT NOW!!
TH...
THERE'S NO WAY I'M SHOWING YOU MY CHEST!!
SO YOU WERE LYING ABOUT HOW BIG YOUR BOOBS ARE!!
I... I MEAN, AKUTSU-KUN IS STANDING RIGHT THERE!!
VWOOM ビュンッ
SAVE YOUR BREATH!!
!!
WHISSH ビュッ
WE'LL ALL SEE THE TRUTH WHEN YOUR BRA COMES OFF!!
?!
パチッ SNAP

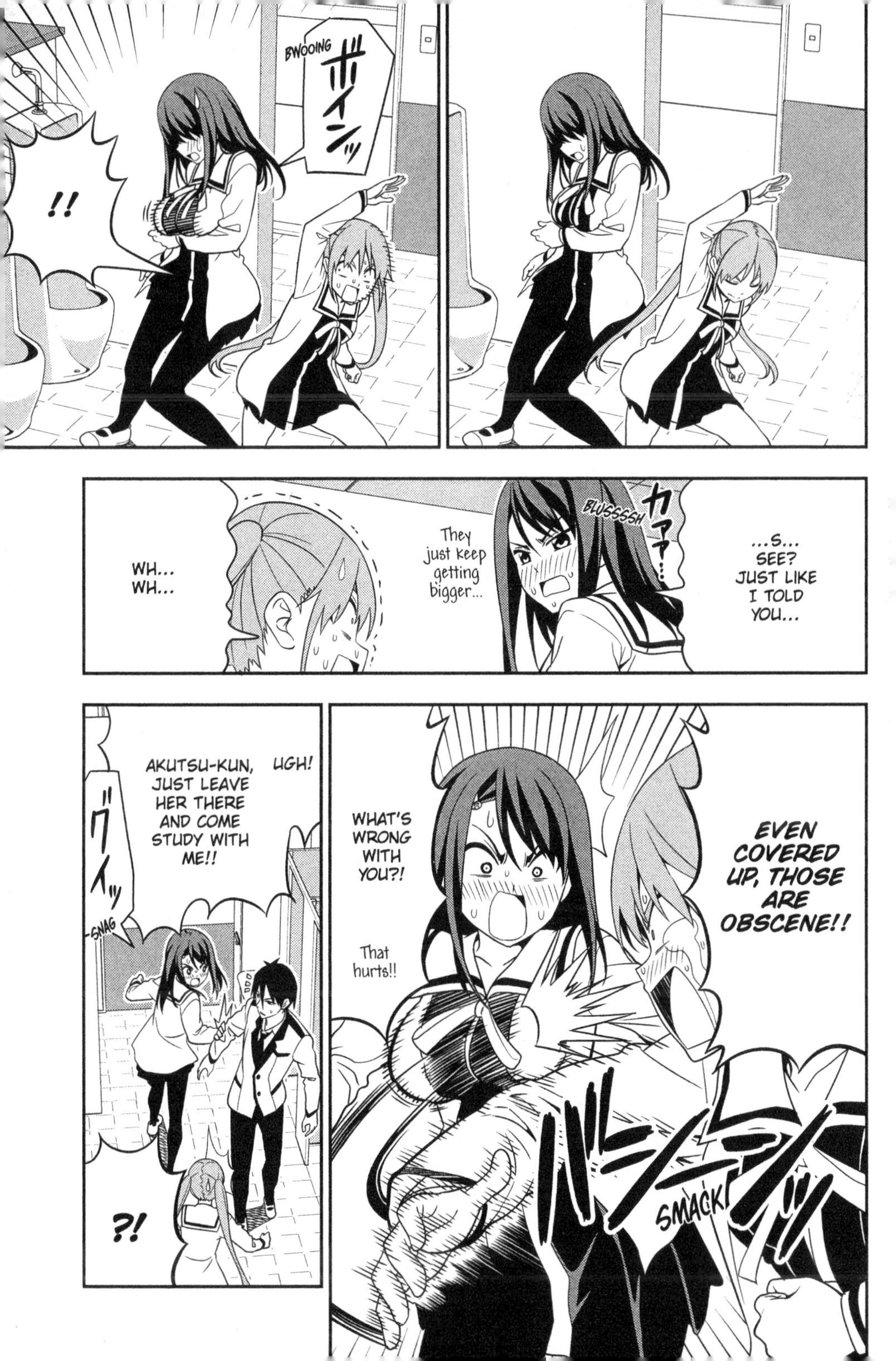
BWOOING
ボインッ
!!
...S... SEE? JUST LIKE I TOLD YOU...
BLUSSSSH
カァァ...
They just keep getting bigger...
WH... WH...
EVEN COVERED UP, THOSE ARE OBSCENE!!
WHAT'S WRONG WITH YOU?!
That hurts!!
SMACK
UGH!
AKUTSU-KUN, JUST LEAVE HER THERE AND COME STUDY WITH ME!!
SNAG
?!

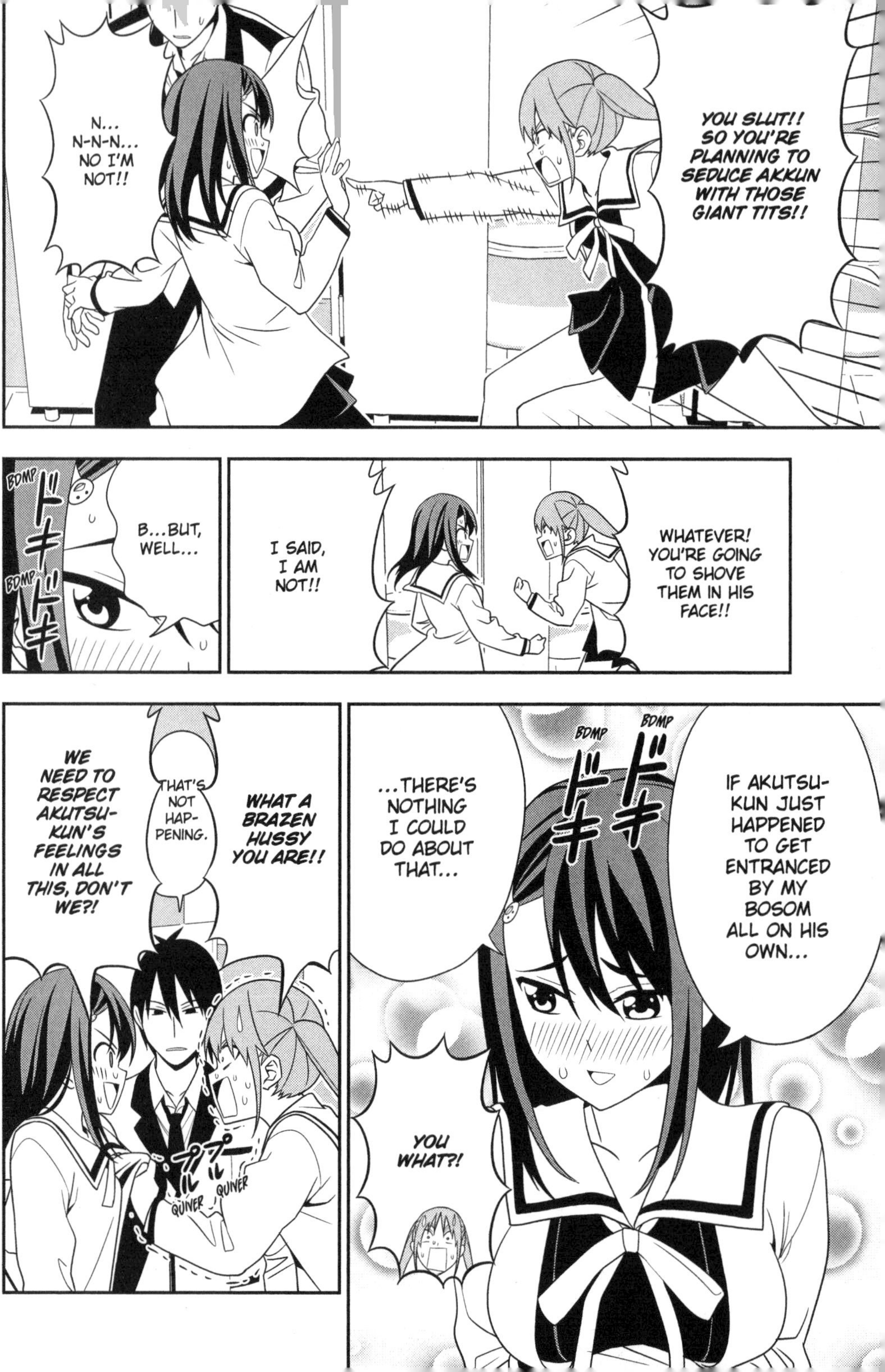
YOU SLUT!! SO YOU'RE PLANNING TO SEDUCE AKKUN WITH THOSE GIANT TITS!!
N... N-N-N... NO I'M NOT!!
WHATEVER! YOU'RE GOING TO SHOVE THEM IN HIS FACE!!
I SAID, I AM NOT!!
B...BUT, WELL...
BDMP
ドキ
BDMP
ドキ
BDMP
ドキ
BDMP
ドキ
IF AKUTSU-KUN JUST HAPPENED TO GET ENTRANCED BY MY BOSOM ALL ON HIS OWN...
...THERE'S NOTHING I COULD DO ABOUT THAT...
YOU WHAT?!
WHAT A BRAZEN HUSSY YOU ARE!!
THAT'S NOT HAP-PENING.
WE NEED TO RESPECT AKUTSU-KUN'S FEELINGS IN ALL THIS, DON'T WE?!
プル
QUIVER
プル
QUIVER

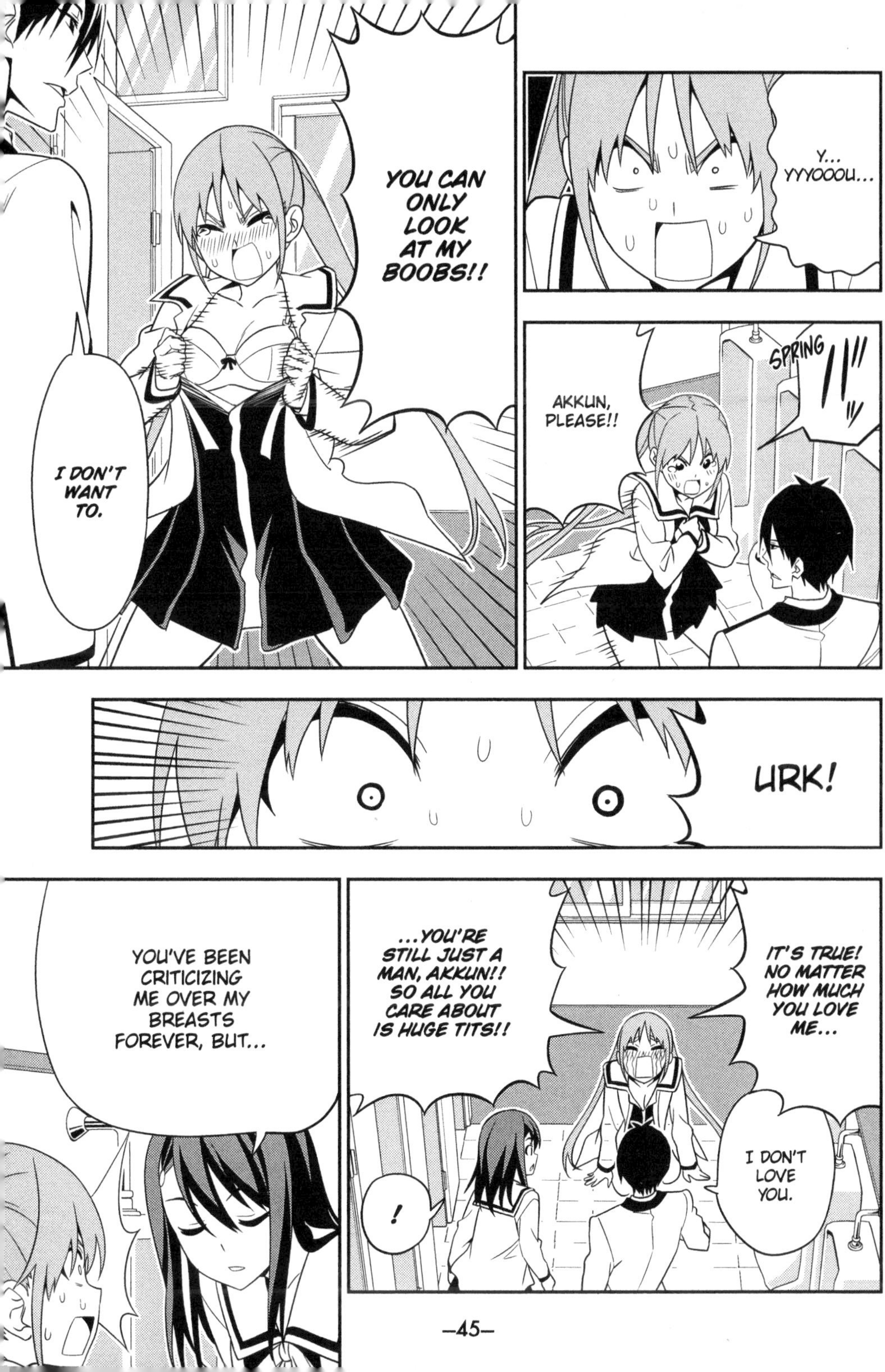

Y... YYYOOOU...
AKKUN, PLEASE!!
SPRING
YOU CAN ONLY LOOK AT MY BOOBS!!
I DON'T WANT TO.
URK!
IT'S TRUE! NO MATTER HOW MUCH YOU LOVE ME...
...YOU'RE STILL JUST A MAN, AKKUN!! SO ALL YOU CARE ABOUT IS HUGE TITS!!
I DON'T LOVE YOU.
!
YOU'VE BEEN CRITICIZING ME OVER MY BREASTS FOREVER, BUT...

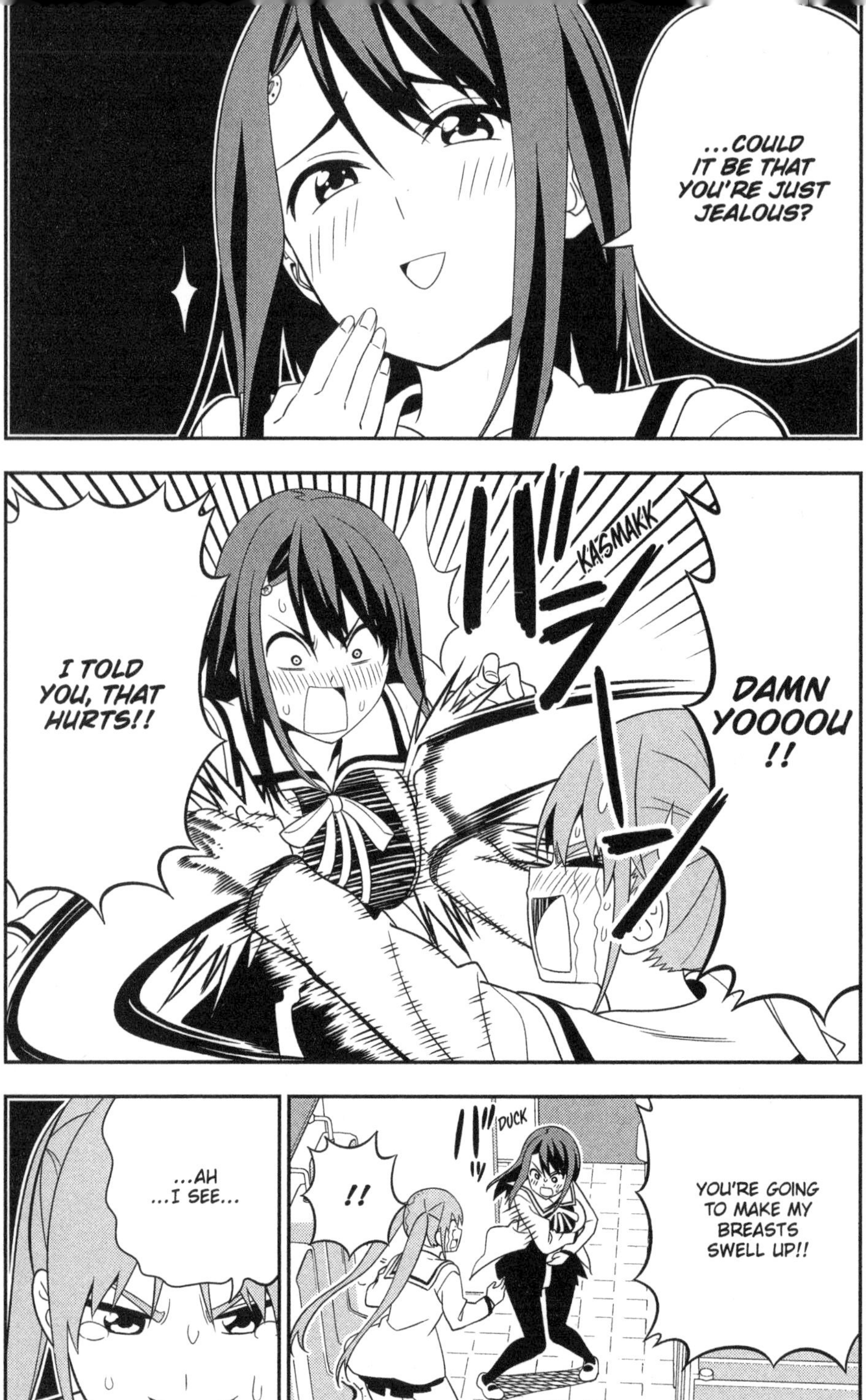
...COULD IT BE THAT YOU'RE JUST JEALOUS?
KA-SMAKK
DAMN YOOOOU !!
I TOLD YOU, THAT HURTS!!
DUCK
YOU'RE GOING TO MAKE MY BREASTS SWELL UP!!
!!
...AH ...I SEE...

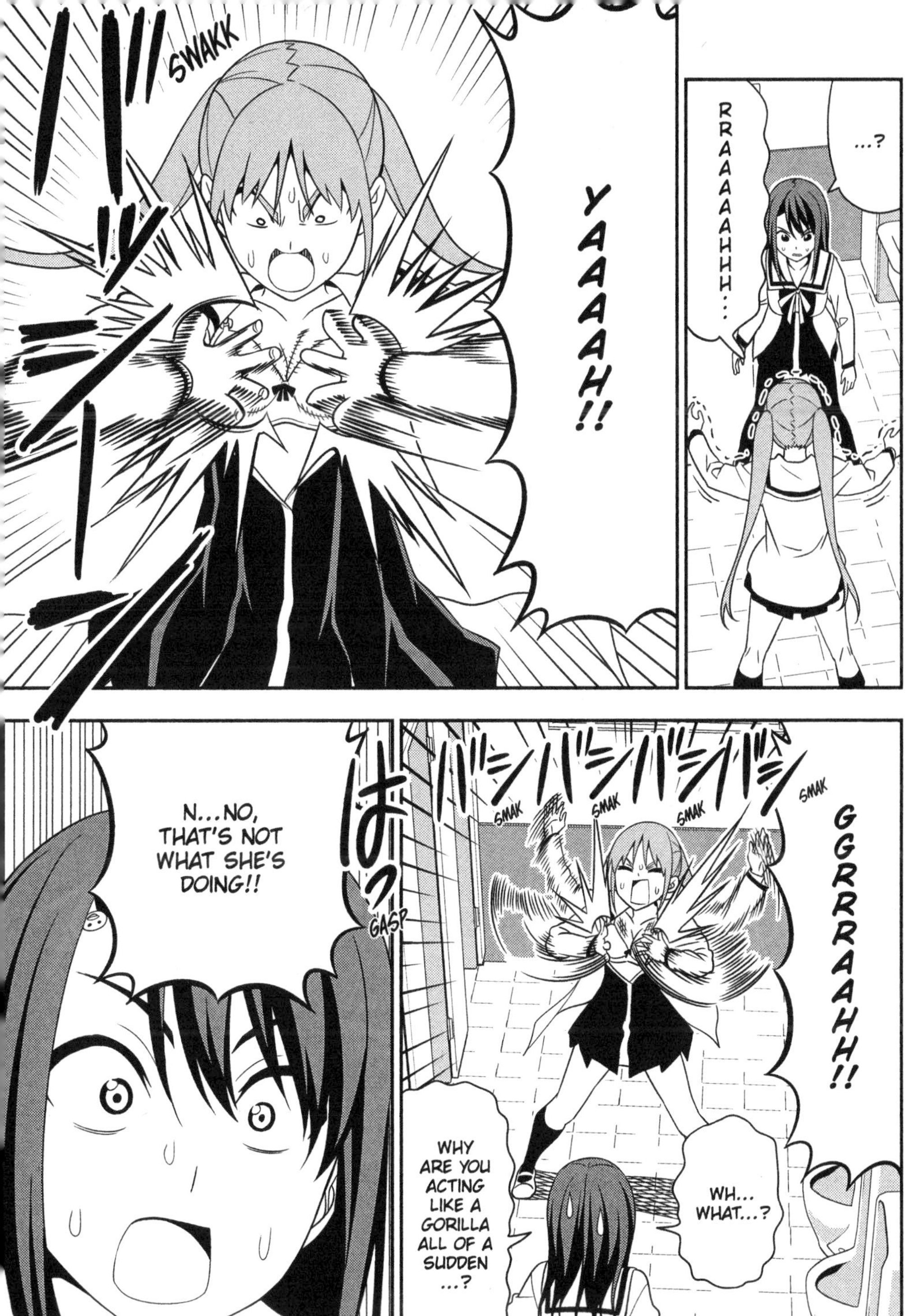
...?
RRAAAAAAHHH...
SWAKK
YAAAAAH!!
SMAK
GGRRRAAHH!!
SMAK
SMAK
SMAK
WH... WHAT...?
WHY ARE YOU ACTING LIKE A GORILLA ALL OF A SUDDEN ...?
GASP
N...NO, THAT'S NOT WHAT SHE'S DOING!!

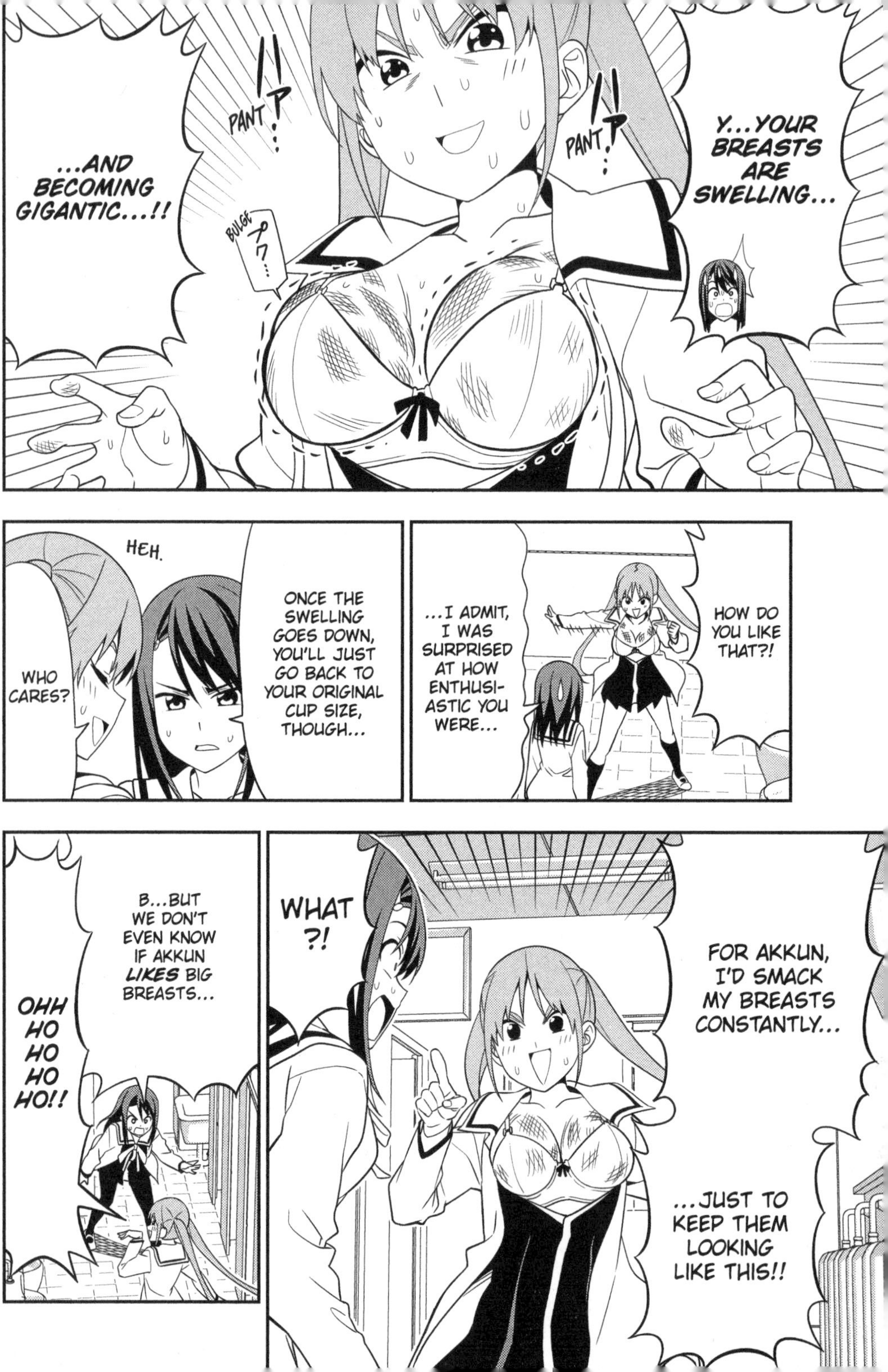
Y…YOUR BREASTS ARE SWELLING…
PANT
PANT
…AND BECOMING GIGANTIC…!!
BULGE
HOW DO YOU LIKE THAT?!
…I ADMIT, I WAS SURPRISED AT HOW ENTHUSI-ASTIC YOU WERE…
ONCE THE SWELLING GOES DOWN, YOU'LL JUST GO BACK TO YOUR ORIGINAL CUP SIZE, THOUGH…
HEH.
WHO CARES?
FOR AKKUN, I'D SMACK MY BREASTS CONSTANTLY…
…JUST TO KEEP THEM LOOKING LIKE THIS!!
WHAT?!
B…BUT WE DON'T EVEN KNOW IF AKKUN *LIKES* BIG BREASTS…
OHH HO HO HO HO!!

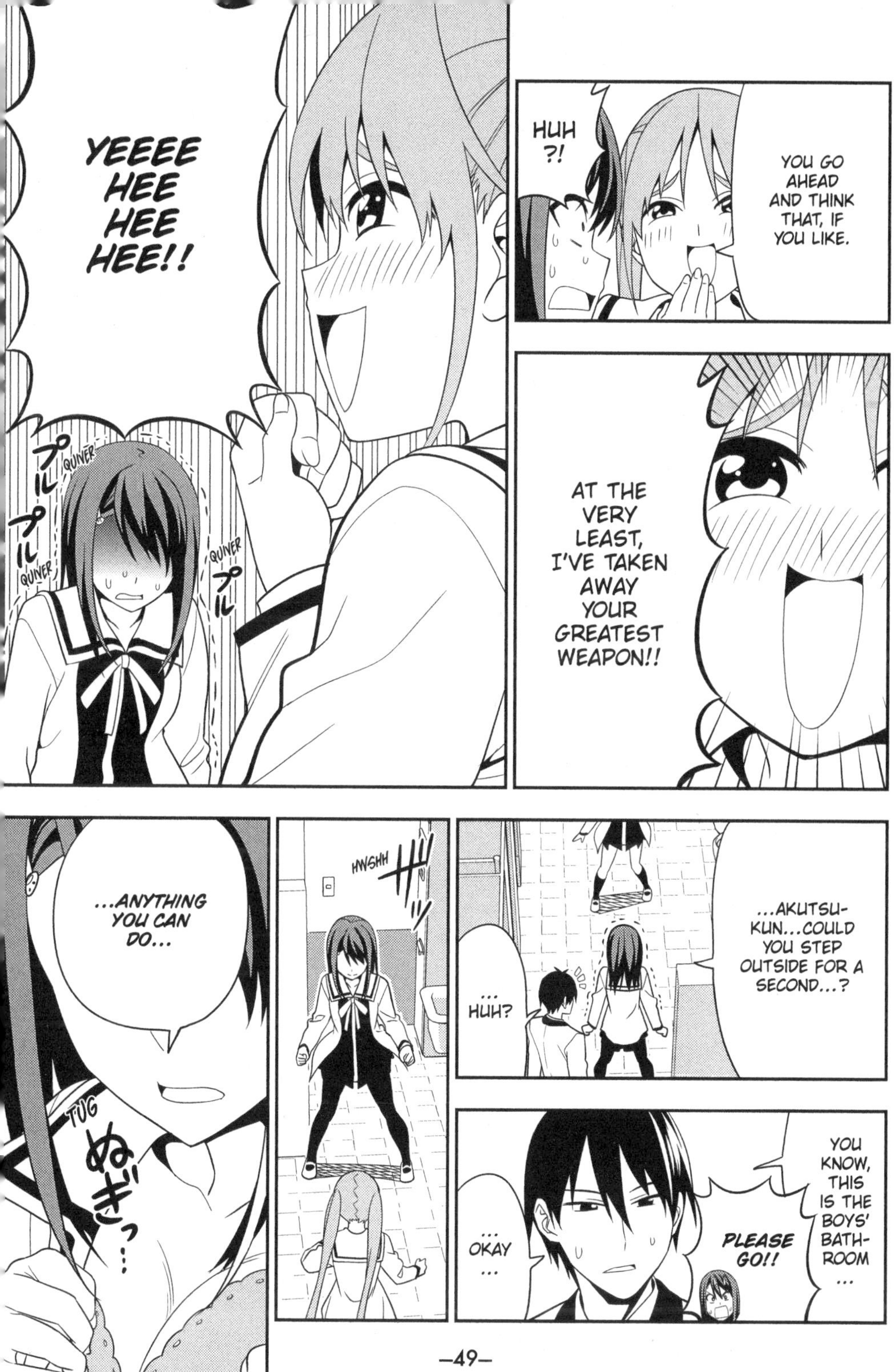
YOU GO AHEAD AND THINK THAT, IF YOU LIKE.
HUH ?!
AT THE VERY LEAST, I'VE TAKEN AWAY YOUR GREATEST WEAPON!!
YEEEEE HEE HEE HEE!!
プル QUIVER
プル QUIVER
プル QUIVER
...AKUTSU-KUN...COULD YOU STEP OUTSIDE FOR A SECOND...?
... HUH?
YOU KNOW, THIS IS THE BOYS' BATH-ROOM ...
PLEASE GO!!
... OKAY ...
HWSHH
...ANYTHING YOU CAN DO...
TUG ぬぎっ...

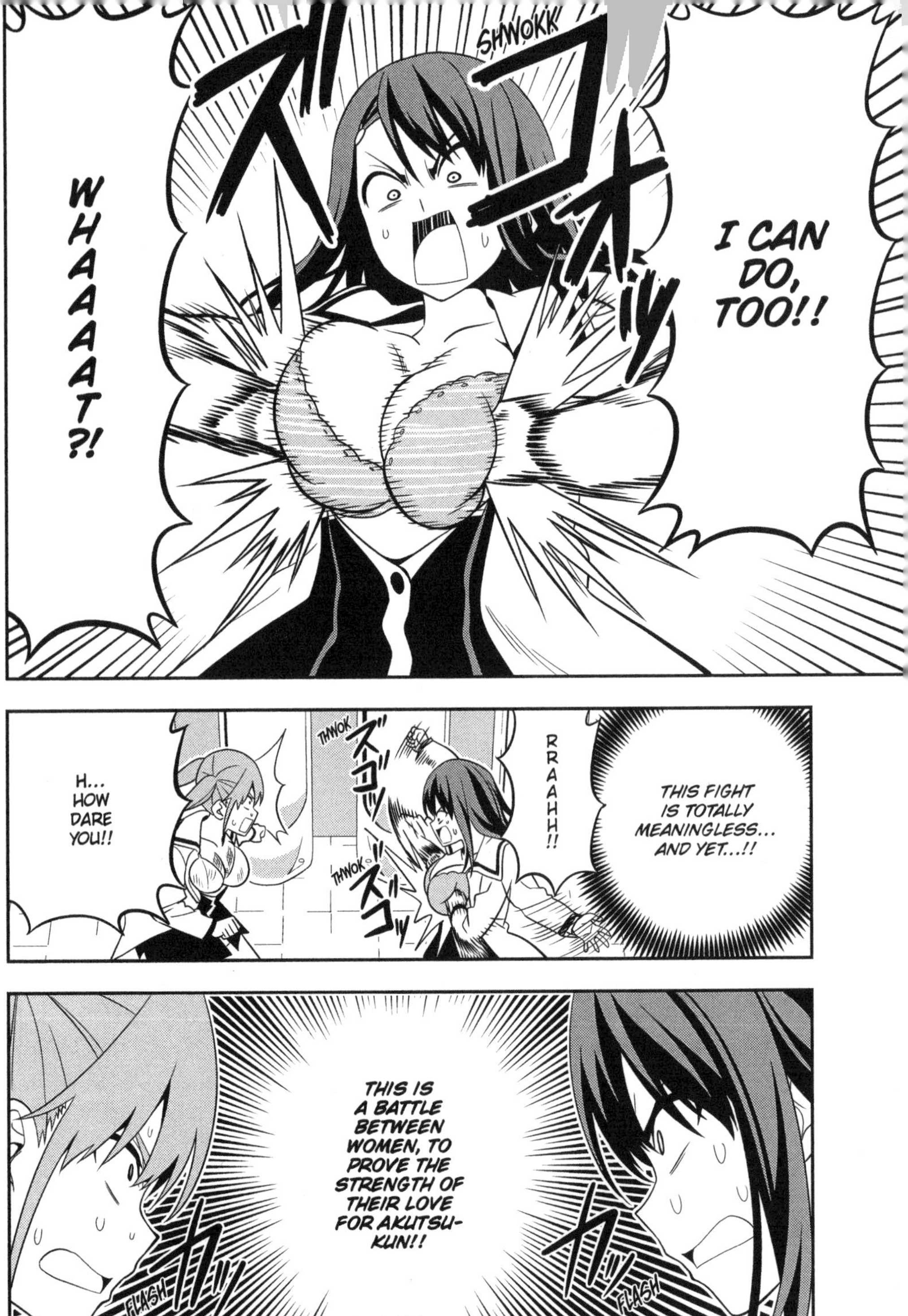
SHWOKK
I CAN DO, TOO!!
WHAAAAAT?!
THIS FIGHT IS TOTALLY MEANINGLESS... AND YET...!!
RRAAHH!!
THWOK
THWOK
H... HOW DARE YOU!!
FLASH
THIS IS A BATTLE BETWEEN WOMEN, TO PROVE THE STRENGTH OF THEIR LOVE FOR AKUTSU-KUN!!
FLASH

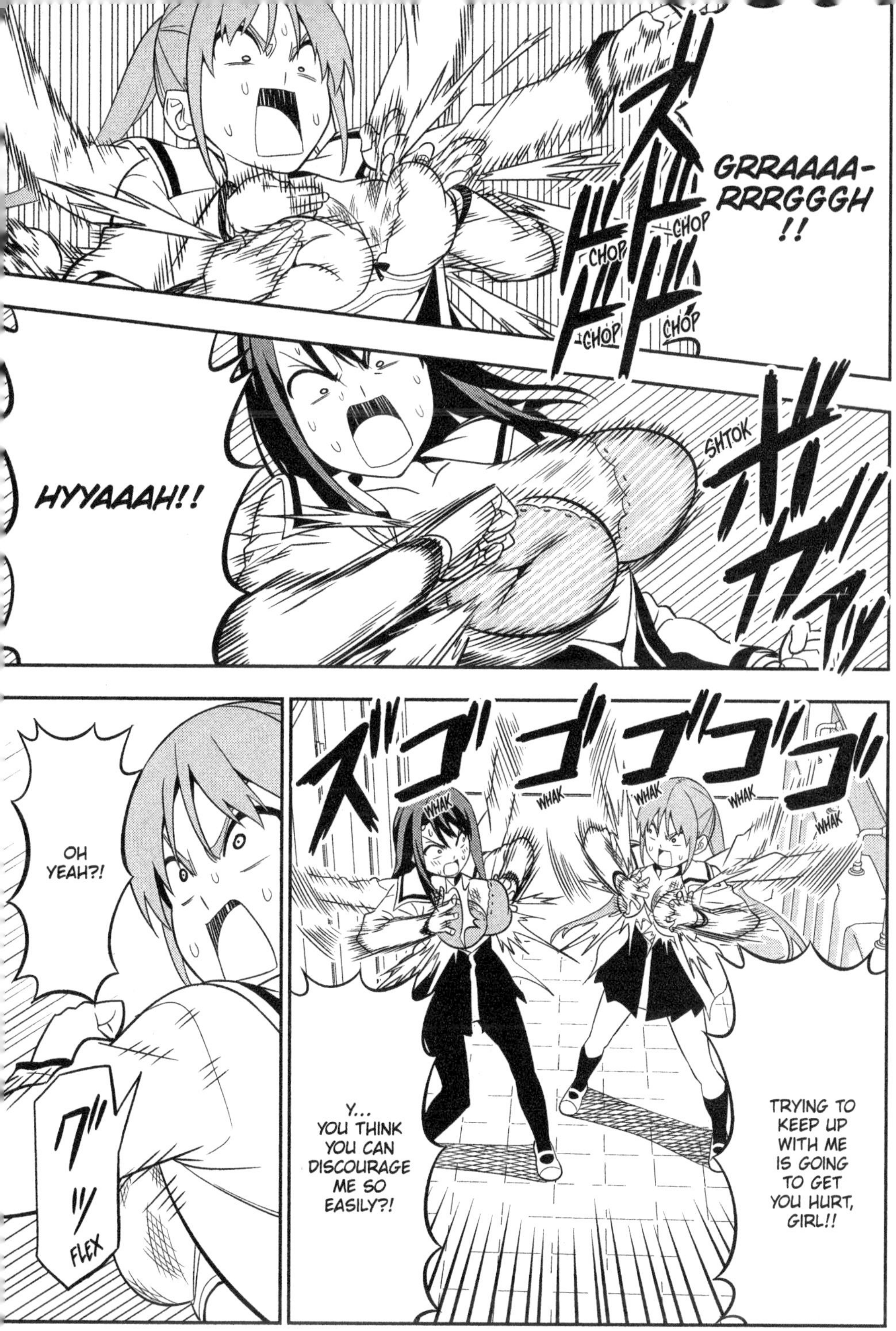

GRRAAAA-RRRGGGH!!
CHOP
CHOP
CHOP
CHOP
SHTOK
HYYAAAH!!
WHAK
WHAK
WHAK
WHAK
WHAK
TRYING TO KEEP UP WITH ME IS GOING TO GET YOU HURT, GIRL!!
Y... YOU THINK YOU CAN DISCOURAGE ME SO EASILY?!
OH YEAH?!
FLEX

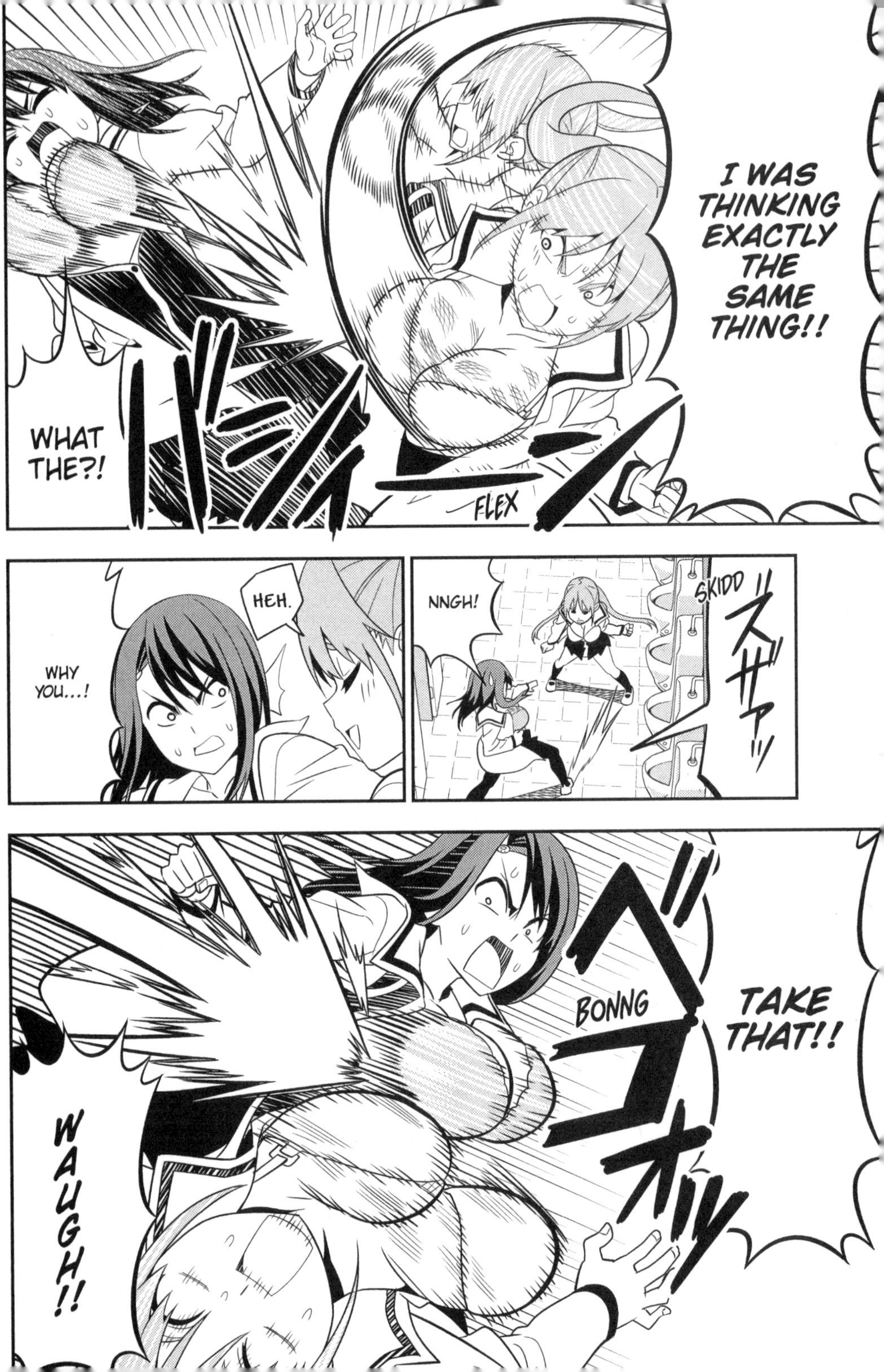
I WAS THINKING EXACTLY THE SAME THING!!
WHAT THE?!
FLEX
SKIDD
NNGH!
HEH.
WHY YOU...!
TAKE THAT!!
BONNG
WAUGH!!

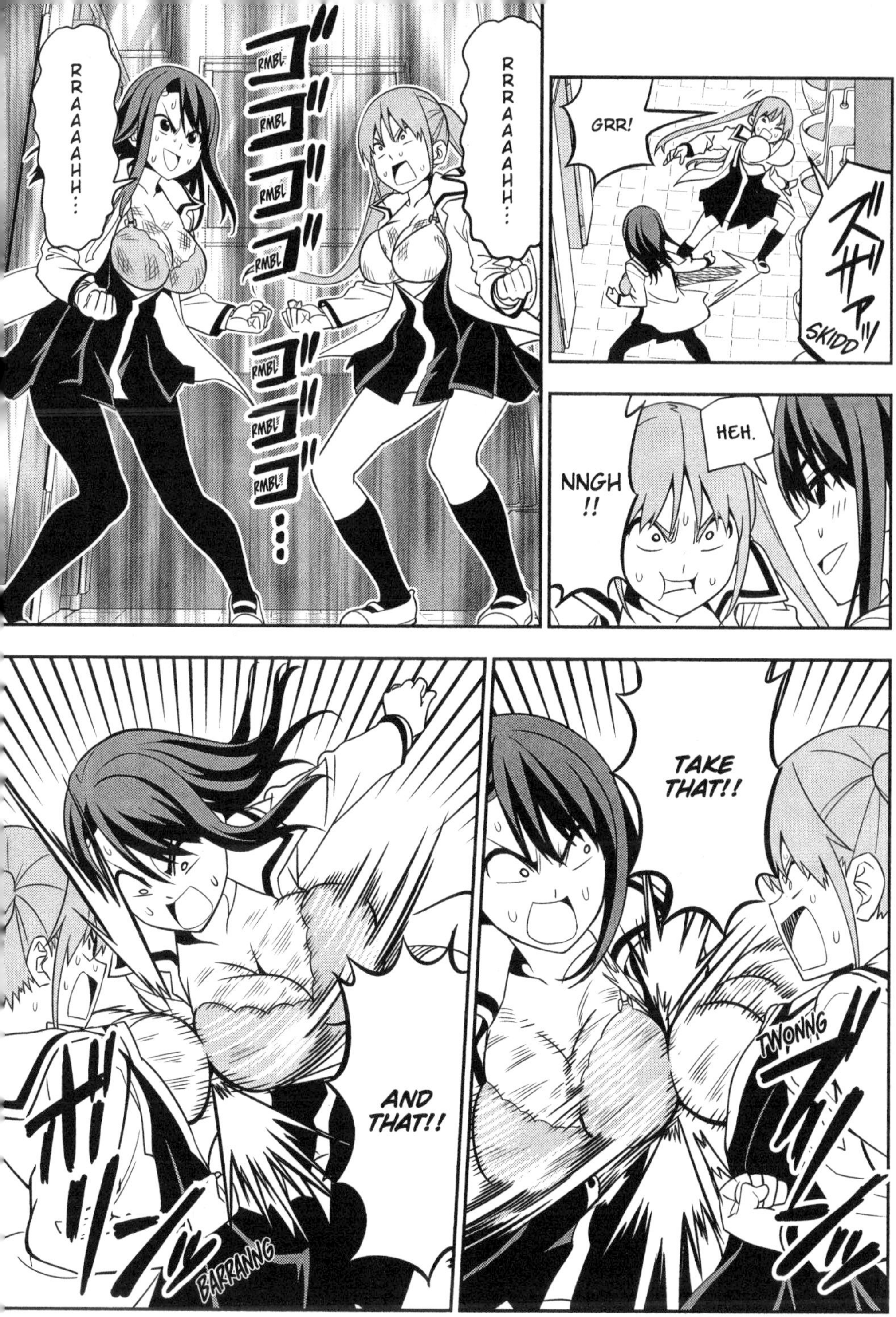
GRR!
SKIDD
HEH.
NNGH !!
RRRAAAAAAHH...
RMBL RMBL RMBL RMBL RMBL RMBL RMBL...
RRAAAAAAHH...
TAKE THAT!!
TWONNG
AND THAT!!
BARRANNG

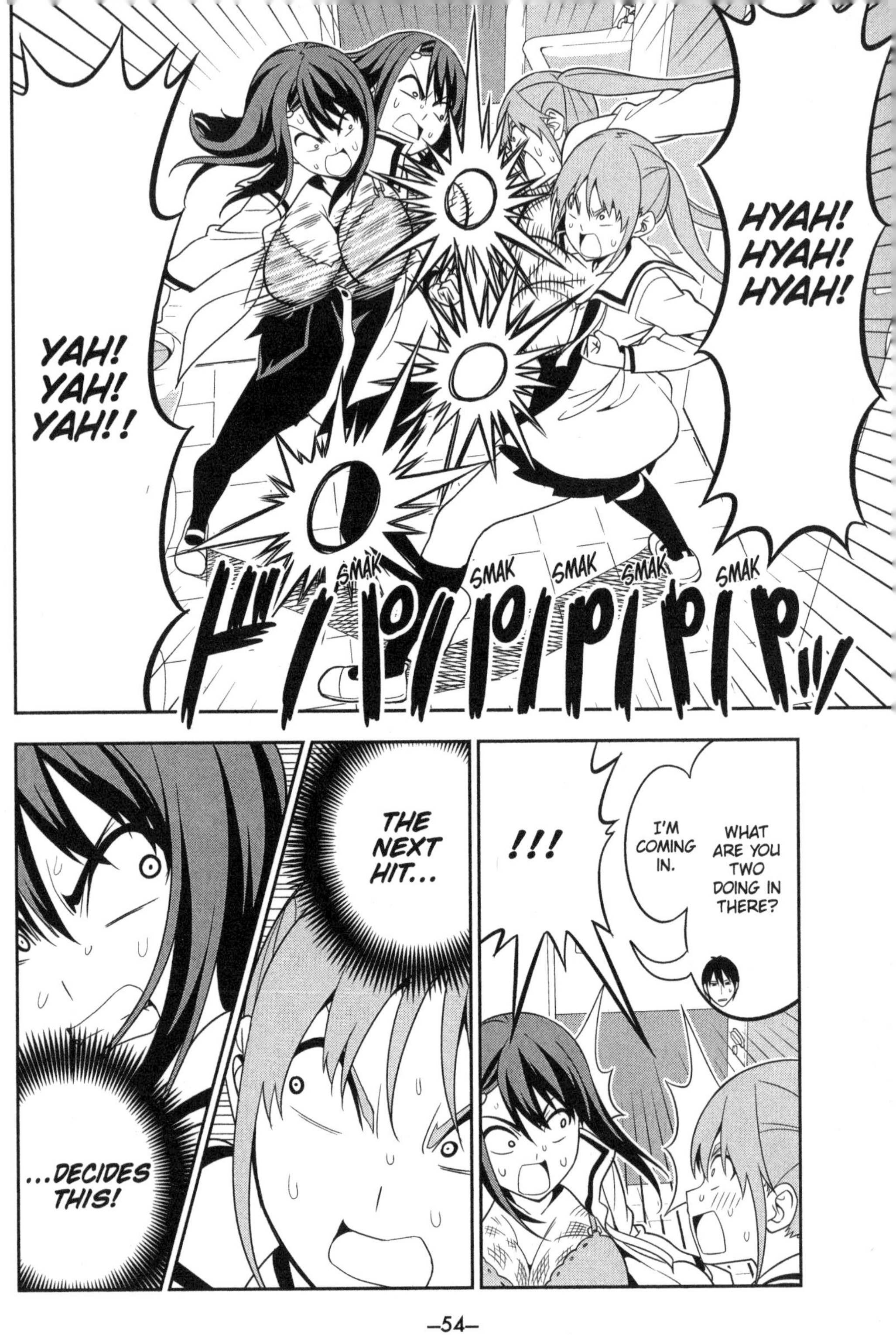
HYAH! HYAH! HYAH!
YAH! YAH! YAH!!
SMAK
SMAK
SMAK
SMAK
SMAK
WHAT ARE YOU TWO DOING IN THERE?
I'M COMING IN.
!!!
THE NEXT HIT...
...DECIDES THIS!

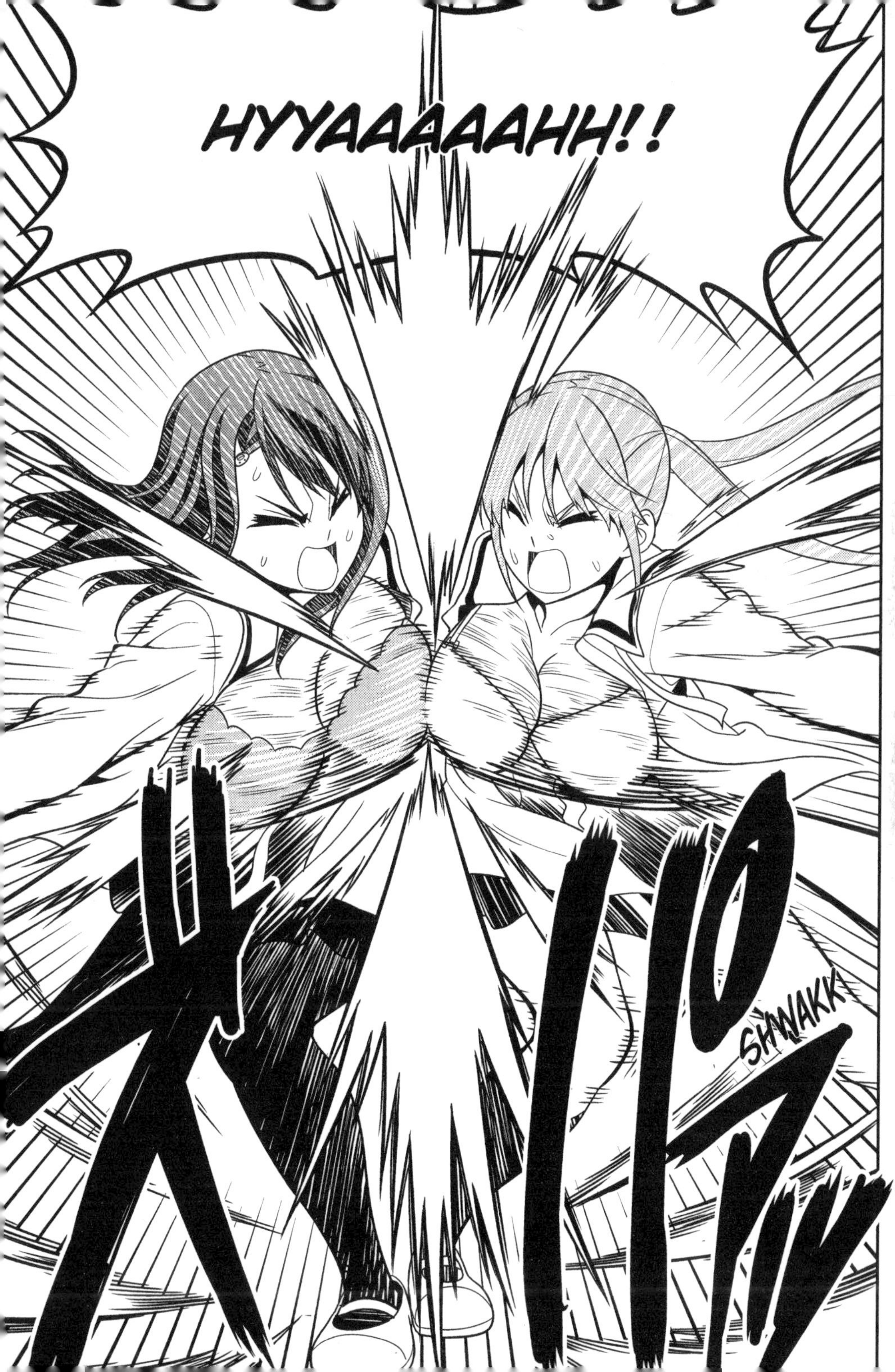
HYYAAAAAAHH!!
SHWAKK

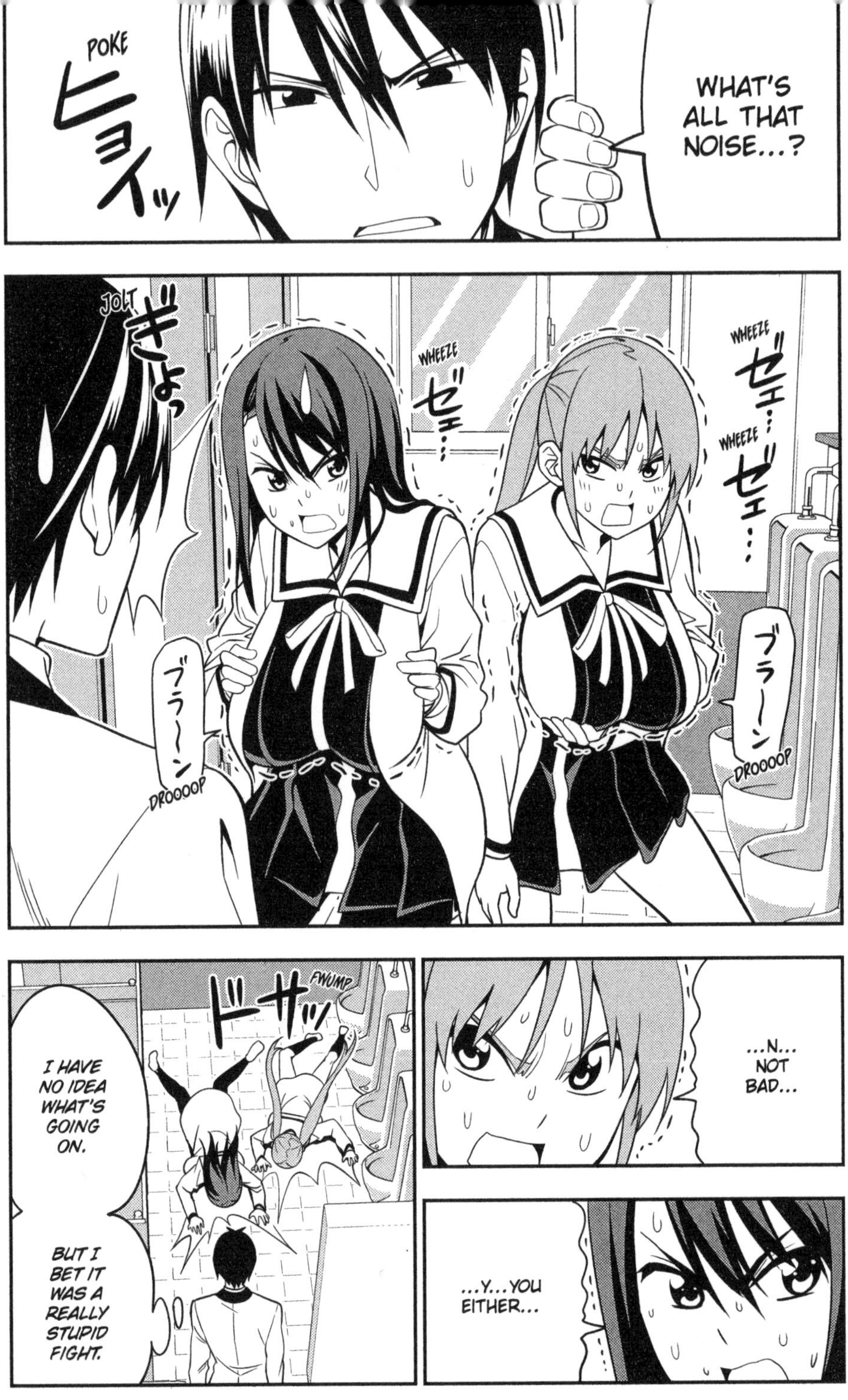
WHAT'S ALL THAT NOISE...?
POKE
ヒョイッ
WHEEZE
ゼェ…
WHEEZE
ゼェ…
ブラ～ン
DROOOOP
WHEEZE
ゼェ…
JOLT
ぎょっ
ブラ～ン
DROOOOP
...N... NOT BAD...
...Y... YOU EITHER...
FWUMP
ドサッ
I HAVE NO IDEA WHAT'S GOING ON.
BUT I BET IT WAS A REALLY STUPID FIGHT.

I Mean, It's The Bathroom Floor

TWITCH
ピクッ
TWITCH
ピクッ
TWITCH
ピクッ
TWITCH
ピクッ
DIS-GUSTING...

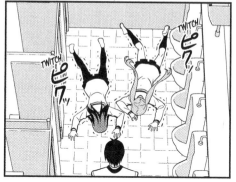

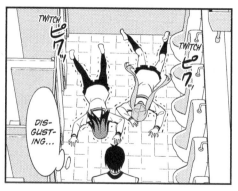

Aho-Girl

\\\'ahô͵gərl\\ *Japanese, noun.*
A clueless girl.

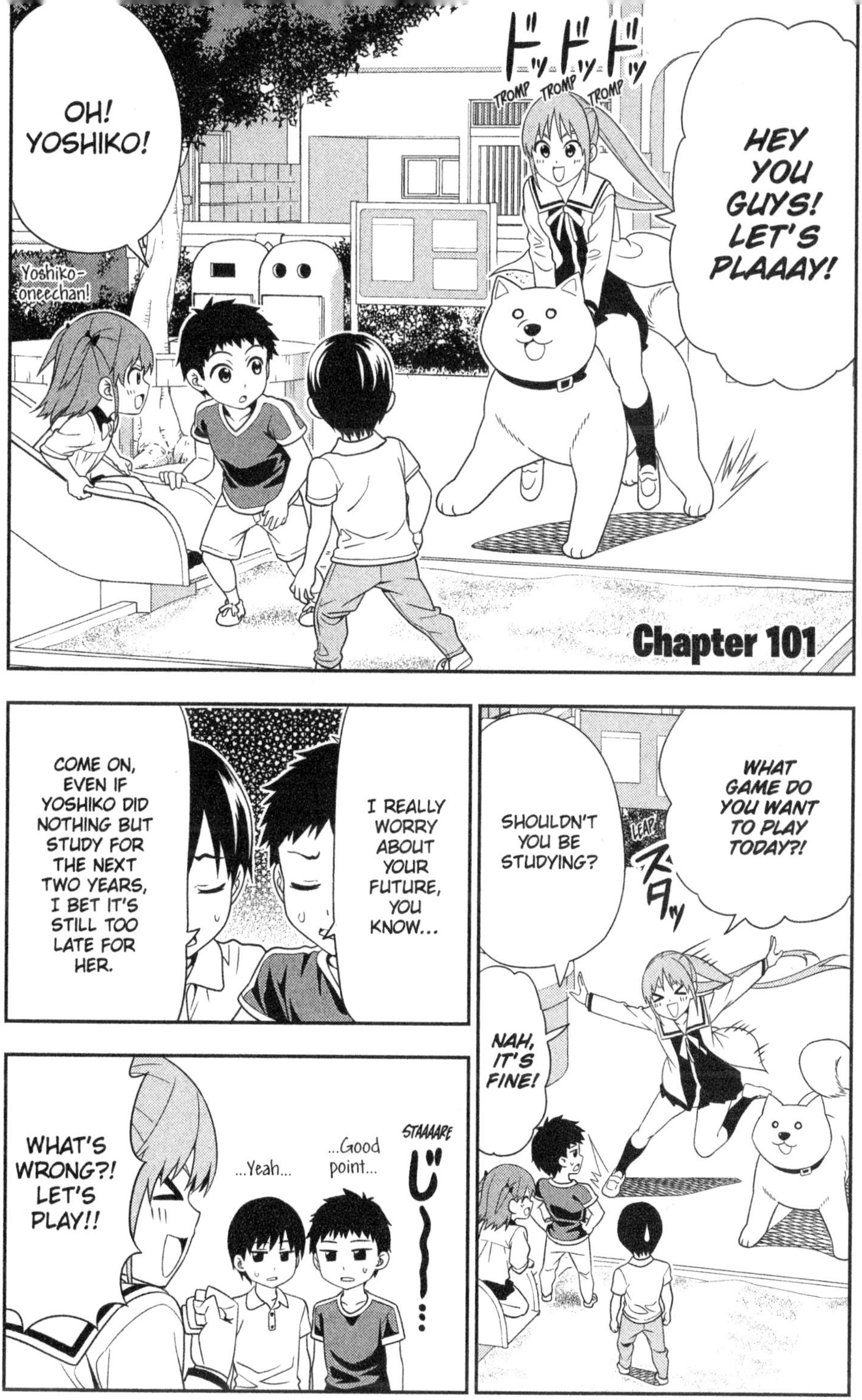
TROMP TROMP TROMP
HEY YOU GUYS! LET'S PLAAAY!
OH! YOSHIKO!
Yoshiko-oneechan!
Chapter 101
WHAT GAME DO YOU WANT TO PLAY TODAY?!
LEAP
SHOULDN'T YOU BE STUDYING?
NAH, IT'S FINE!
I REALLY WORRY ABOUT YOUR FUTURE, YOU KNOW...
COME ON, EVEN IF YOSHIKO DID NOTHING BUT STUDY FOR THE NEXT TWO YEARS, I BET IT'S STILL TOO LATE FOR HER.
STAAAARE
...Good point...
...Yeah...
WHAT'S WRONG?! LET'S PLAY!!

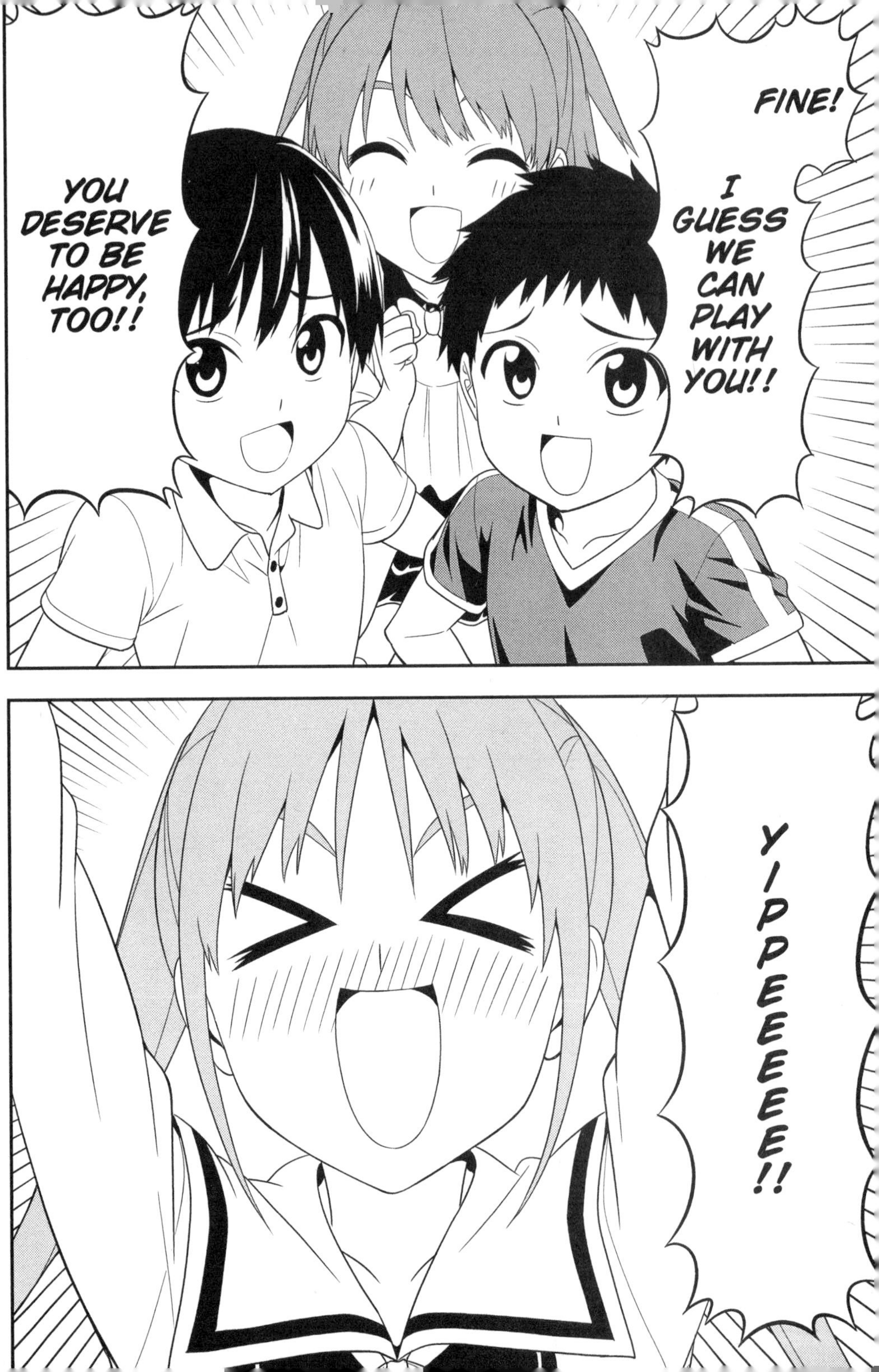
FINE! I GUESS WE CAN PLAY WITH YOU!!
YOU DESERVE TO BE HAPPY, TOO!!
YIPPEEEEE!!

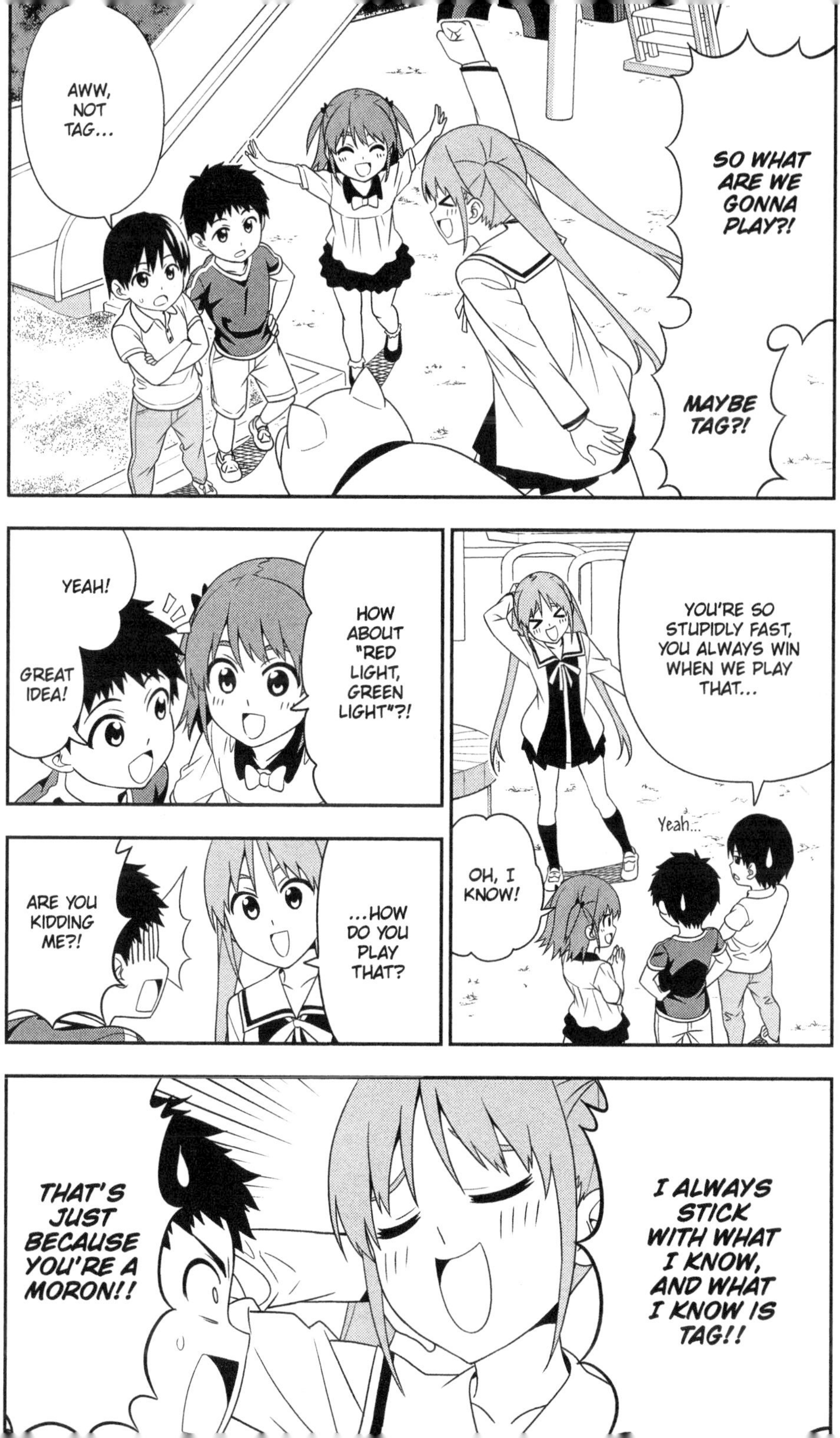
SO WHAT ARE WE GONNA PLAY?!
MAYBE TAG?!
AWW, NOT TAG...
YOU'RE SO STUPIDLY FAST, YOU ALWAYS WIN WHEN WE PLAY THAT...
Yeah...
OH, I KNOW!
HOW ABOUT "RED LIGHT, GREEN LIGHT"?!
YEAH!
GREAT IDEA!
...HOW DO YOU PLAY THAT?
ARE YOU KIDDING ME?!
I ALWAYS STICK WITH WHAT I KNOW, AND WHAT I KNOW IS TAG!!
THAT'S JUST BECAUSE YOU'RE A MORON!!

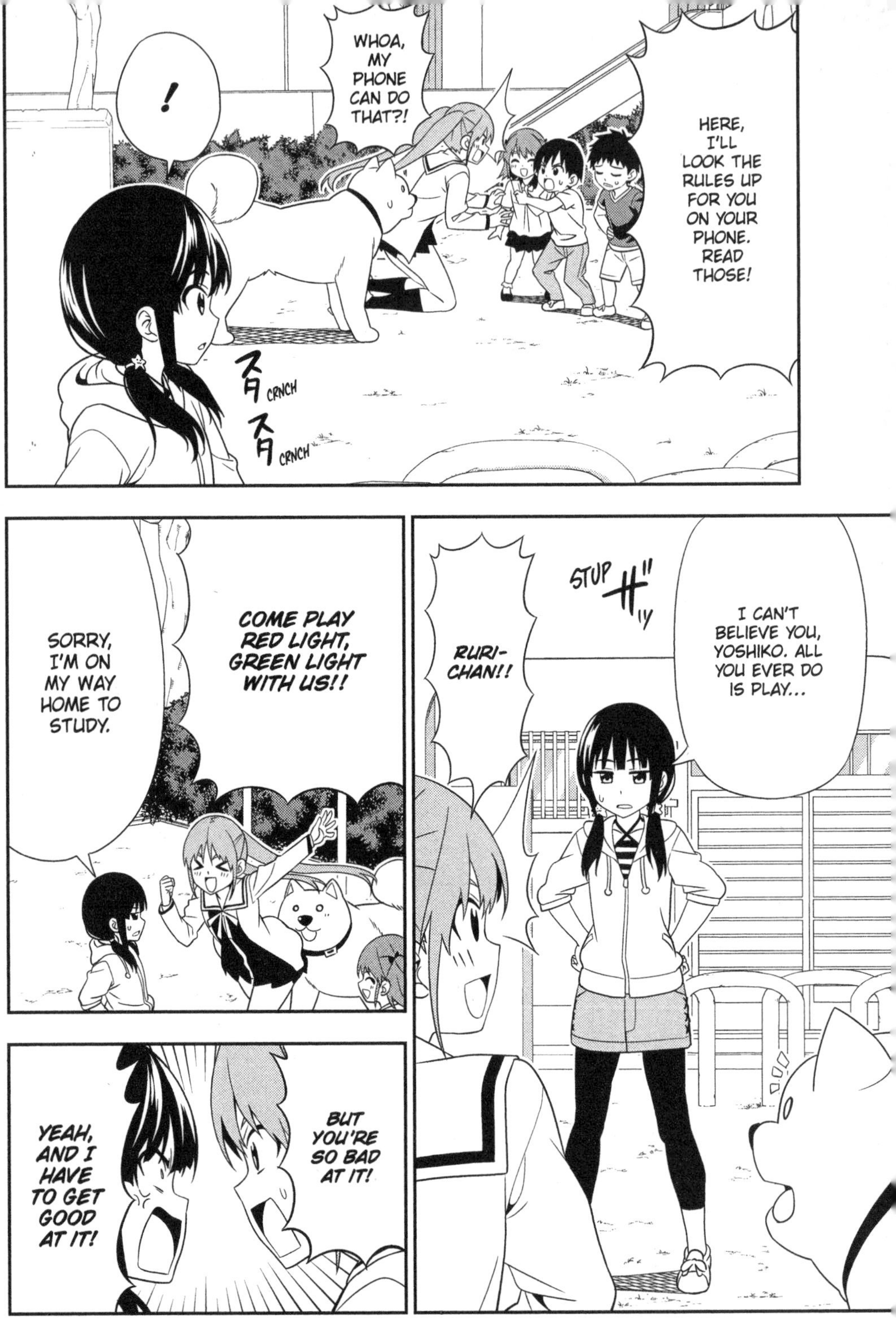
HERE, I'LL LOOK THE RULES UP FOR YOU ON YOUR PHONE. READ THOSE!
WHOA, MY PHONE CAN DO THAT?!
!
CRNCH
CRNCH
I CAN'T BELIEVE YOU, YOSHIKO. ALL YOU EVER DO IS PLAY...
STUP
RURI-CHAN!!
COME PLAY RED LIGHT, GREEN LIGHT WITH US!!
SORRY, I'M ON MY WAY HOME TO STUDY.
BUT YOU'RE SO BAD AT IT!
YEAH, AND I HAVE TO GET GOOD AT IT!

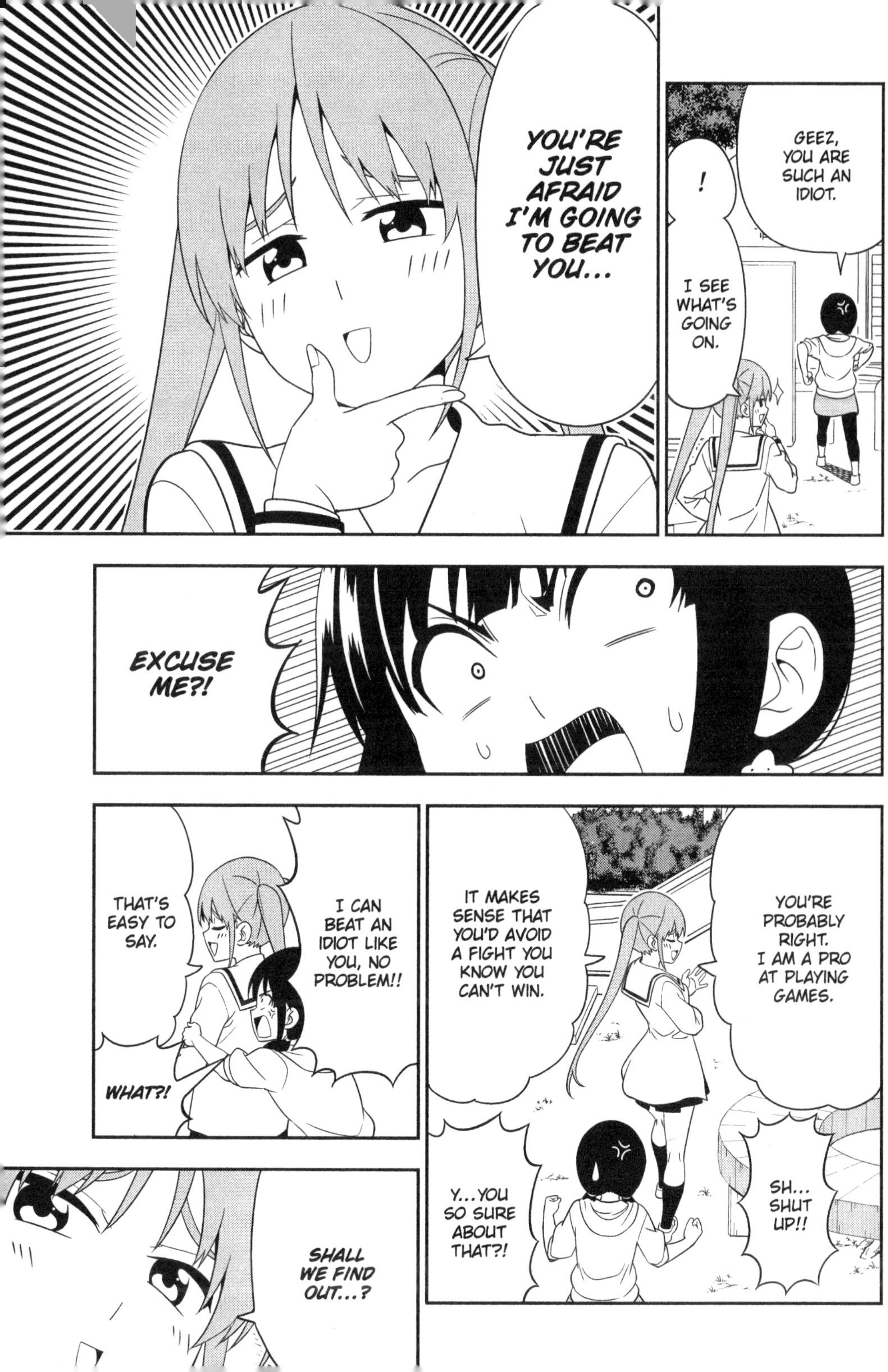
GEEZ, YOU ARE SUCH AN IDIOT.
!
I SEE WHAT'S GOING ON.
YOU'RE JUST AFRAID I'M GOING TO BEAT YOU...
EXCUSE ME?!
YOU'RE PROBABLY RIGHT. I AM A PRO AT PLAYING GAMES.
IT MAKES SENSE THAT YOU'D AVOID A FIGHT YOU KNOW YOU CAN'T WIN.
SH... SHUT UP!!
Y...YOU SO SURE ABOUT THAT?!
I CAN BEAT AN IDIOT LIKE YOU, NO PROBLEM!!
THAT'S EASY TO SAY.
WHAT?!
SHALL WE FIND OUT...?

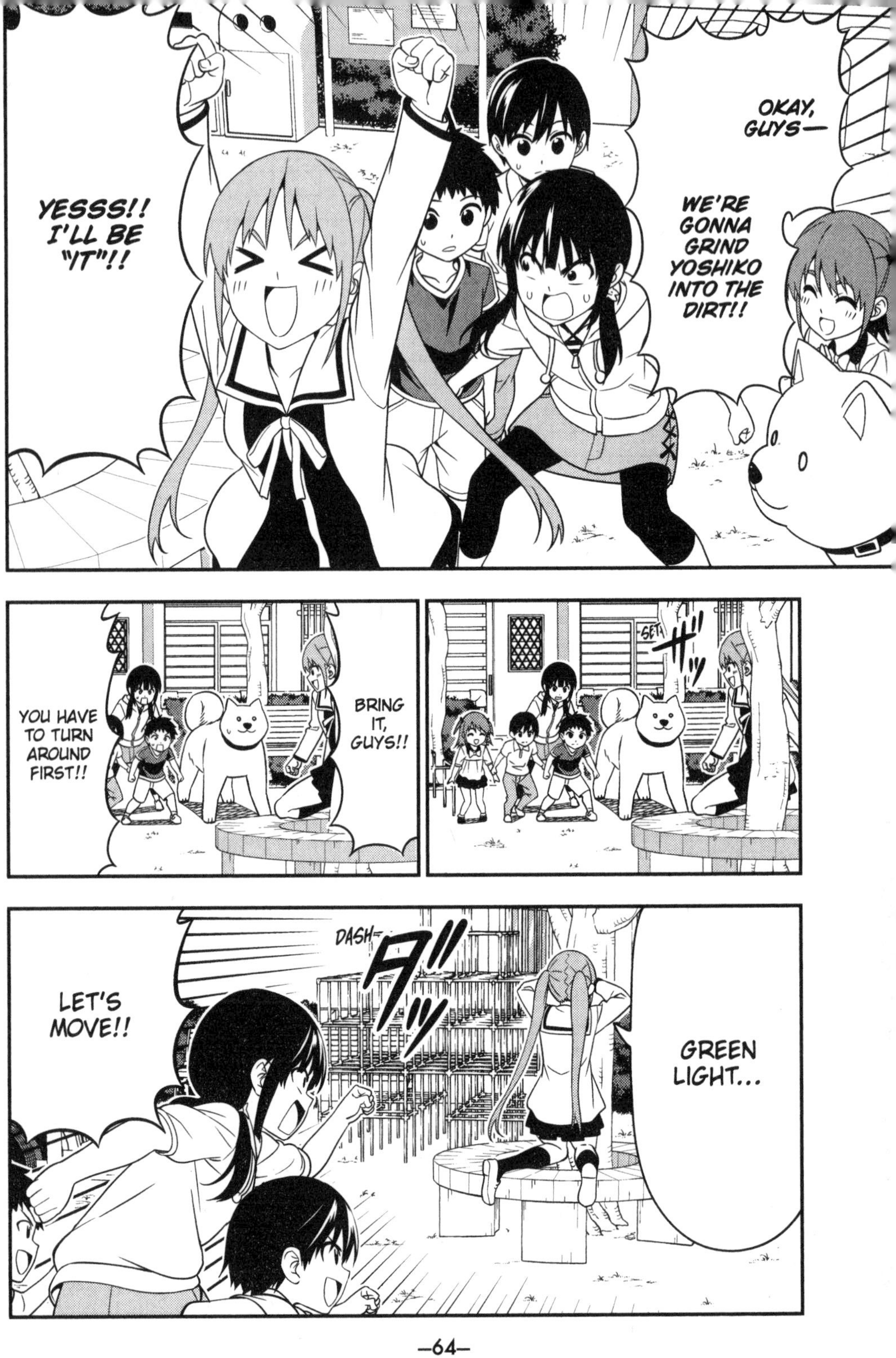
OKAY, GUYS—
WE'RE GONNA GRIND YOSHIKO INTO THE DIRT!!
YESSS!! I'LL BE "IT"!!
SET
BRING IT, GUYS!!
YOU HAVE TO TURN AROUND FIRST!!
GREEN LIGHT...
DASH
LET'S MOVE!!

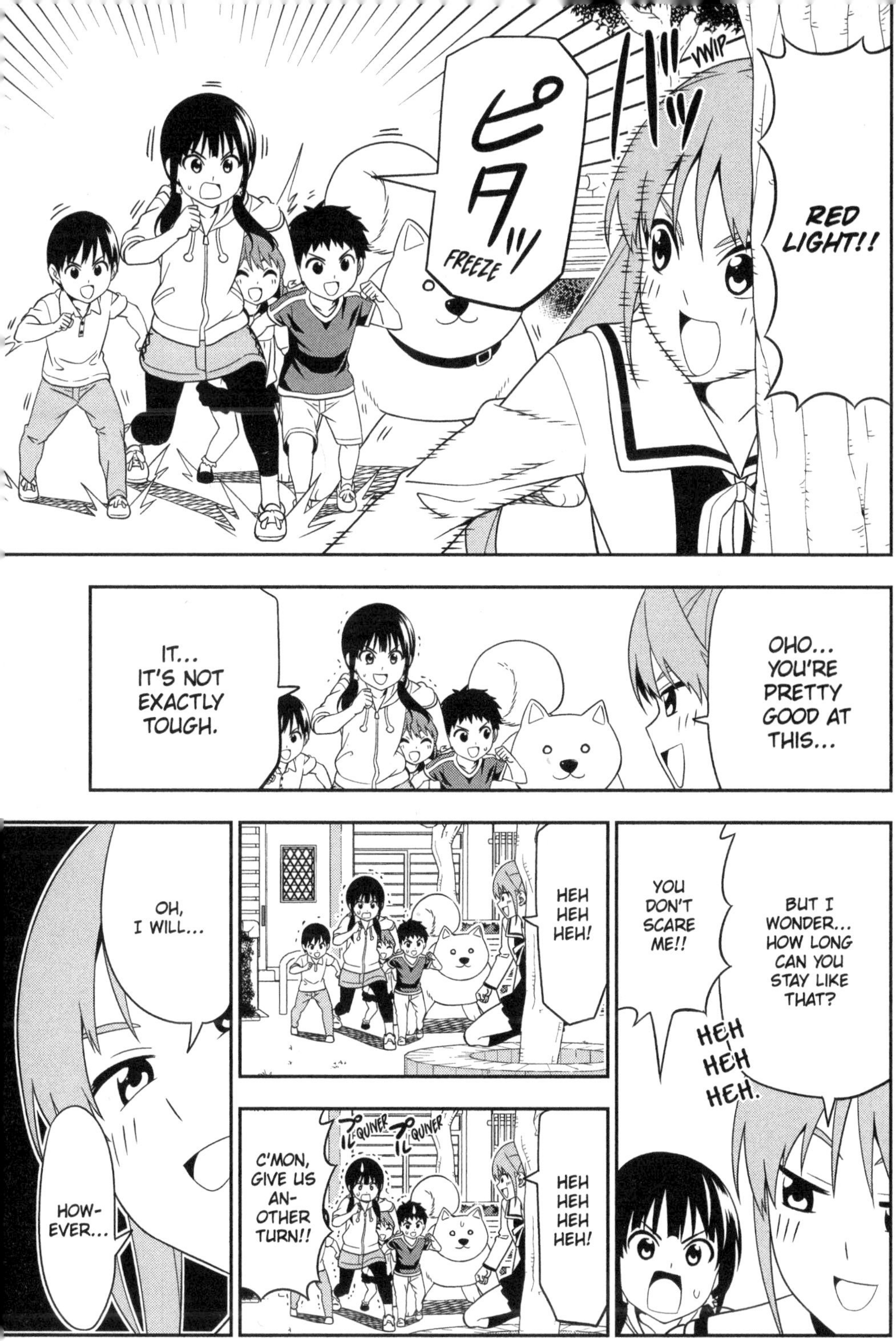
RED LIGHT!!
バッ VWIP
ピタッ FREEZE
OHO... YOU'RE PRETTY GOOD AT THIS...
IT... IT'S NOT EXACTLY TOUGH.
BUT I WONDER... HOW LONG CAN YOU STAY LIKE THAT?
HEH HEH HEH.
YOU DON'T SCARE ME!!
HEH HEH HEH!
HEH HEH HEH HEH!
プル QUIVER プル QUIVER
C'MON, GIVE US AN-OTHER TURN!!
OH, I WILL...
HOW-EVER...

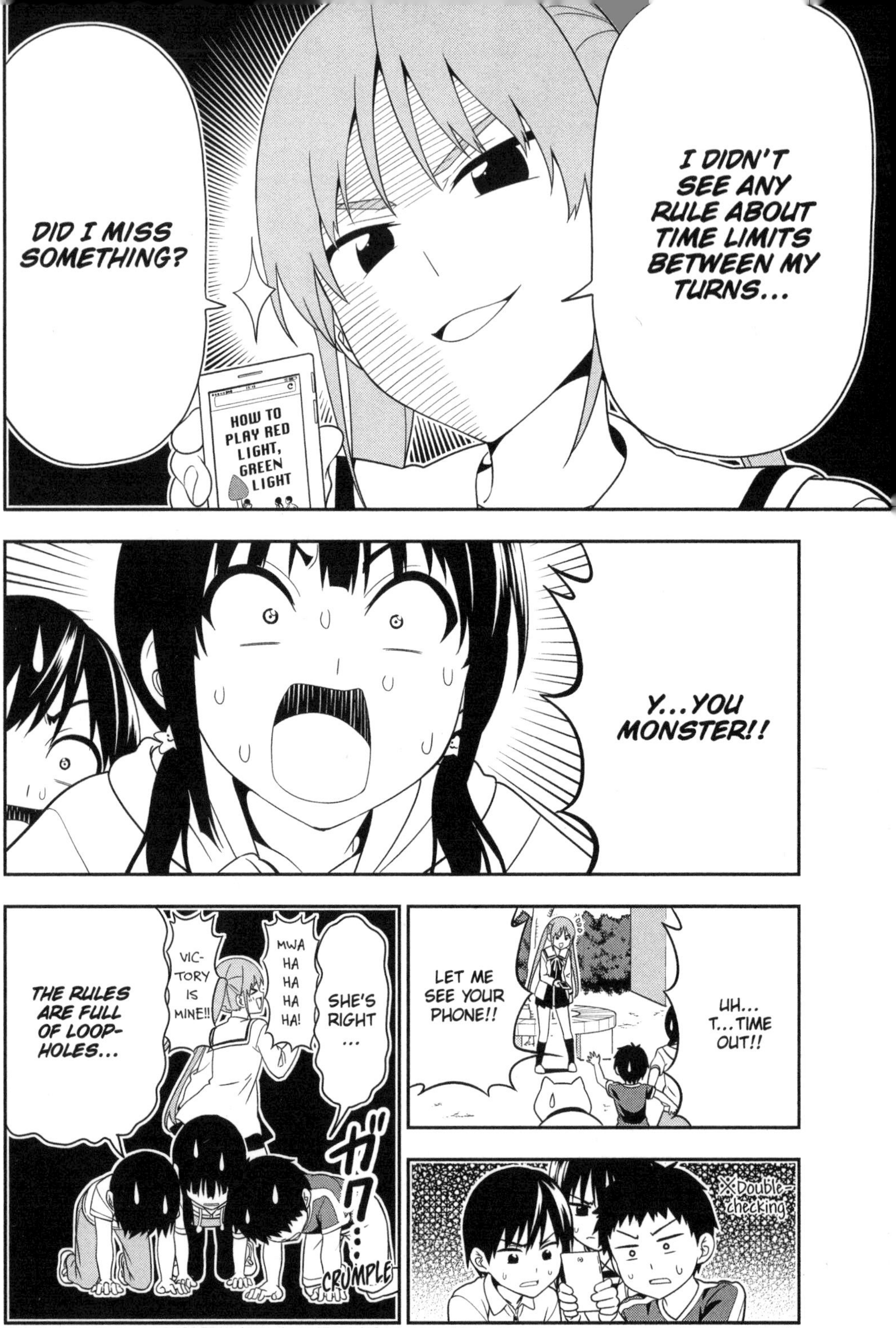
I DIDN'T SEE ANY RULE ABOUT TIME LIMITS BETWEEN MY TURNS...
DID I MISS SOMETHING?
HOW TO PLAY RED LIGHT, GREEN LIGHT
Y...YOU MONSTER!!
UH... T...TIME OUT!!
LET ME SEE YOUR PHONE!!
※Double-checking
SHE'S RIGHT...
MWA HA HA HA HA!
VICTORY IS MINE!!
THE RULES ARE FULL OF LOOP-HOLES...
CRUMPLE
※THERE REALLY WASN'T ANY RULE FOR IT.

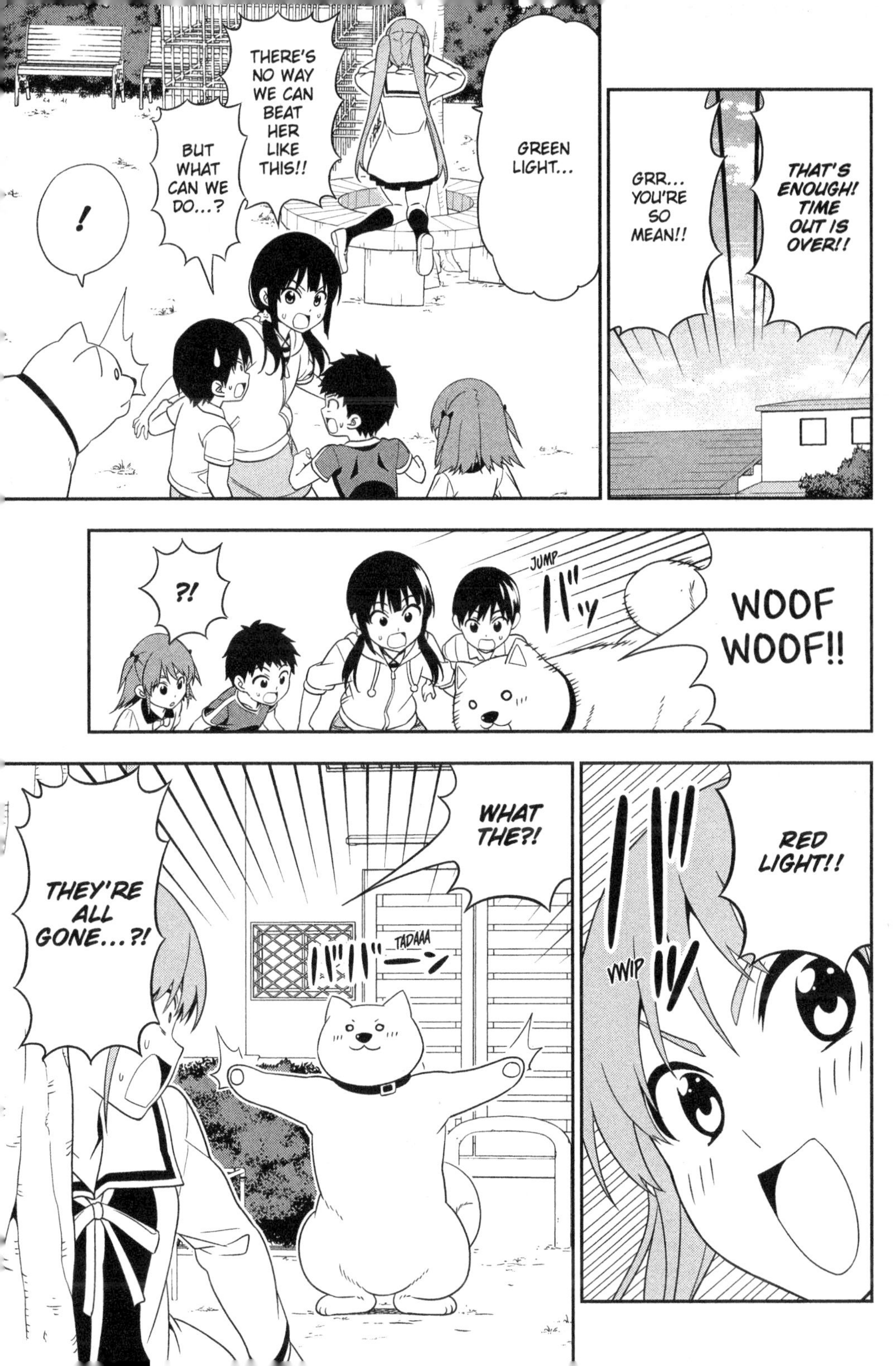
THAT'S ENOUGH! TIME OUT IS OVER!!
GRR... YOU'RE SO MEAN!!
GREEN LIGHT...
THERE'S NO WAY WE CAN BEAT HER LIKE THIS!!
BUT WHAT CAN WE DO...?
!
WOOF WOOF!!
JUMP
?!
RED LIGHT!!
VWIP
WHAT THE?!
TADAAA
THEY'RE ALL GONE...?!

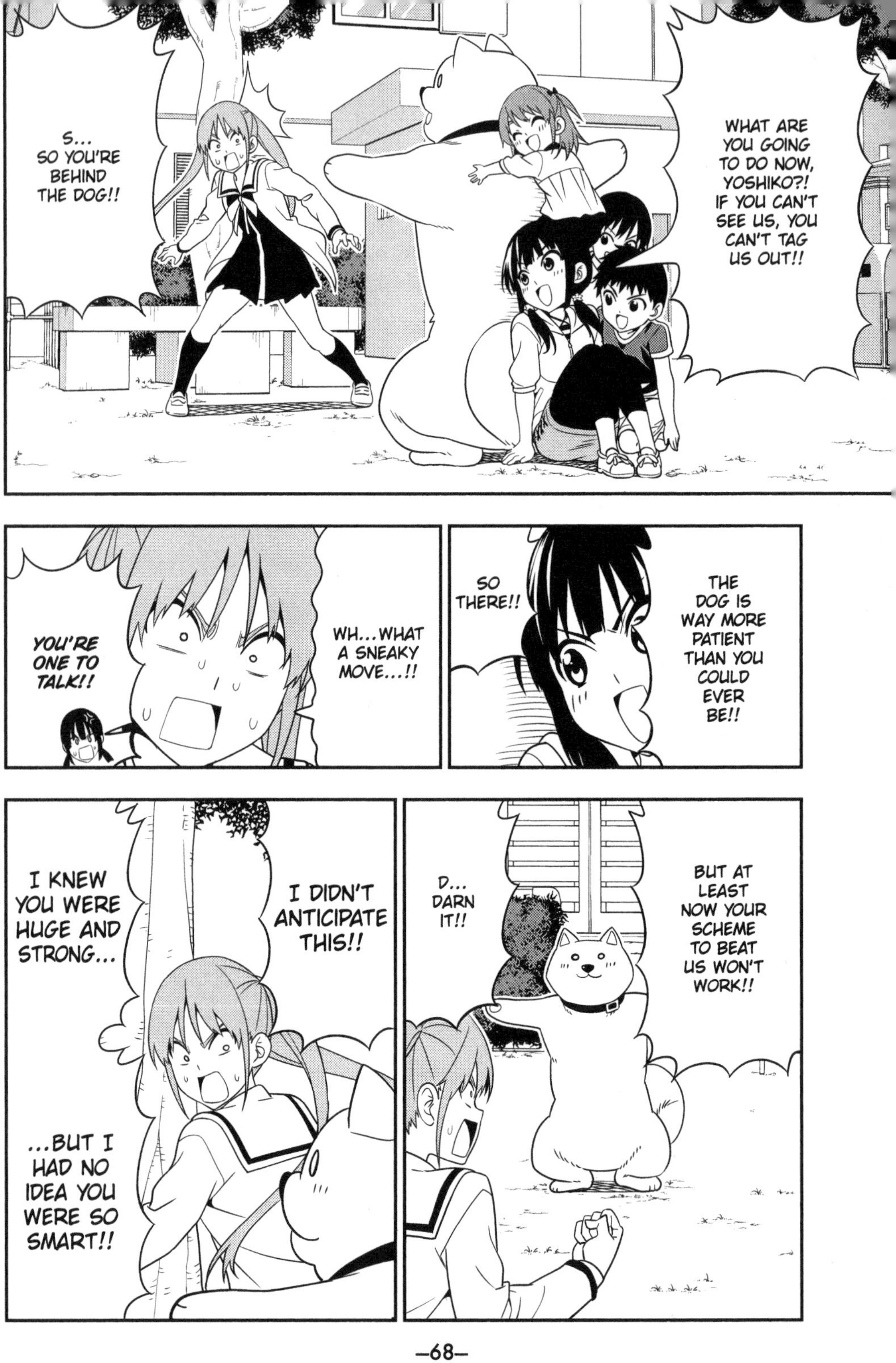
WHAT ARE YOU GOING TO DO NOW, YOSHIKO?! IF YOU CAN'T SEE US, YOU CAN'T TAG US OUT!!
S... SO YOU'RE BEHIND THE DOG!!
THE DOG IS WAY MORE PATIENT THAN YOU COULD EVER BE!!
SO THERE!!
WH...WHAT A SNEAKY MOVE...!!
YOU'RE ONE TO TALK!!
BUT AT LEAST NOW YOUR SCHEME TO BEAT US WON'T WORK!!
D... DARN IT!!
I DIDN'T ANTICIPATE THIS!!
I KNEW YOU WERE HUGE AND STRONG...
...BUT I HAD NO IDEA YOU WERE SO SMART!!

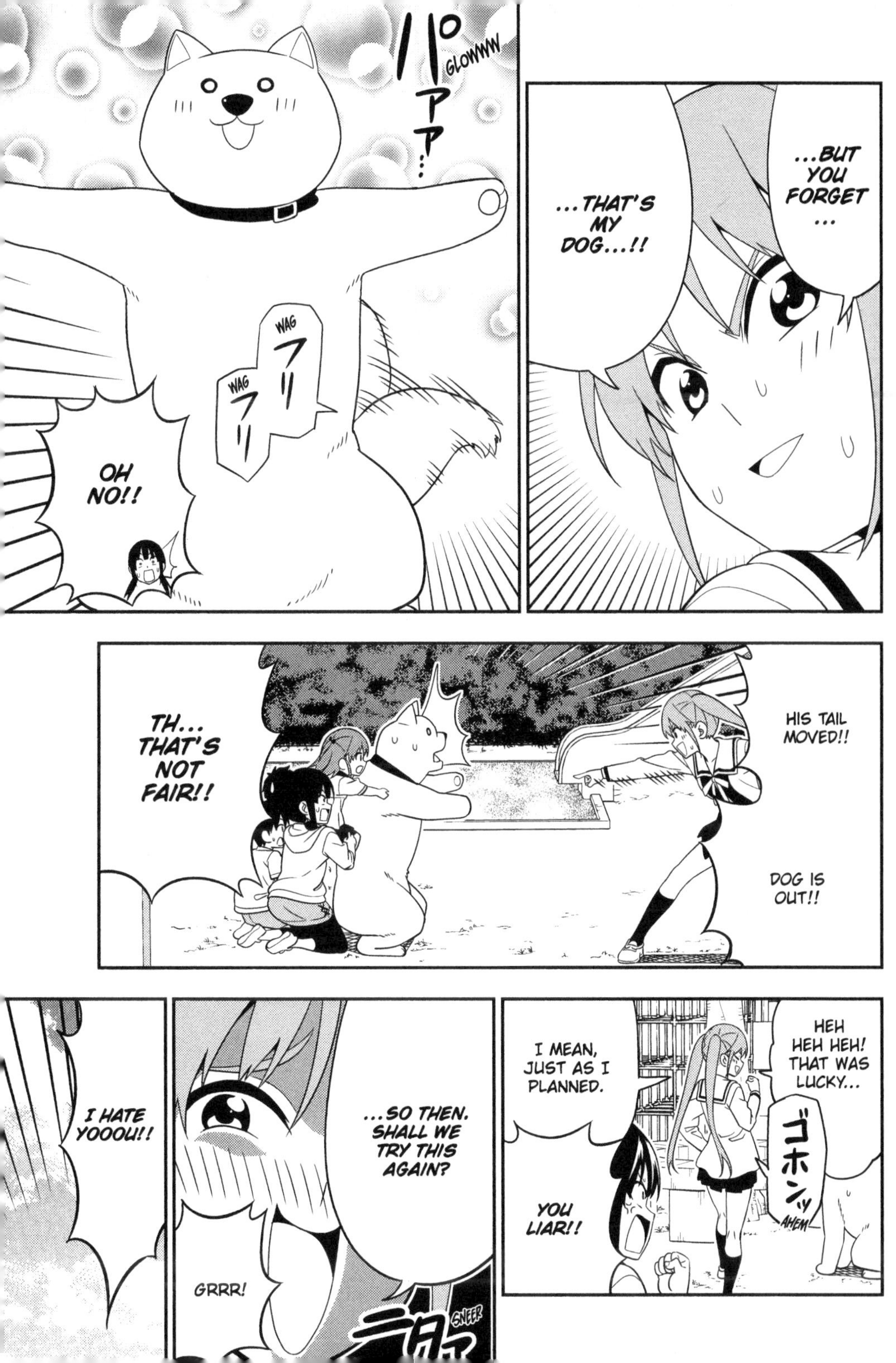
...BUT YOU FORGET...
...THAT'S MY DOG...!!
パァァ...
GLOWWW
フリ
WAG
フリ
WAG
OH NO!!
HIS TAIL MOVED!!
DOG IS OUT!!
TH... THAT'S NOT FAIR!!
HEH HEH HEH! THAT WAS LUCKY...
ゴホンッ
AHEM
I MEAN, JUST AS I PLANNED.
YOU LIAR!!
...SO THEN. SHALL WE TRY THIS AGAIN?
GRRR!
SNEER
I HATE YOOOU!!

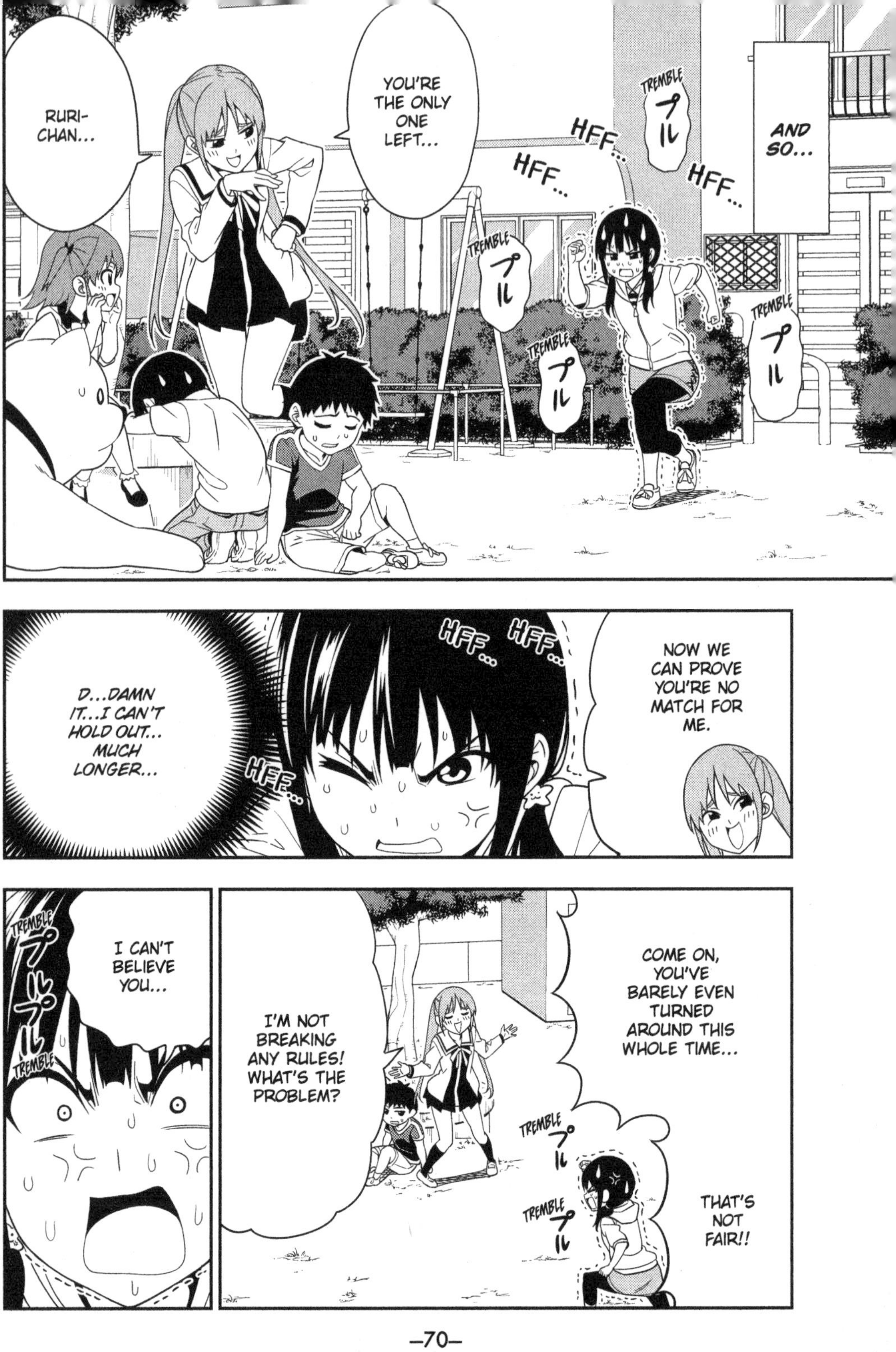
AND SO...
HFF...
TREMBLE
プル
HFF...
HFF...
TREMBLE
プル
TREMBLE
プル
TREMBLE
プル
YOU'RE THE ONLY ONE LEFT...
RURI-CHAN...
NOW WE CAN PROVE YOU'RE NO MATCH FOR ME.
HFF... HFF...
HFF...
D...DAMN IT...I CAN'T HOLD OUT... MUCH LONGER...
COME ON, YOU'VE BARELY EVEN TURNED AROUND THIS WHOLE TIME...
THAT'S NOT FAIR!!
TREMBLE
プル
TREMBLE
プル
I'M NOT BREAKING ANY RULES! WHAT'S THE PROBLEM?
I CAN'T BELIEVE YOU...
TREMBLE
プルプル
TREMBLE

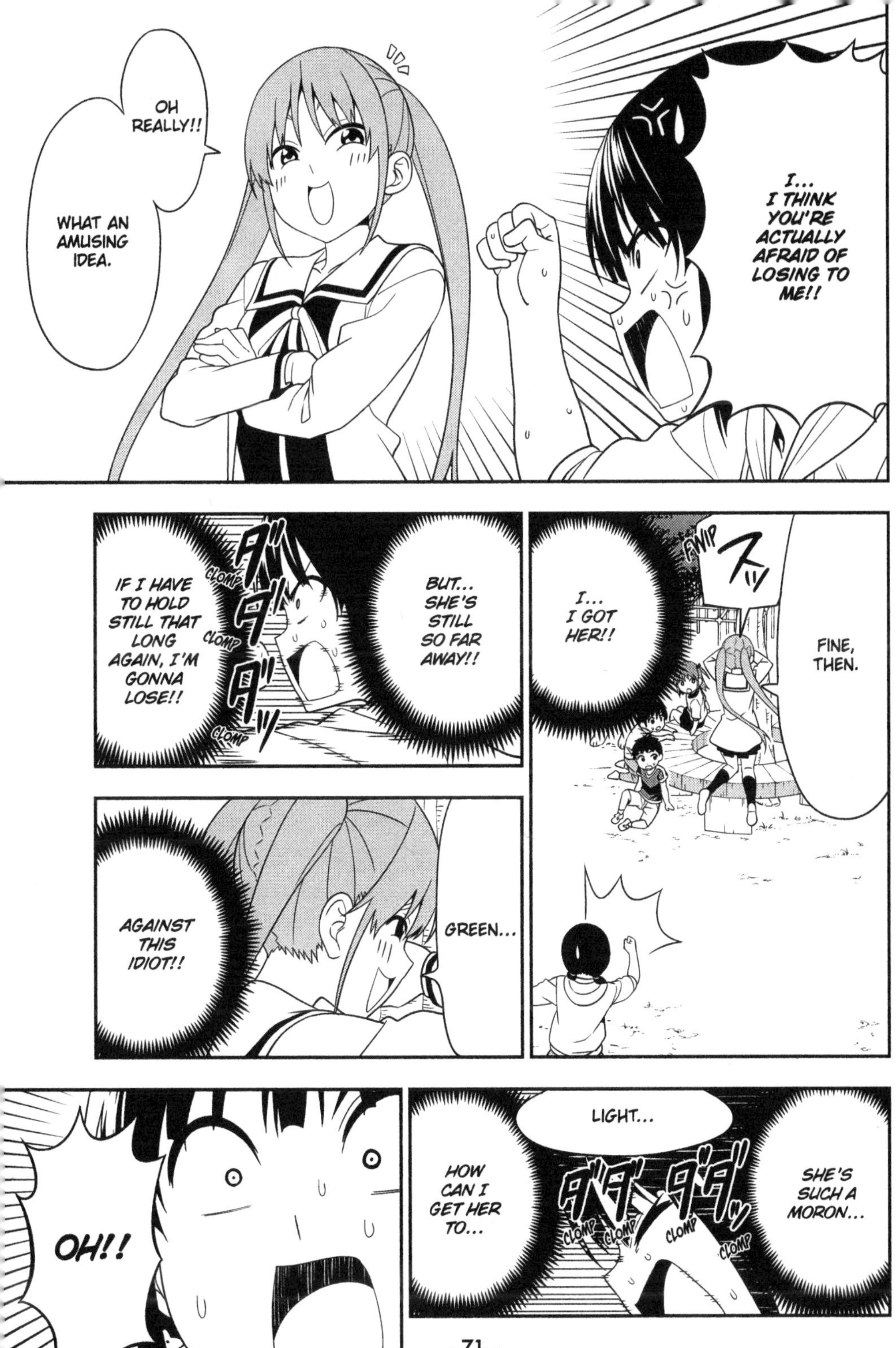

I... I THINK YOU'RE ACTUALLY AFRAID OF LOSING TO ME!!
OH REALLY!!
WHAT AN AMUSING IDEA.
FWIP
スッ
FINE, THEN.
I... I GOT HER!!
BUT... SHE'S STILL SO FAR AWAY!!
ダダダダッ
CLOMP CLOMP CLOMP
IF I HAVE TO HOLD STILL THAT LONG AGAIN, I'M GONNA LOSE!!
GREEN...
AGAINST THIS IDIOT!!
LIGHT...
SHE'S SUCH A MORON...
ダダダダッ
CLOMP CLOMP CLOMP CLOMP
HOW CAN I GET HER TO...
OH!!

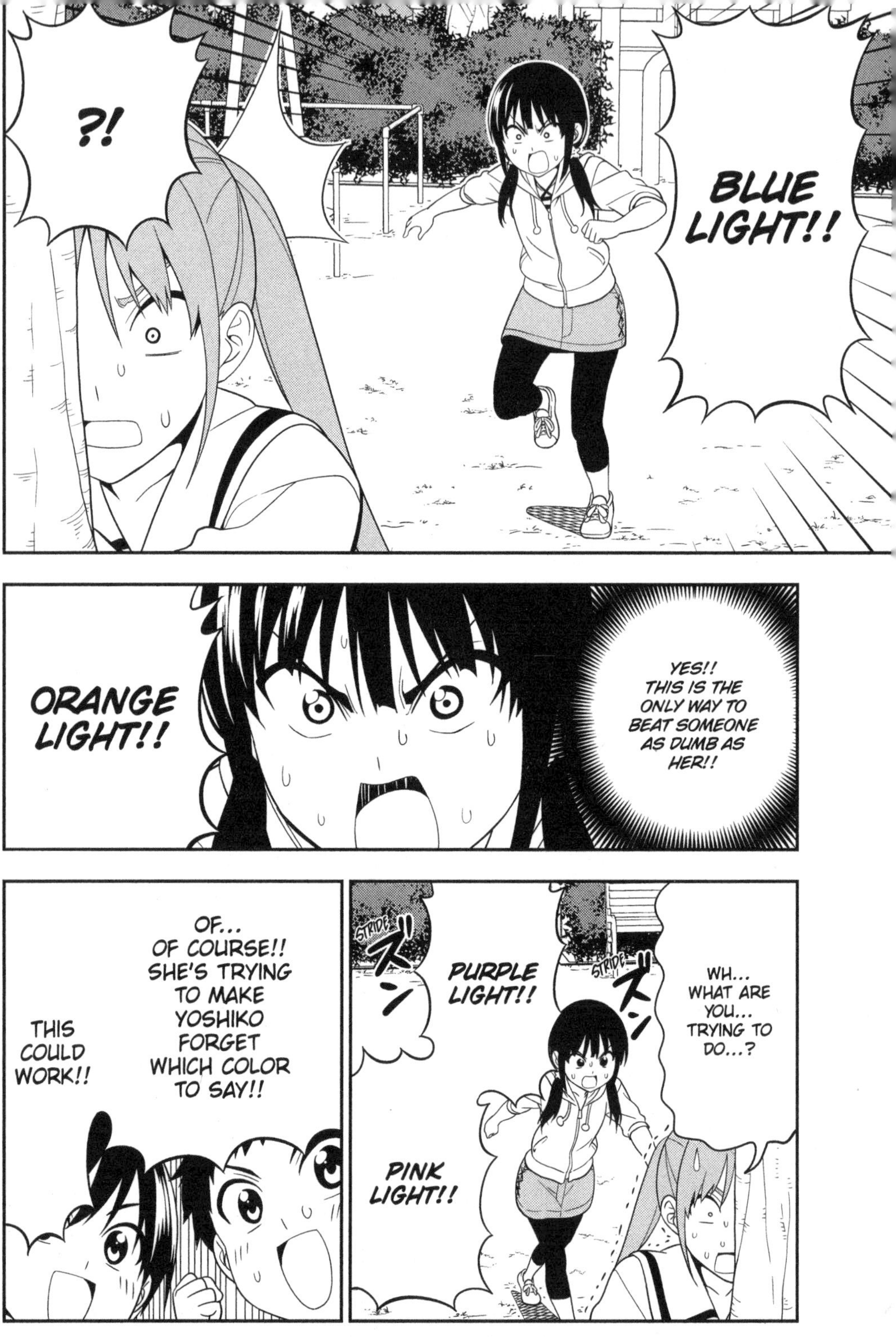
BLUE LIGHT!!
?!
YES!! THIS IS THE ONLY WAY TO BEAT SOMEONE AS DUMB AS HER!!
ORANGE LIGHT!!
WH... WHAT ARE YOU... TRYING TO DO...?
STRIDE
STRIDE
PURPLE LIGHT!!
PINK LIGHT!!
OF... OF COURSE!! SHE'S TRYING TO MAKE YOSHIKO FORGET WHICH COLOR TO SAY!!
THIS COULD WORK!!

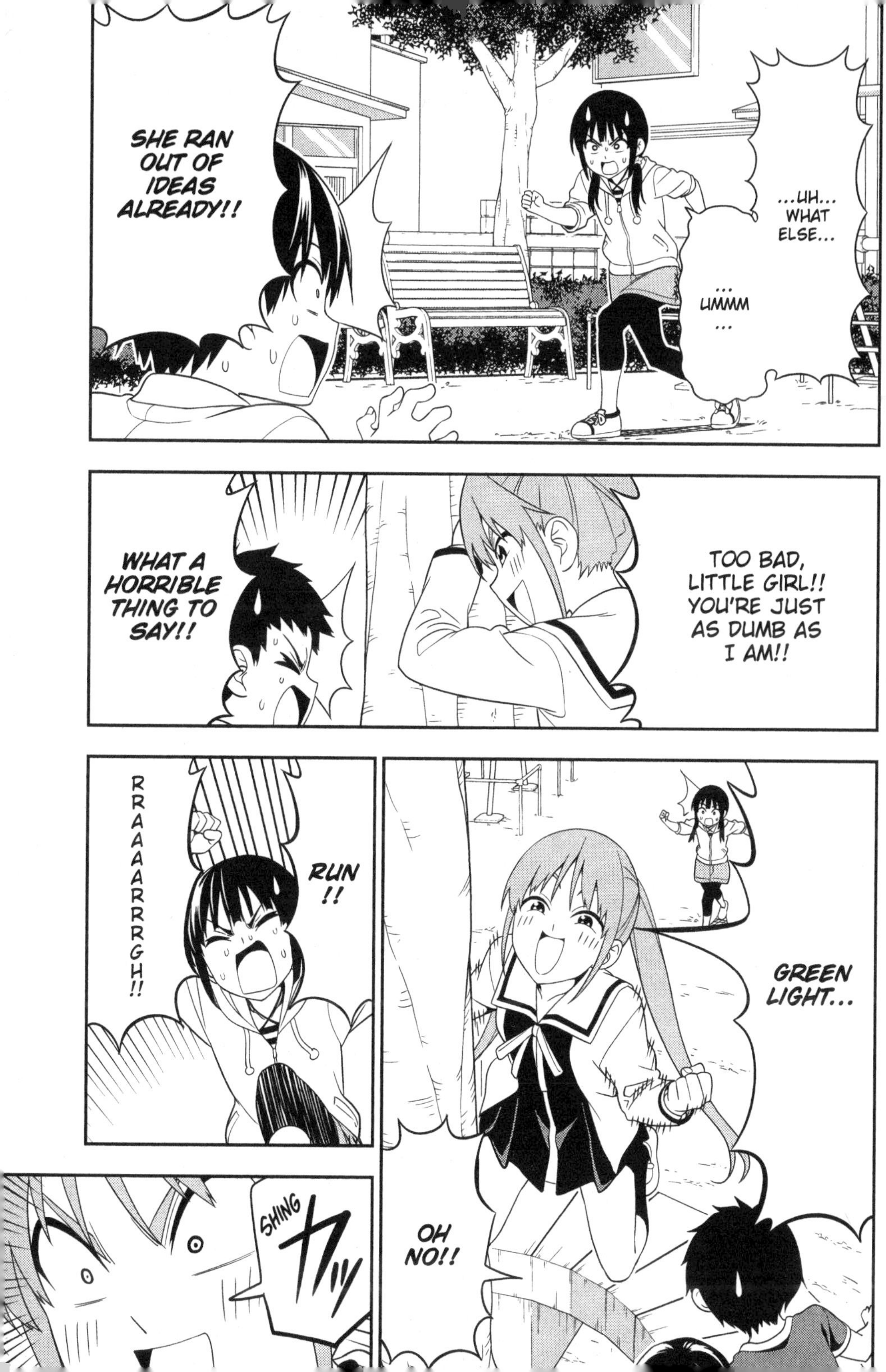
...UH... WHAT ELSE...
... UMMM ...
SHE RAN OUT OF IDEAS ALREADY!!
TOO BAD, LITTLE GIRL!! YOU'RE JUST AS DUMB AS I AM!!
WHAT A HORRIBLE THING TO SAY!!
GREEN LIGHT...
OH NO!!
RUN!!
RRAAAARRRGH!!
SHING

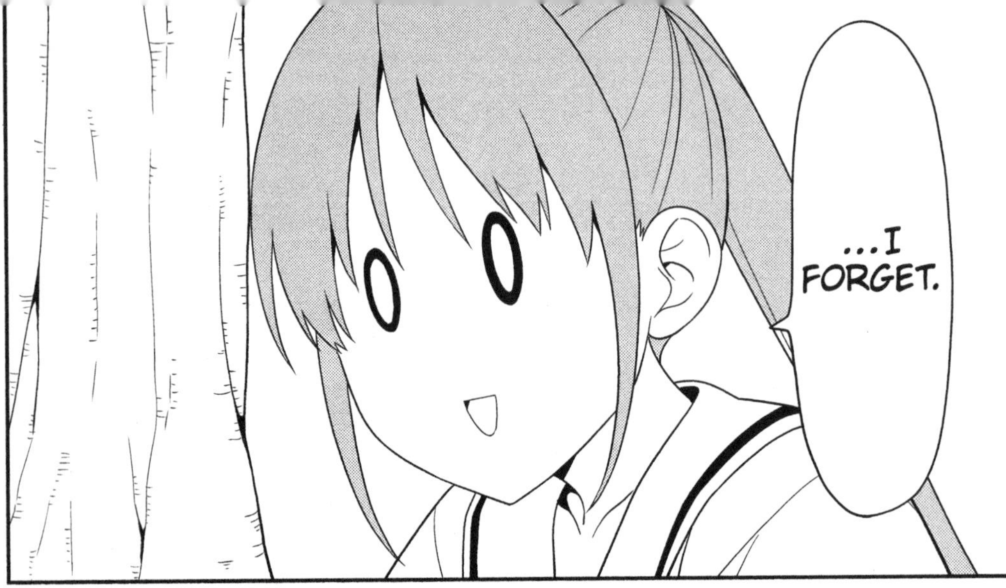
...I FORGET.

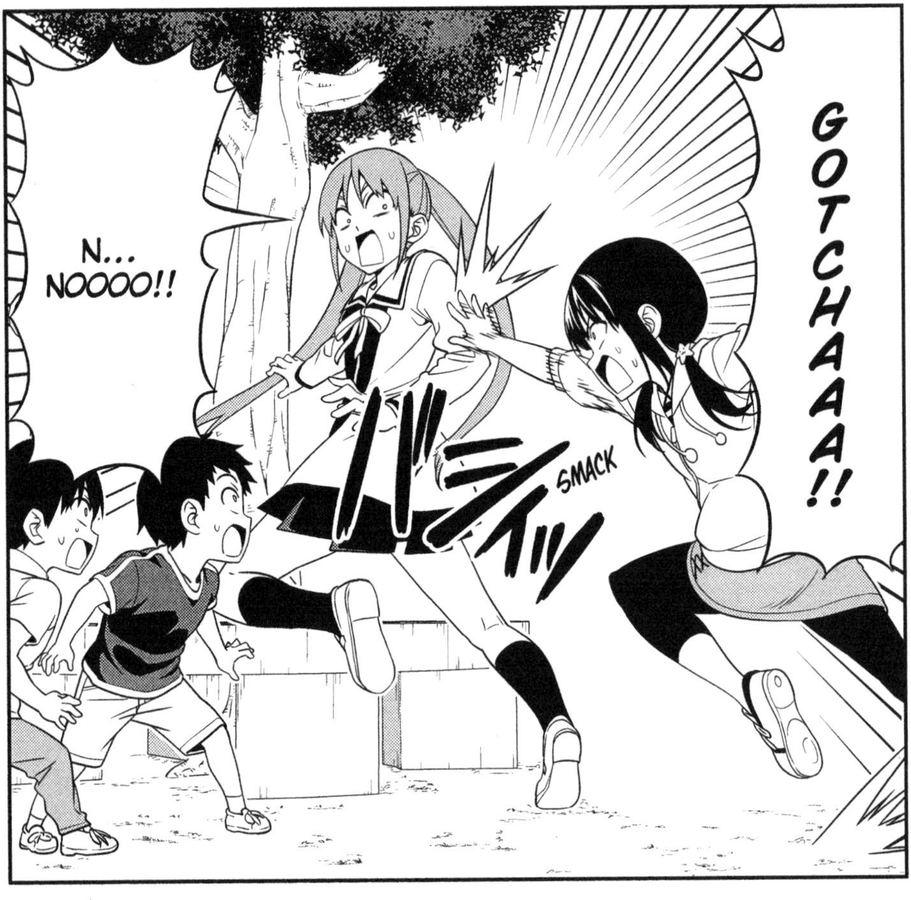
GOTCHAAAA!!
SMACK
N... NOOOO!!

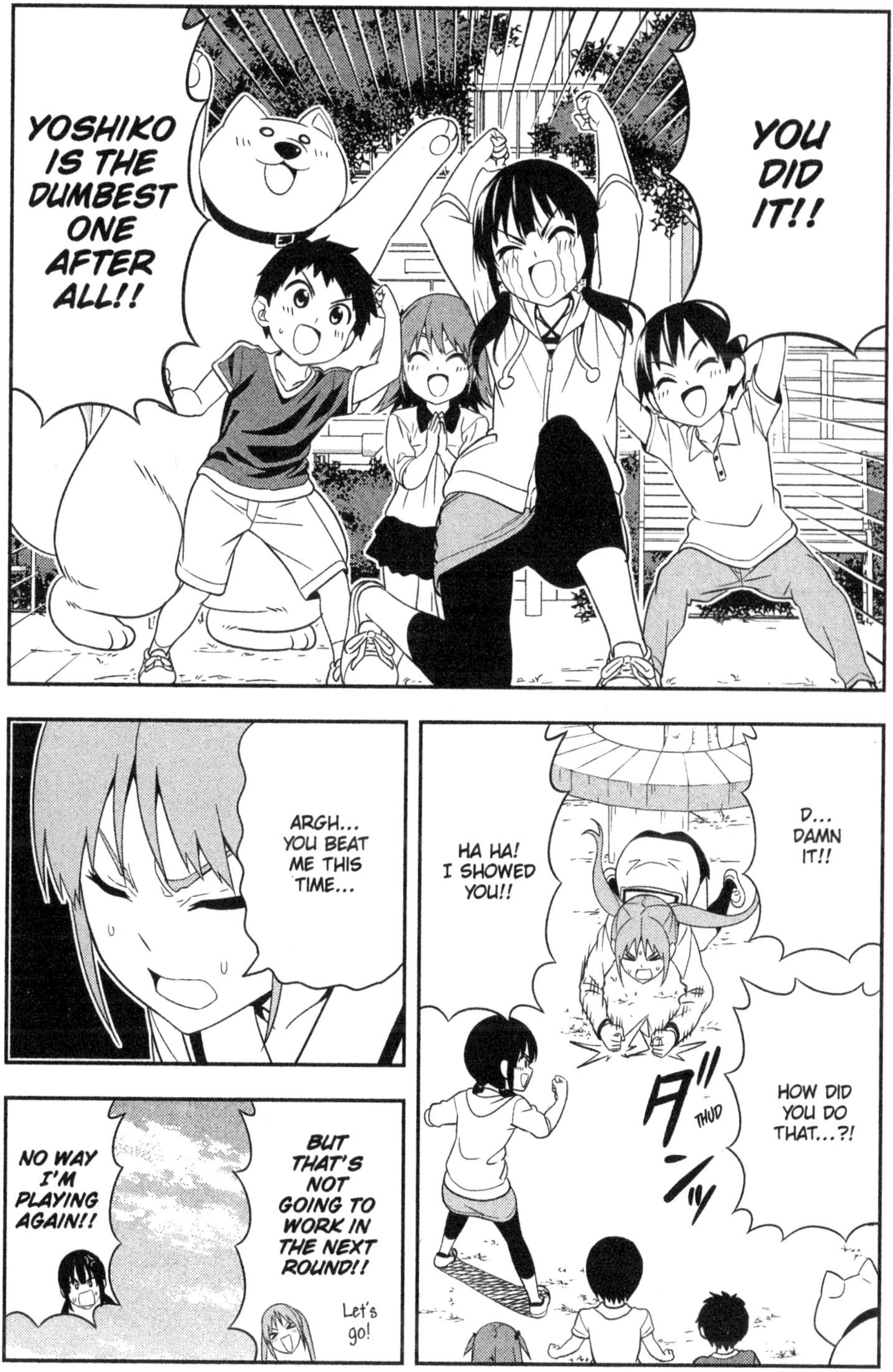
YOU DID IT!!
YOSHIKO IS THE DUMBEST ONE AFTER ALL!!
D... DAMN IT!!
HA HA! I SHOWED YOU!!
THUD
HOW DID YOU DO THAT...?!
ARGH... YOU BEAT ME THIS TIME...
BUT THAT'S NOT GOING TO WORK IN THE NEXT ROUND!!
Let's go!
NO WAY I'M PLAYING AGAIN!!

Fatal Blow

YOU DON'T WANT TO PLAY WITH US ANYMORE, RURI-ONEECHAN?
I ALREADY SAID, I HAVE TO GO DO HOME-WORK!!
SNIFFLE
しゅ～ん
J... JUST ONE MORE ROUND, GOT IT?!

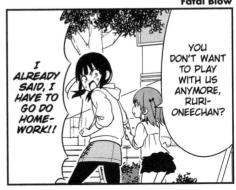

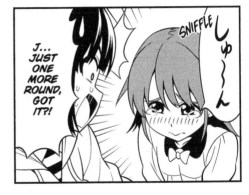

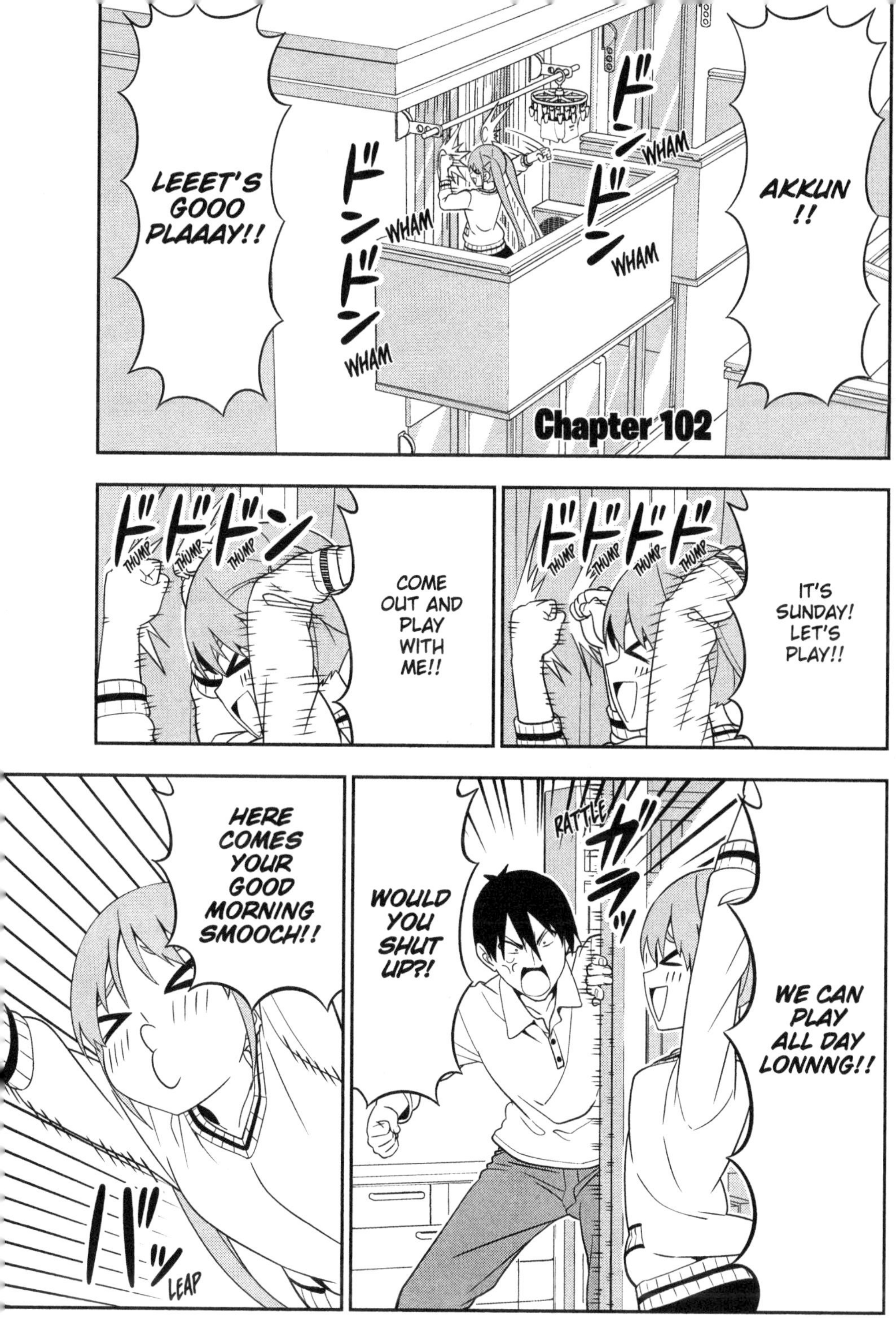
AKKUN !!
ドン ドン
WHAM
WHAM
ドン ドン
WHAM
WHAM
LEEET'S GOOO PLAAAY!!
Chapter 102
ドドドド
THUMP THUMP THUMP THUMP
IT'S SUNDAY! LET'S PLAY!!
ドドドン
THUMP THUMP THUMP
COME OUT AND PLAY WITH ME!!
WE CAN PLAY ALL DAY LONNNG!!
ガラッ
RATTLE
WOULD YOU SHUT UP?!
HERE COMES YOUR GOOD MORNING SMOOCH!!
バッ
LEAP

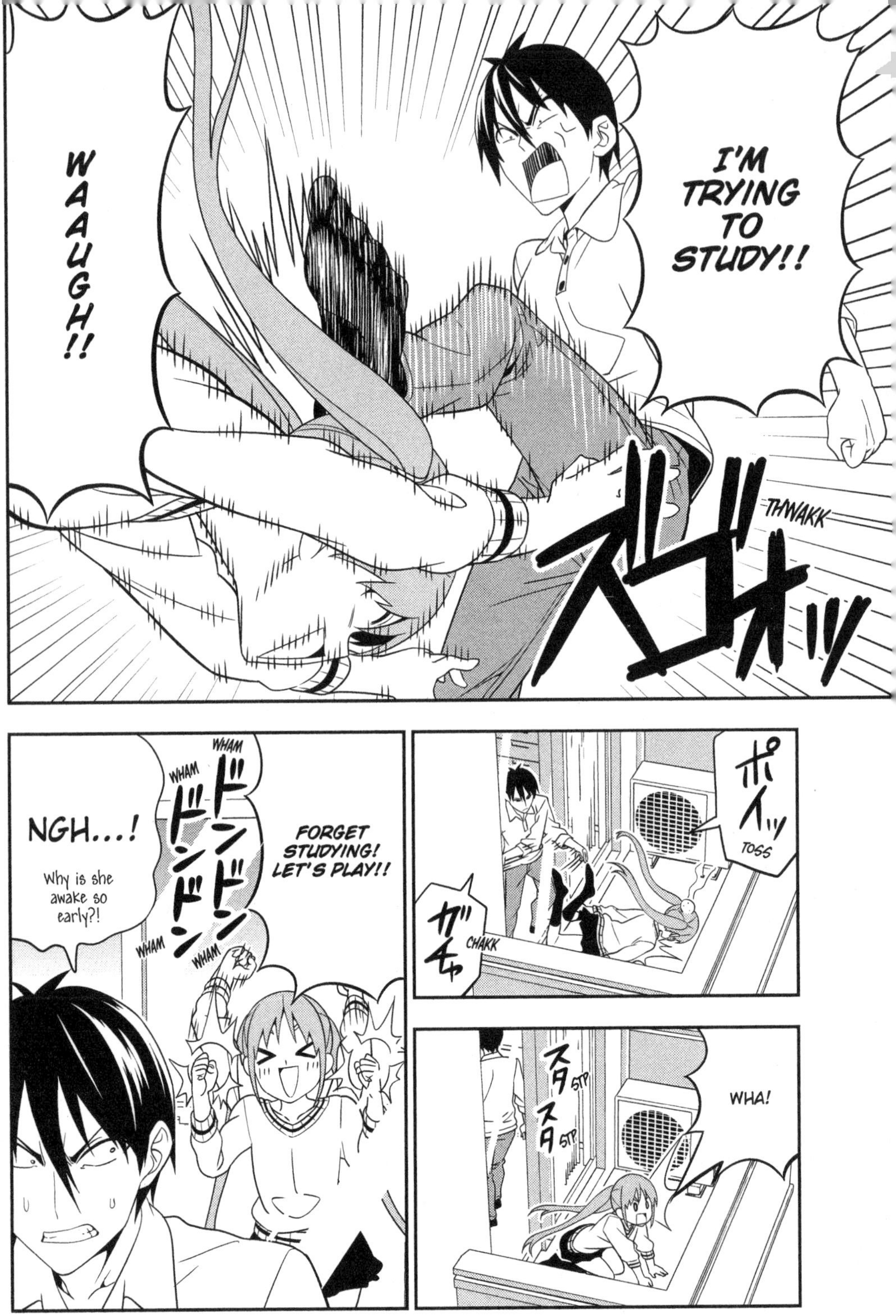

I'M TRYING TO STUDY!!
WAAAUGH!!
ズゴオッ
THWAKK
ポイッ
TOSS
ガチャ
CHAKK
WHA!
スタスタ
STP STP
ドンドン ドンドン
WHAM WHAM WHAM WHAM
FORGET STUDYING! LET'S PLAY!!
NGH...!
Why is she awake so early?!

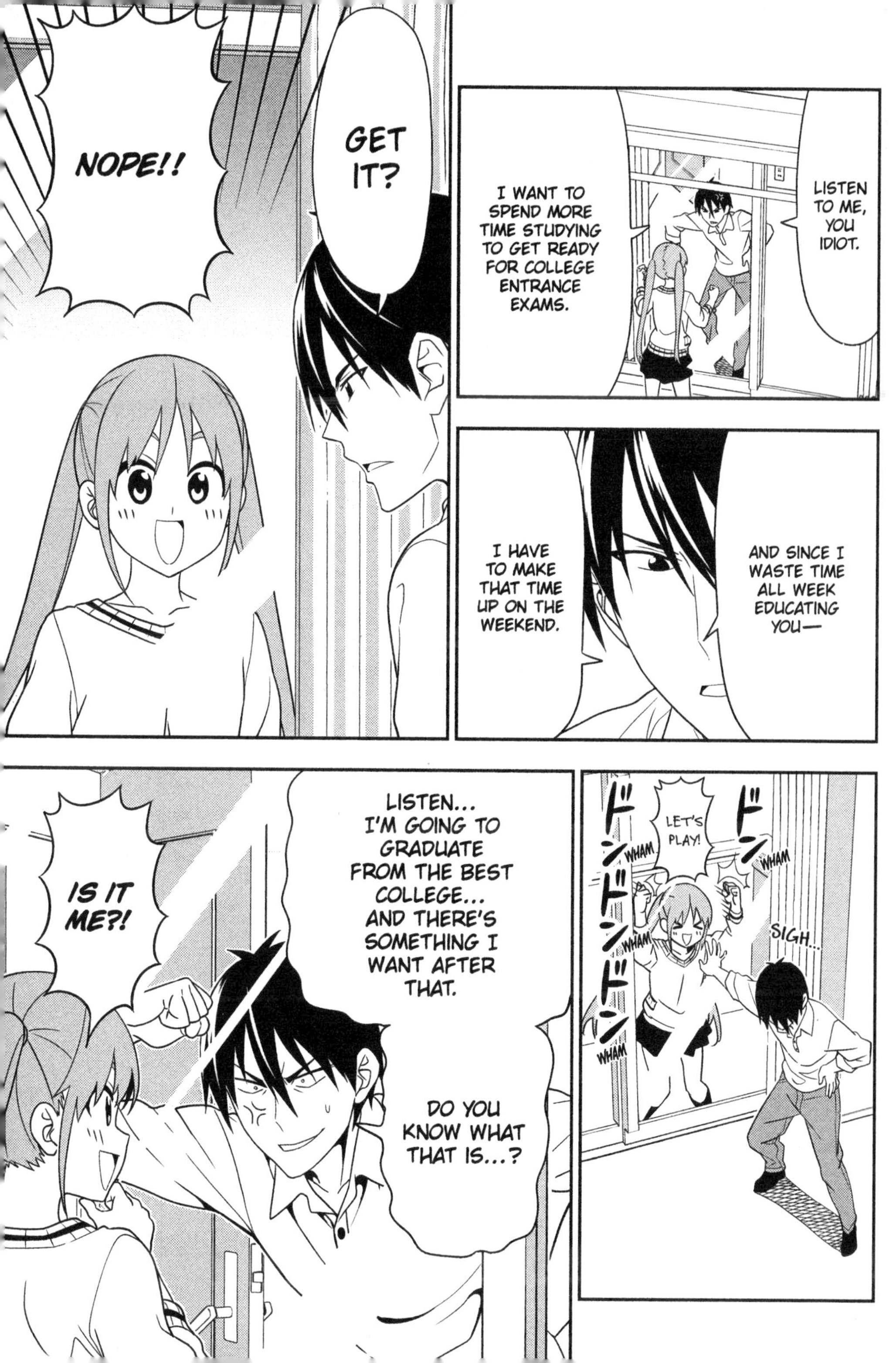
LISTEN TO ME, YOU IDIOT.
I WANT TO SPEND MORE TIME STUDYING TO GET READY FOR COLLEGE ENTRANCE EXAMS.
AND SINCE I WASTE TIME ALL WEEK EDUCATING YOU—
I HAVE TO MAKE THAT TIME UP ON THE WEEKEND.
GET IT?
NOPE!!
ドン
WHAM
LET'S PLAY!
ドンドンドン
WHAM
WHAM
WHAM
SIGH...
LISTEN... I'M GOING TO GRADUATE FROM THE BEST COLLEGE... AND THERE'S SOMETHING I WANT AFTER THAT.
DO YOU KNOW WHAT THAT IS...?
IS IT ME?!

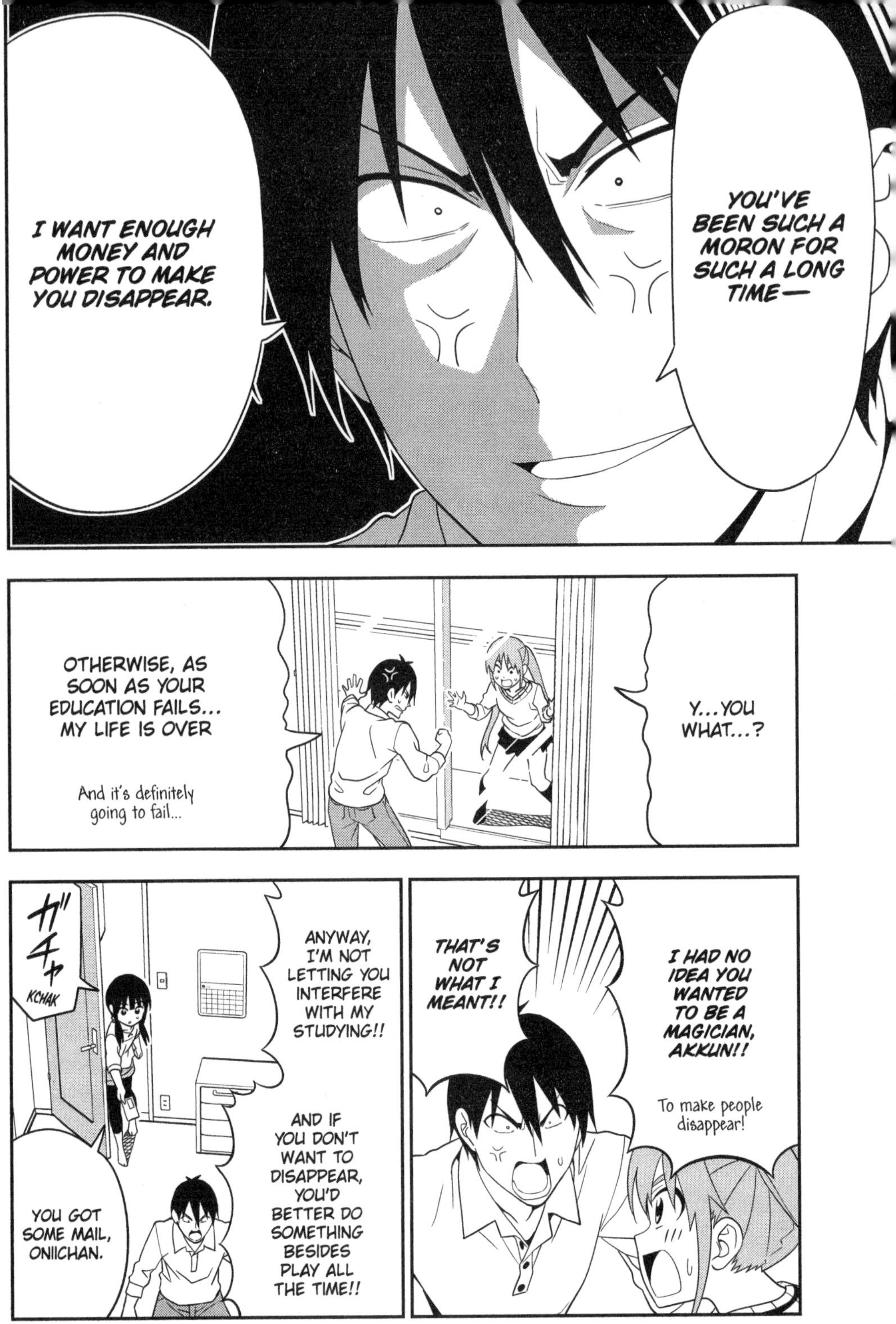
YOU'VE BEEN SUCH A MORON FOR SUCH A LONG TIME—
I WANT ENOUGH MONEY AND POWER TO MAKE YOU DISAPPEAR.
Y...YOU WHAT...?
OTHERWISE, AS SOON AS YOUR EDUCATION FAILS... MY LIFE IS OVER
And it's definitely going to fail...
I HAD NO IDEA YOU WANTED TO BE A MAGICIAN, AKKUN!!
To make people disappear!
THAT'S NOT WHAT I MEANT!!
ANYWAY, I'M NOT LETTING YOU INTERFERE WITH MY STUDYING!!
AND IF YOU DON'T WANT TO DISAPPEAR, YOU'D BETTER DO SOMETHING BESIDES PLAY ALL THE TIME!!
ガチャ
KCHAK
YOU GOT SOME MAIL, ONIICHAN.

ペラ FLIP

TEST SCORES

AKURU AKUTSU

EVALUATION

DESIRED SCHOOL	EVALUATION	SUCCESS RATE
KYO SCHOOL OF LIBERAL ARTS	C	40%

It is very unlikely you will be accepted at your preferred school.

I'LL PROBABLY BE AROUND A B...

THESE ARE THE RESULTS FROM THE PRACTICE TEST I TOOK!

POMPUS TESTING

I HAVEN'T HAD TIME TO PRACTICE MY TEST-TAKING TECHNIQUES...

YOSHIKO'S BEEN DISTRACTING ME SO MUCH...

ビリ!! RRIP

Come onnn!! Let's go!!

THUMP THUMP THUMP THUMP

Let's go play, Akkun!!

THUMP THUMP THUMP THUMP

Let's go plaaay!! Let's go plaaay!!

THUMP THUMP THUMP

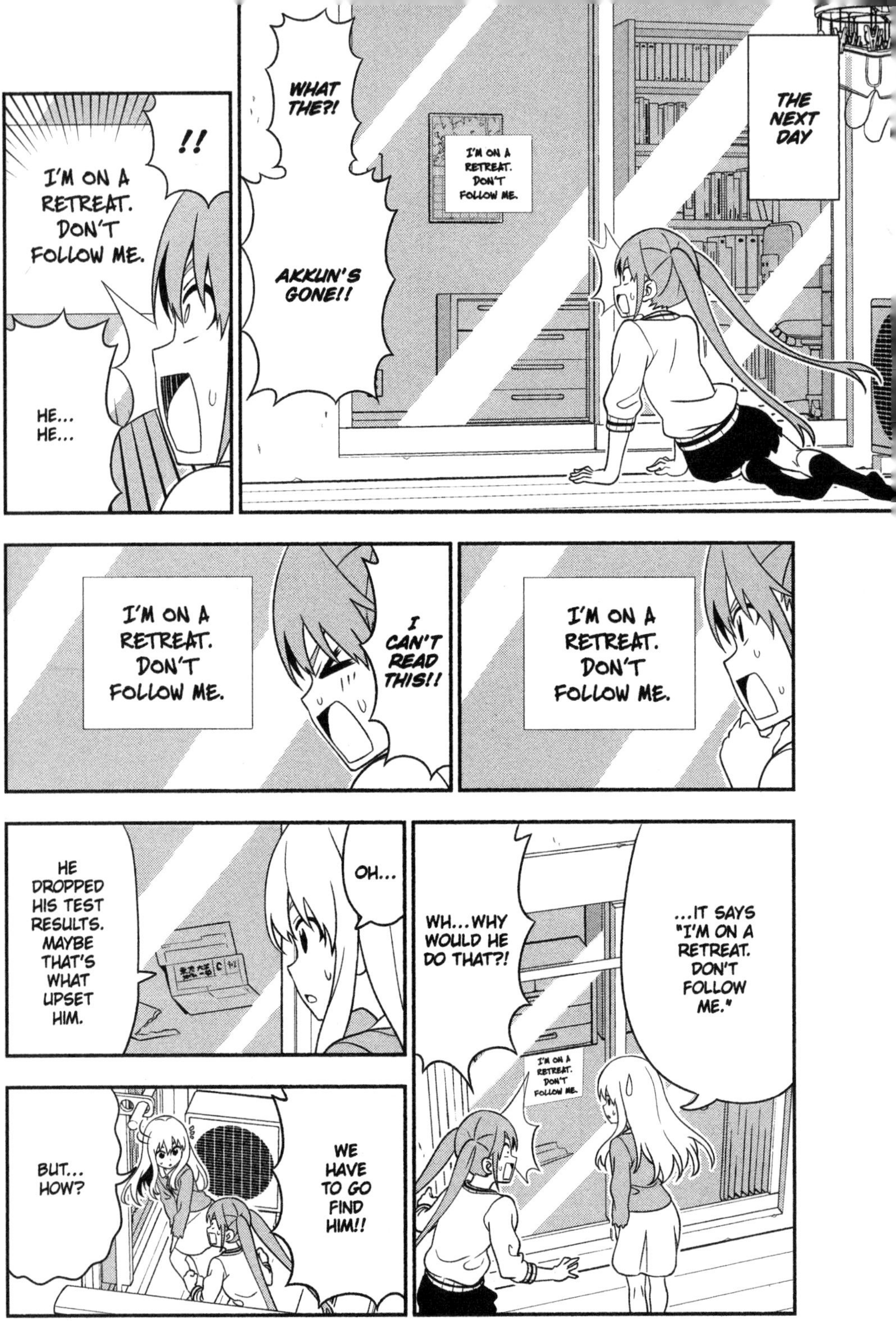
THE NEXT DAY
I'M ON A RETREAT. DON'T FOLLOW ME.
WHAT THE?!
AKKUN'S GONE!!
!!
I'M ON A RETREAT. DON'T FOLLOW ME.
HE... HE...
I'M ON A RETREAT. DON'T FOLLOW ME.
I CAN'T READ THIS!!
I'M ON A RETREAT. DON'T FOLLOW ME.
...IT SAYS "I'M ON A RETREAT. DON'T FOLLOW ME."
WH...WHY WOULD HE DO THAT?!
I'M ON A RETREAT. DON'T FOLLOW ME.
OH...
HE DROPPED HIS TEST RESULTS. MAYBE THAT'S WHAT UPSET HIM.
WE HAVE TO GO FIND HIM!!
BUT... HOW?

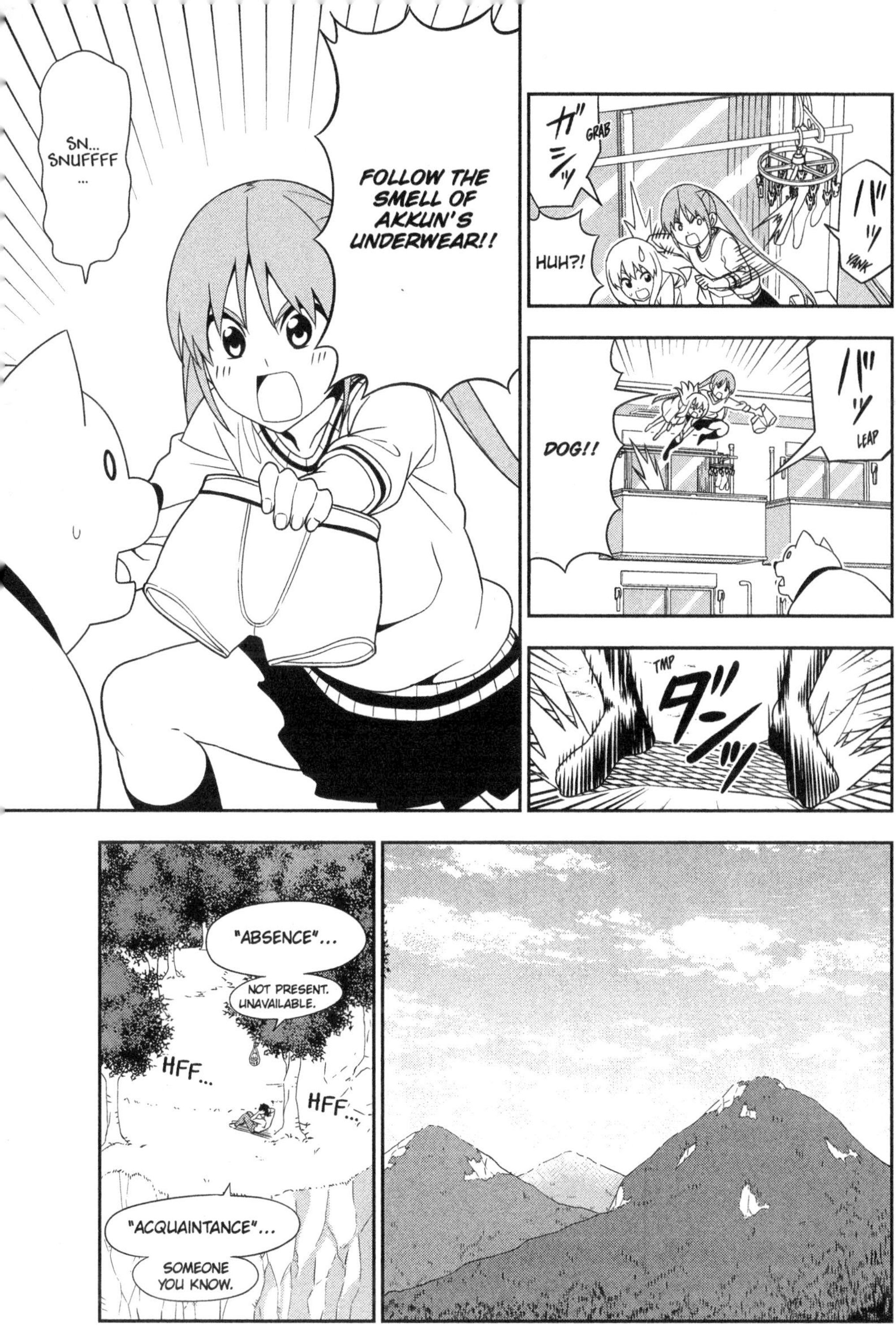
ガシッ
GRAB
バッ
YANK
HUH?!
バッ
LEAP
DOG!!
TMP
ダン
FOLLOW THE SMELL OF AKKUN'S UNDERWEAR!!
SN... SNUFFFF...
"ABSENCE"...
NOT PRESENT. UNAVAILABLE.
HFF...
HFF...
"ACQUAINTANCE"...
SOMEONE YOU KNOW.

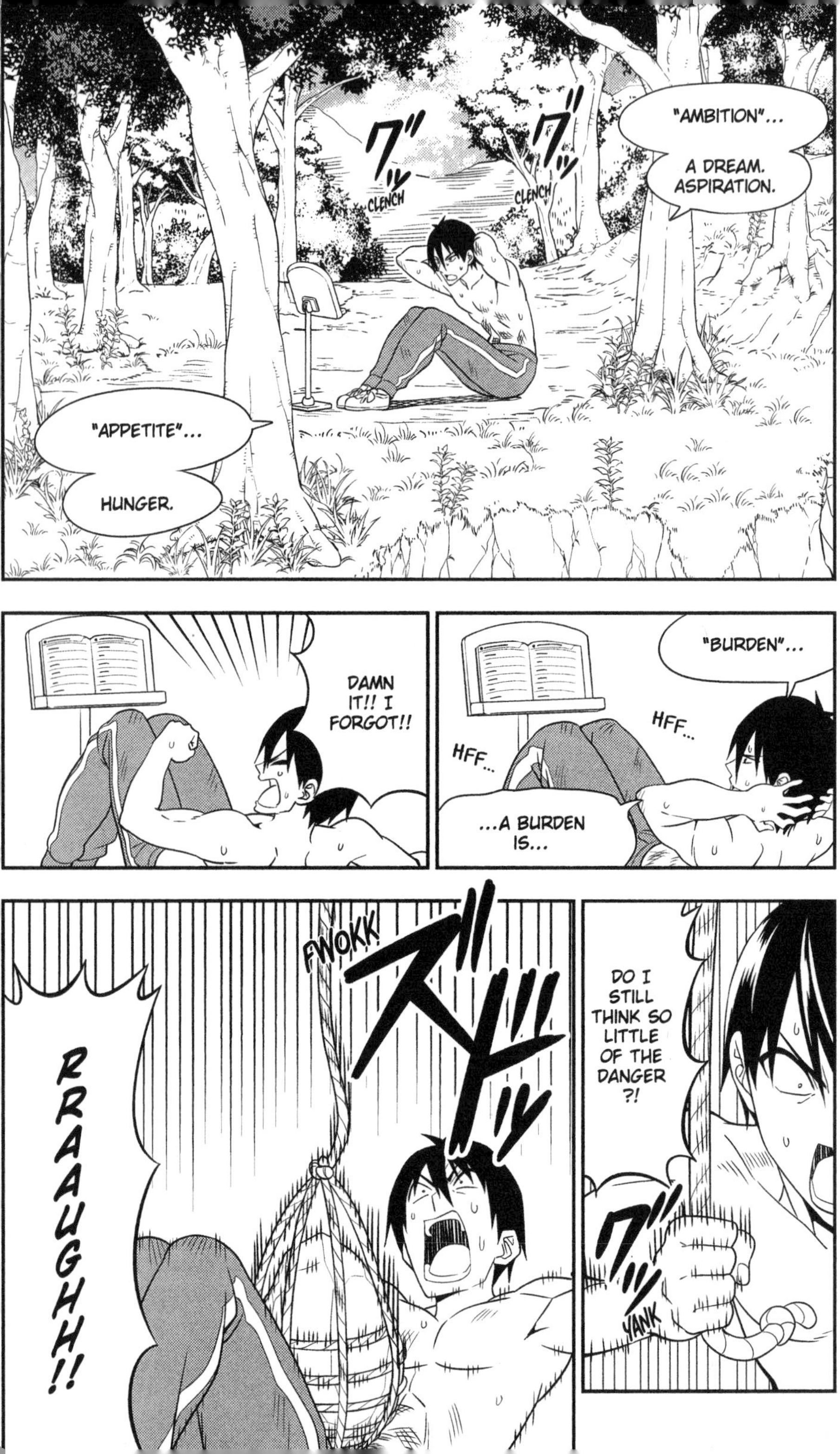
"AMBITION"...
A DREAM. ASPIRATION.
グッ
CLENCH
グッ
CLENCH
"APPETITE"...
HUNGER.
"BURDEN"...
HFF...
HFF...
...A BURDEN IS...
DAMN IT!! I FORGOT!!
DO I STILL THINK SO LITTLE OF THE DANGER ?!
グッ
YANK
ズッ
FWOKK
RRAAUGHH!!

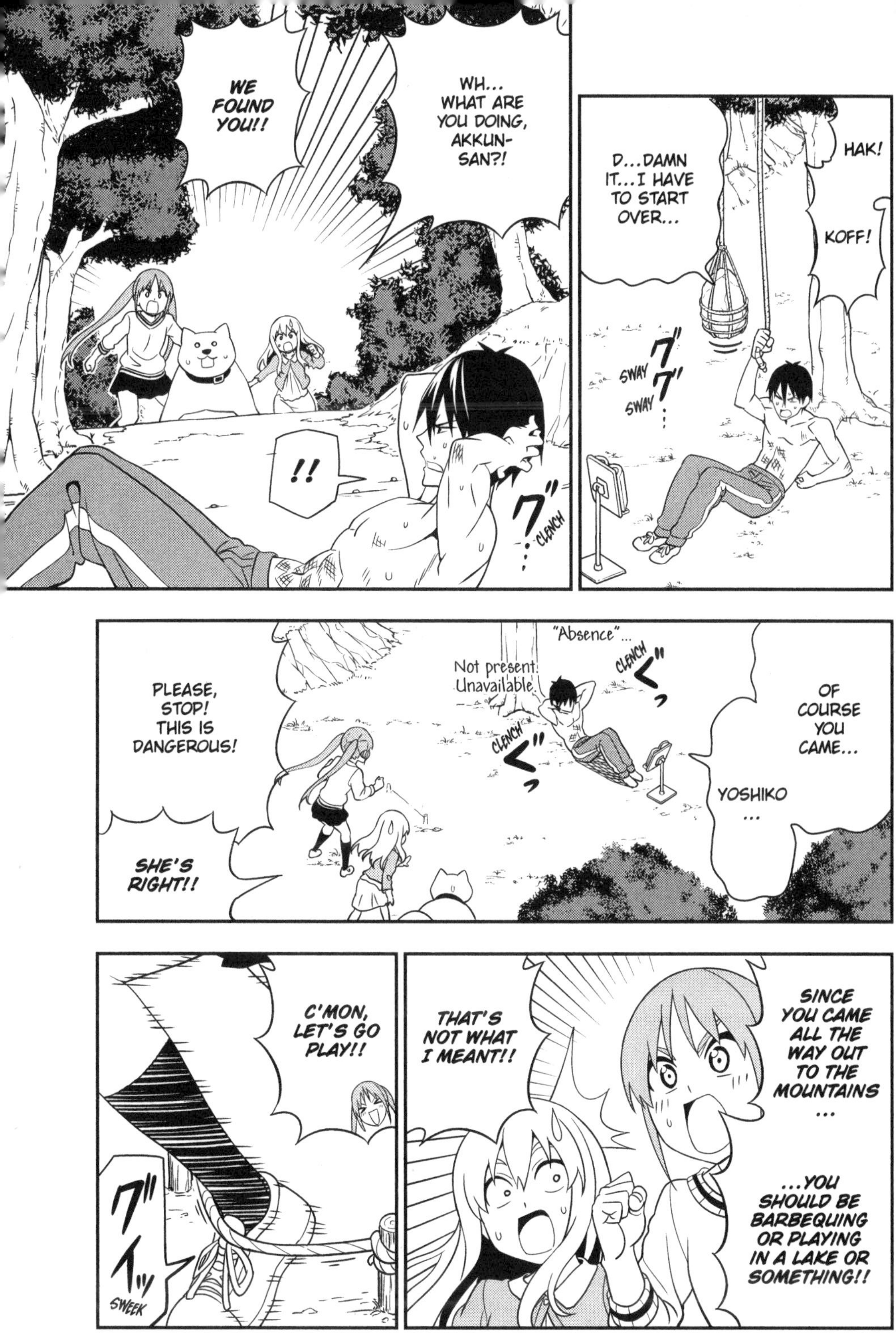
HAK!
KOFF!
D...DAMN IT...I HAVE TO START OVER...
SWAY SWAY
WH... WHAT ARE YOU DOING, AKKUN-SAN?!
WE FOUND YOU!!
!!
CLENCH
OF COURSE YOU CAME...
YOSHIKO...
"Absence"...
CLENCH
Not present. Unavailable.
CLENCH
PLEASE, STOP! THIS IS DANGEROUS!
SHE'S RIGHT!!
SINCE YOU CAME ALL THE WAY OUT TO THE MOUNTAINS...
...YOU SHOULD BE BARBEQUING OR PLAYING IN A LAKE OR SOMETHING!!
THAT'S NOT WHAT I MEANT!!
C'MON, LET'S GO PLAY!!
SWEEK

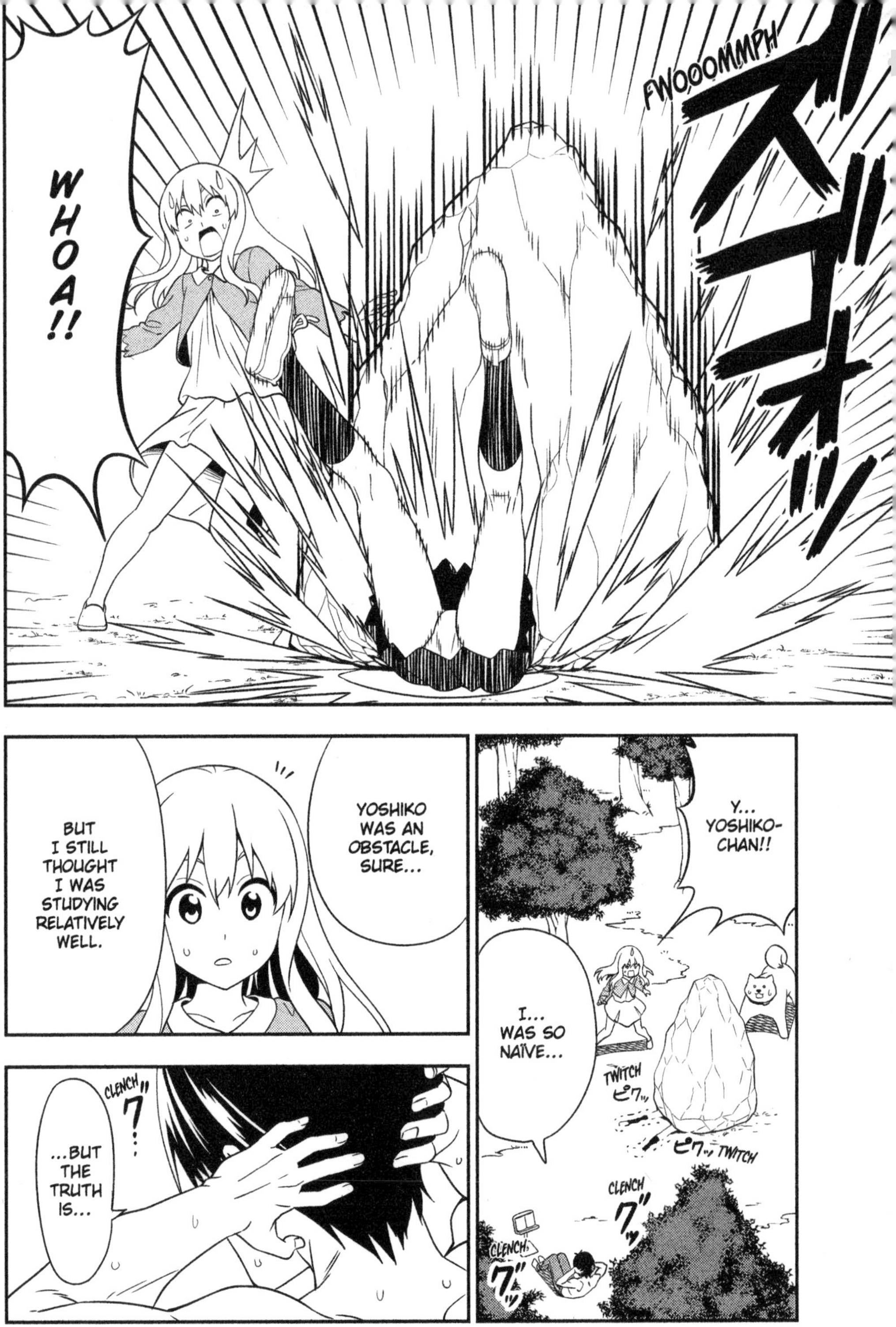
FWOOOMMPH
ズゴオッ
WHOA!!
Y... YOSHIKO-CHAN!!
I... WAS SO NAÏVE...
TWITCH
ピクッ
ピクッ
TWITCH
CLENCH
グッ
CLENCH
グッ
YOSHIKO WAS AN OBSTACLE, SURE...
BUT I STILL THOUGHT I WAS STUDYING RELATIVELY WELL.
CLENCH
グ...
...BUT THE TRUTH IS...

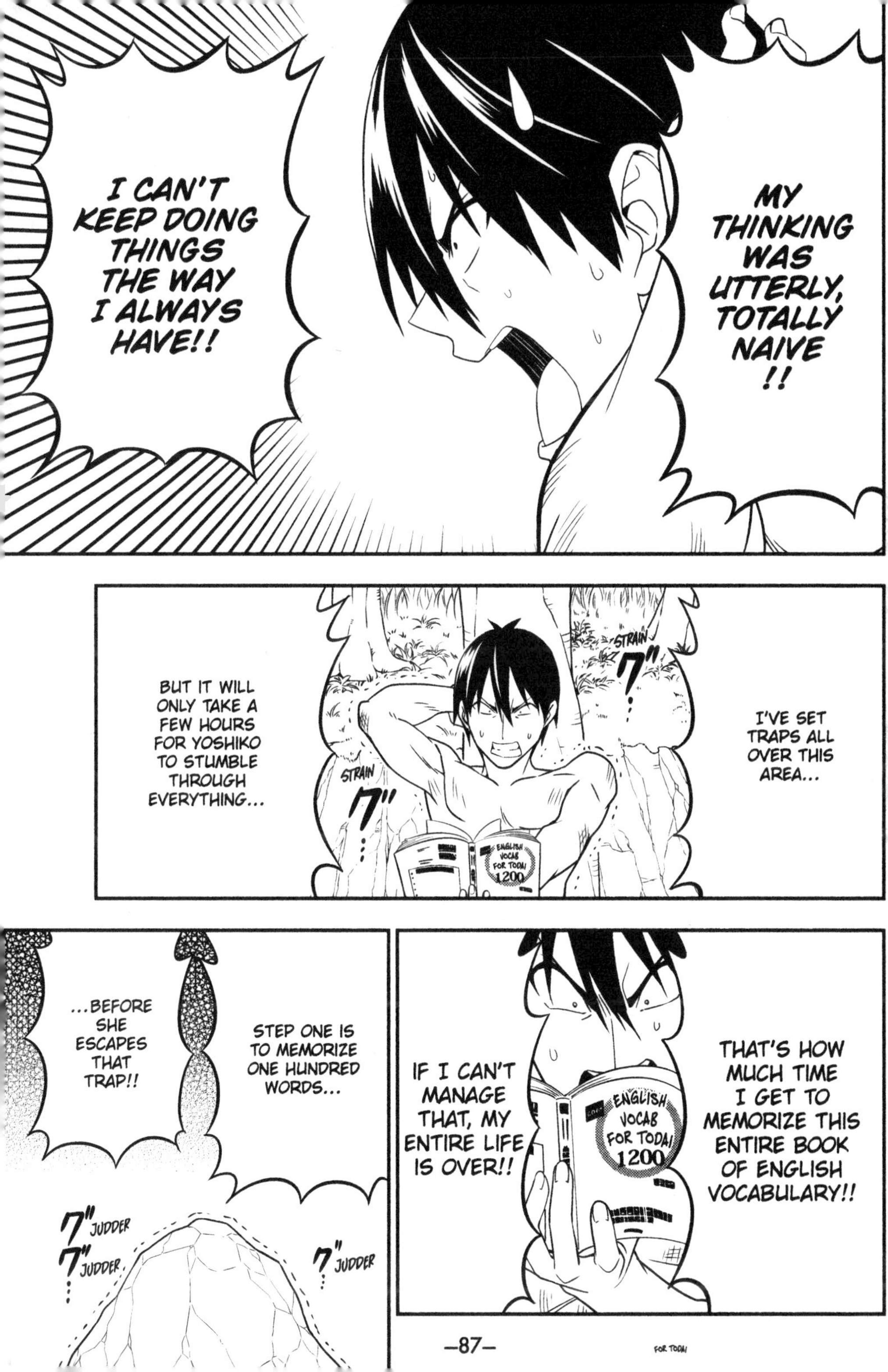
MY THINKING WAS UTTERLY, TOTALLY NAIVE!!
I CAN'T KEEP DOING THINGS THE WAY I ALWAYS HAVE!!
I'VE SET TRAPS ALL OVER THIS AREA...
STRAIN
ENGLISH VOCAB FOR TODAI 1200
STRAIN
BUT IT WILL ONLY TAKE A FEW HOURS FOR YOSHIKO TO STUMBLE THROUGH EVERYTHING...
THAT'S HOW MUCH TIME I GET TO MEMORIZE THIS ENTIRE BOOK OF ENGLISH VOCABULARY!!
ENGLISH VOCAB FOR TODAI 1200
IF I CAN'T MANAGE THAT, MY ENTIRE LIFE IS OVER!!
STEP ONE IS TO MEMORIZE ONE HUNDRED WORDS...
...BEFORE SHE ESCAPES THAT TRAP!!
JUDDER
JUDDER
JUDDER

FOR TODAI

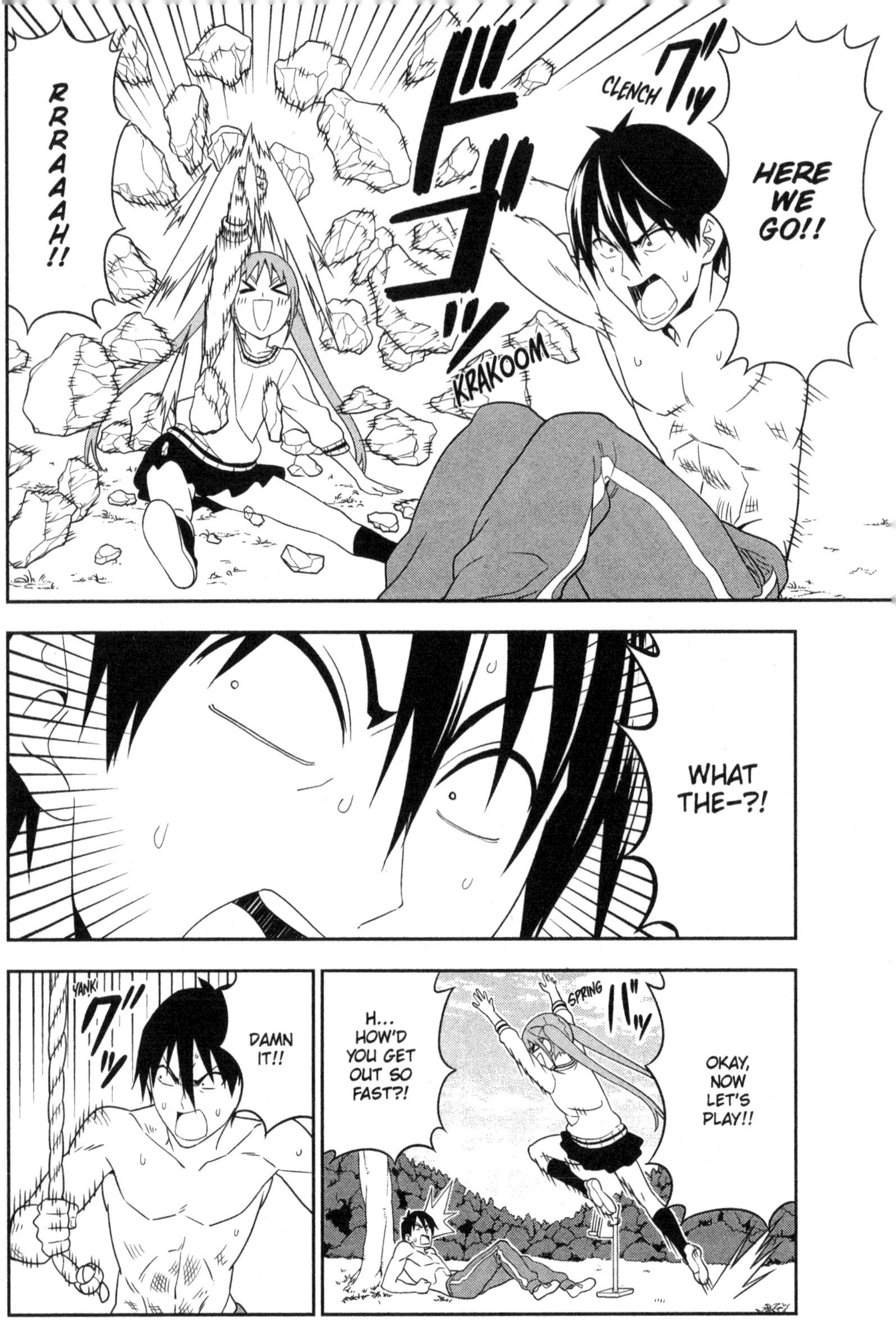
HERE WE GO!!
CLENCH
KRAKOOM
RRRAAAAH!!
WHAT THE–?!
OKAY, NOW LET'S PLAY!!
SPRING
H... HOW'D YOU GET OUT SO FAST?!
DAMN IT!!
YANK

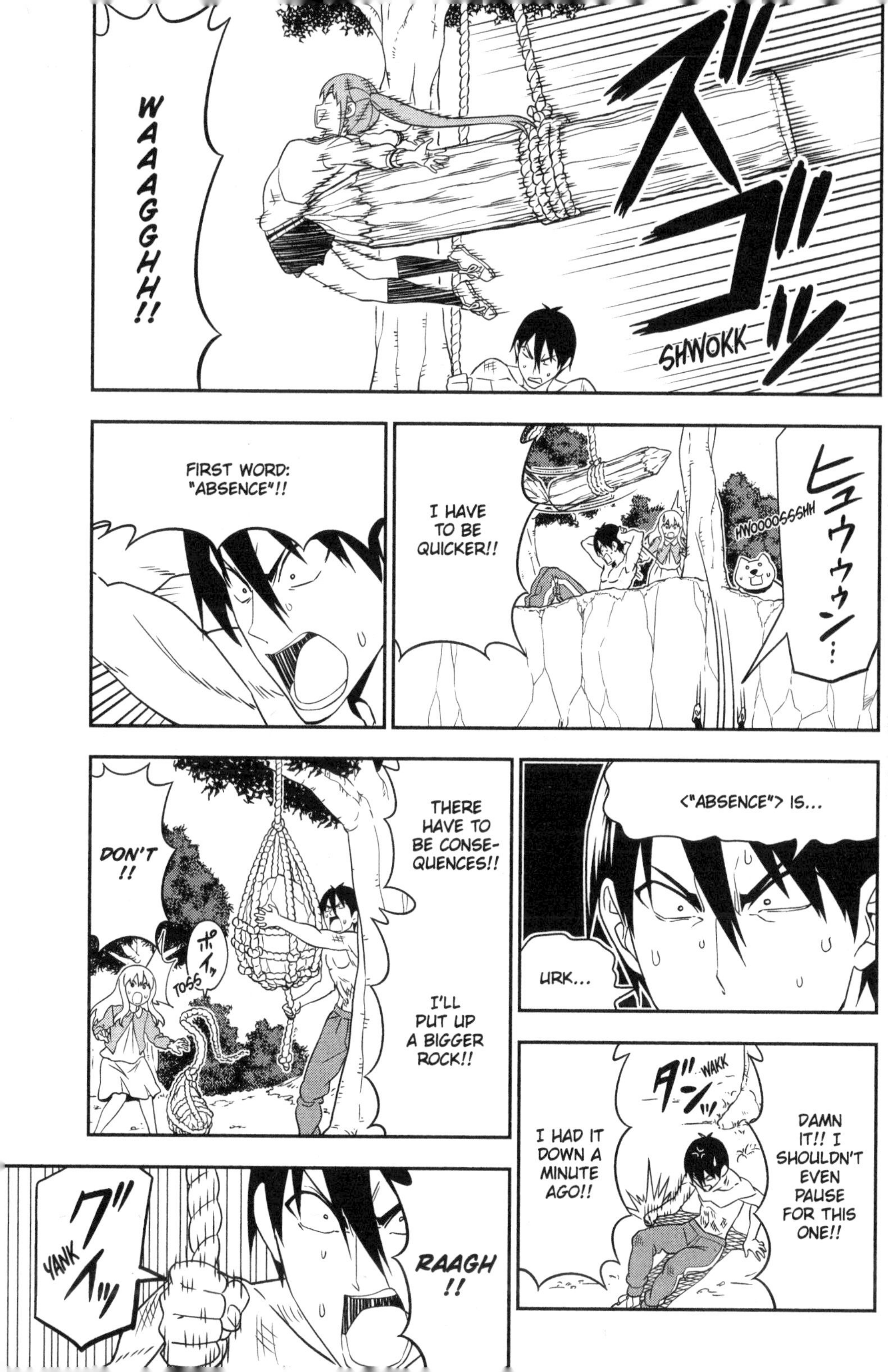
ズゴッ
SHWOKK
WAAAAGGHH!!
ヒュウウウン…
HWOOOOSSSHH
I HAVE TO BE QUICKER!!
FIRST WORD: "ABSENCE"!!
<"ABSENCE"> IS...
URK...
ダンッ
WAKK
DAMN IT!! I SHOULDN'T EVEN PAUSE FOR THIS ONE!!
I HAD IT DOWN A MINUTE AGO!!
THERE HAVE TO BE CONSE-QUENCES!!
I'LL PUT UP A BIGGER ROCK!!
ポイッ
TOSS
DON'T!!
RAAGH!!
グイッ
YANK

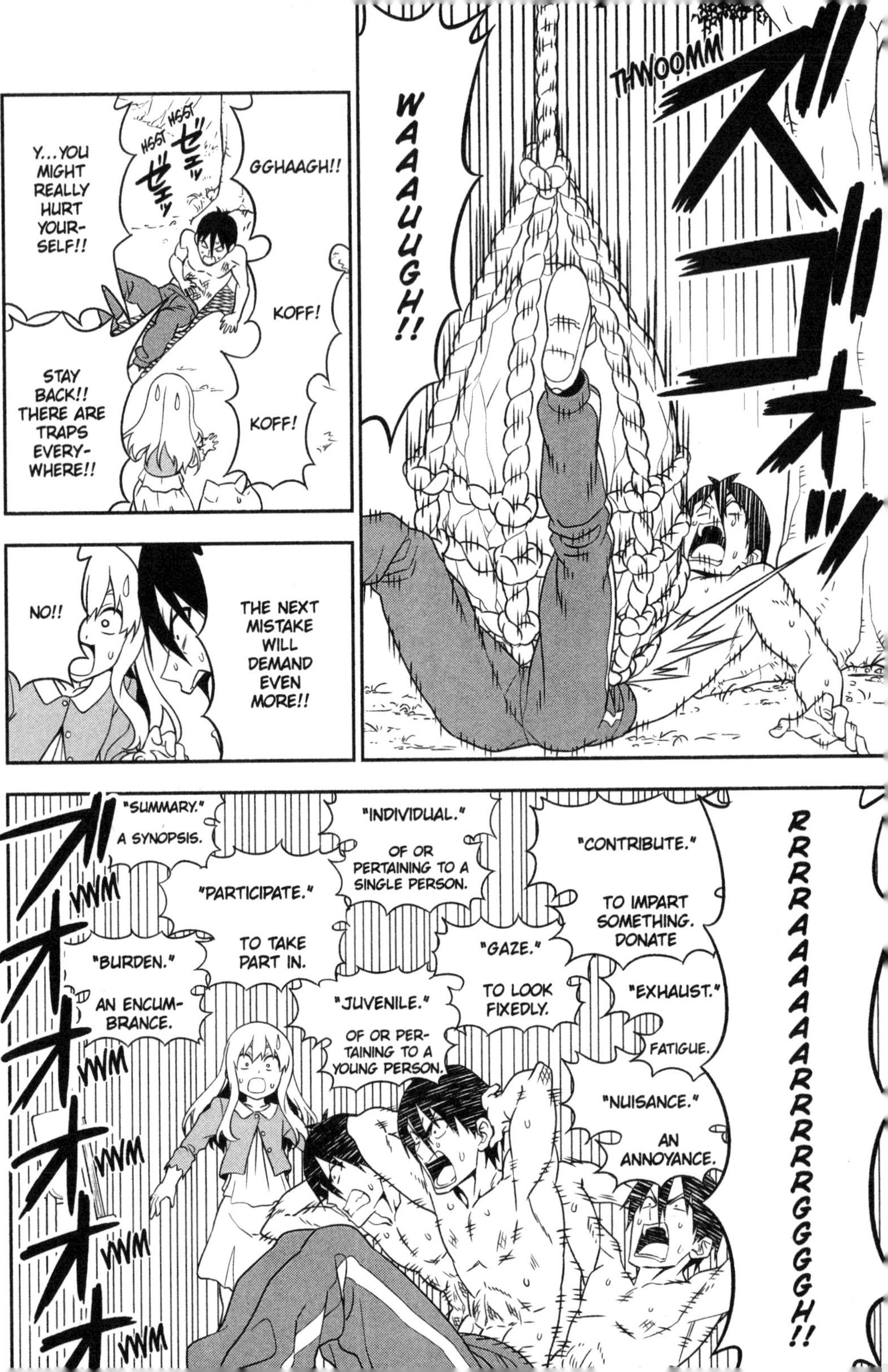
ズゴオッ
THWOOMM
WAAAUUGH!!
GGHAAGH!!
KOFF!
KOFF!
ゼェ ゼェッ
HSST HSST
Y...YOU MIGHT REALLY HURT YOUR-SELF!!
STAY BACK!! THERE ARE TRAPS EVERY-WHERE!!
THE NEXT MISTAKE WILL DEMAND EVEN MORE!!
NO!!
RRRRAAAAARRRRGGGGH!!
"CONTRIBUTE."
TO IMPART SOMETHING. DONATE
"EXHAUST."
FATIGUE.
"NUISANCE."
AN ANNOYANCE.
"INDIVIDUAL."
OF OR PERTAINING TO A SINGLE PERSON.
"GAZE."
TO LOOK FIXEDLY.
"JUVENILE."
OF OR PER-TAINING TO A YOUNG PERSON.
"SUMMARY."
A SYNOPSIS.
"PARTICIPATE."
TO TAKE PART IN.
"BURDEN."
AN ENCUM-BRANCE.
ゴオオオオ
VVVM
VVVM
VVVM
VVVM
VVVM

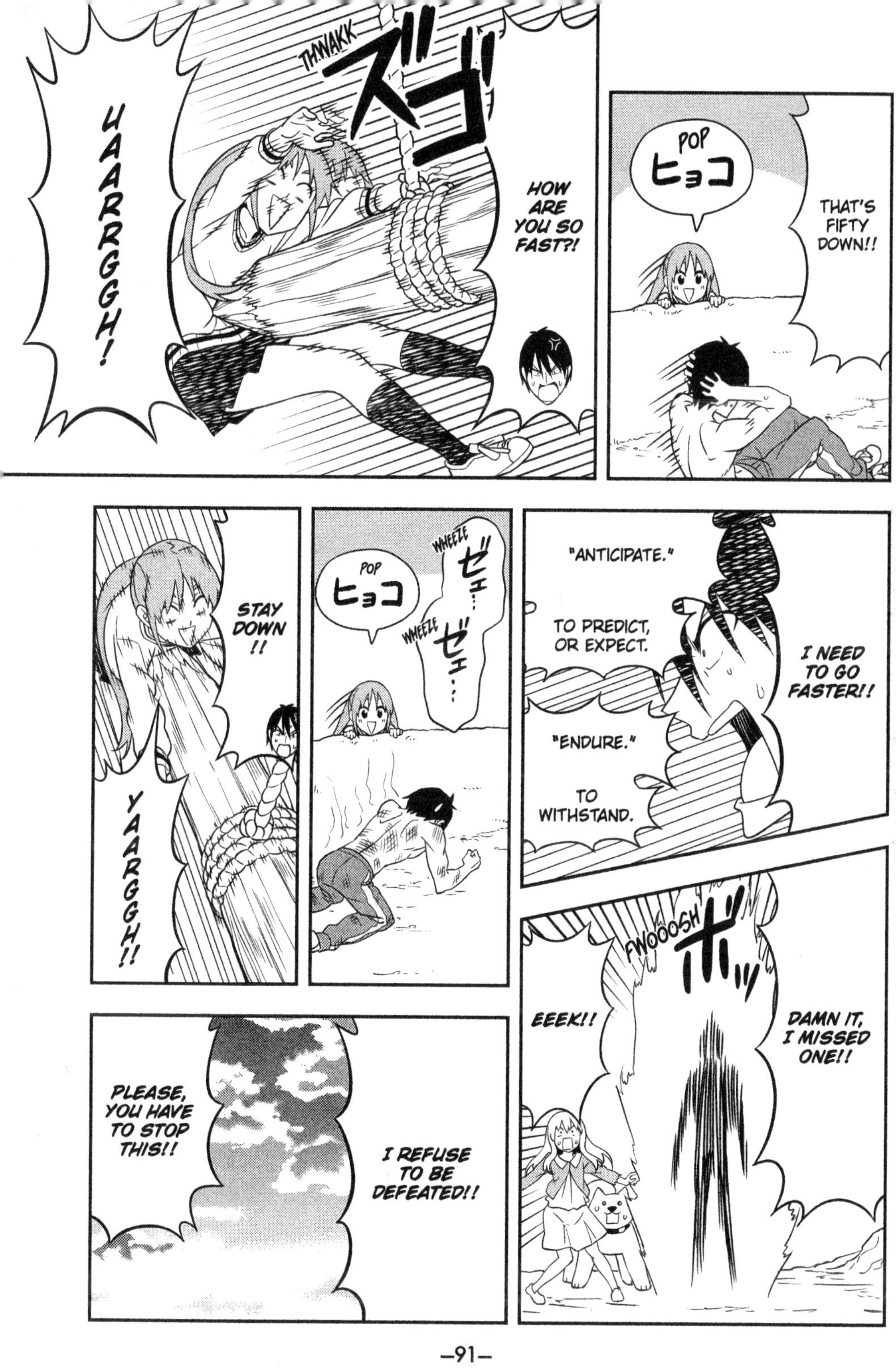
THAT'S FIFTY DOWN!!
POP
ヒョコ
THWAKK
ズゴ
HOW ARE YOU SO FAST?!
UAARRGGH!
"ANTICIPATE."
TO PREDICT, OR EXPECT.
"ENDURE."
TO WITHSTAND.
I NEED TO GO FASTER!!
WHEEZE
ゼェ…
WHEEZE
ゼェ…
POP
ヒョコ
STAY DOWN!!
YAARRGGH!!
FWOOOSH
ボッ
DAMN IT, I MISSED ONE!!
EEEK!!
I REFUSE TO BE DEFEATED!!
PLEASE, YOU HAVE TO STOP THIS!!

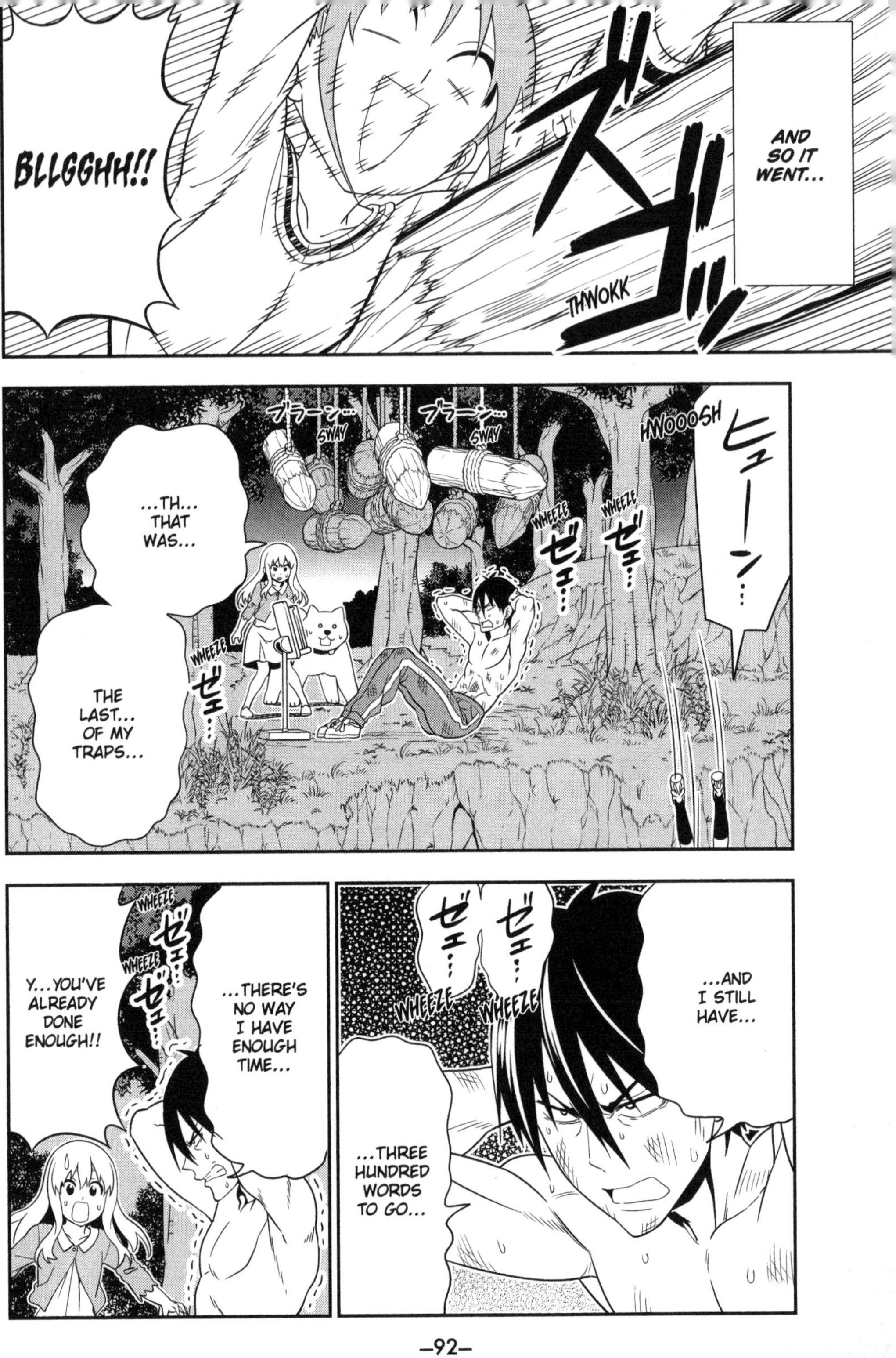

AND SO IT WENT...
ズゴ
THWOKK
BLLGGHH!!
HWOOOSH
ヒューーン...
WHEEZE
ゼェ...
WHEEZE
ゼェ...
ブラーン...
SWAY
ブラーン...
SWAY
...TH... THAT WAS...
THE LAST... OF MY TRAPS...
WHEEZE
ゼェ...
...AND I STILL HAVE...
ゼェ...
ゼェ...
WHEEZE
WHEEZE
...THREE HUNDRED WORDS TO GO...
...THERE'S NO WAY I HAVE ENOUGH TIME...
WHEEZE
ゼェ...
WHEEZE
ゼェ...
Y...YOU'VE ALREADY DONE ENOUGH!!

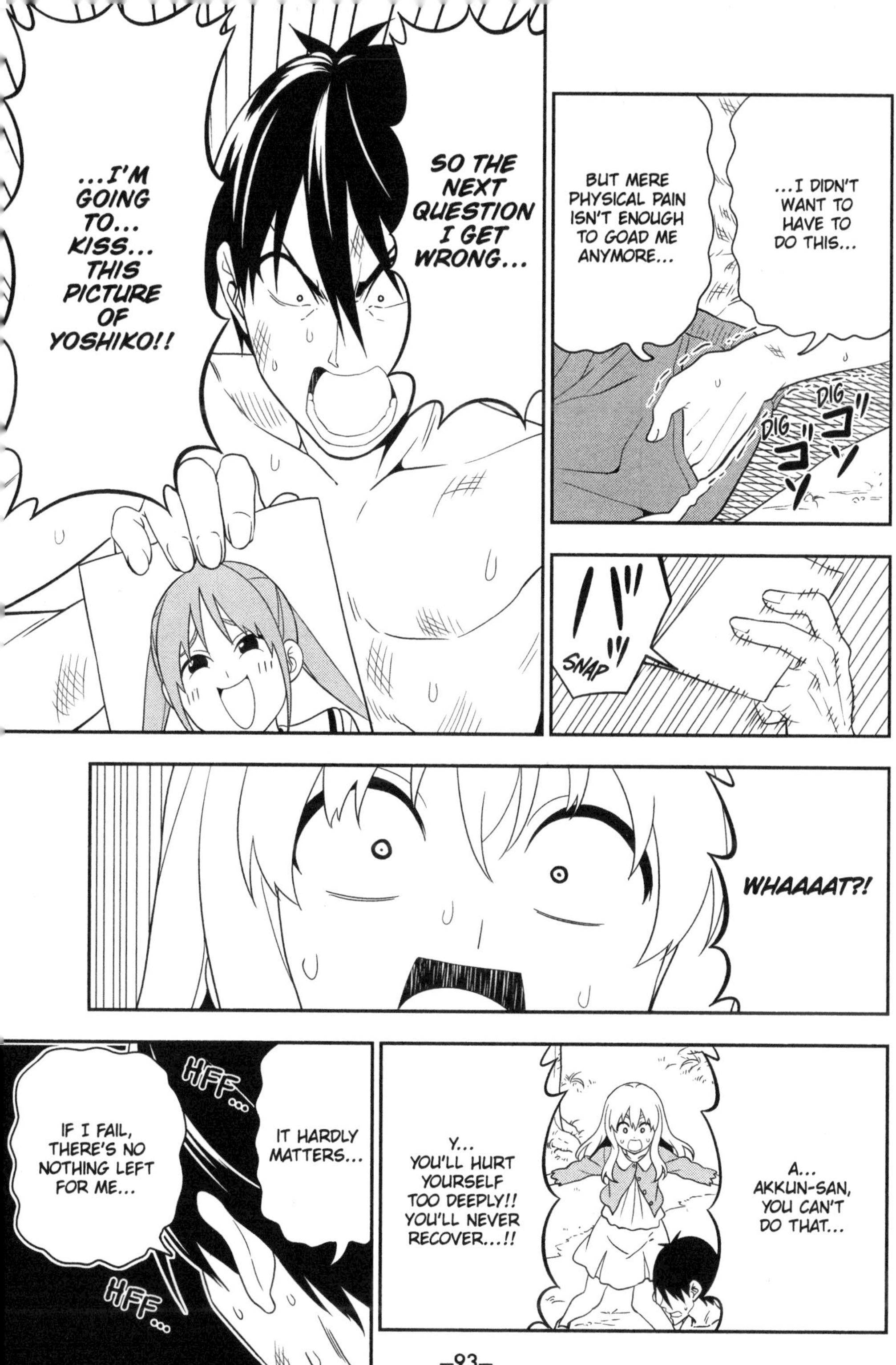
...I DIDN'T WANT TO HAVE TO DO THIS...
BUT MERE PHYSICAL PAIN ISN'T ENOUGH TO GOAD ME ANYMORE...
DIG
DIG
SNAP
SO THE NEXT QUESTION I GET WRONG...
...I'M GOING TO... KISS... THIS PICTURE OF YOSHIKO!!
WHAAAAT?!
A... AKKUN-SAN, YOU CAN'T DO THAT...
Y... YOU'LL HURT YOURSELF TOO DEEPLY!! YOU'LL NEVER RECOVER...!!
HFF...
IT HARDLY MATTERS...
IF I FAIL, THERE'S NO NOTHING LEFT FOR ME...
HFF...

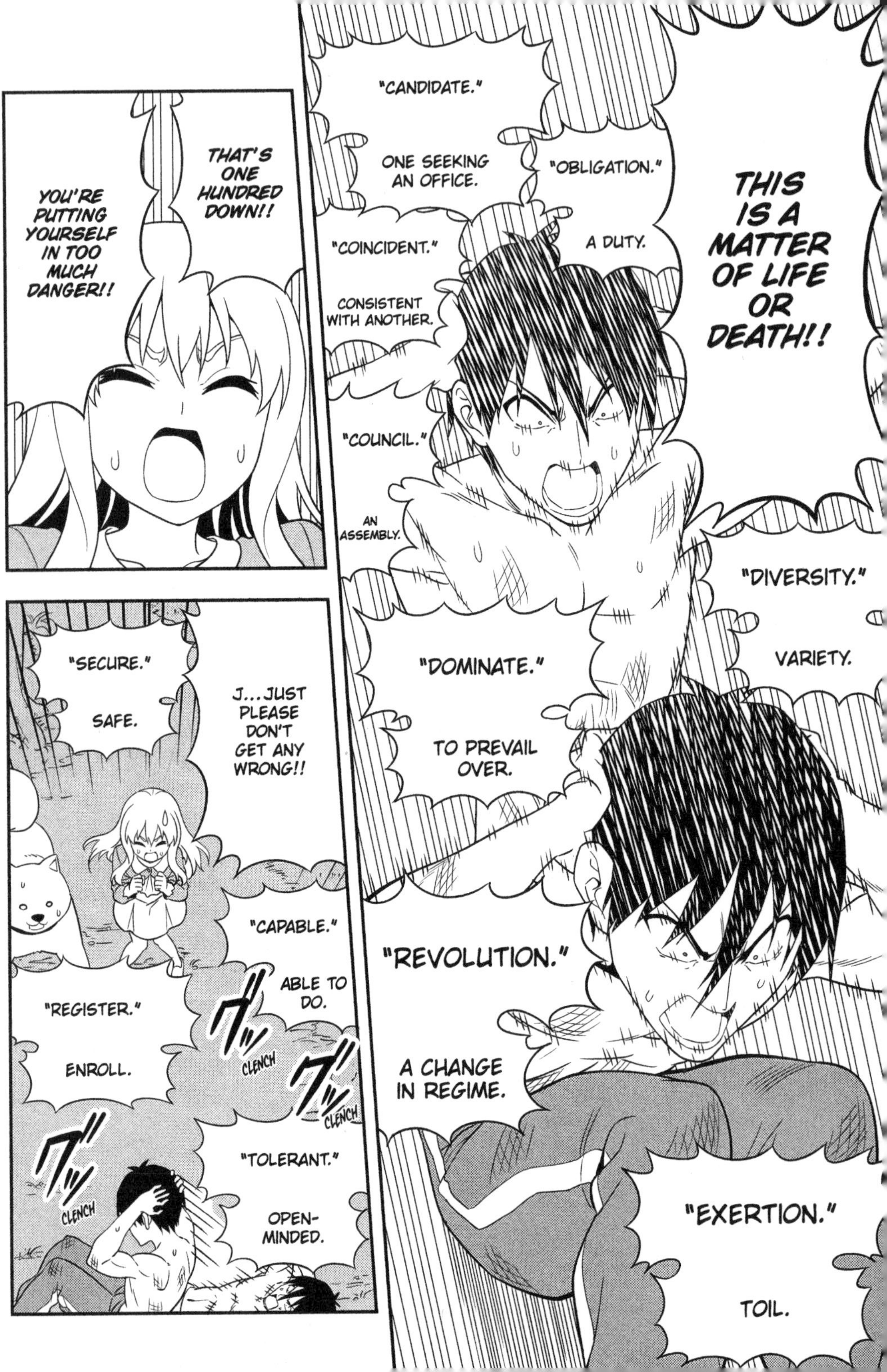
THIS IS A MATTER OF LIFE OR DEATH!!
"OBLIGATION."
A DUTY.
"CANDIDATE."
ONE SEEKING AN OFFICE.
"COINCIDENT."
CONSISTENT WITH ANOTHER.
"COUNCIL."
AN ASSEMBLY.
"DIVERSITY."
VARIETY.
"DOMINATE."
TO PREVAIL OVER.
"REVOLUTION."
A CHANGE IN REGIME.
"EXERTION."
TOIL.
THAT'S ONE HUNDRED DOWN!!
YOU'RE PUTTING YOURSELF IN TOO MUCH DANGER!!
J...JUST PLEASE DON'T GET ANY WRONG!!
"SECURE."
SAFE.
"CAPABLE."
ABLE TO DO.
"REGISTER."
ENROLL.
CLENCH
CLENCH
CLENCH
"TOLERANT."
OPEN-MINDED.

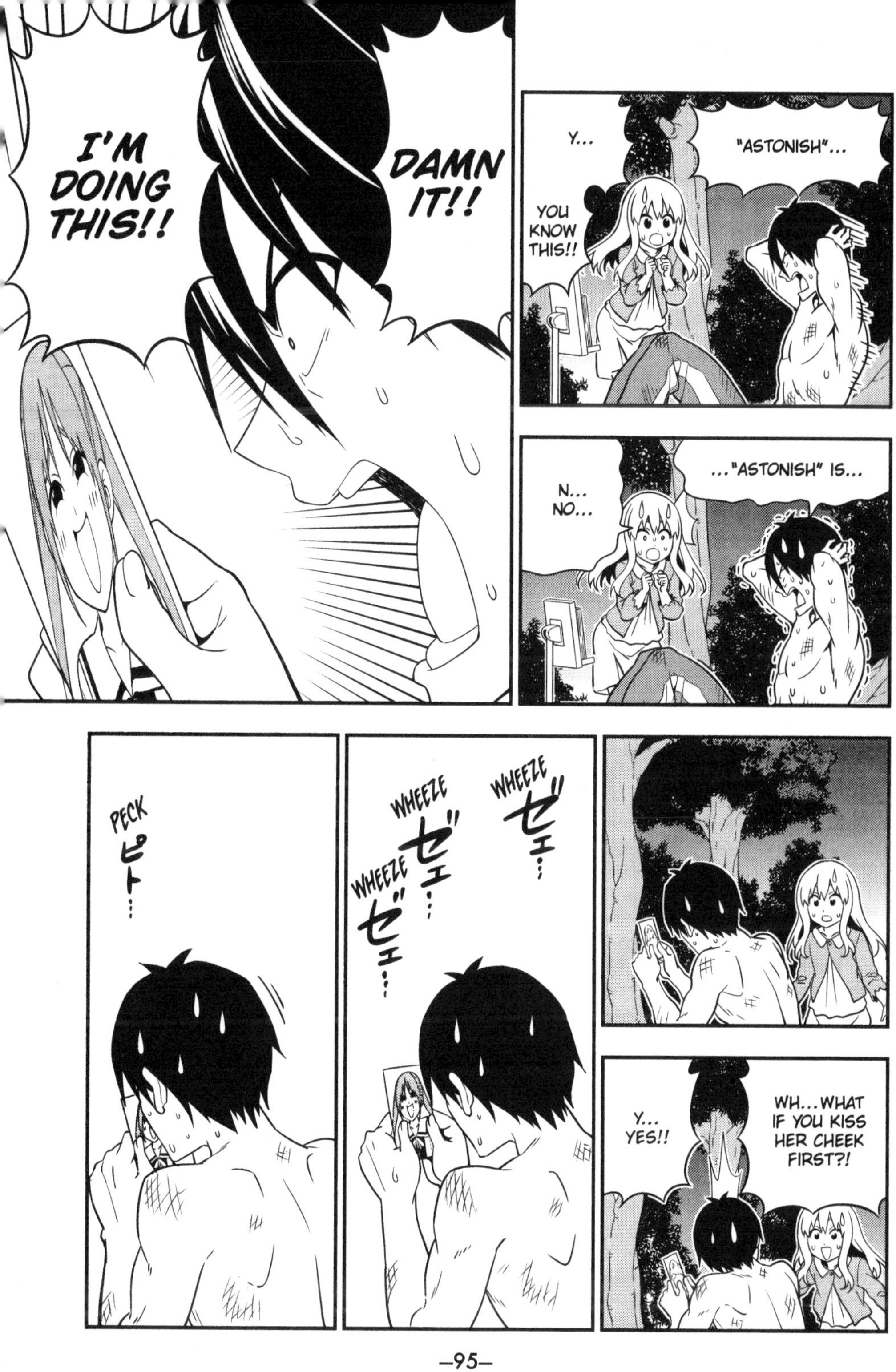
"ASTONISH"...
Y...
YOU KNOW THIS!!
..."ASTONISH" IS...
N... NO...
DAMN IT!!
I'M DOING THIS!!
WH...WHAT IF YOU KISS HER CHEEK FIRST?!
Y... YES!!
WHEEZE ゼェ…
WHEEZE ゼェ…
WHEEZE ゼェ…
PECK ピト…

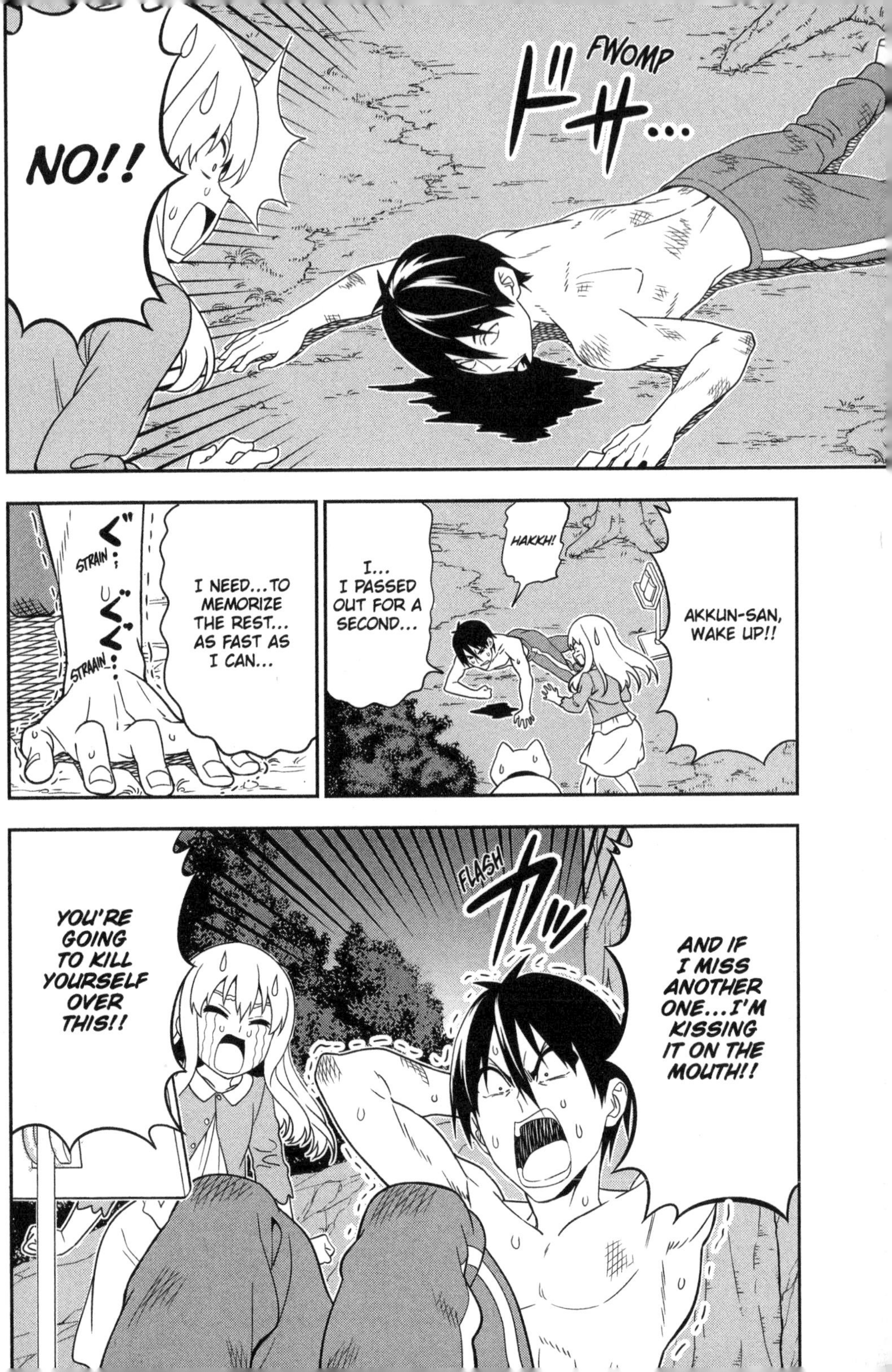

ドサ…
FWOMP
NO!!
AKKUN-SAN, WAKE UP!!
HAKKH!
I... I PASSED OUT FOR A SECOND...
STRAIN
STRAAIN
I NEED...TO MEMORIZE THE REST... AS FAST AS I CAN...
カッ
FLASH
AND IF I MISS ANOTHER ONE...I'M KISSING IT ON THE MOUTH!!
YOU'RE GOING TO KILL YOURSELF OVER THIS!!

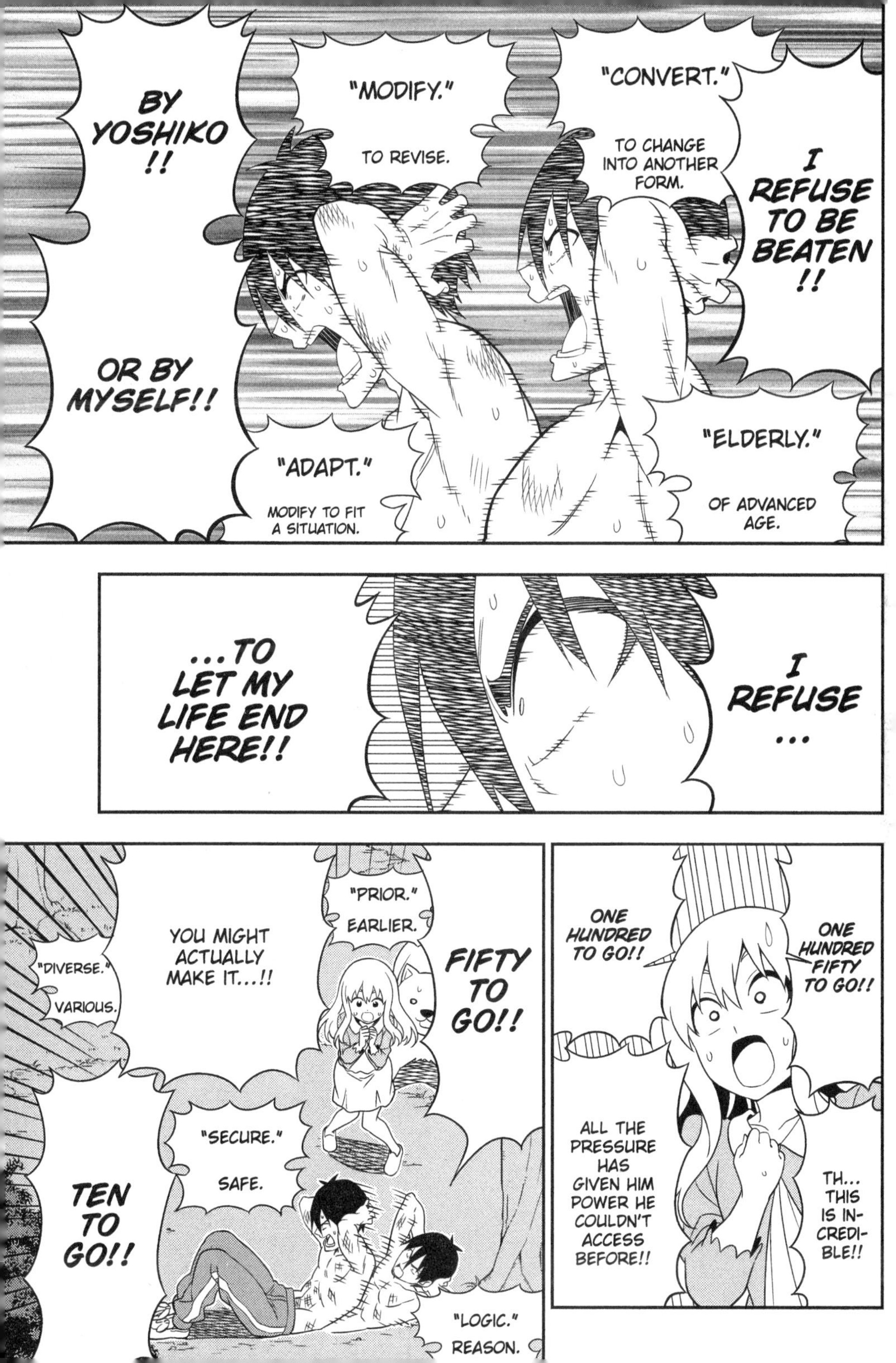
I REFUSE TO BE BEATEN!!
"CONVERT."
TO CHANGE INTO ANOTHER FORM.
"MODIFY."
TO REVISE.
BY YOSHIKO!!
"ELDERLY."
OF ADVANCED AGE.
"ADAPT."
MODIFY TO FIT A SITUATION.
OR BY MYSELF!!
I REFUSE...
...TO LET MY LIFE END HERE!!
ONE HUNDRED FIFTY TO GO!!
ONE HUNDRED TO GO!!
TH... THIS IS IN-CREDI-BLE!!
ALL THE PRESSURE HAS GIVEN HIM POWER HE COULDN'T ACCESS BEFORE!!
FIFTY TO GO!!
"PRIOR."
EARLIER.
YOU MIGHT ACTUALLY MAKE IT...!!
"DIVERSE."
VARIOUS.
"SECURE."
SAFE.
TEN TO GO!!
"LOGIC."
REASON.

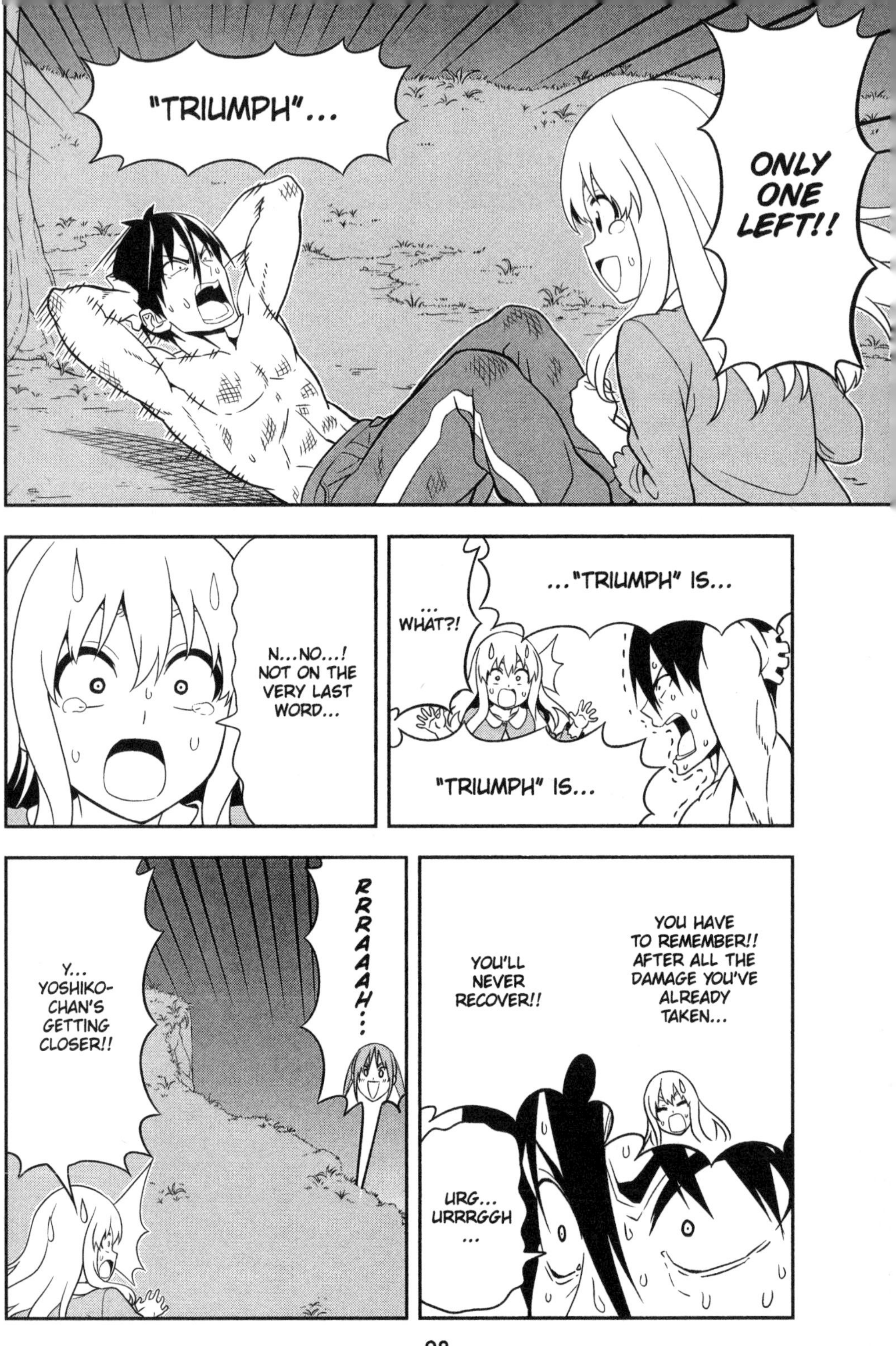
ONLY ONE LEFT!!
"TRIUMPH"...
..."TRIUMPH" IS...
... WHAT?!
"TRIUMPH" IS...
N...NO...! NOT ON THE VERY LAST WORD...
YOU HAVE TO REMEMBER!! AFTER ALL THE DAMAGE YOU'VE ALREADY TAKEN...
YOU'LL NEVER RECOVER!!
URG... URRRGGH ...
RRRAAAAH...
Y... YOSHIKO-CHAN'S GETTING CLOSER!!

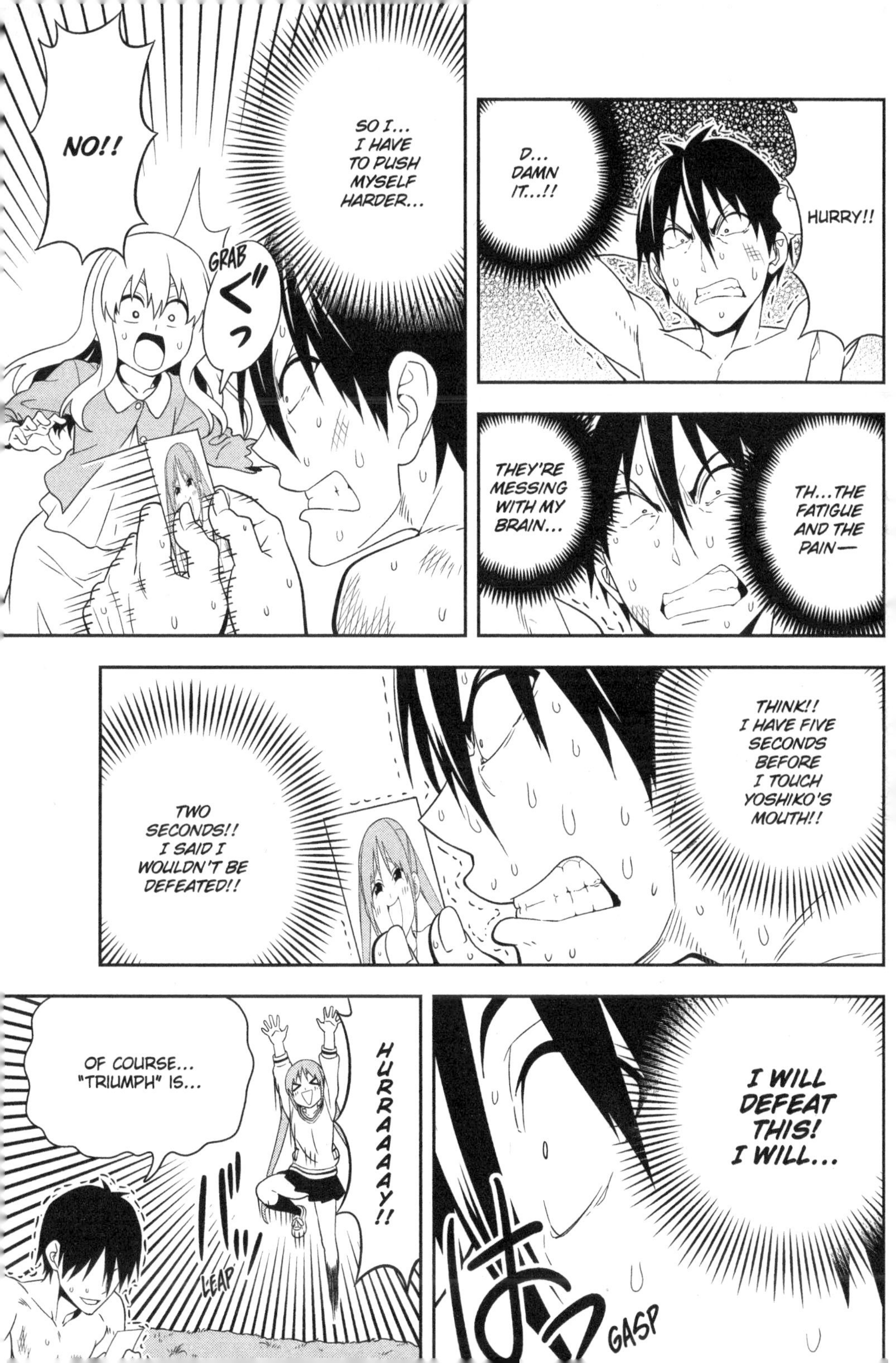

D... DAMN IT...!!
HURRY!!
TH...THE FATIGUE AND THE PAIN—
THEY'RE MESSING WITH MY BRAIN...
SO I... I HAVE TO PUSH MYSELF HARDER...
GRAB
ぐっ
NO!!
THINK!! I HAVE FIVE SECONDS BEFORE I TOUCH YOSHIKO'S MOUTH!!
TWO SECONDS!! I SAID I WOULDN'T BE DEFEATED!!
I WILL DEFEAT THIS! I WILL...
はっ
GASP
HURRAAAAAY!!
OF COURSE... "TRIUMPH" IS...
LEAP

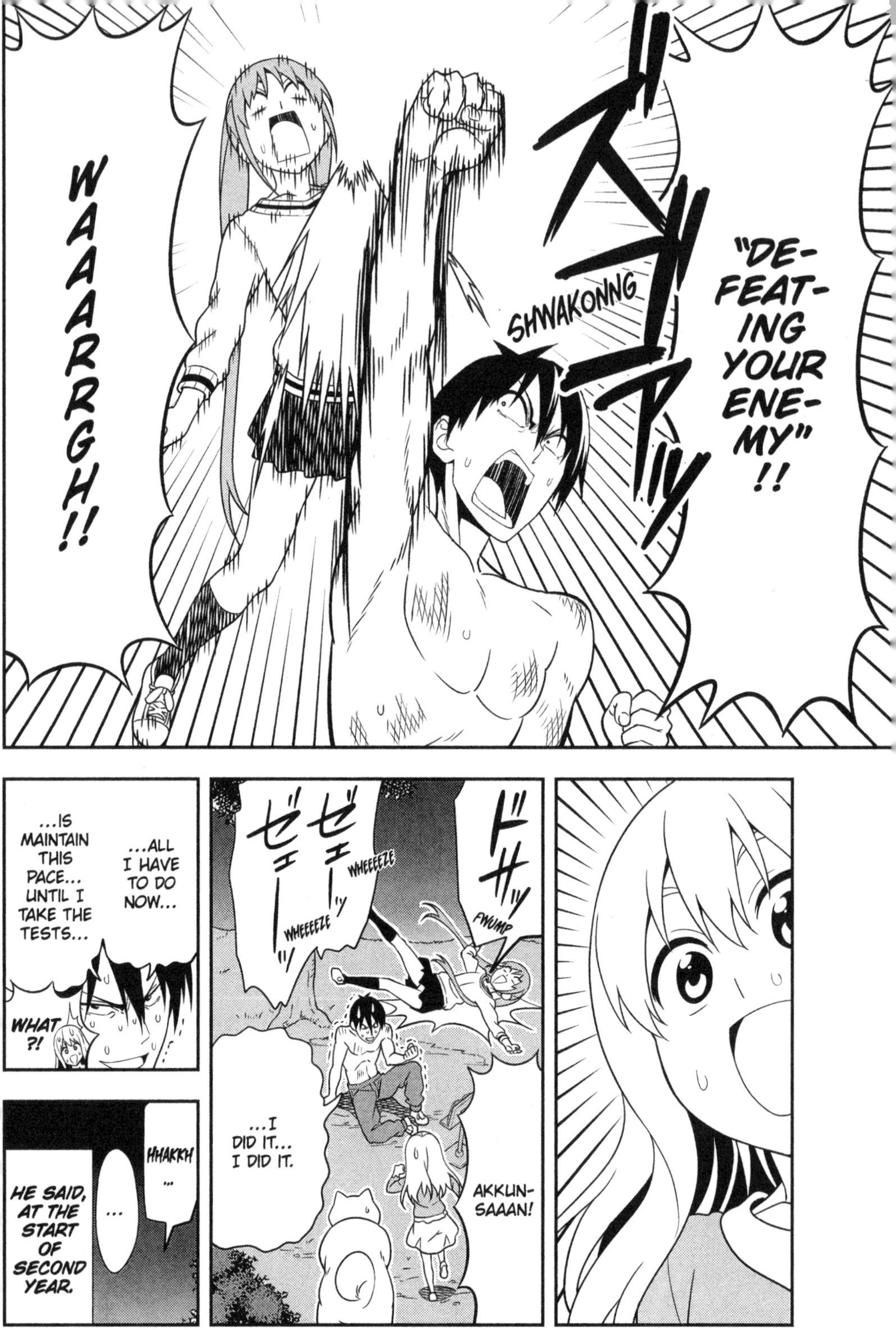
"DE-FEAT-ING YOUR ENE-MY"!!
SHWAKONNG
WAAAARRGH!!
FWUMP
WHEEEEZE
WHEEEEZE
...I DID IT... I DID IT.
AKKUN-SAAAN!
...ALL I HAVE TO DO NOW...
...IS MAINTAIN THIS PACE... UNTIL I TAKE THE TESTS...
WHAT?!
HHAKKH...
...
HE SAID, AT THE START OF SECOND YEAR.

Absolute Certainty

I'M... GOING TO DO IT...
I'M GOING TO KEEP... GOING... UNTIL THE... TESTS...
HE'LL DIE BEFORE THAT...

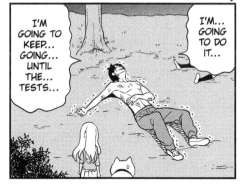

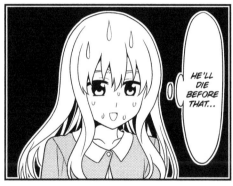

Aho-Girl

\\ˈɑhô͵gərl\\ *Japanese, noun.*
A clueless girl.

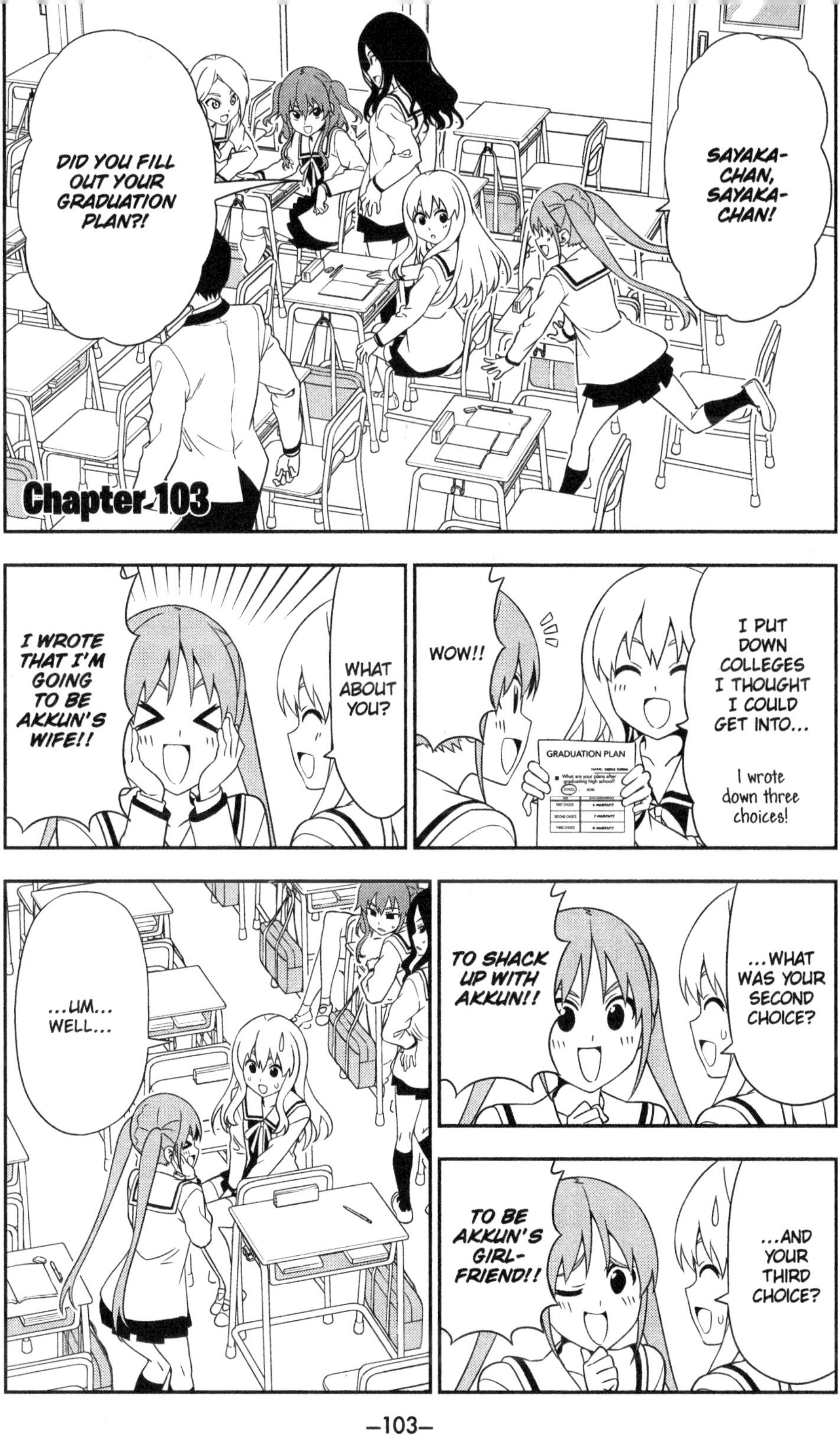
SAYAKA-CHAN, SAYAKA-CHAN!
DID YOU FILL OUT YOUR GRADUATION PLAN?!
Chapter 103
I PUT DOWN COLLEGES I THOUGHT I COULD GET INTO...
I wrote down three choices!
GRADUATION PLAN
WOW!!
WHAT ABOUT YOU?
I WROTE THAT I'M GOING TO BE AKKUN'S WIFE!!
...WHAT WAS YOUR SECOND CHOICE?
TO SHACK UP WITH AKKUN!!
...AND YOUR THIRD CHOICE?
TO BE AKKUN'S GIRL-FRIEND!!
...UM... WELL...

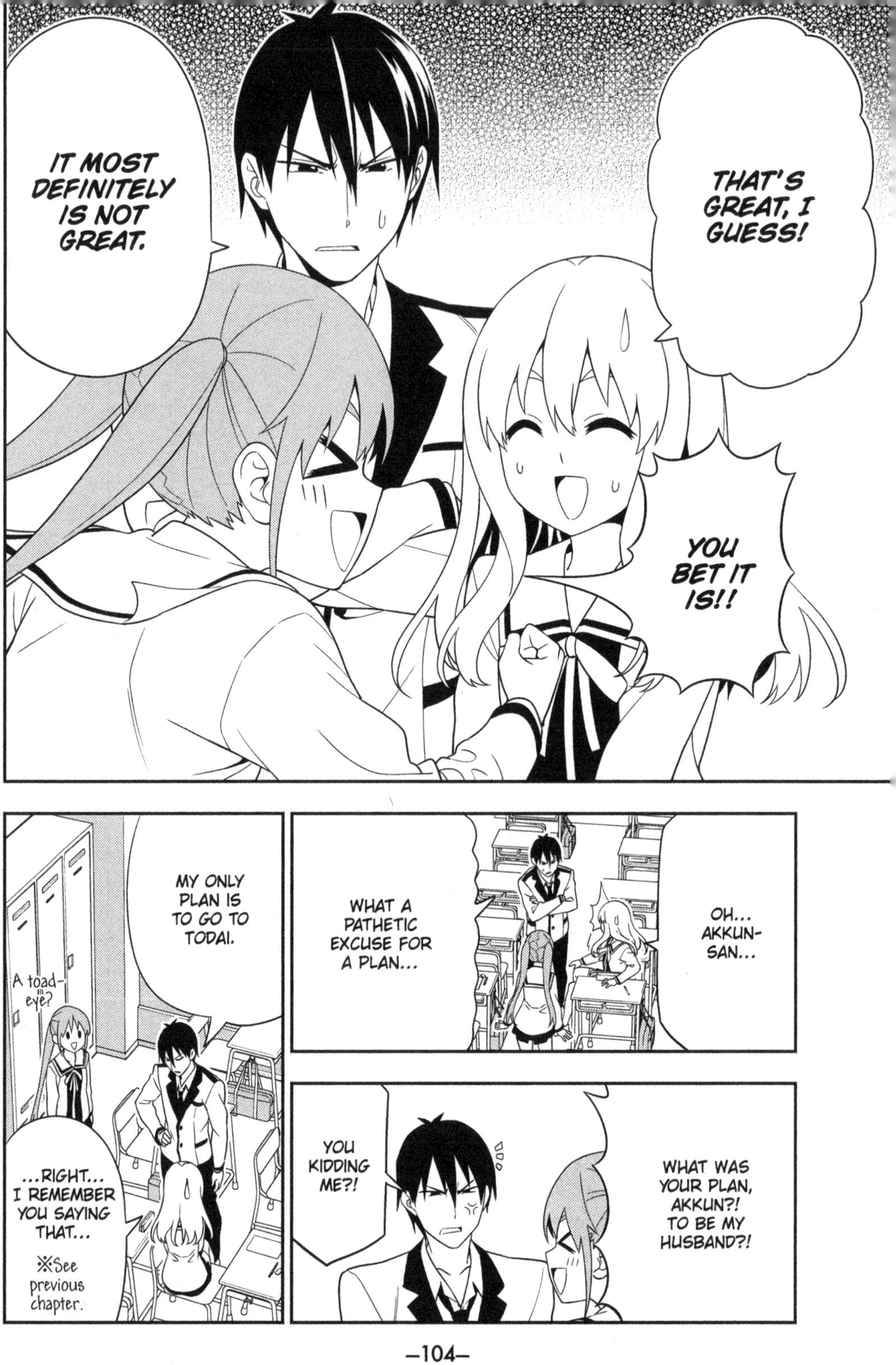
THAT'S GREAT, I GUESS!
YOU BET IT IS!!
IT MOST DEFINITELY IS NOT GREAT.
OH... AKKUN-SAN...
WHAT A PATHETIC EXCUSE FOR A PLAN...
WHAT WAS YOUR PLAN, AKKUN?! TO BE MY HUSBAND?!
YOU KIDDING ME?!
MY ONLY PLAN IS TO GO TO TODAI.
A toad-eye?
...RIGHT... I REMEMBER YOU SAYING THAT...
※See previous chapter.

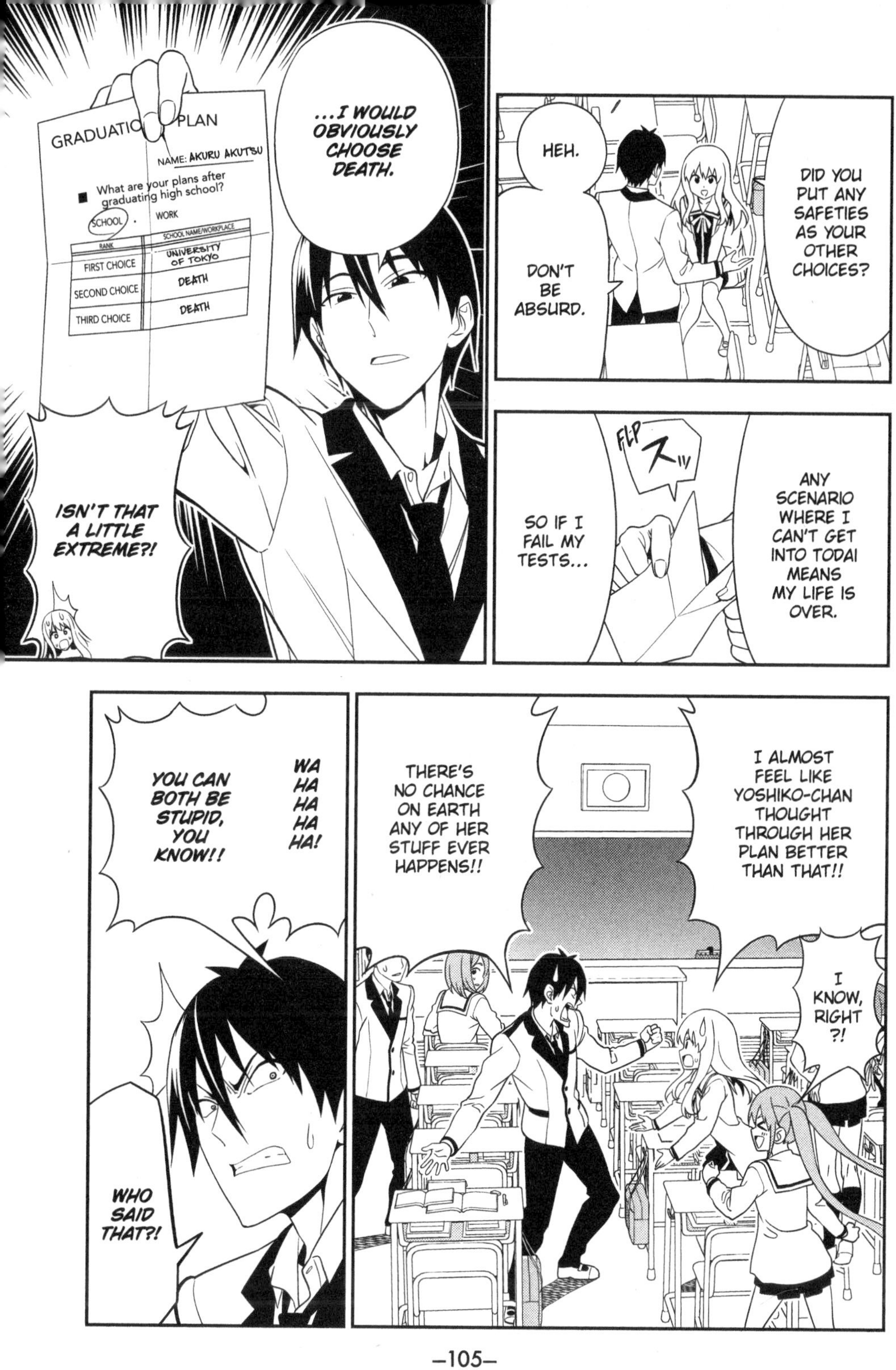
DID YOU PUT ANY SAFETIES AS YOUR OTHER CHOICES?
HEH.
DON'T BE ABSURD.
ANY SCENARIO WHERE I CAN'T GET INTO TODAI MEANS MY LIFE IS OVER.
FLIP
ス
SO IF I FAIL MY TESTS...
...I WOULD OBVIOUSLY CHOOSE DEATH.
GRADUATION PLAN
NAME: AKURU AKUTSU
What are your plans after graduating high school?
SCHOOL · WORK
RANK
SCHOOL NAME/WORKPLACE
FIRST CHOICE
UNIVERSITY OF TOKYO
SECOND CHOICE
DEATH
THIRD CHOICE
DEATH
ISN'T THAT A LITTLE EXTREME?!
I ALMOST FEEL LIKE YOSHIKO-CHAN THOUGHT THROUGH HER PLAN BETTER THAN THAT!!
THERE'S NO CHANCE ON EARTH ANY OF HER STUFF EVER HAPPENS!!
I KNOW, RIGHT?!
WA HA HA HA HA!
YOU CAN BOTH BE STUPID, YOU KNOW!!
WHO SAID THAT?!

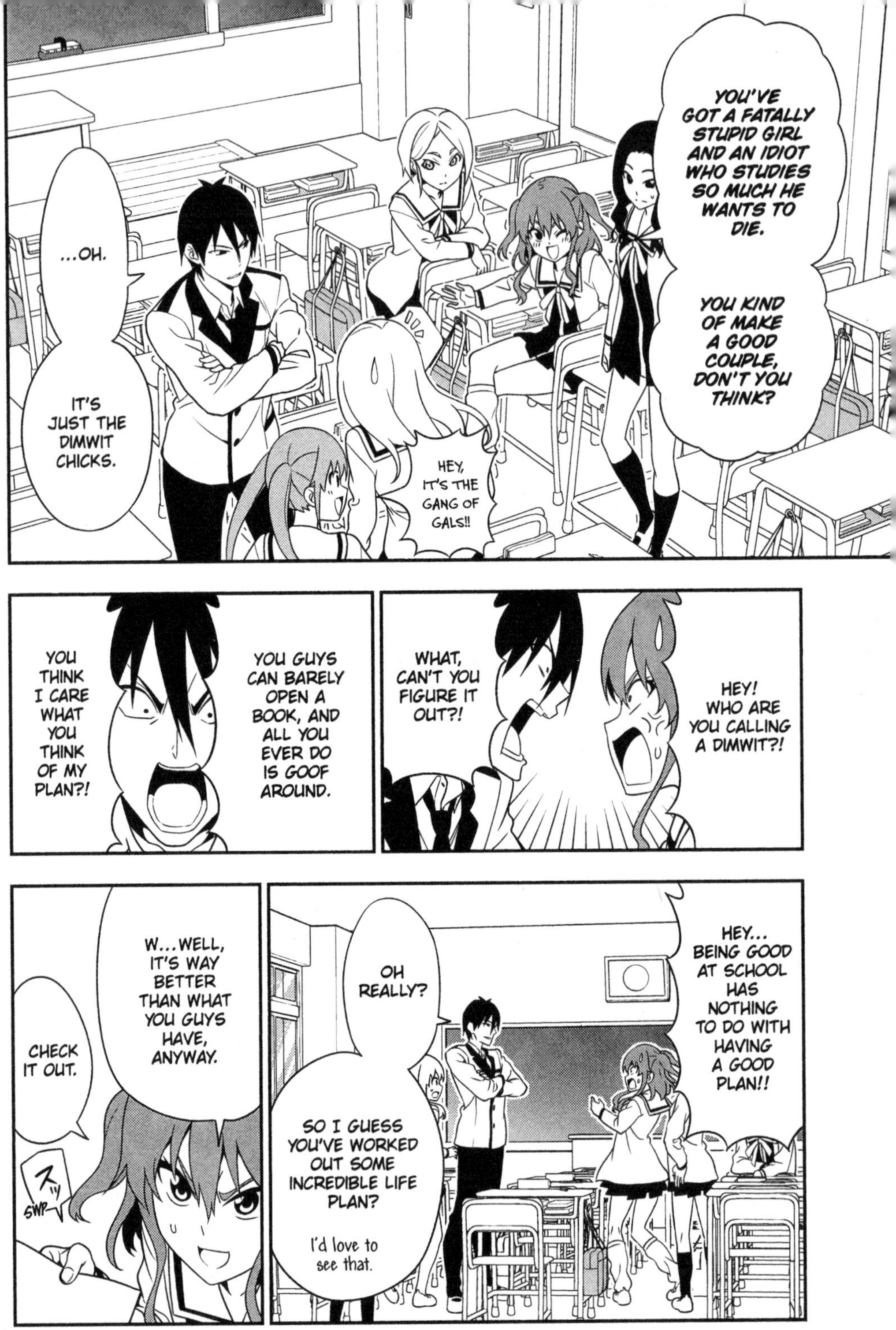
YOU'VE GOT A FATALLY STUPID GIRL AND AN IDIOT WHO STUDIES SO MUCH HE WANTS TO DIE.
YOU KIND OF MAKE A GOOD COUPLE, DON'T YOU THINK?
HEY, IT'S THE GANG OF GALS!!
...OH.
IT'S JUST THE DIMWIT CHICKS.
HEY! WHO ARE YOU CALLING A DIMWIT?!
WHAT, CAN'T YOU FIGURE IT OUT?!
YOU GUYS CAN BARELY OPEN A BOOK, AND ALL YOU EVER DO IS GOOF AROUND.
YOU THINK I CARE WHAT YOU THINK OF MY PLAN?!
HEY... BEING GOOD AT SCHOOL HAS NOTHING TO DO WITH HAVING A GOOD PLAN!!
OH REALLY?
SO I GUESS YOU'VE WORKED OUT SOME INCREDIBLE LIFE PLAN?
I'd love to see that.
W...WELL, IT'S WAY BETTER THAN WHAT YOU GUYS HAVE, ANYWAY.
CHECK IT OUT.
スッ
SWP

THIS IS A JOKE!!

GRADUATION PLAN

NAME: AKANE EIMURA

■ What are your plans after graduating high school?

SCHOOL · (WORK)

RANK	SCHOOL NAME/WORKPLACE
FIRST CHOICE	RUN A FLOWER SHOP
SECOND CHOICE	RUN A CAKE SHOP
THIRD CHOICE	PET-SITTER

...A FLOWER SHOP...

...A CAKE SHOP...

...AND PET-SITTER.

HUH?!

WHAT'S SO WEIRD ABOUT THAT?!

I didn't know that about you!

Is that what you wrote down...?

How cute!!

I EXPECTED IT TO BE DUMB, BUT THIS IS TOTALLY IMBECILIC!!

ARE YOU SOME KIND OF STARRY-EYED LITTLE GIRL?!

WHAT'S SO HARD TO UNDER-STAND?!

GO ON, TELL US WHAT DEEP THOUGHTS YOU WERE THINKING WHEN YOU PICKED THOSE JOBS.

THIS IS LIKE ASKING A GRADE-SCHOOL KID WHAT SHE WANTS TO BE...

FOR ONE THING, THEY HAVE ABSOLUTELY NOTHING TO DO WITH EACH OTHER...

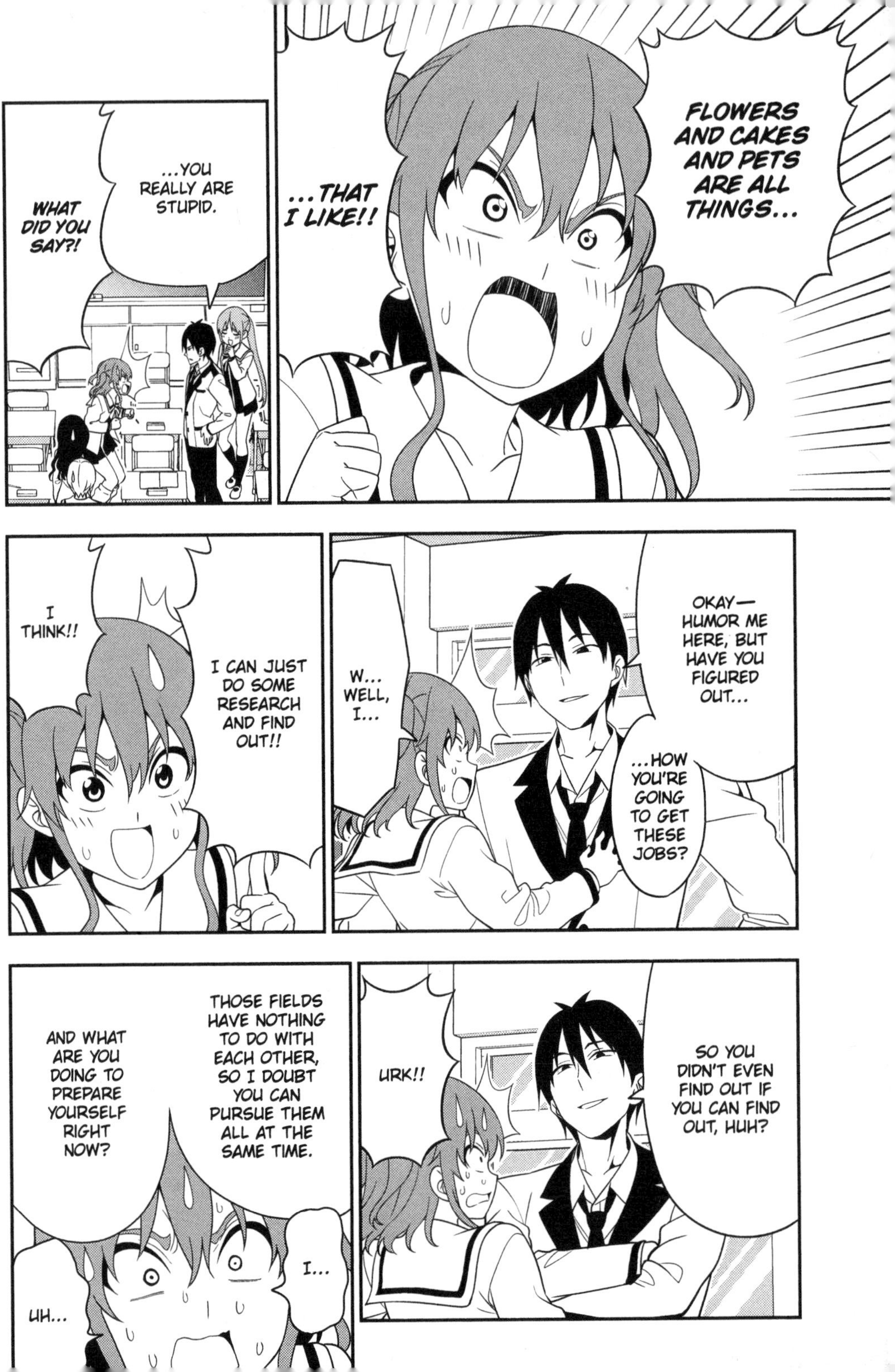
FLOWERS AND CAKES AND PETS ARE ALL THINGS...
...THAT I LIKE!!
...YOU REALLY ARE STUPID.
WHAT DID YOU SAY?!
OKAY—HUMOR ME HERE, BUT HAVE YOU FIGURED OUT...
...HOW YOU'RE GOING TO GET THESE JOBS?
W... WELL, I...
I CAN JUST DO SOME RESEARCH AND FIND OUT!!
I THINK!!
SO YOU DIDN'T EVEN FIND OUT IF YOU CAN FIND OUT, HUH?
URK!!
THOSE FIELDS HAVE NOTHING TO DO WITH EACH OTHER, SO I DOUBT YOU CAN PURSUE THEM ALL AT THE SAME TIME.
AND WHAT ARE YOU DOING TO PREPARE YOURSELF RIGHT NOW?
I...
UH...

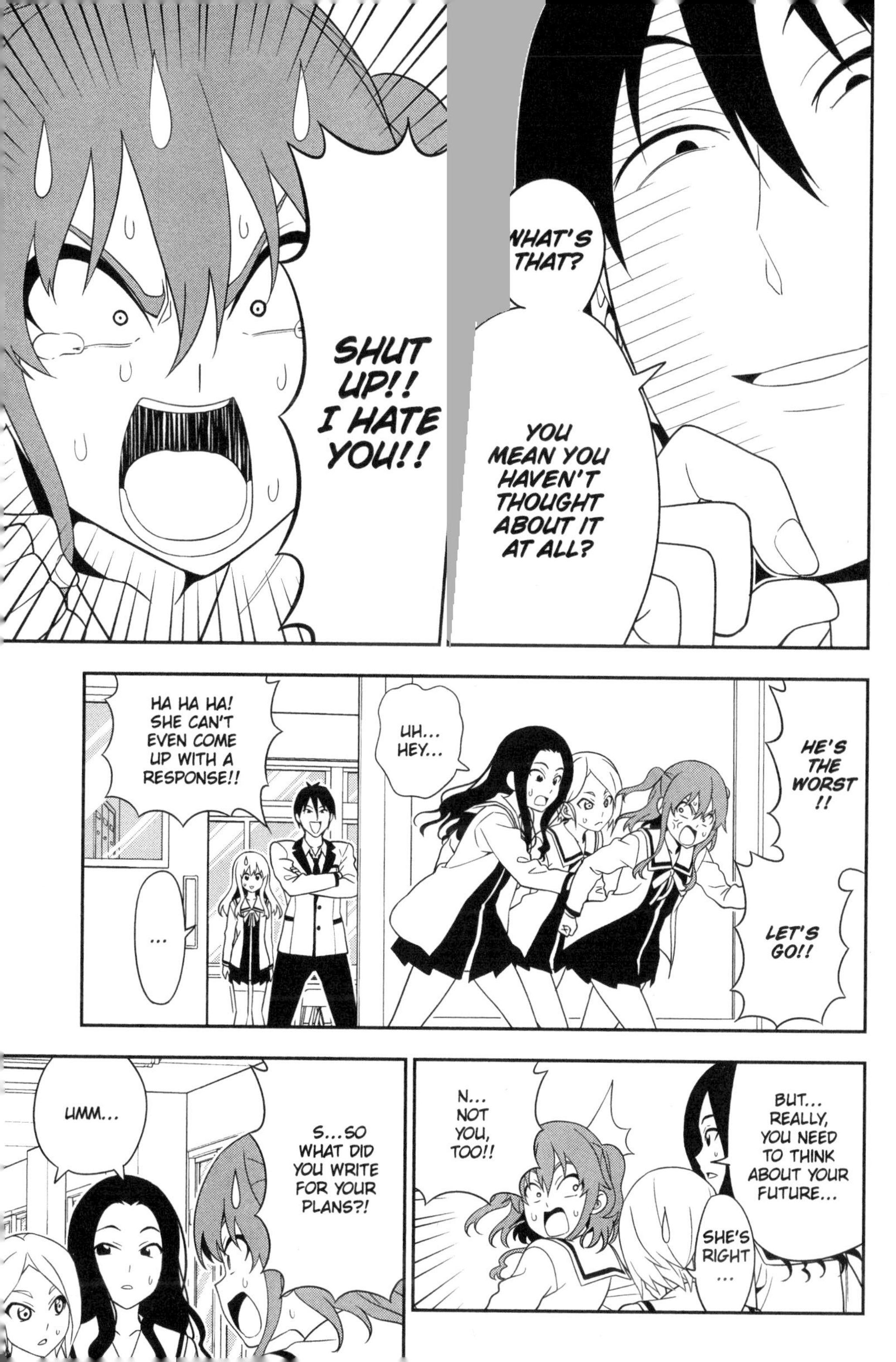
WHAT'S THAT?
YOU MEAN YOU HAVEN'T THOUGHT ABOUT IT AT ALL?
SHUT UP!! I HATE YOU!!
HE'S THE WORST!!
LET'S GO!!
UH... HEY...
HA HA HA! SHE CAN'T EVEN COME UP WITH A RESPONSE!!
...
BUT... REALLY, YOU NEED TO THINK ABOUT YOUR FUTURE...
SHE'S RIGHT...
N... NOT YOU, TOO!!
S...SO WHAT DID YOU WRITE FOR YOUR PLANS?!
UMM...

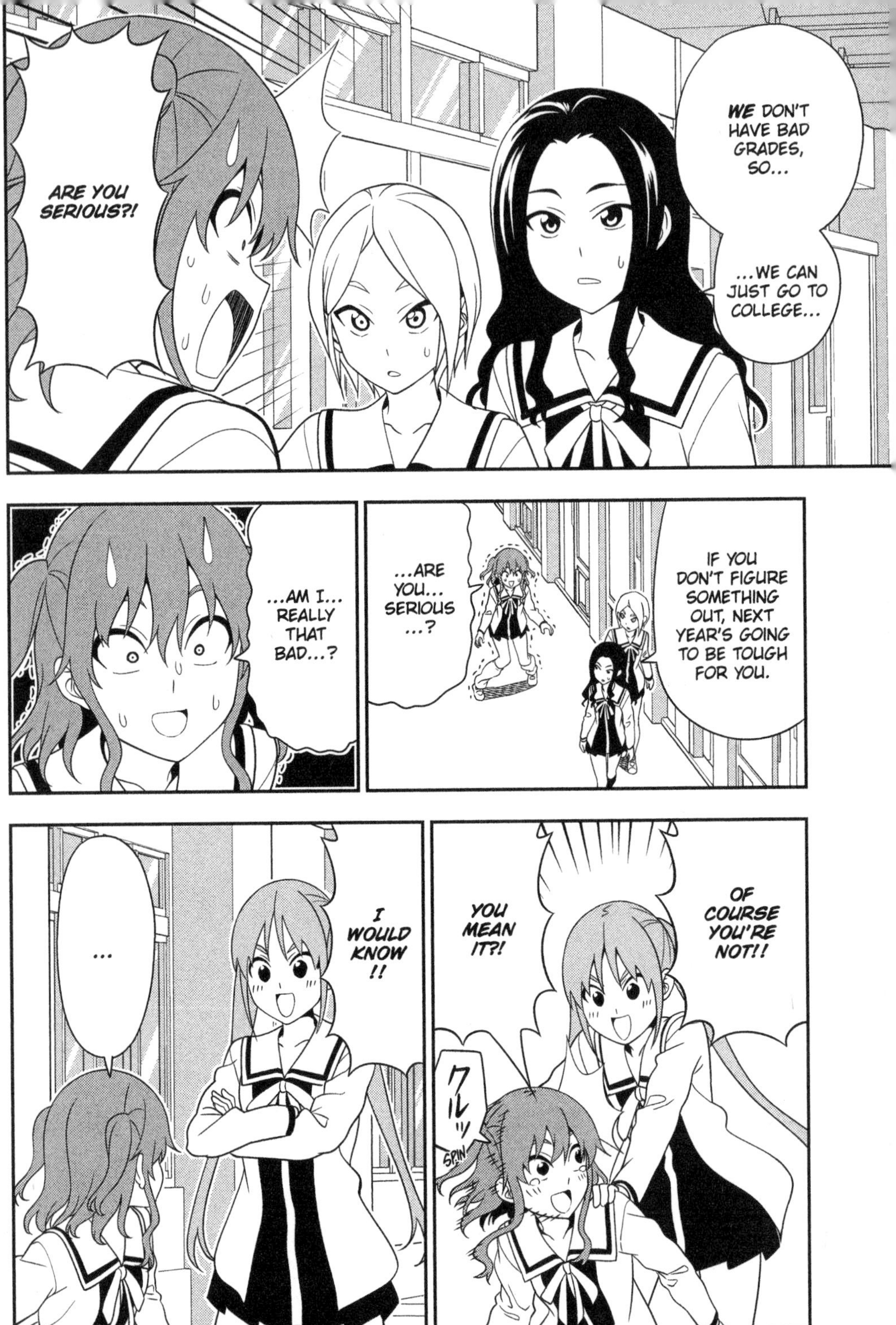
WE DON'T HAVE BAD GRADES, SO...
...WE CAN JUST GO TO COLLEGE...
ARE YOU SERIOUS?!
IF YOU DON'T FIGURE SOMETHING OUT, NEXT YEAR'S GOING TO BE TOUGH FOR YOU.
...ARE YOU... SERIOUS ...?
...AM I... REALLY THAT BAD...?
OF COURSE YOU'RE NOT!!
YOU MEAN IT?!
クルッ
SPIN
I WOULD KNOW !!
...

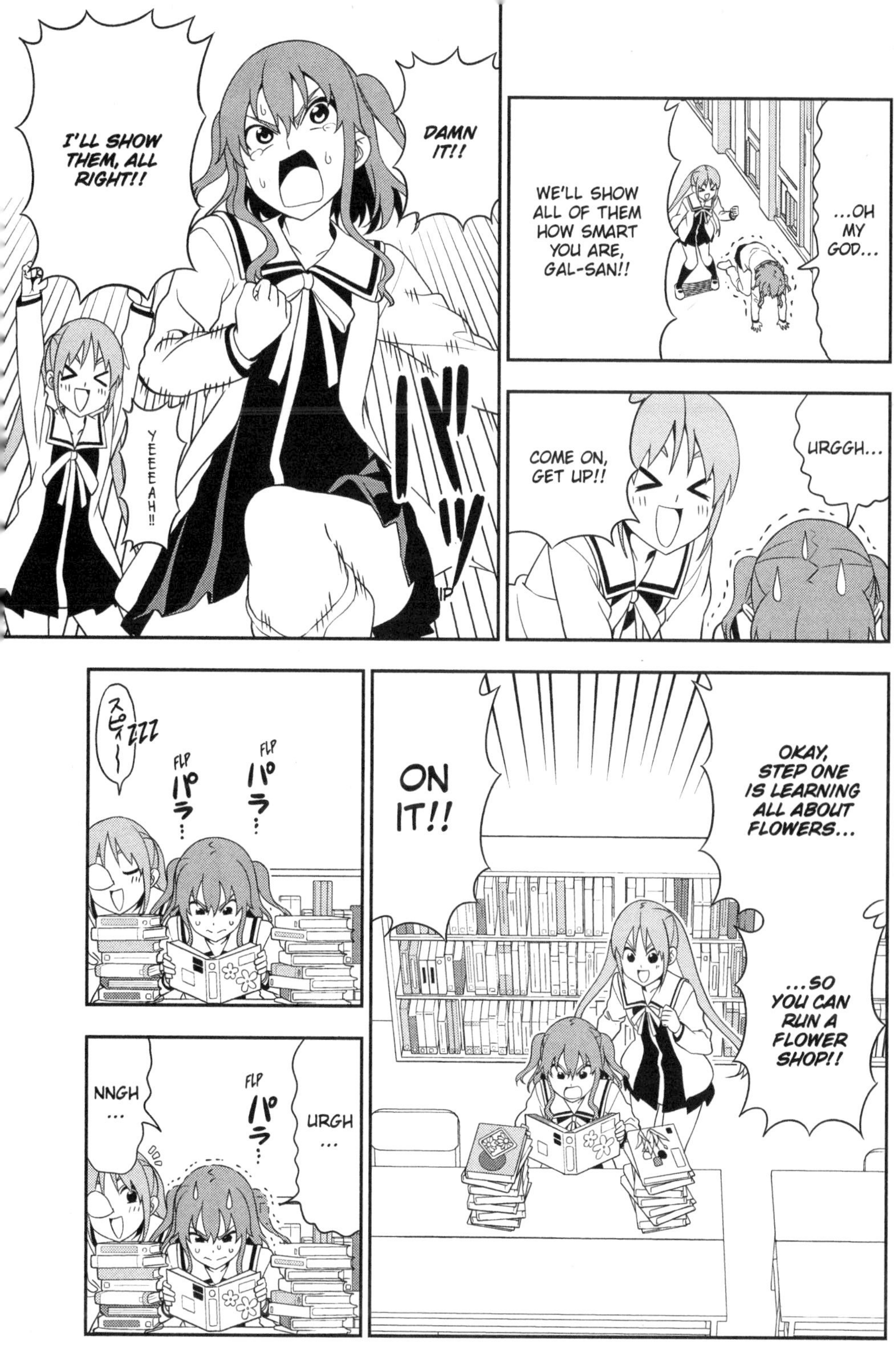
...OH MY GOD...
WE'LL SHOW ALL OF THEM HOW SMART YOU ARE, GAL-SAN!!
URGGH...
COME ON, GET UP!!
DAMN IT!!
I'LL SHOW THEM, ALL RIGHT!!
YEEEAH!!
OKAY, STEP ONE IS LEARNING ALL ABOUT FLOWERS...
...SO YOU CAN RUN A FLOWER SHOP!!
ON IT!!
FLP パラ...
FLP パラ...
スピィ～ ZZZ
URGH ...
FLP パラ...
NNGH ...

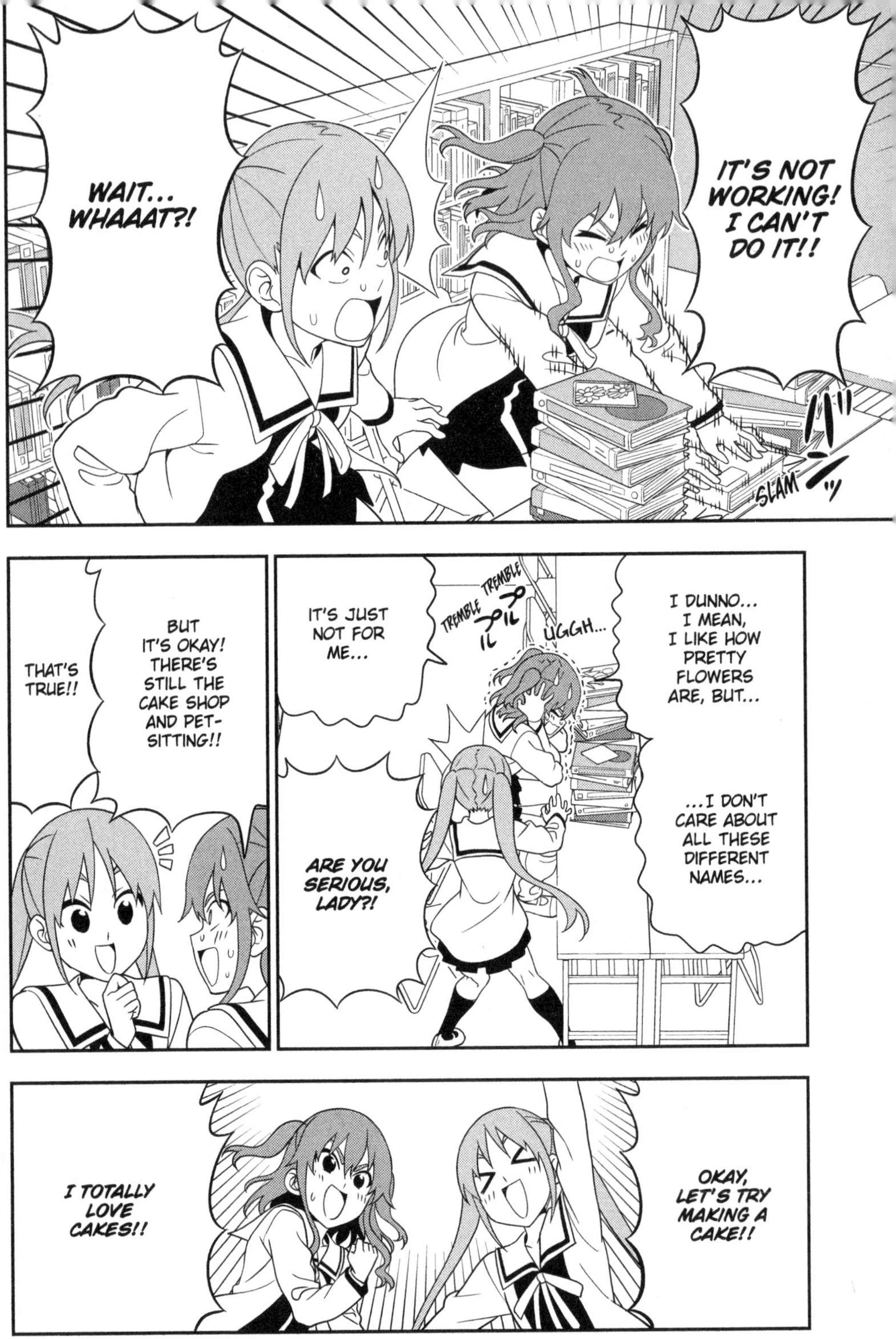
IT'S NOT WORKING! I CAN'T DO IT!!
WAIT... WHAAAT?!
SLAM
I DUNNO... I MEAN, I LIKE HOW PRETTY FLOWERS ARE, BUT...
...I DON'T CARE ABOUT ALL THESE DIFFERENT NAMES...
UGGH...
TREMBLE TREMBLE
IT'S JUST NOT FOR ME...
ARE YOU SERIOUS, LADY?!
BUT IT'S OKAY! THERE'S STILL THE CAKE SHOP AND PET-SITTING!!
THAT'S TRUE!!
OKAY, LET'S TRY MAKING A CAKE!!
I TOTALLY LOVE CAKES!!

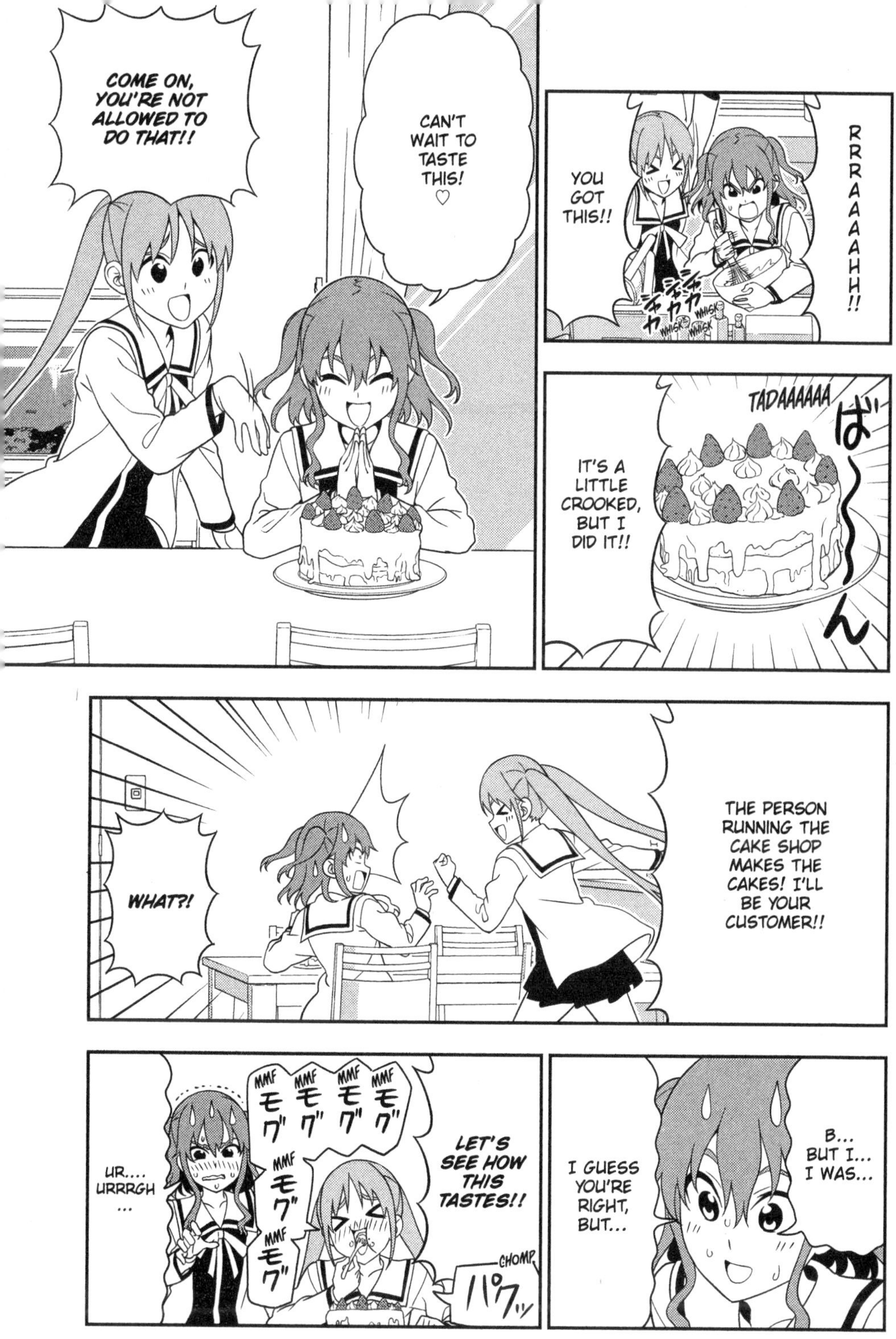
RRRAAAAHH!!
YOU GOT THIS!!
シャカシャカ
WHISK WHISK
ば~~ん
TADAAAAAA
IT'S A LITTLE CROOKED, BUT I DID IT!!
CAN'T WAIT TO TASTE THIS! ♡
COME ON, YOU'RE NOT ALLOWED TO DO THAT!!
THE PERSON RUNNING THE CAKE SHOP MAKES THE CAKES! I'LL BE YOUR CUSTOMER!!
WHAT?!
B... BUT I... I WAS...
I GUESS YOU'RE RIGHT, BUT...
LET'S SEE HOW THIS TASTES!!
パクッ
CHOMP
モグモグモグモグモグモグ
MMF MMF MMF MMF MMF MMF
UR.... URRRGH ...

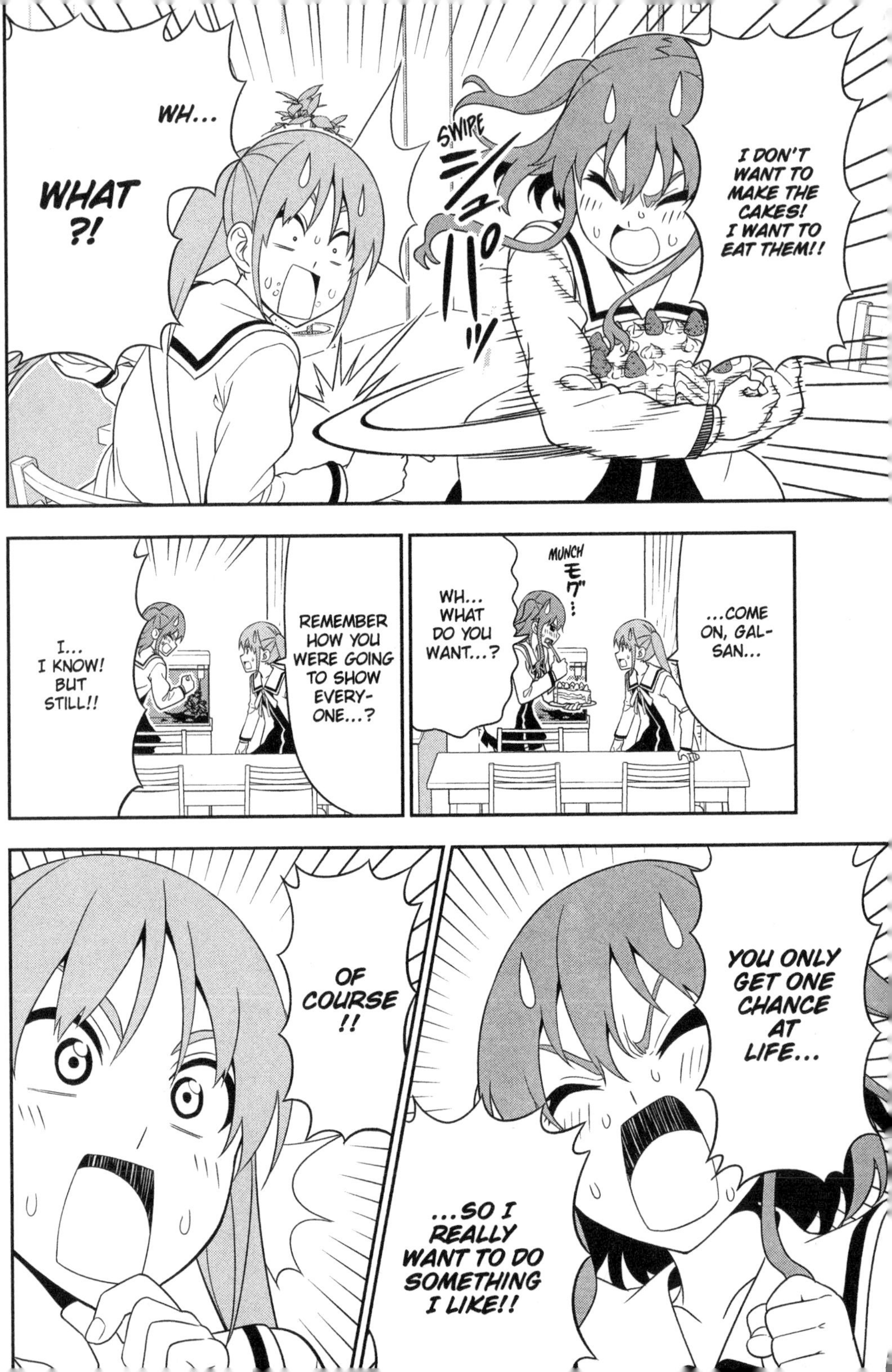
I DON'T WANT TO MAKE THE CAKES! I WANT TO EAT THEM!!
SWIPE
WH...
WHAT ?!
...COME ON, GAL-SAN...
MUNCH
モグ…
WH... WHAT DO YOU WANT...?
REMEMBER HOW YOU WERE GOING TO SHOW EVERY-ONE...?
I... I KNOW! BUT STILL!!
YOU ONLY GET ONE CHANCE AT LIFE...
...SO I REALLY WANT TO DO SOMETHING I LIKE!!
OF COURSE!!

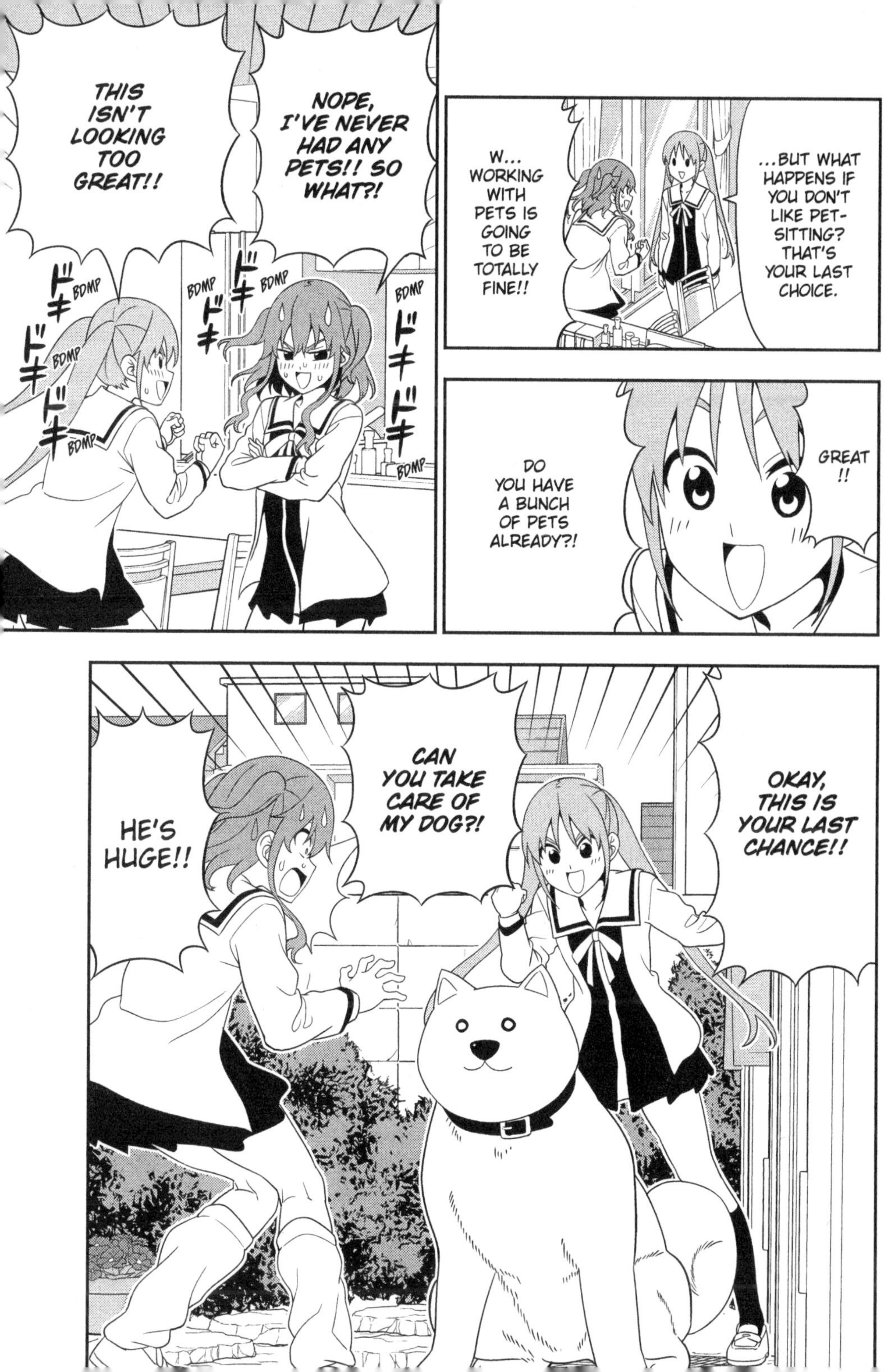
...BUT WHAT HAPPENS IF YOU DON'T LIKE PET-SITTING? THAT'S YOUR LAST CHOICE.
W... WORKING WITH PETS IS GOING TO BE TOTALLY FINE!!
GREAT !!
DO YOU HAVE A BUNCH OF PETS ALREADY?!
NOPE, I'VE NEVER HAD ANY PETS!! SO WHAT?!
THIS ISN'T LOOKING TOO GREAT!!
ドキ BDMP
ドキ BDMP
ドキ BDMP
ドキ BDMP
ドキ BDMP
ドキ BDMP
ドキ BDMP
ドキ BDMP
OKAY, THIS IS YOUR LAST CHANCE!!
CAN YOU TAKE CARE OF MY DOG?!
HE'S HUGE!!

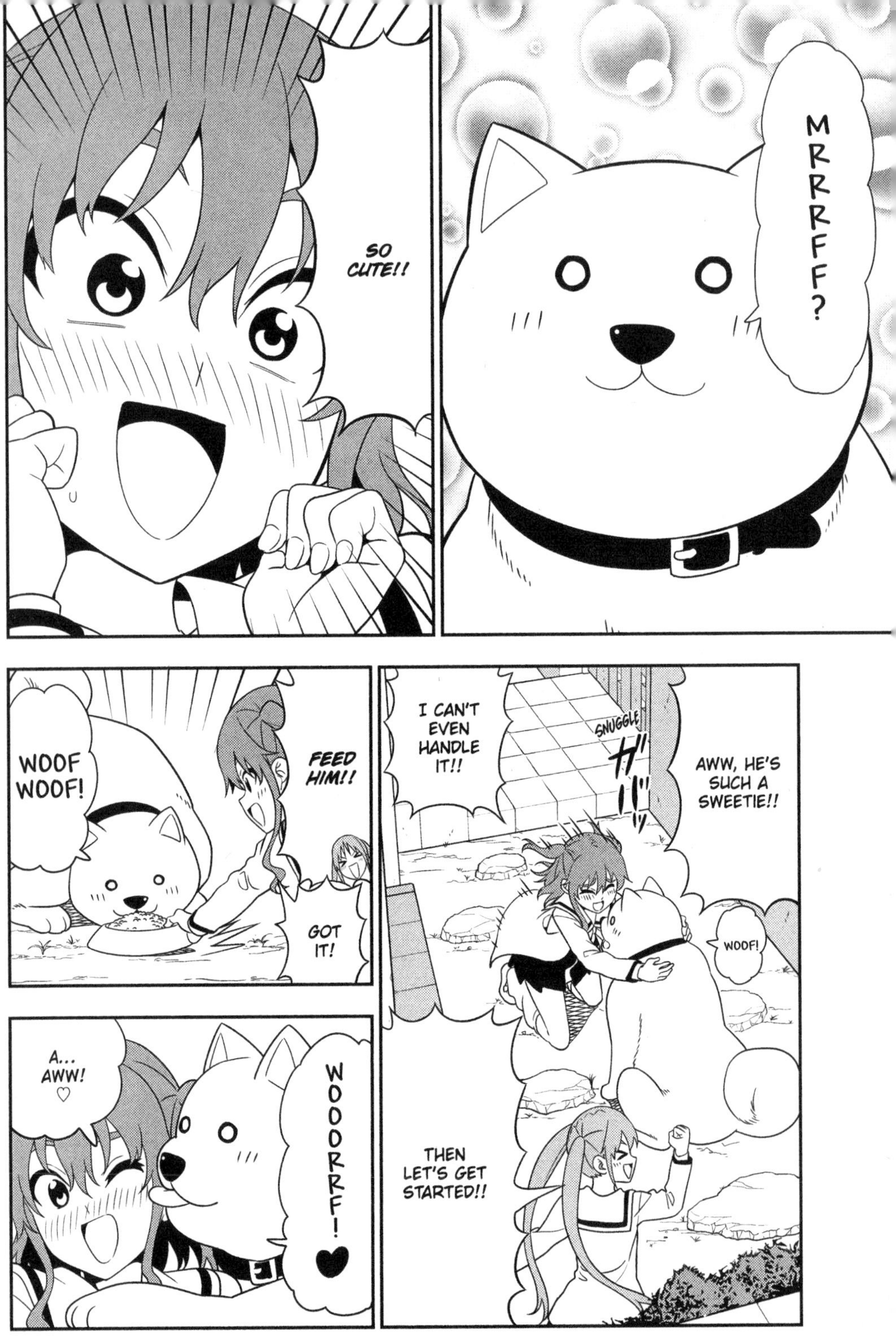
MRRRFF?
SO CUTE!!
AWW, HE'S SUCH A SWEETIE!!
SNUGGLE
I CAN'T EVEN HANDLE IT!!
WOOF!
THEN LET'S GET STARTED!!
FEED HIM!!
WOOF WOOF!
GOT IT!
WOOOORRF! ♥
A... AWW! ♡

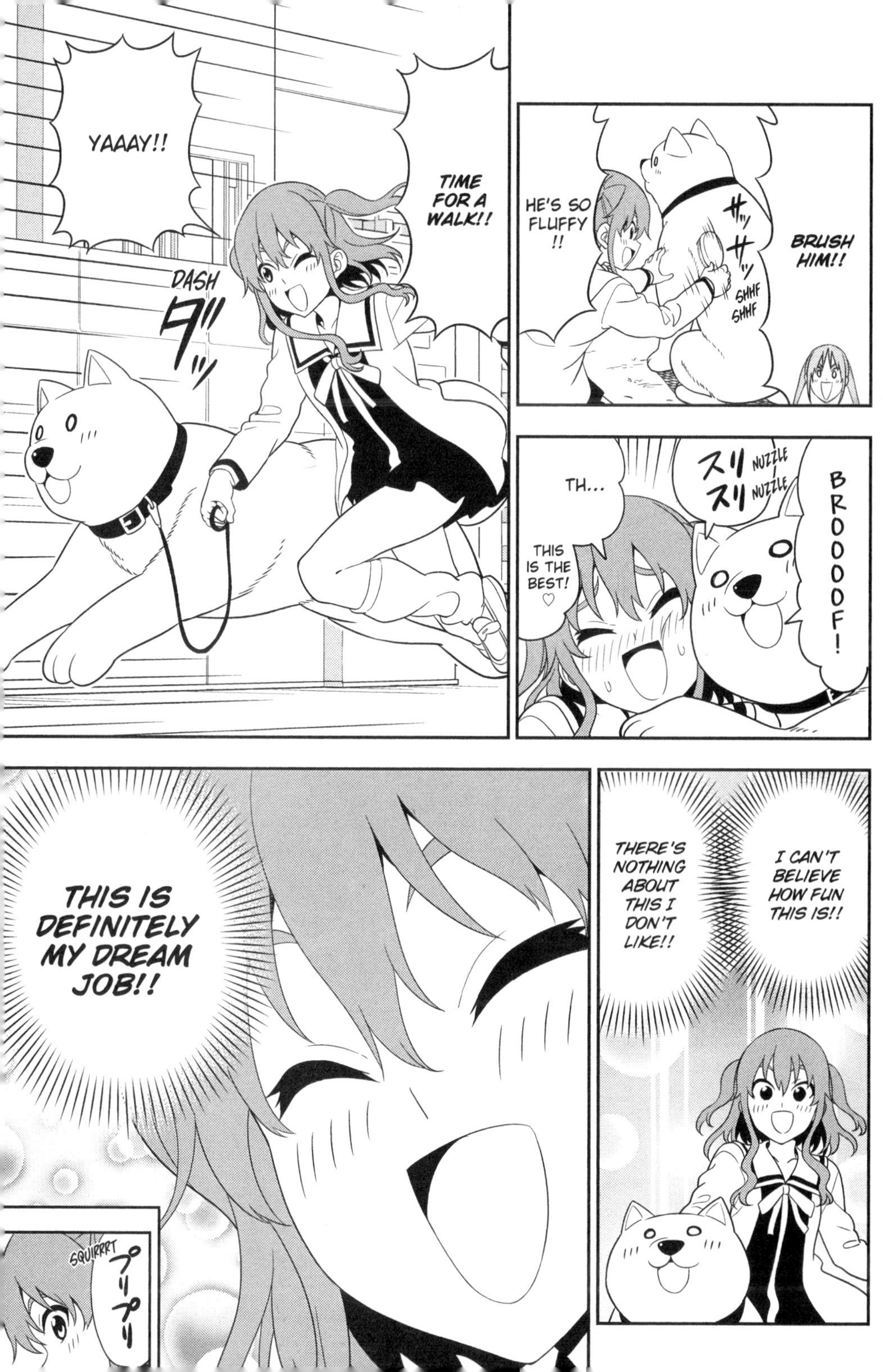
BRUSH HIM!!
ザッザッ
SHHF SHHF
HE'S SO FLUFFY!!
BROOOOOF!
スリスリ
NUZZLE NUZZLE
TH...
THIS IS THE BEST! ♡
TIME FOR A WALK!!
YAAAY!!
DASH
ダッ
I CAN'T BELIEVE HOW FUN THIS IS!!
THERE'S NOTHING ABOUT THIS I DON'T LIKE!!
THIS IS DEFINITELY MY DREAM JOB!!
SQUIRRRT
プリプリ

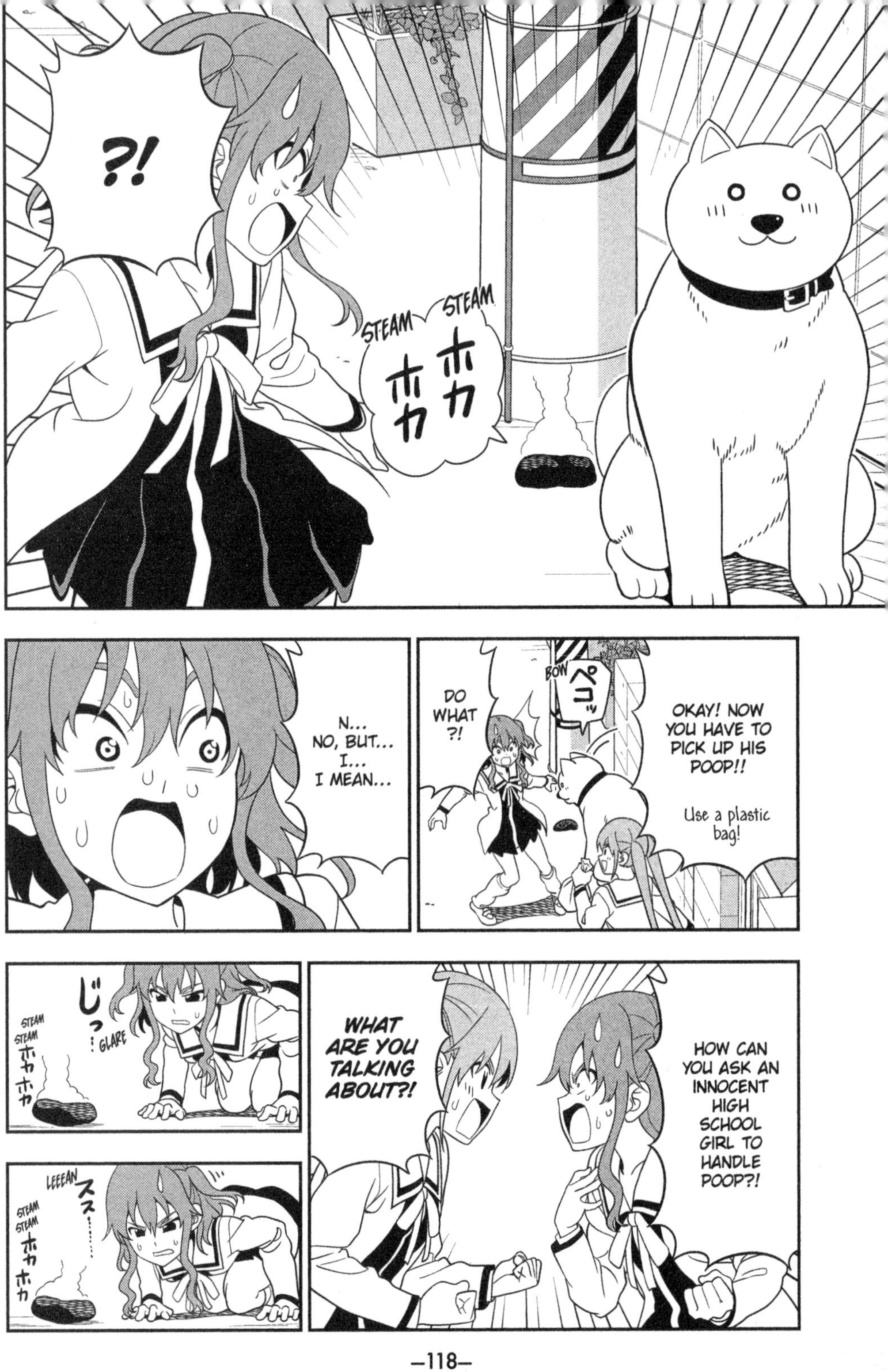
?!
STEAM STEAM
ホカホカ
OKAY! NOW YOU HAVE TO PICK UP HIS POOP!!
Use a plastic bag!
BOW
ペコッ
DO WHAT ?!
N... NO, BUT... I... I MEAN...
HOW CAN YOU ASK AN INNOCENT HIGH SCHOOL GIRL TO HANDLE POOP?!
WHAT ARE YOU TALKING ABOUT?!
じっ
GLARE
STEAM STEAM
ホカホカ
LEEEAN
スス……
STEAM STEAM
ホカホカ

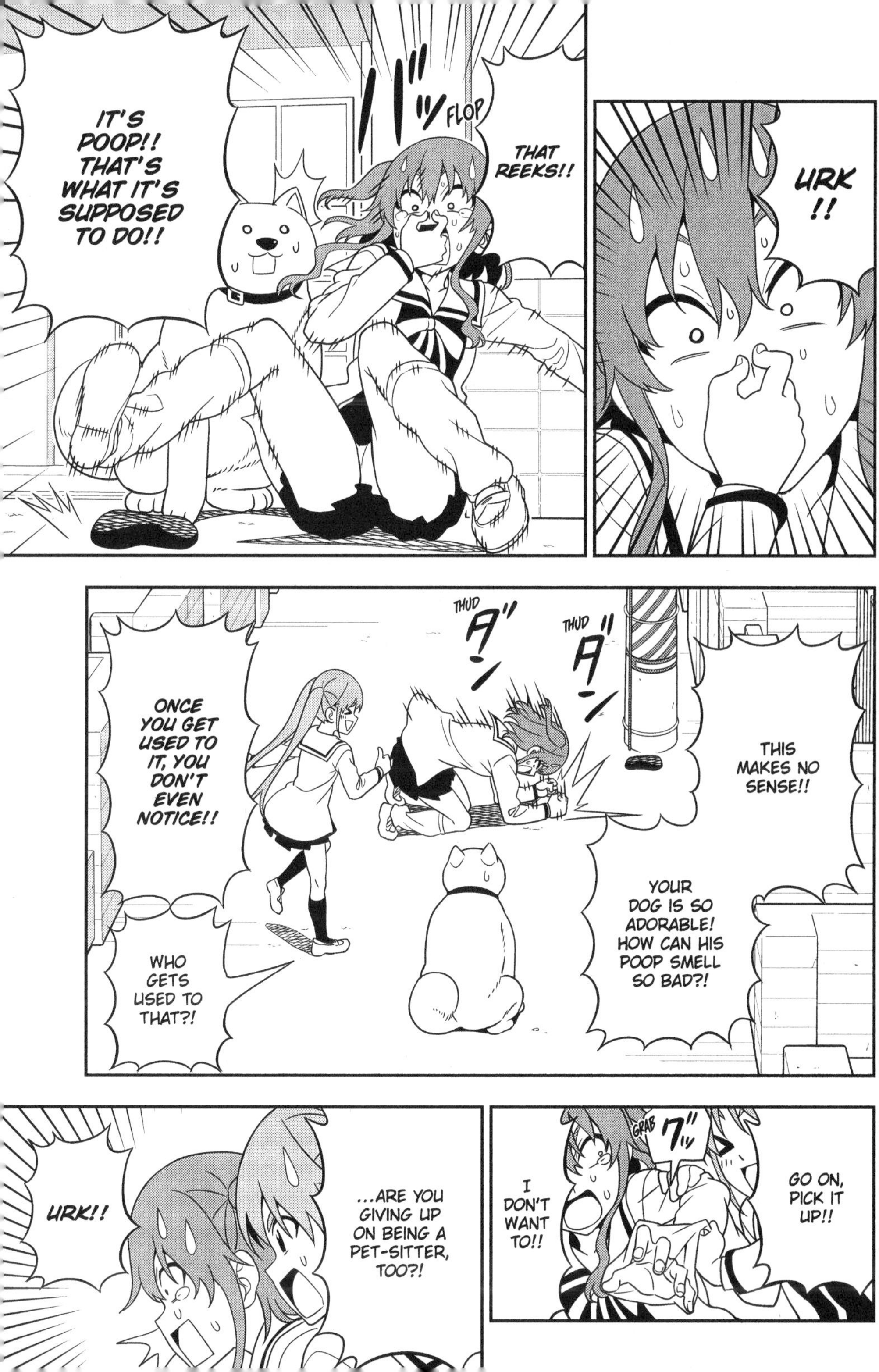
URK !!
FLOP
THAT REEKS!!
IT'S POOP!! THAT'S WHAT IT'S SUPPOSED TO DO!!
THUD
THUD
THIS MAKES NO SENSE!!
ONCE YOU GET USED TO IT, YOU DON'T EVEN NOTICE!!
YOUR DOG IS SO ADORABLE! HOW CAN HIS POOP SMELL SO BAD?!
WHO GETS USED TO THAT?!
GRAB
GO ON, PICK IT UP!!
I DON'T WANT TO!!
...ARE YOU GIVING UP ON BEING A PET-SITTER, TOO?!
URK!!

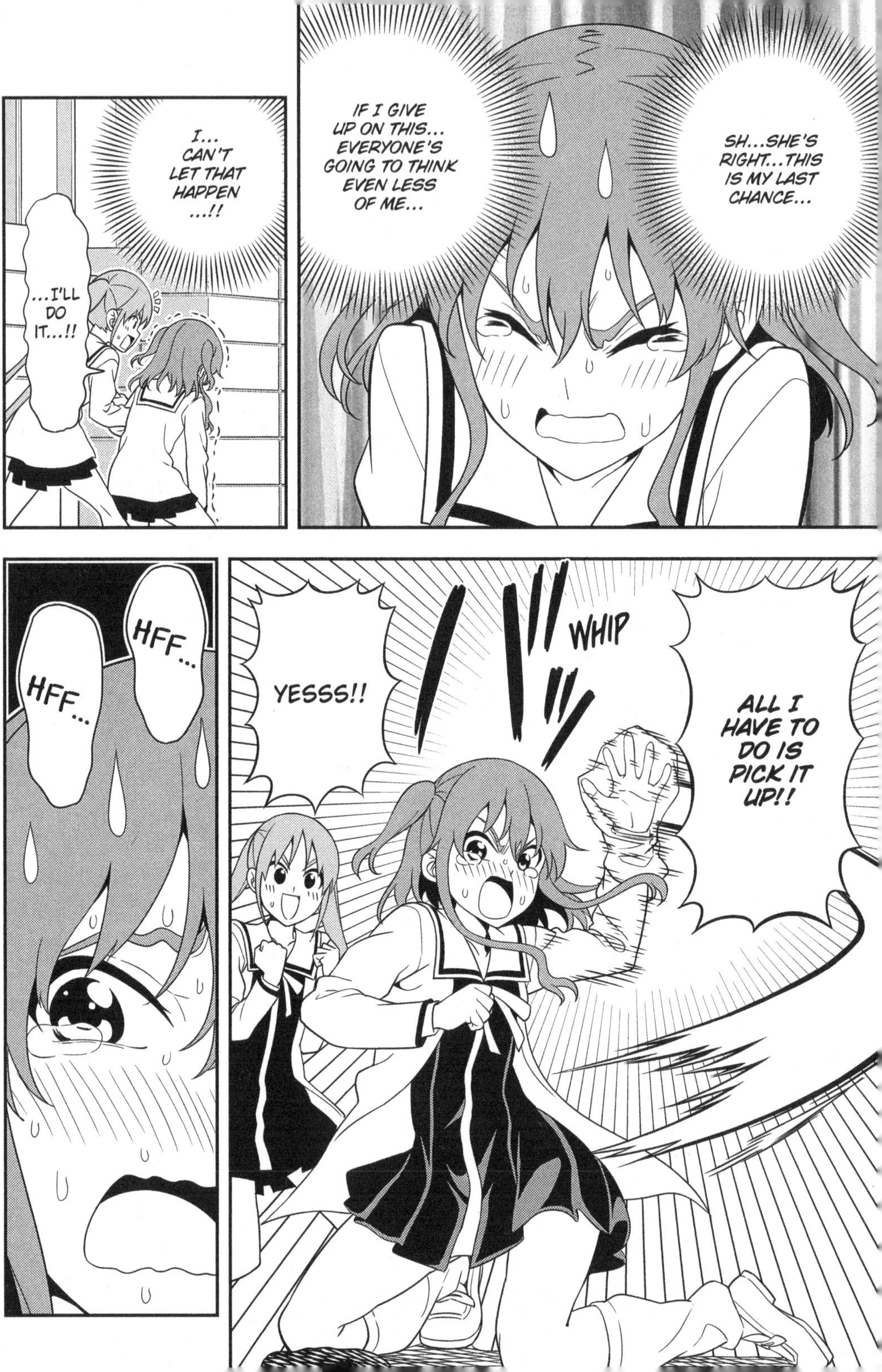
SH...SHE'S RIGHT...THIS IS MY LAST CHANCE...
IF I GIVE UP ON THIS... EVERYONE'S GOING TO THINK EVEN LESS OF ME...
I... CAN'T LET THAT HAPPEN ...!!
...I'LL DO IT...!!
ALL I HAVE TO DO IS PICK IT UP!!
WHIP
YESSS!!
HFF...
HFF...

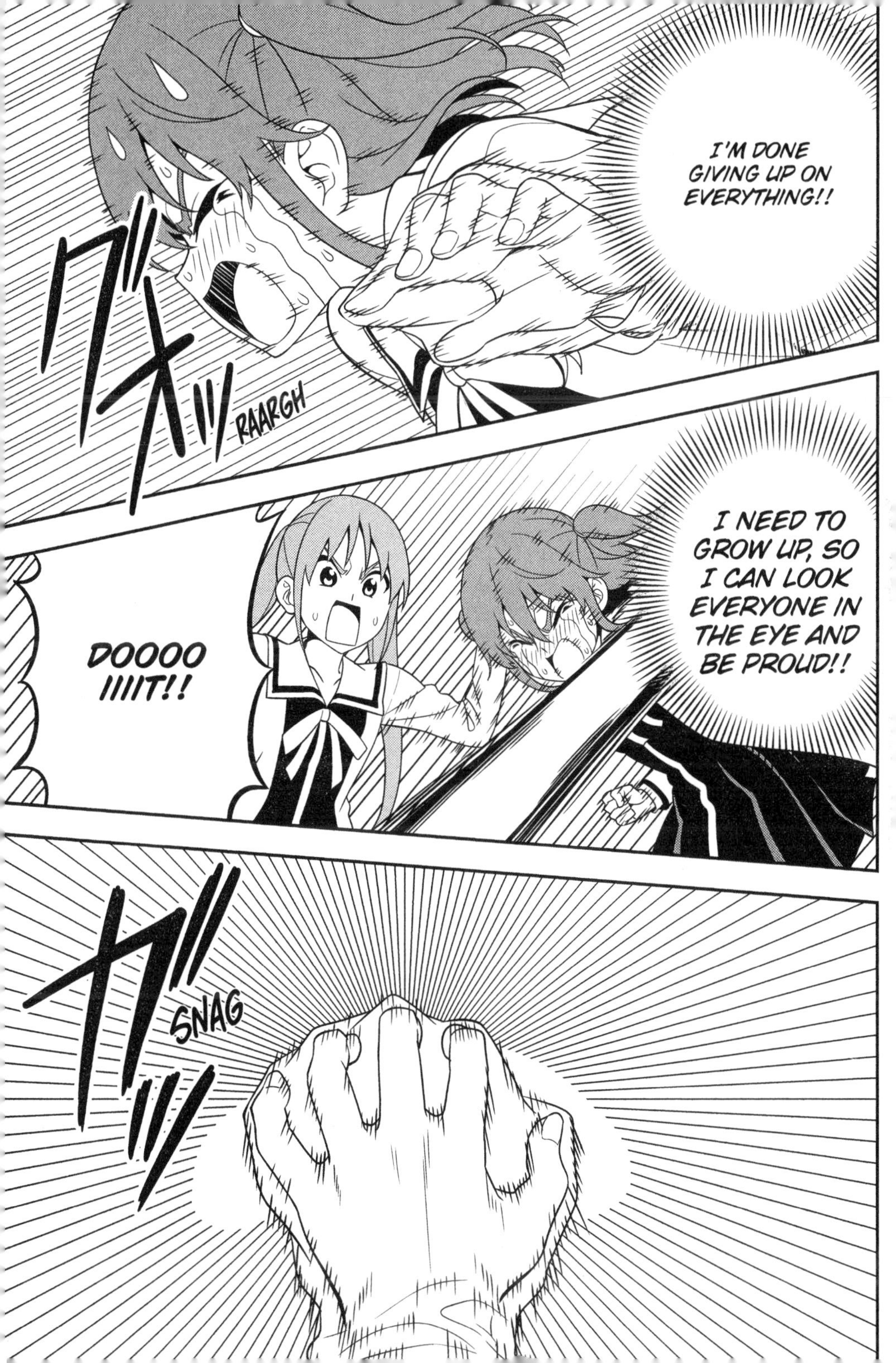
I'M DONE GIVING UP ON EVERYTHING!!
RAARGH
I NEED TO GROW UP, SO I CAN LOOK EVERYONE IN THE EYE AND BE PROUD!!
DOOOO IIIIT!!
SNAG

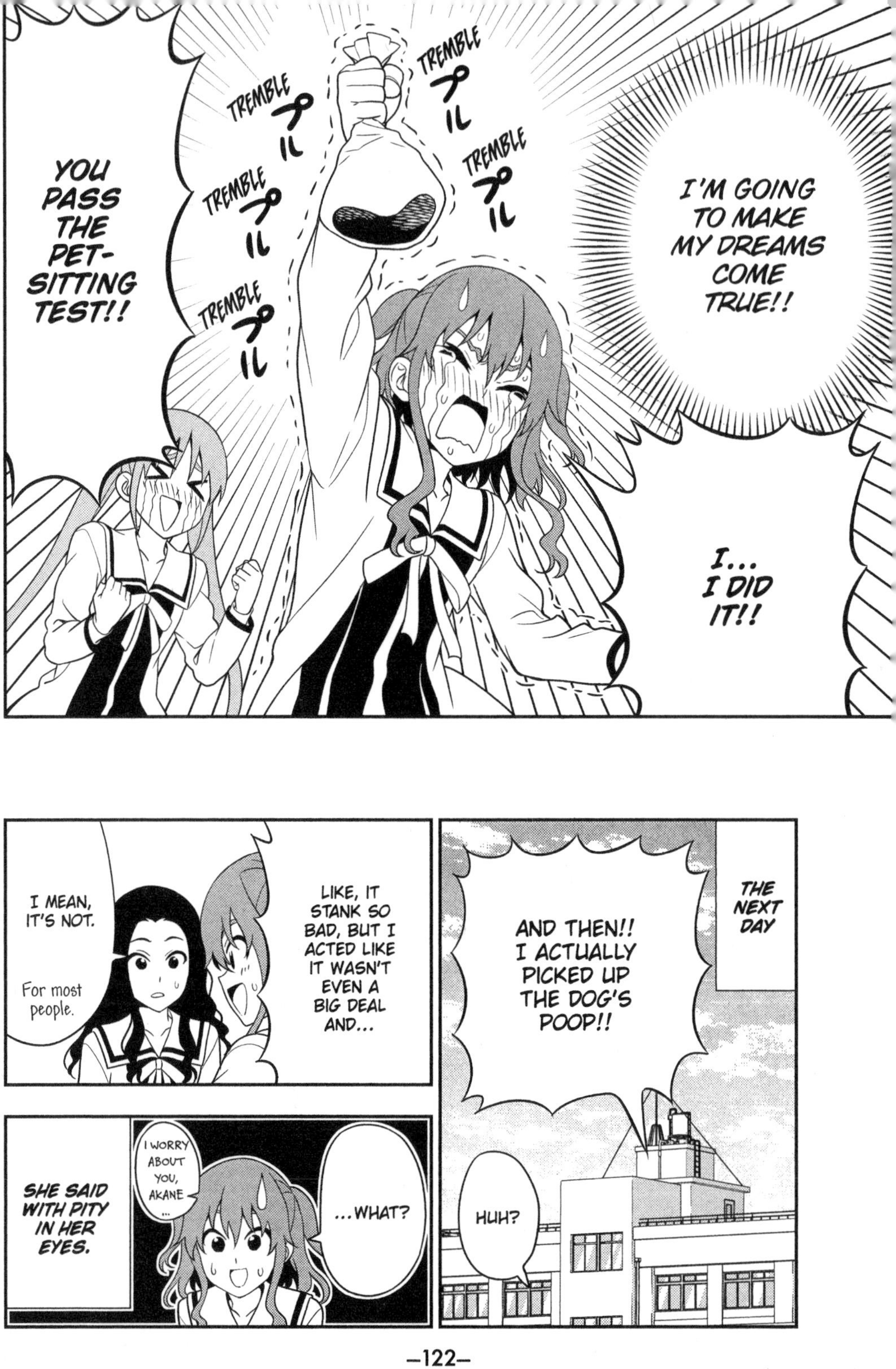
I'M GOING TO MAKE MY DREAMS COME TRUE!!
TREMBLE プル
TREMBLE プル
TREMBLE プル
TREMBLE プル
TREMBLE プル
YOU PASS THE PET-SITTING TEST!!
I... I DID IT!!
THE NEXT DAY
AND THEN!! I ACTUALLY PICKED UP THE DOG'S POOP!!
HUH?
LIKE, IT STANK SO BAD, BUT I ACTED LIKE IT WASN'T EVEN A BIG DEAL AND...
I MEAN, IT'S NOT.
For most people.
...WHAT?
I WORRY ABOUT YOU, AKANE...
SHE SAID WITH PITY IN HER EYES.

Dog Has Feelings, Too

SHE JUST WENT ON AND ON ABOUT HOW MUCH HE STANK...
HOP
ヒョコ
DOGGY! YOU WANT TO PLAY?
!
DUCK
プイッ
WHA?!
...SO THE DOG WAS MORTI-FIED.

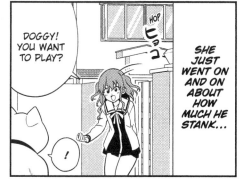

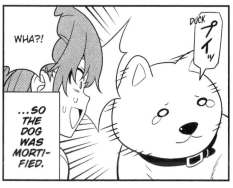

(wat does that even meen? srsly, i just)

Aho-Girl

\ˈahôˌgərl\ *Japanese, noun*.
A clueless girl.

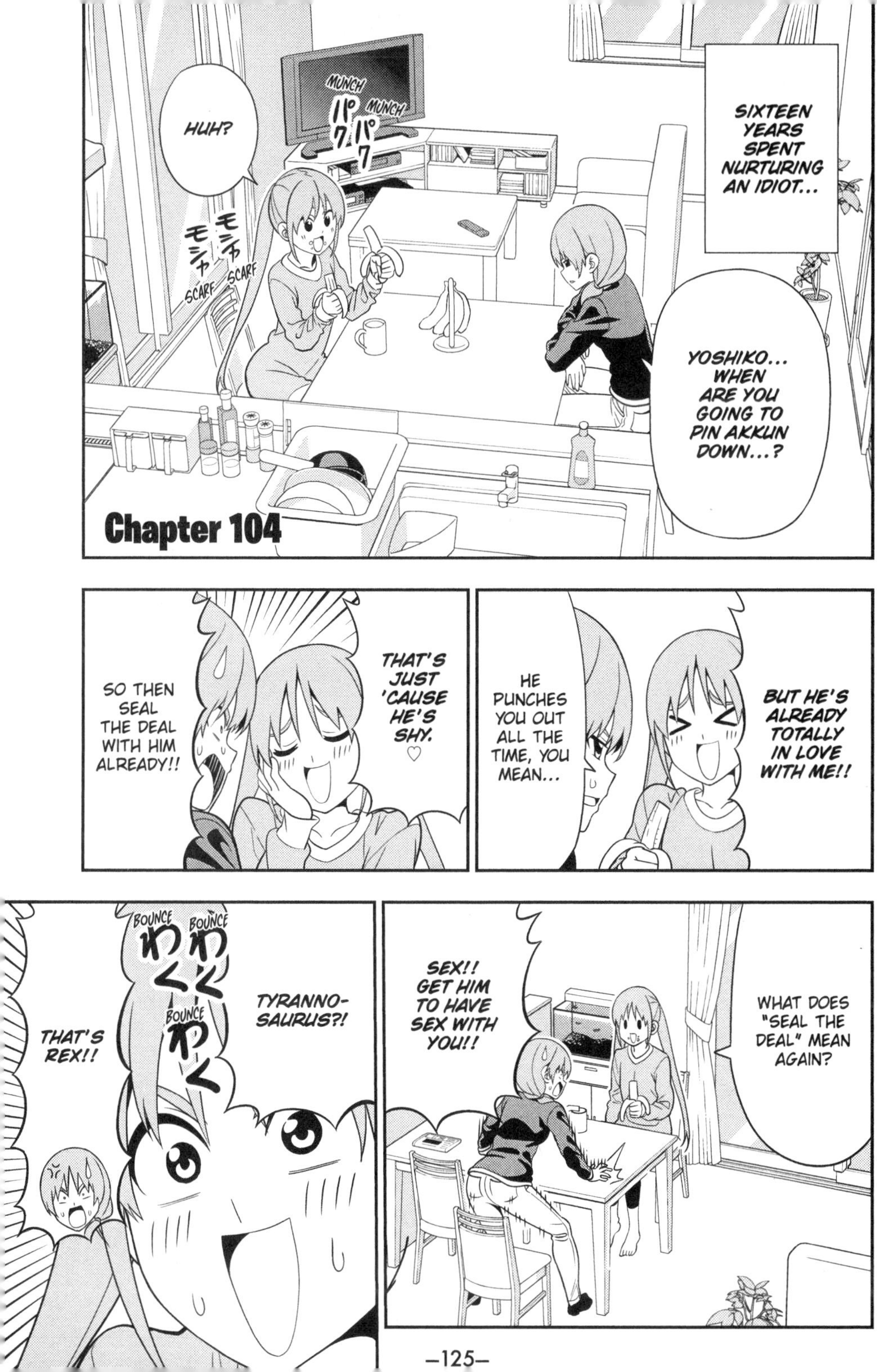
SIXTEEN YEARS SPENT NURTURING AN IDIOT...
YOSHIKO... WHEN ARE YOU GOING TO PIN AKKUN DOWN...?
MUNCH MUNCH
パクパク
HUH?
モシャモシャ
SCARF SCARF
Chapter 104
BUT HE'S ALREADY TOTALLY IN LOVE WITH ME!!
HE PUNCHES YOU OUT ALL THE TIME, YOU MEAN...
THAT'S JUST 'CAUSE HE'S SHY. ♡
SO THEN SEAL THE DEAL WITH HIM ALREADY!!
WHAT DOES "SEAL THE DEAL" MEAN AGAIN?
SEX!! GET HIM TO HAVE SEX WITH YOU!!
TYRANNO-SAURUS?!
BOUNCE BOUNCE BOUNCE
わくわくわく
THAT'S REX!!

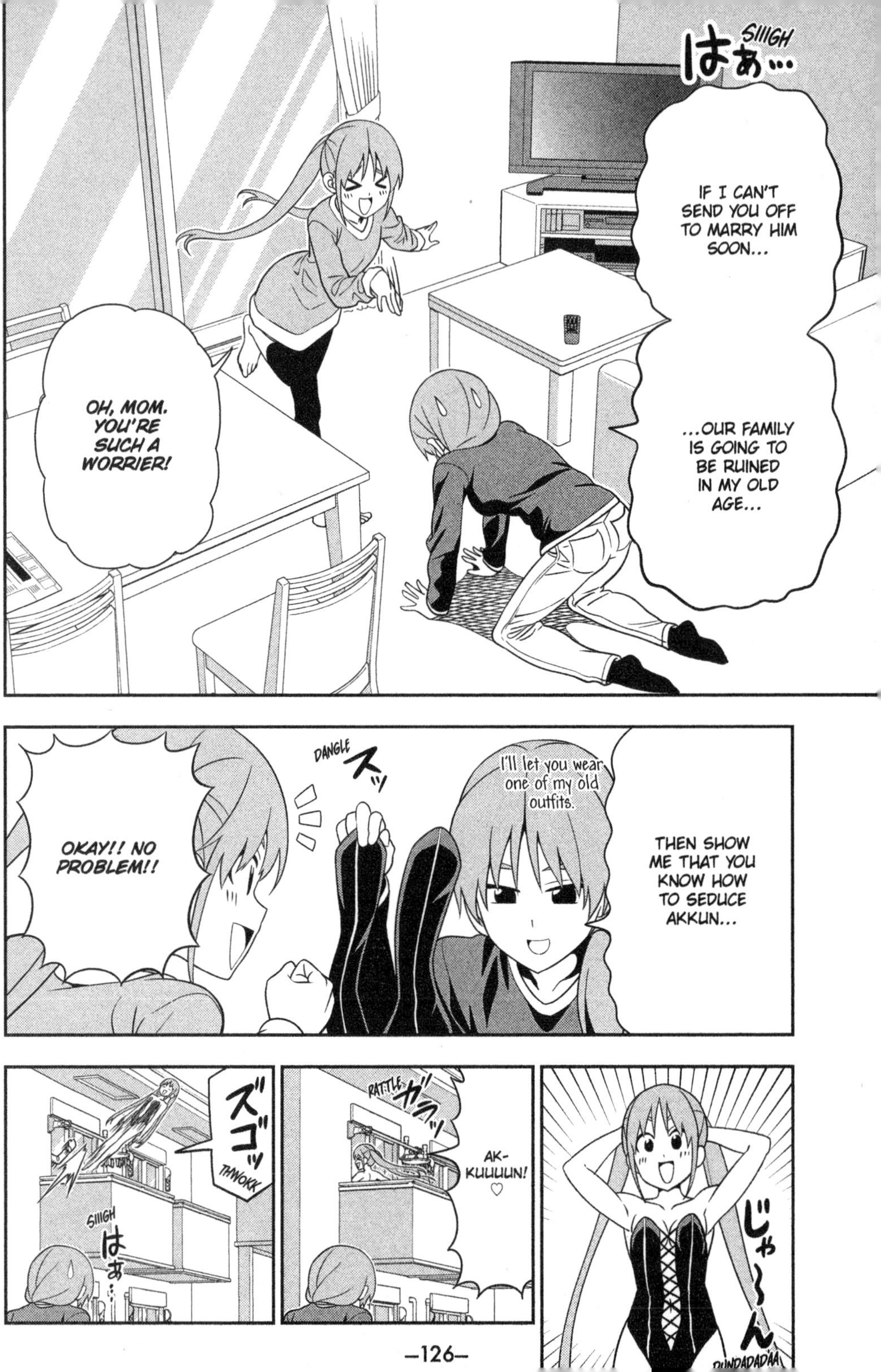
SIIIGH
はぁ…
IF I CAN'T SEND YOU OFF TO MARRY HIM SOON…
…OUR FAMILY IS GOING TO BE RUINED IN MY OLD AGE…
OH, MOM. YOU'RE SUCH A WORRIER!
THEN SHOW ME THAT YOU KNOW HOW TO SEDUCE AKKUN…
I'll let you wear one of my old outfits.
DANGLE
スッ
OKAY!! NO PROBLEM!!
じゃ～ん
DUNDADADAA
RATTLE
ガラッ
AK-KUUUUN! ♡
ズゴッ
THWOKK
SIIIGH
はぁ…

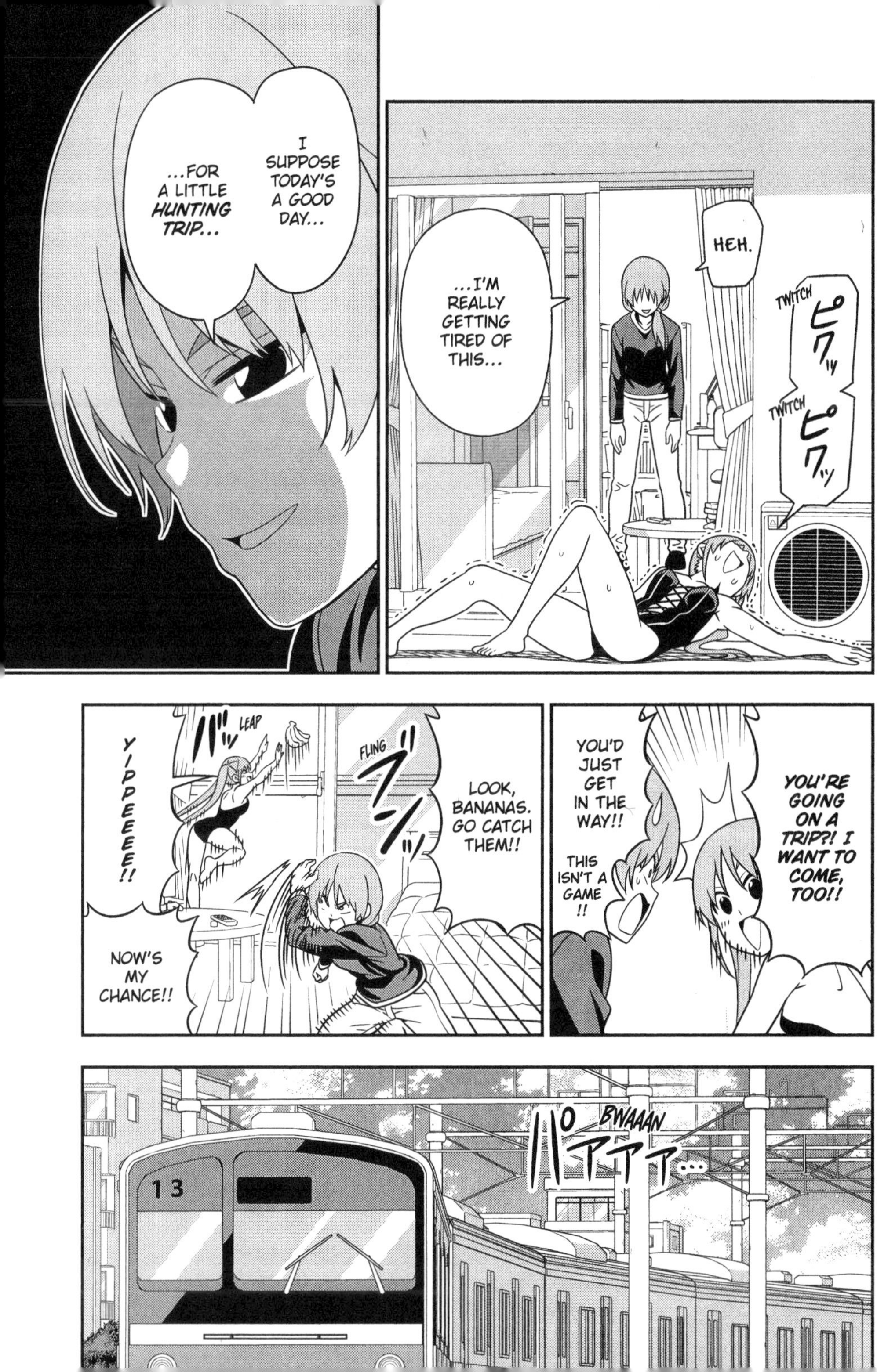
HEH.
TWITCH
ピクッ
TWITCH
ピクッ
...I'M REALLY GETTING TIRED OF THIS...
I SUPPOSE TODAY'S A GOOD DAY...
...FOR A LITTLE HUNTING TRIP...
YOU'RE GOING ON A TRIP?! I WANT TO COME, TOO!!
YOU'D JUST GET IN THE WAY!!
THIS ISN'T A GAME!!
LOOK, BANANAS. GO CATCH THEM!!
FLING
ブンッ
LEAP
バッ
YIPPEEEEE!!
NOW'S MY CHANCE!!
BWAAAN
パアァァ…
13

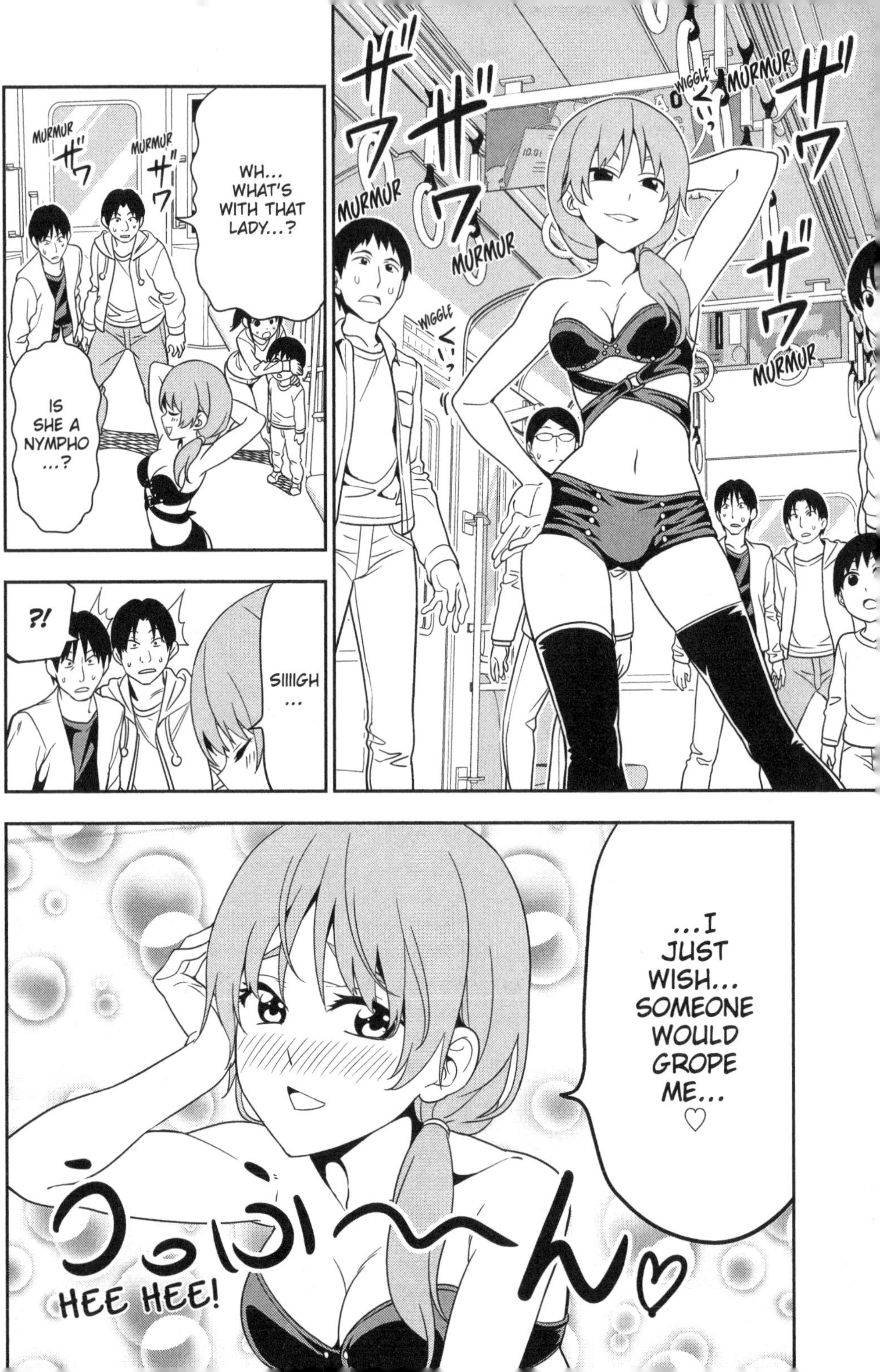
ザワ
MURMUR
WIGGLE
くいっ
ザワ
MURMUR
ザワ ザワ
MURMUR
ザワ
MURMUR
WIGGLE
くいっ
WH... WHAT'S WITH THAT LADY...?
MURMUR
ザワ
MURMUR
ザワ
IS SHE A NYMPHO...?
SIIIGH...
?!
...I JUST WISH... SOMEONE WOULD GROPE ME... ♡
うっふ〜ん♡
HEE HEE!

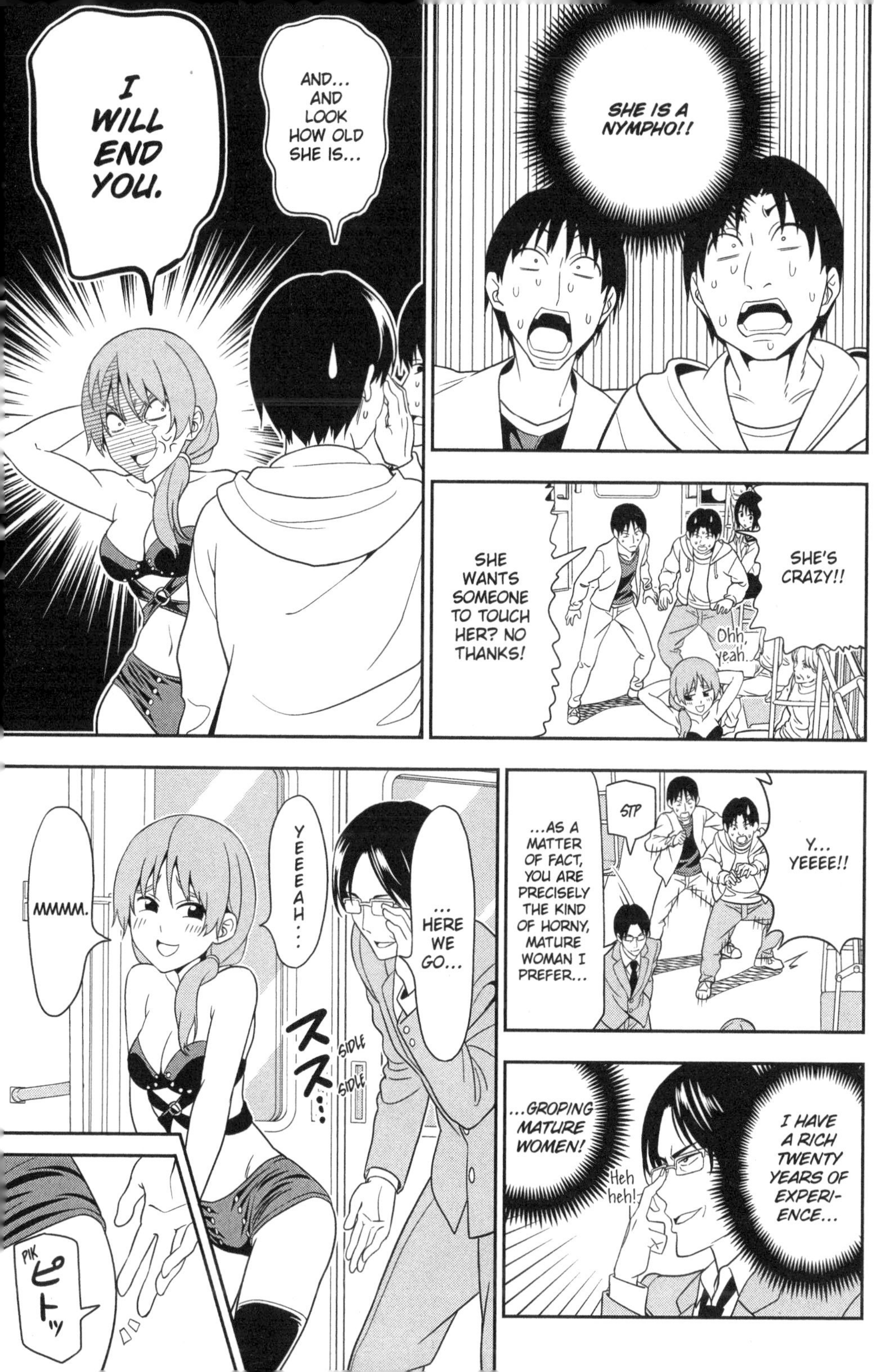
SHE IS A NYMPHO!!
SHE'S CRAZY!!
Ohh, yeah..
SHE WANTS SOMEONE TO TOUCH HER? NO THANKS!
AND... AND LOOK HOW OLD SHE IS...
I WILL END YOU.
Y... YEEEE!!
STP
...AS A MATTER OF FACT, YOU ARE PRECISELY THE KIND OF HORNY, MATURE WOMAN I PREFER...
I HAVE A RICH TWENTY YEARS OF EXPERI-ENCE...
Heh heh!
...GROPING MATURE WOMEN!
... HERE WE GO...
YEEEAH...
MMMM.
SIDLE SIDLE
PIK

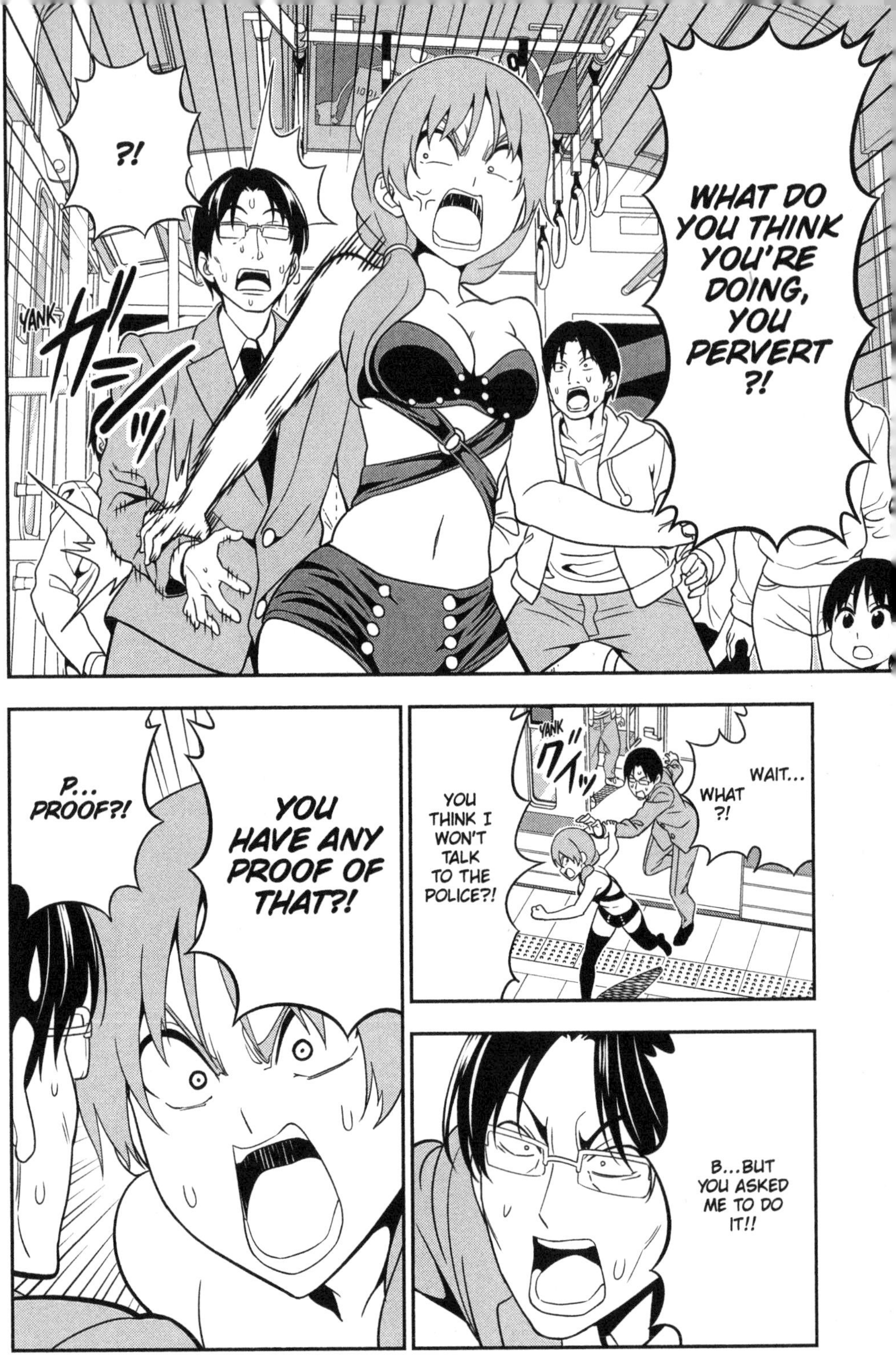
WHAT DO YOU THINK YOU'RE DOING, YOU PERVERT ?!
?!
YANK
WAIT... WHAT ?!
YANK
YOU THINK I WON'T TALK TO THE POLICE?!
B...BUT YOU ASKED ME TO DO IT!!
YOU HAVE ANY PROOF OF THAT?!
P... PROOF?!

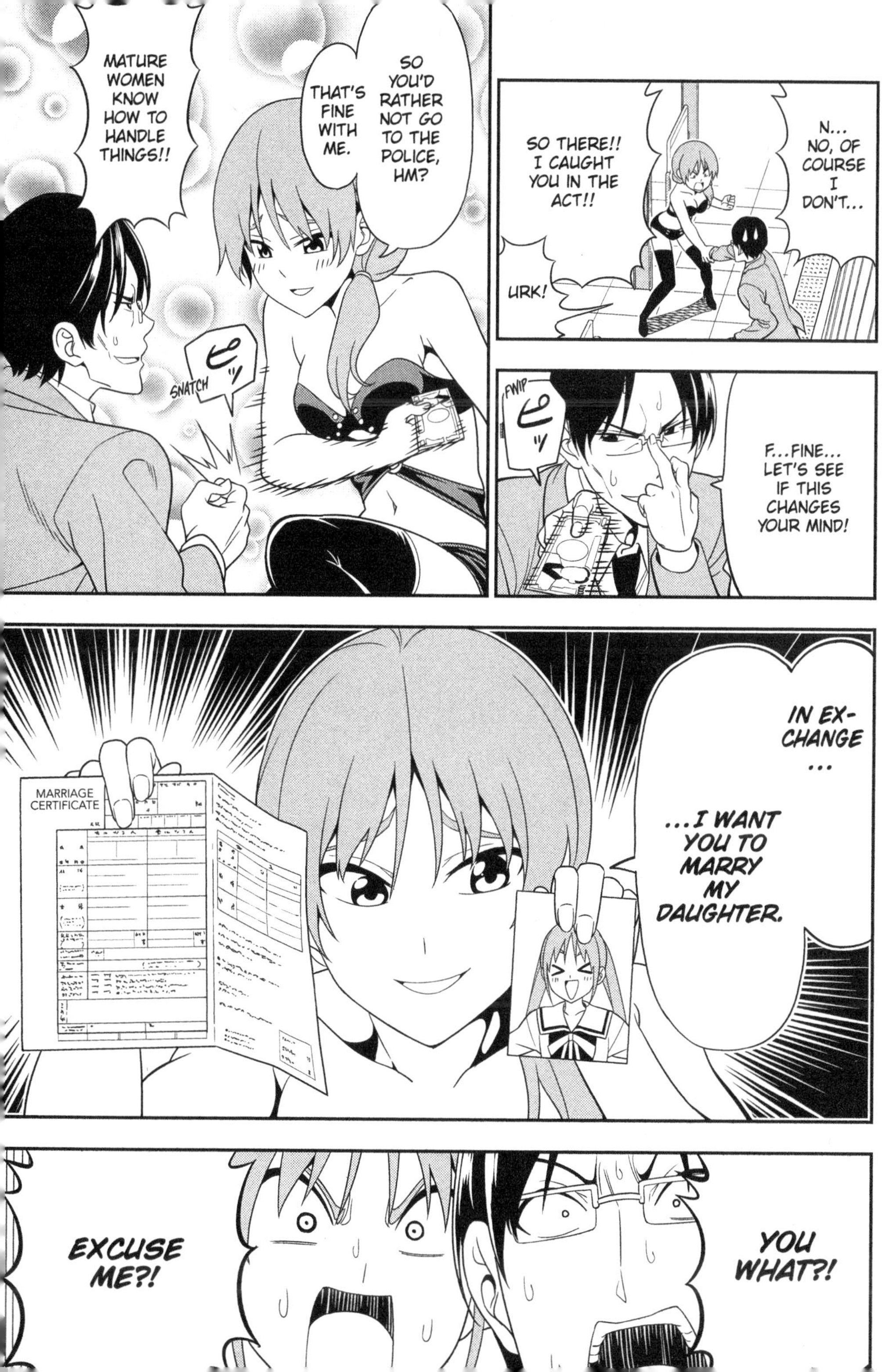
N... NO, OF COURSE I DON'T...
SO THERE!! I CAUGHT YOU IN THE ACT!!
URK!
FWIP ピッ
F...FINE... LET'S SEE IF THIS CHANGES YOUR MIND!
SO YOU'D RATHER NOT GO TO THE POLICE, HM?
THAT'S FINE WITH ME.
SNATCH ピッ
MATURE WOMEN KNOW HOW TO HANDLE THINGS!!
IN EX-CHANGE...
...I WANT YOU TO MARRY MY DAUGHTER.
MARRIAGE CERTIFICATE
YOU WHAT?!
EXCUSE ME?!

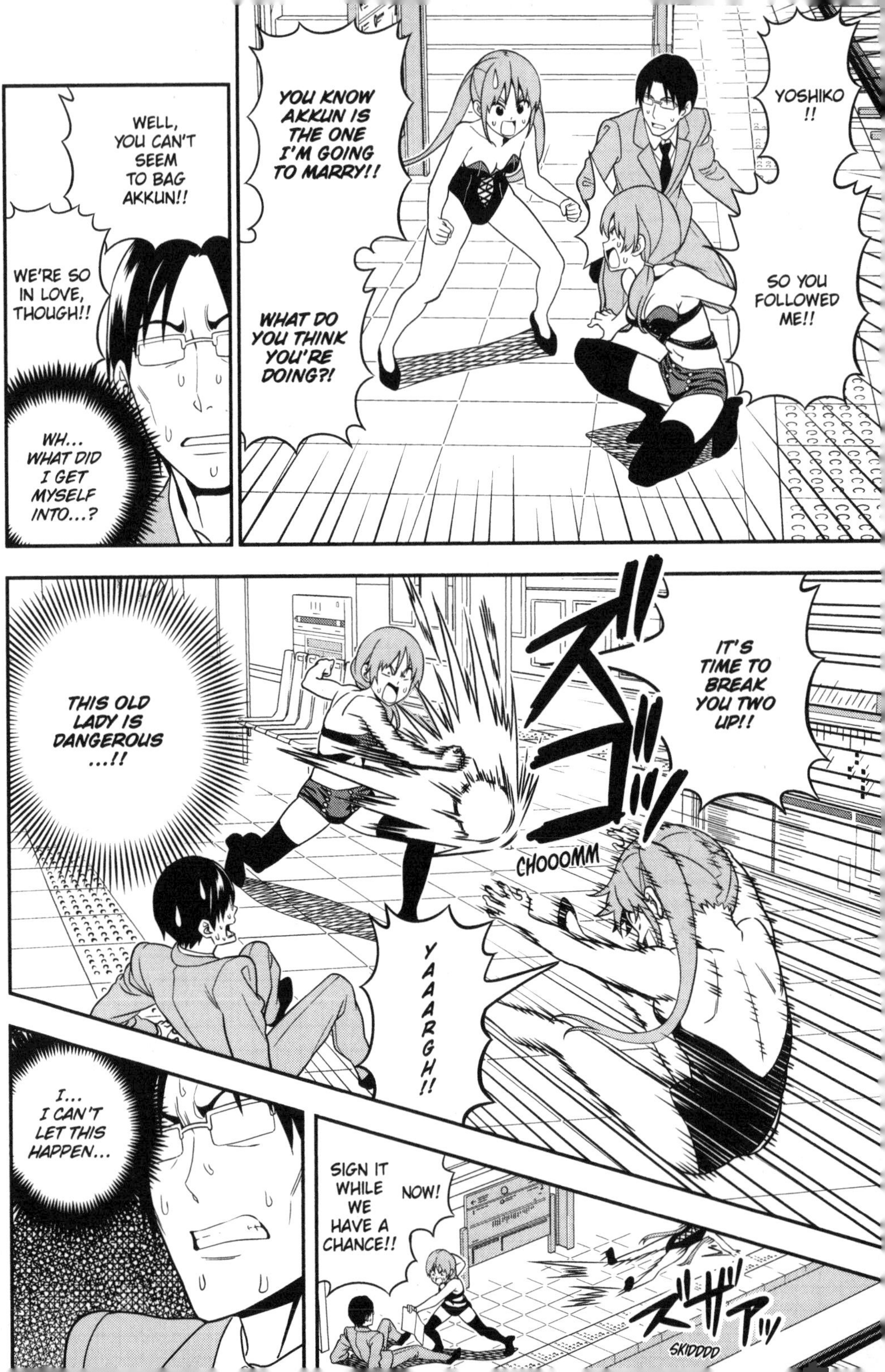
YOSHIKO!!
SO YOU FOLLOWED ME!!
YOU KNOW AKKUN IS THE ONE I'M GOING TO MARRY!!
WHAT DO YOU THINK YOU'RE DOING?!
WELL, YOU CAN'T SEEM TO BAG AKKUN!!
WE'RE SO IN LOVE, THOUGH!!
WH... WHAT DID I GET MYSELF INTO...?
IT'S TIME TO BREAK YOU TWO UP!!
ズゴッ
CHOOOMM
YAAAARGH!!
THIS OLD LADY IS DANGEROUS...!!
NOW!
SIGN IT WHILE WE HAVE A CHANCE!!
ズザアッ
SKIDDDD
I... I CAN'T LET THIS HAPPEN...

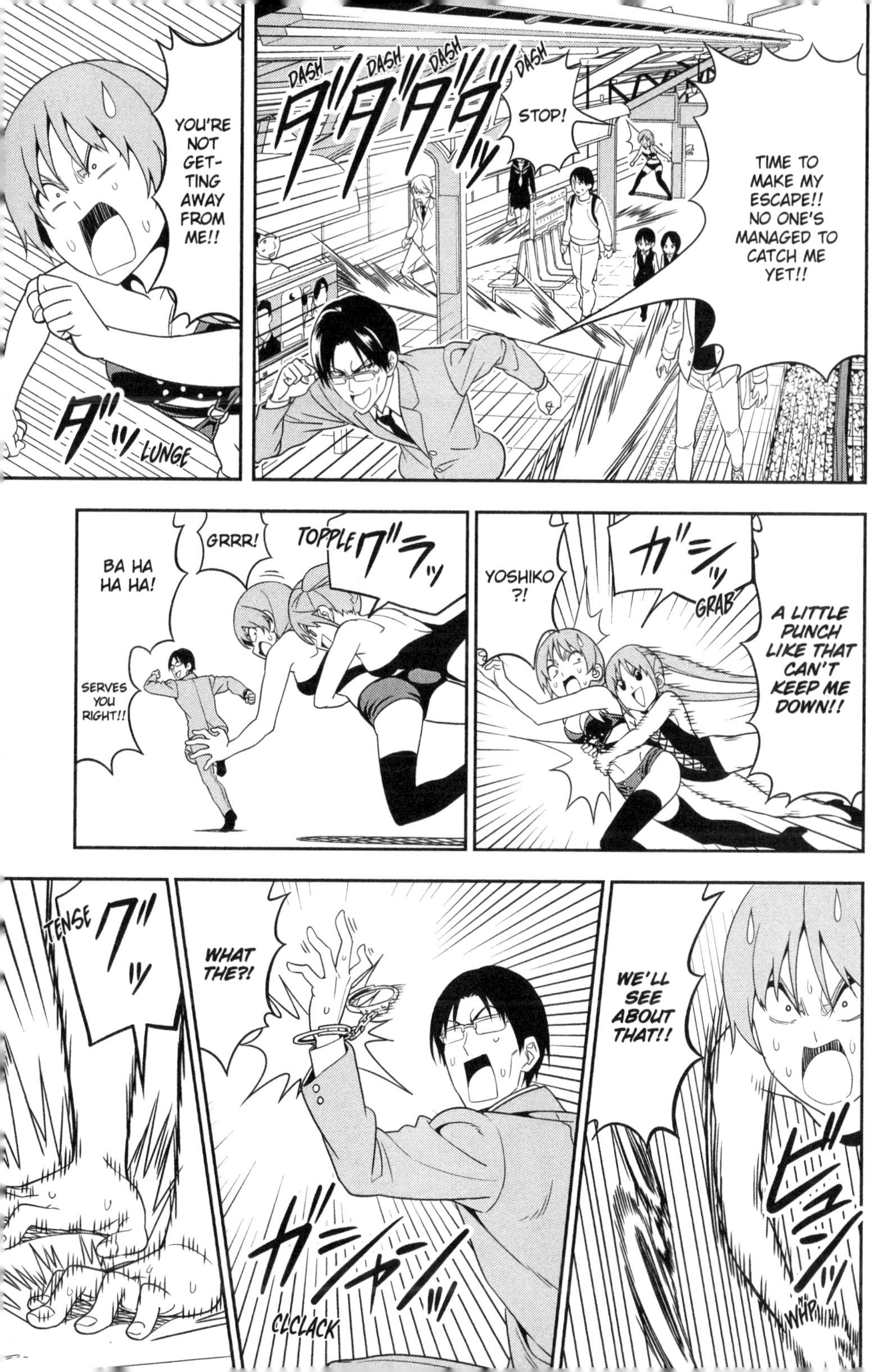
TIME TO MAKE MY ESCAPE!! NO ONE'S MANAGED TO CATCH ME YET!!
DASH DASH DASH DASH
STOP!
YOU'RE NOT GET-TING AWAY FROM ME!!
LUNGE
A LITTLE PUNCH LIKE THAT CAN'T KEEP ME DOWN!!
GRAB
YOSHIKO ?!
TOPPLE
GRRR!
BA HA HA HA!
SERVES YOU RIGHT!!
WE'LL SEE ABOUT THAT!!
WHIP
WHAT THE?!
CLCLACK
TENSE

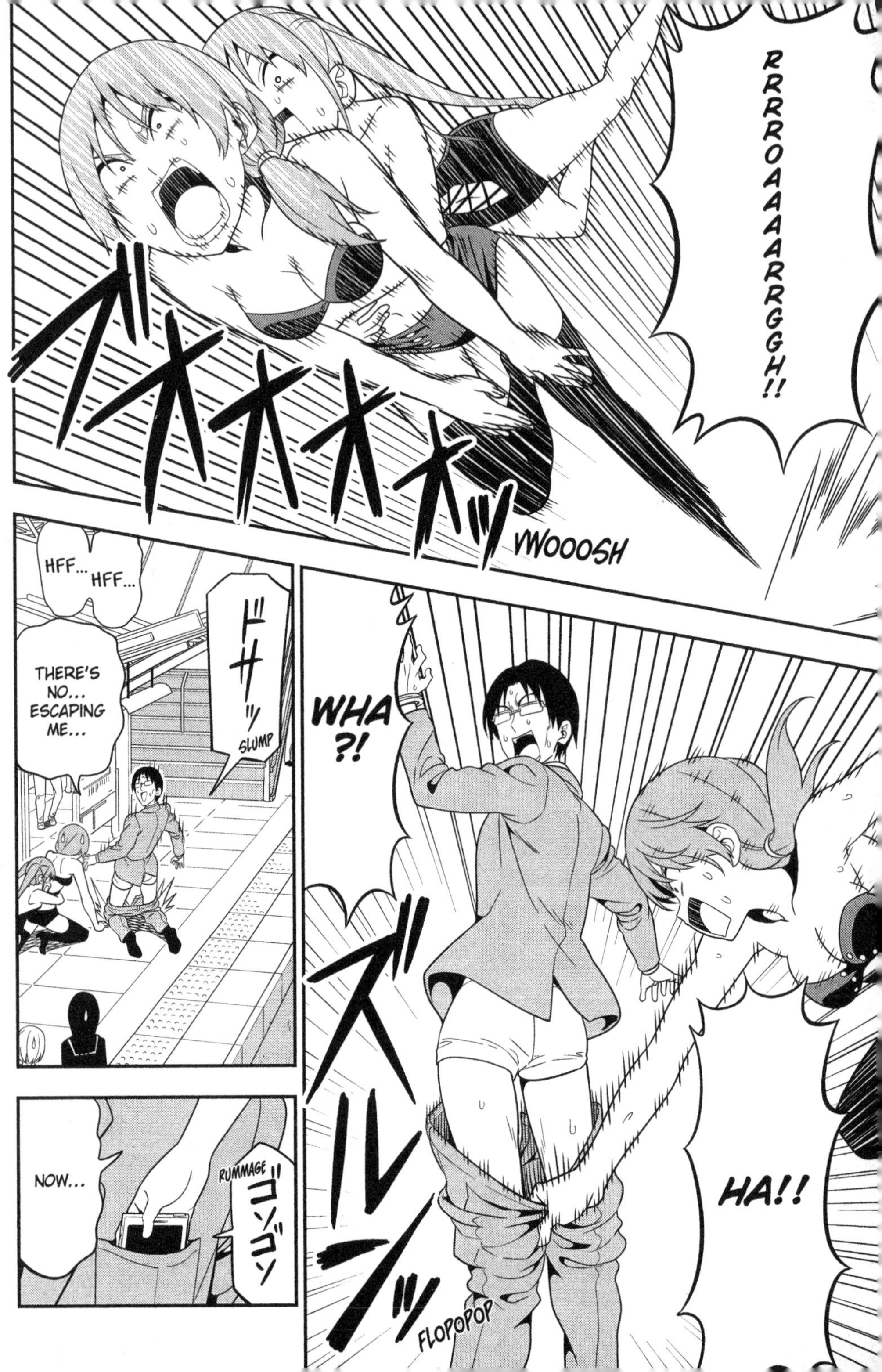
RRRROAAAARRGGH!!
ズオオオオッ
VWOOOSH
WHA?!
HA!!
ズルッ
FLOPOPOP
HFF... HFF...
THERE'S NO... ESCAPING ME...
ドサッ
SLUMP
NOW...
ゴソゴソ
RUMMAGE

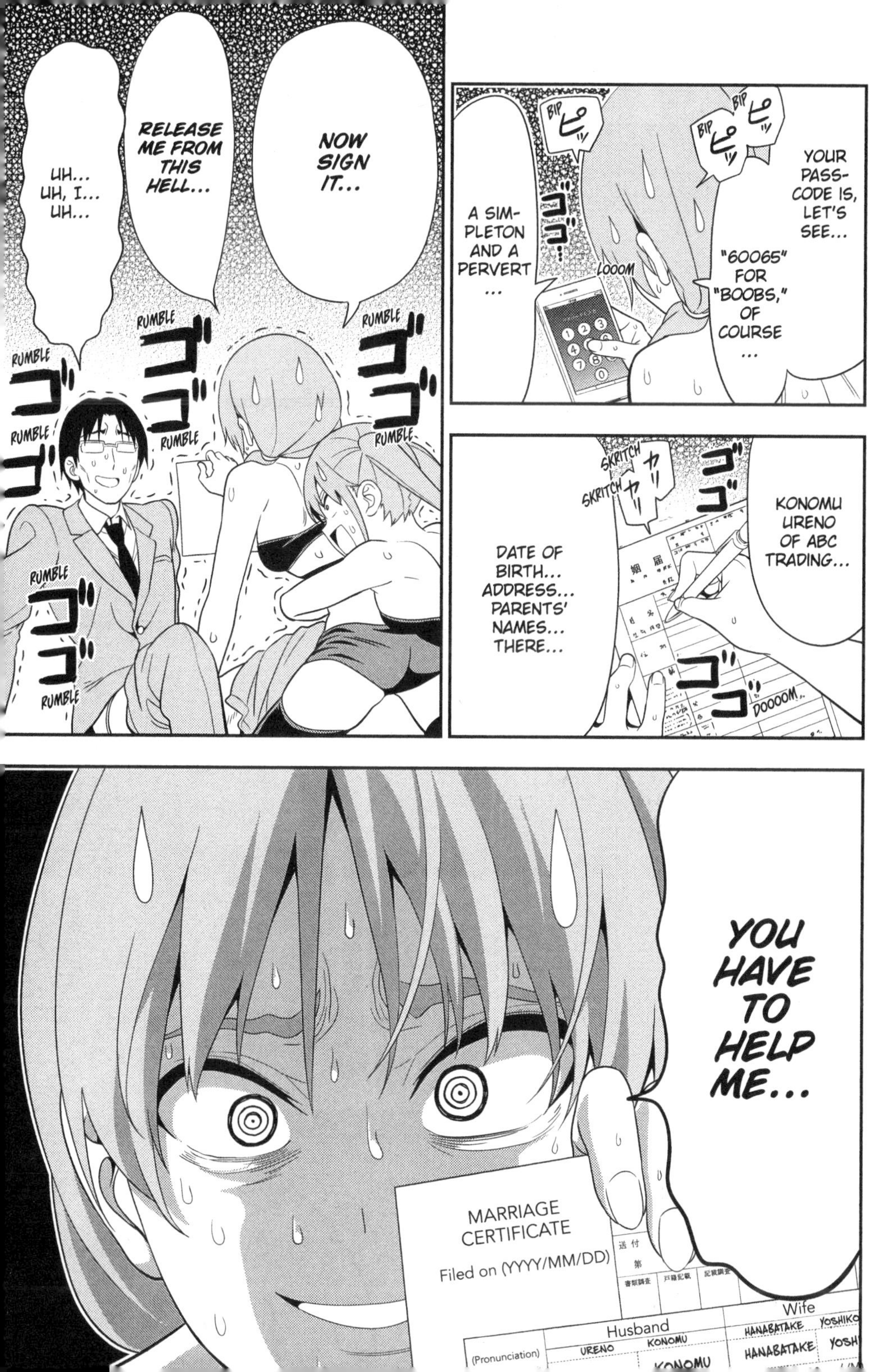
BIP
BIP
BIP
YOUR PASS-CODE IS, LET'S SEE...
"60065" FOR "BOOBS," OF COURSE...
A SIM-PLETON AND A PERVERT...
LOOOM
SKRITCH
SKRITCH
KONOMU URENO OF ABC TRADING...
DATE OF BIRTH... ADDRESS... PARENTS' NAMES... THERE...
DOOOOM
NOW SIGN IT...
RELEASE ME FROM THIS HELL...
UH... UH, I... UH...
RUMBLE
RUMBLE
RUMBLE
RUMBLE
RUMBLE
RUMBLE
RUMBLE
YOU HAVE TO HELP ME...
MARRIAGE CERTIFICATE
Filed on (YYYY/MM/DD)
Husband
Wife
(Pronunciation)
URENO
KONOMU
HANABATAKE
YOSHIKO
HANABATAKE
KONOMU

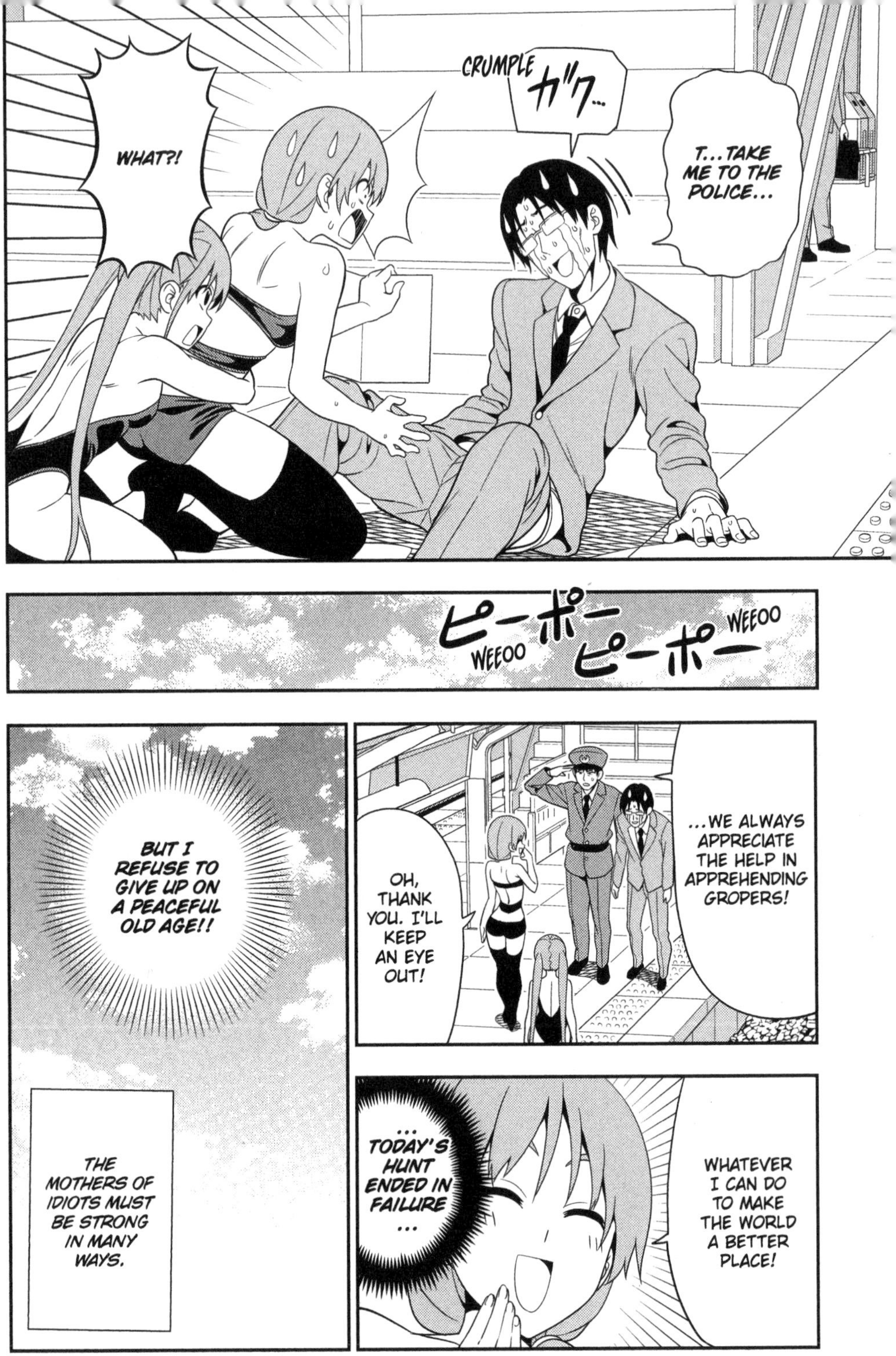
T...TAKE ME TO THE POLICE...
CRUMPLE
ガク...
WHAT?!
ピーポー
WEEOO
ピーポー
WEEOO
...WE ALWAYS APPRECIATE THE HELP IN APPREHENDING GROPERS!
OH, THANK YOU. I'LL KEEP AN EYE OUT!
WHATEVER I CAN DO TO MAKE THE WORLD A BETTER PLACE!
...TODAY'S HUNT ENDED IN FAILURE...
BUT I REFUSE TO GIVE UP ON A PEACEFUL OLD AGE!!
THE MOTHERS OF IDIOTS MUST BE STRONG IN MANY WAYS.

This Is How It Always Goes

NOW LET'S USE THIS MONEY HE GAVE ME AND GET SOME YAKINIKU!!

REALLY?! HURRAAY !!

Aho-Girl

\ˈahôˌgərl\ *Japanese, noun.*
A clueless girl.

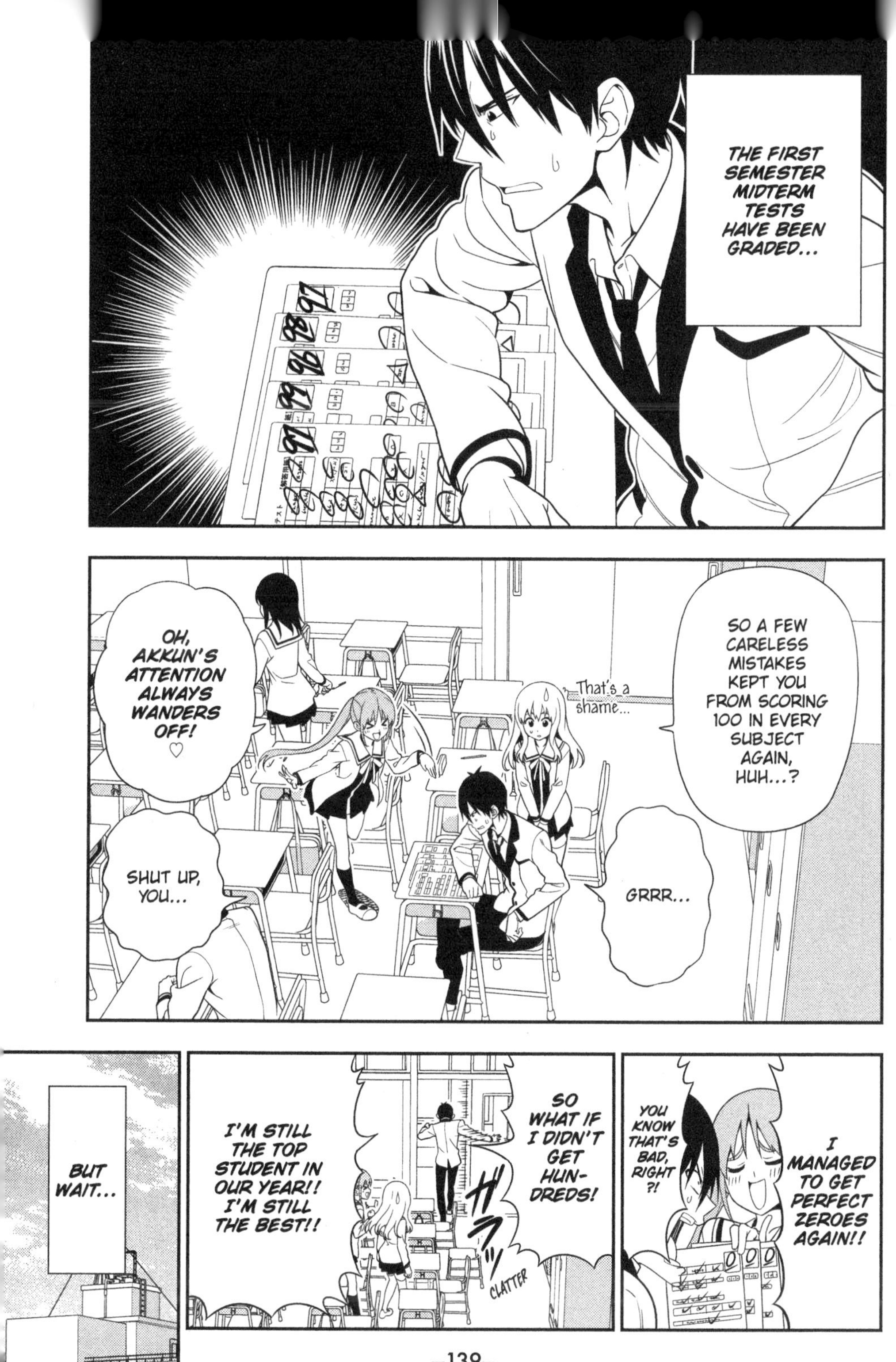
THE FIRST SEMESTER MIDTERM TESTS HAVE BEEN GRADED...
SO A FEW CARELESS MISTAKES KEPT YOU FROM SCORING 100 IN EVERY SUBJECT AGAIN, HUH...?
That's a shame...
OH, AKKUN'S ATTENTION ALWAYS WANDERS OFF! ♡
GRRR...
SHUT UP, YOU...
I MANAGED TO GET PERFECT ZEROES AGAIN!!
YOU KNOW THAT'S BAD, RIGHT?!
SO WHAT IF I DIDN'T GET HUN-DREDS!
I'M STILL THE TOP STUDENT IN OUR YEAR!! I'M STILL THE BEST!!
CLATTER
BUT WAIT...

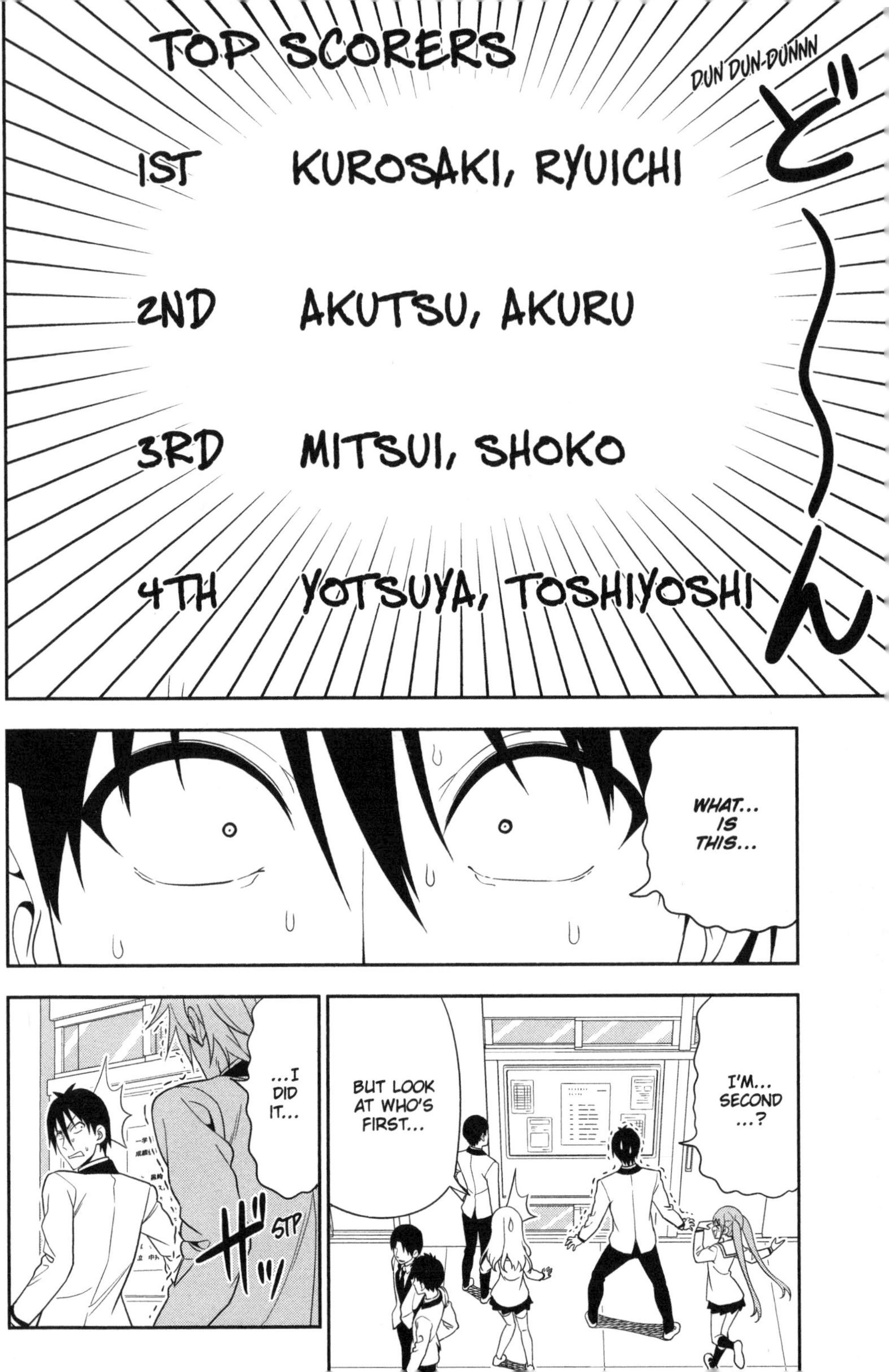
TOP SCORERS
DUN DUN-DUNNN
1ST KUROSAKI, RYUICHI
2ND AKUTSU, AKURU
3RD MITSUI, SHOKO
4TH YOTSUYA, TOSHIYOSHI
WHAT... IS THIS...
I'M... SECOND ...?
BUT LOOK AT WHO'S FIRST...
...I DID IT...
STP

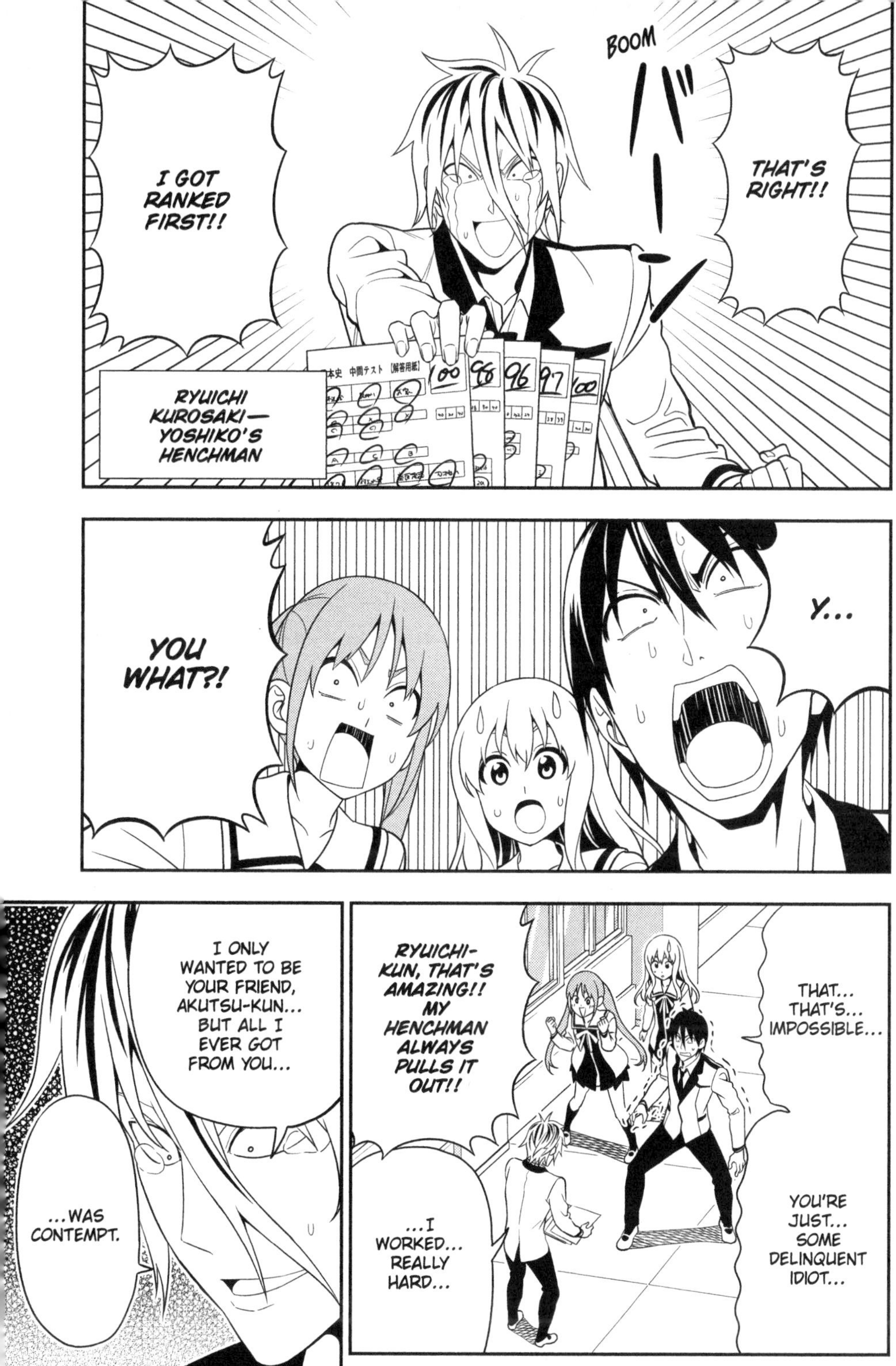
BOOM
THAT'S RIGHT!!
I GOT RANKED FIRST!!
RYUICHI KUROSAKI—YOSHIKO'S HENCHMAN
Y...
YOU WHAT?!
THAT... THAT'S... IMPOSSIBLE...
RYUICHI-KUN, THAT'S AMAZING!! MY HENCHMAN ALWAYS PULLS IT OUT!!
YOU'RE JUST... SOME DELINQUENT IDIOT...
...I WORKED... REALLY HARD...
I ONLY WANTED TO BE YOUR FRIEND, AKUTSU-KUN... BUT ALL I EVER GOT FROM YOU...
...WAS CONTEMPT.

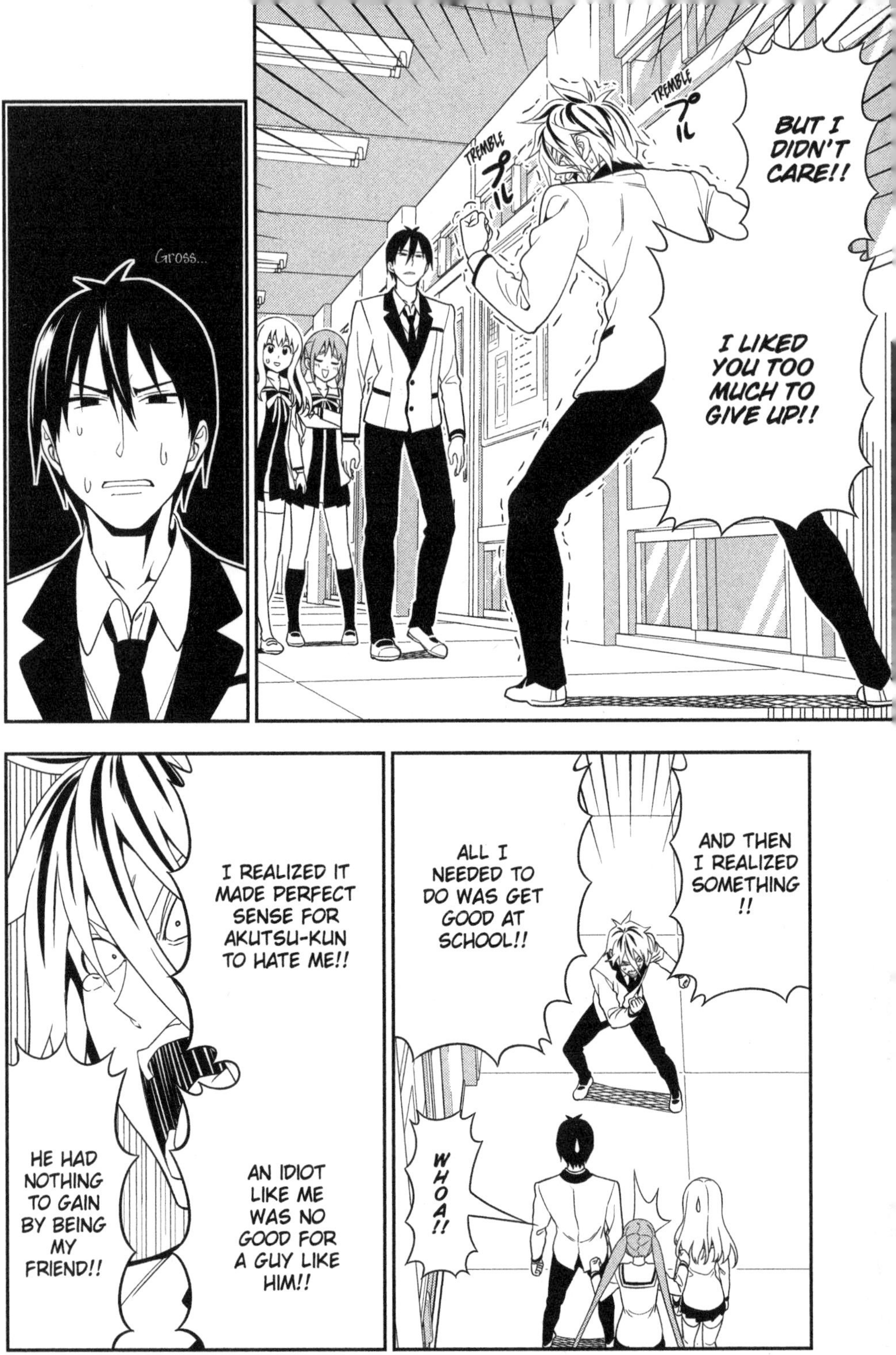
TREMBLE
プル
BUT I DIDN'T CARE!!
TREMBLE
プル
I LIKED YOU TOO MUCH TO GIVE UP!!
Gross...
AND THEN I REALIZED SOMETHING!!
ALL I NEEDED TO DO WAS GET GOOD AT SCHOOL!!
WHOA!!
I REALIZED IT MADE PERFECT SENSE FOR AKUTSU-KUN TO HATE ME!!
AN IDIOT LIKE ME WAS NO GOOD FOR A GUY LIKE HIM!!
HE HAD NOTHING TO GAIN BY BEING MY FRIEND!!

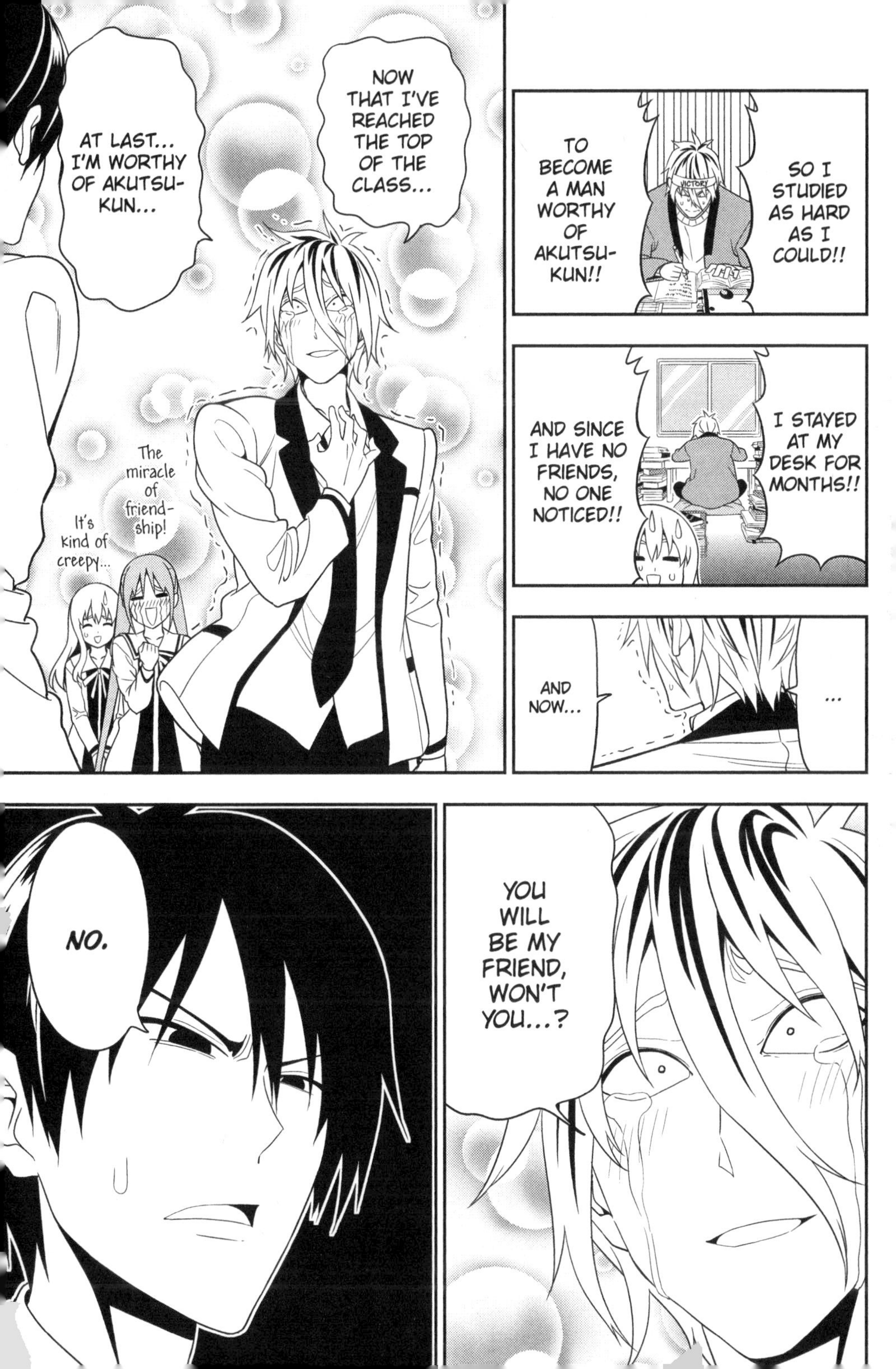
SO I STUDIED AS HARD AS I COULD!!
TO BECOME A MAN WORTHY OF AKUTSU-KUN!!
VICTORY
I STAYED AT MY DESK FOR MONTHS!!
AND SINCE I HAVE NO FRIENDS, NO ONE NOTICED!!
...
AND NOW...
NOW THAT I'VE REACHED THE TOP OF THE CLASS...
AT LAST... I'M WORTHY OF AKUTSU-KUN...
The miracle of friend-ship!
It's kind of creepy...
YOU WILL BE MY FRIEND, WON'T YOU...?
NO.

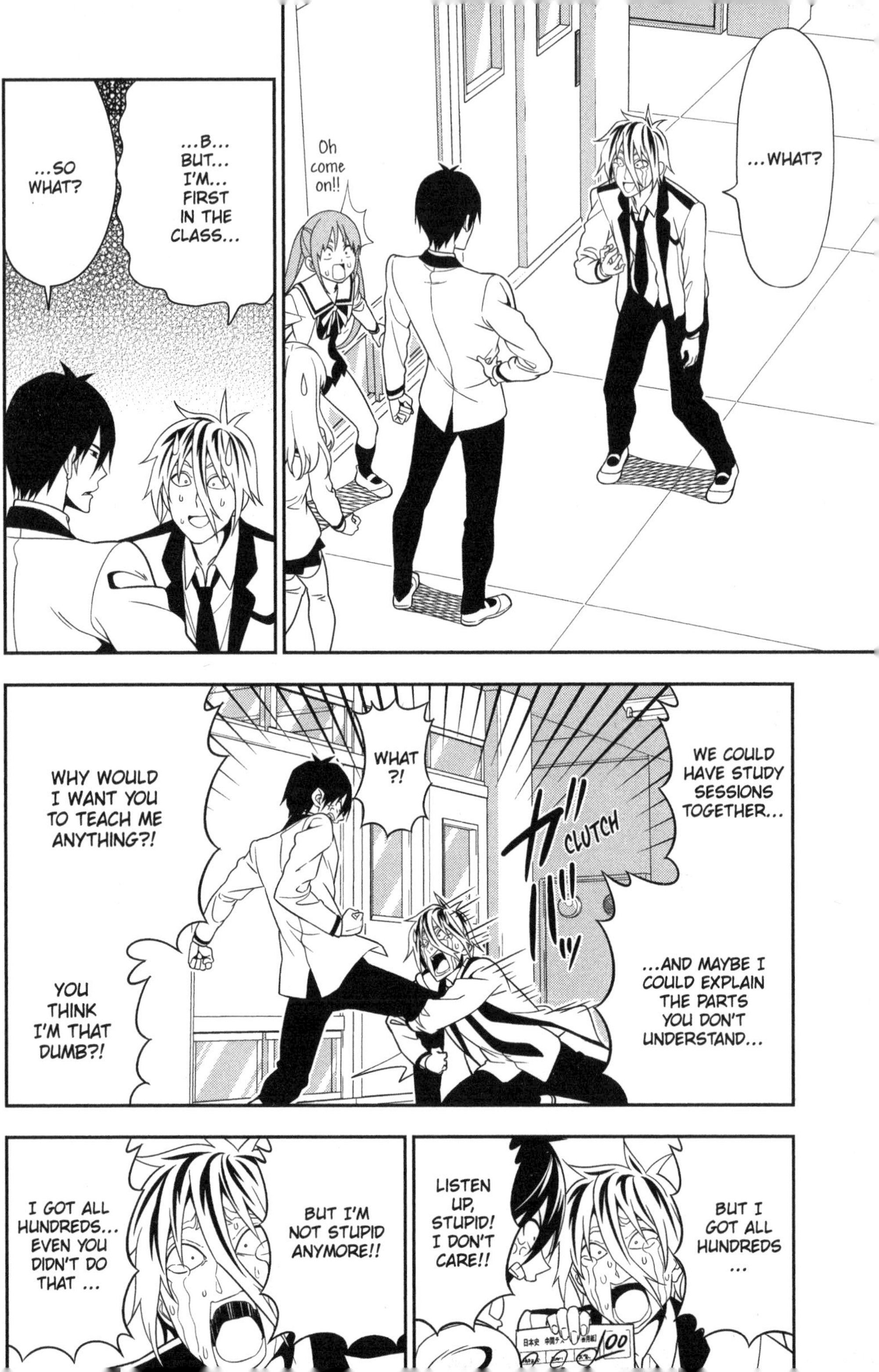

...WHAT?
Oh come on!!
...B... BUT... I'M... FIRST IN THE CLASS...
...SO WHAT?
WE COULD HAVE STUDY SESSIONS TOGETHER...
...AND MAYBE I COULD EXPLAIN THE PARTS YOU DON'T UNDERSTAND...
CLUTCH
WHAT?!
WHY WOULD I WANT YOU TO TEACH ME ANYTHING?!
YOU THINK I'M THAT DUMB?!
BUT I GOT ALL HUNDREDS ...
LISTEN UP, STUPID! I DON'T CARE!!
100
BUT I'M NOT STUPID ANYMORE!!
I GOT ALL HUNDREDS... EVEN YOU DIDN'T DO THAT ...

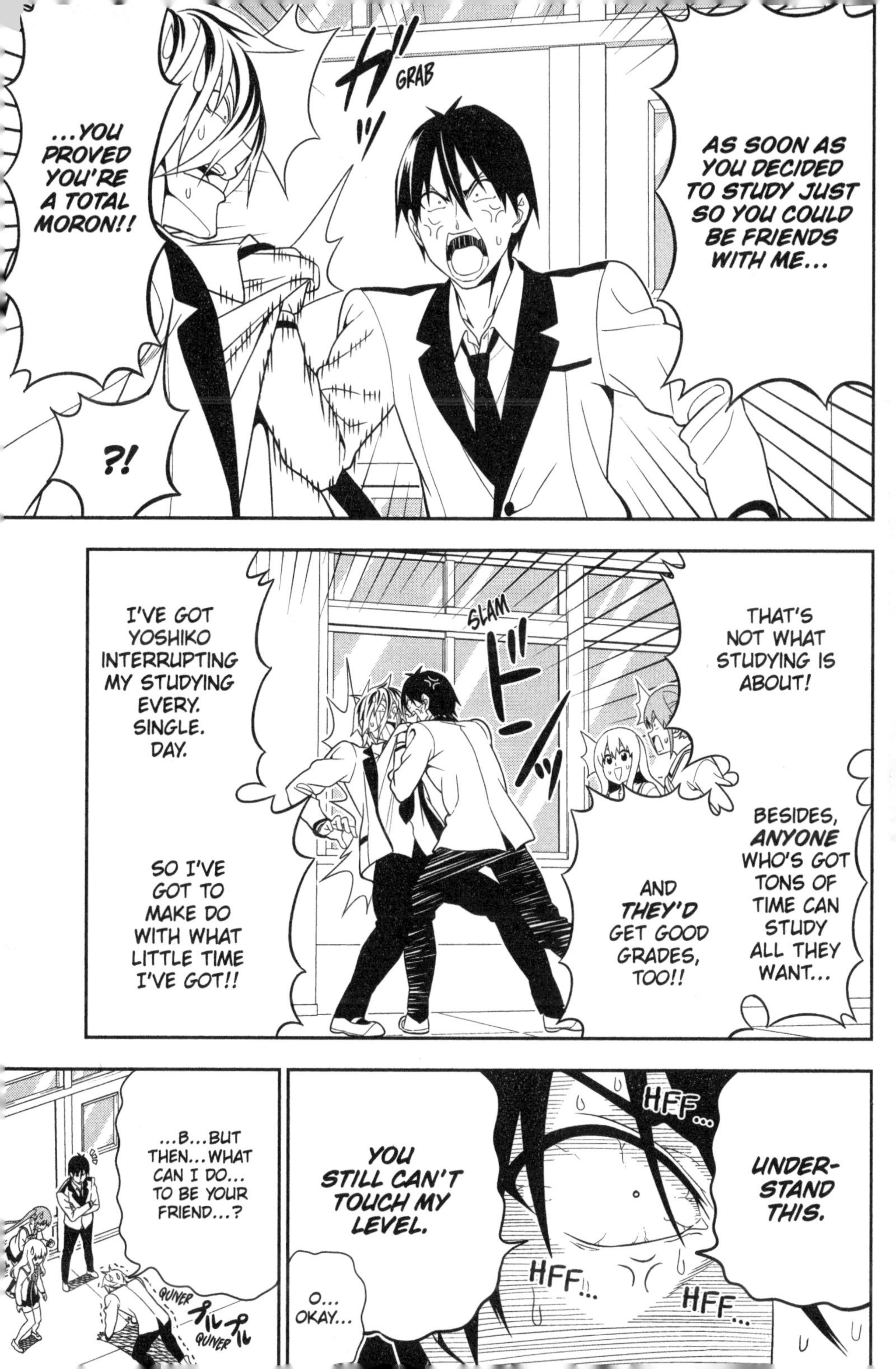
AS SOON AS YOU DECIDED TO STUDY JUST SO YOU COULD BE FRIENDS WITH ME...
GRAB
...YOU PROVED YOU'RE A TOTAL MORON!!
?!
THAT'S NOT WHAT STUDYING IS ABOUT!
BESIDES, *ANYONE* WHO'S GOT TONS OF TIME CAN STUDY ALL THEY WANT...
AND *THEY'D* GET GOOD GRADES, TOO!!
SLAM
I'VE GOT YOSHIKO INTERRUPTING MY STUDYING EVERY. SINGLE. DAY.
SO I'VE GOT TO MAKE DO WITH WHAT LITTLE TIME I'VE GOT!!
HFF...
UNDER-STAND THIS.
YOU STILL CAN'T TOUCH MY LEVEL.
HFF!...
HFF...
O... OKAY...
...B...BUT THEN...WHAT CAN I DO... TO BE YOUR FRIEND...?
QUIVER
QUIVER

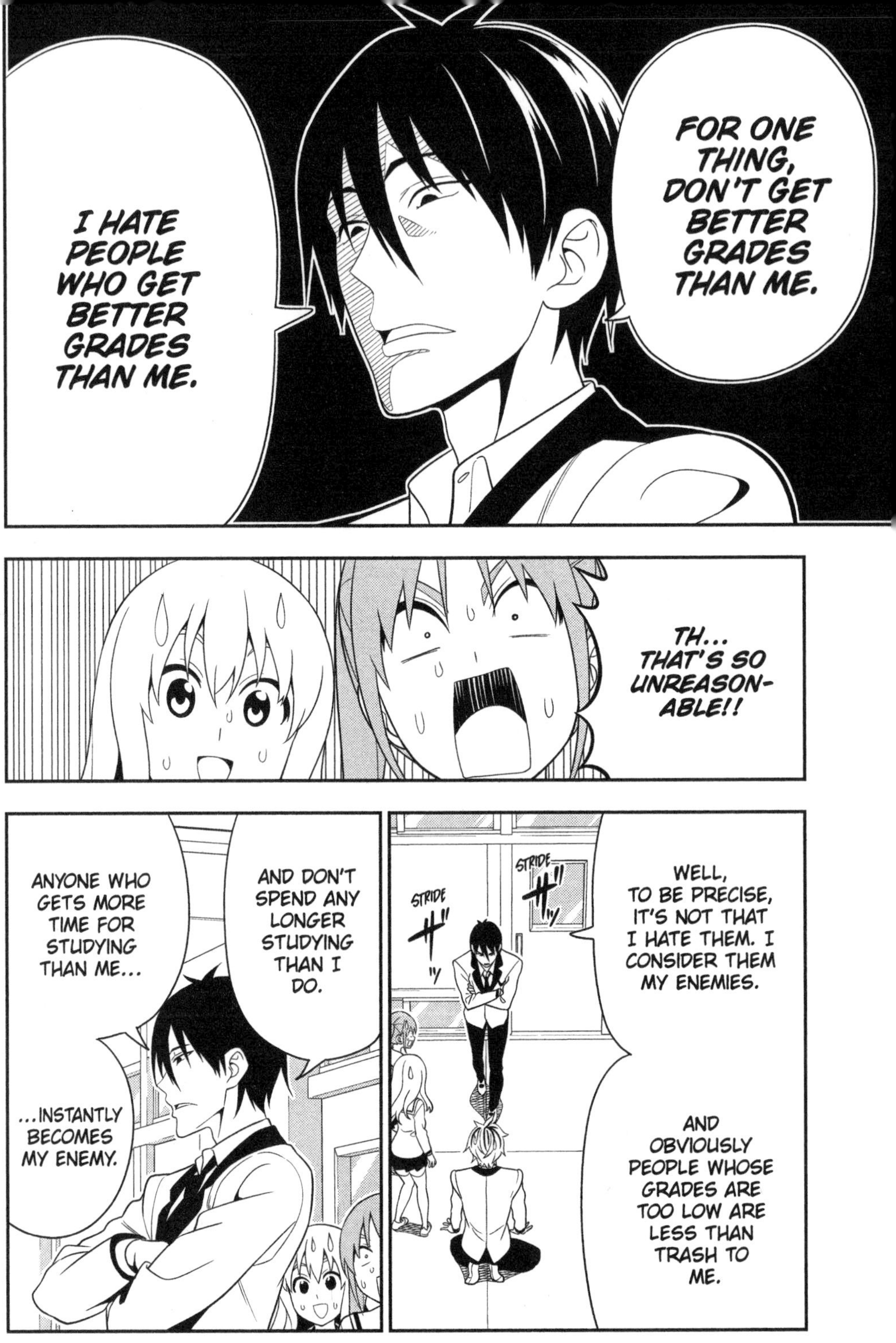
FOR ONE THING, DON'T GET BETTER GRADES THAN ME.
I HATE PEOPLE WHO GET BETTER GRADES THAN ME.
TH... THAT'S SO UNREASON-ABLE!!
STRIDE
STRIDE
WELL, TO BE PRECISE, IT'S NOT THAT I HATE THEM. I CONSIDER THEM MY ENEMIES.
AND OBVIOUSLY PEOPLE WHOSE GRADES ARE TOO LOW ARE LESS THAN TRASH TO ME.
AND DON'T SPEND ANY LONGER STUDYING THAN I DO.
ANYONE WHO GETS MORE TIME FOR STUDYING THAN ME...
...INSTANTLY BECOMES MY ENEMY.

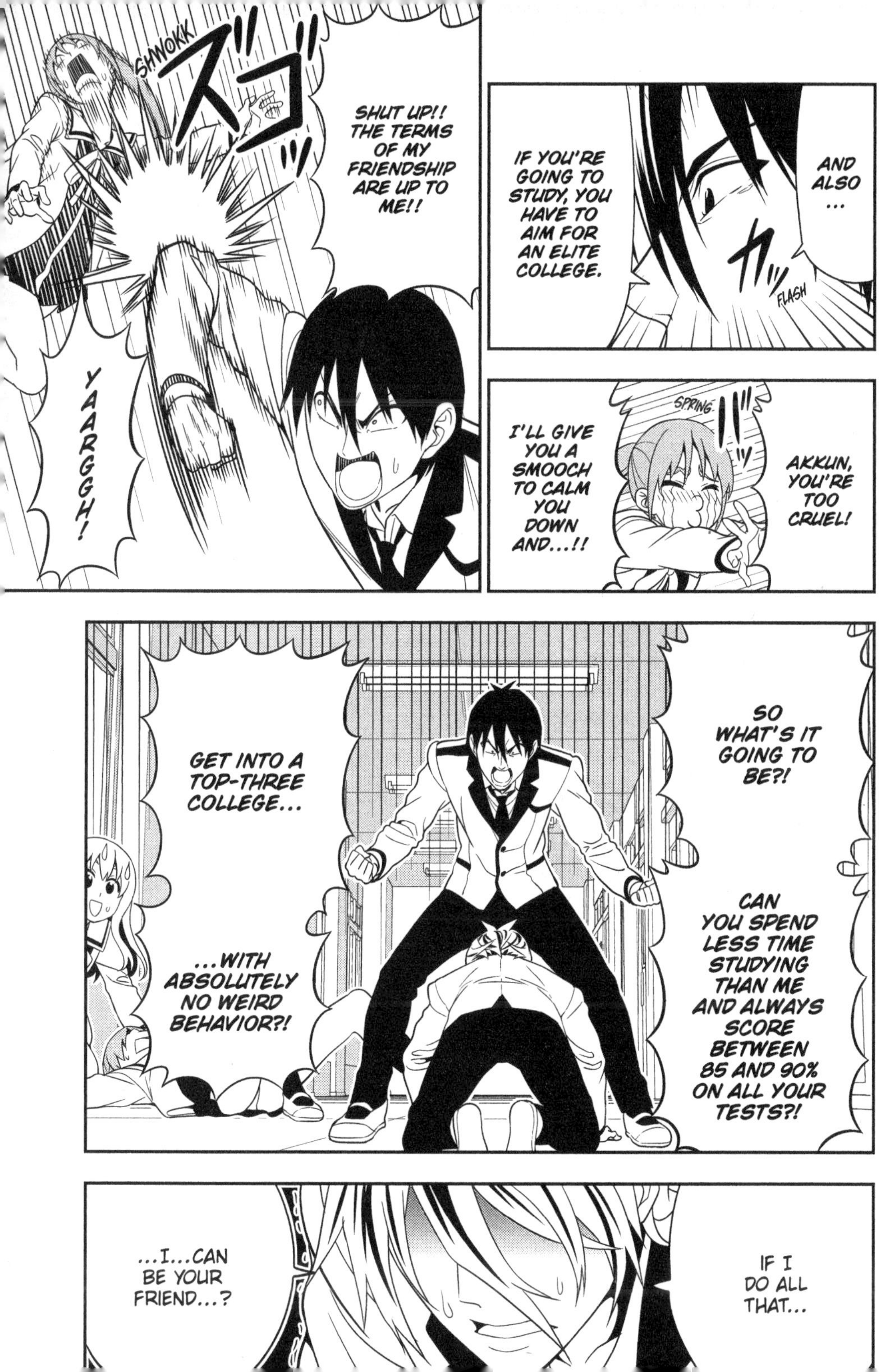
IF YOU'RE GOING TO STUDY, YOU HAVE TO AIM FOR AN ELITE COLLEGE.
AND ALSO...
FLASH
AKKUN, YOU'RE TOO CRUEL!
SPRING
I'LL GIVE YOU A SMOOCH TO CALM YOU DOWN AND...!!
SHWOKK
SHUT UP!! THE TERMS OF MY FRIENDSHIP ARE UP TO ME!!
YAARGGH!
SO WHAT'S IT GOING TO BE?!
CAN YOU SPEND LESS TIME STUDYING THAN ME AND ALWAYS SCORE BETWEEN 85 AND 90% ON ALL YOUR TESTS?!
GET INTO A TOP-THREE COLLEGE...
...WITH ABSOLUTELY NO WEIRD BEHAVIOR?!
IF I DO ALL THAT...
...I...CAN BE YOUR FRIEND...?

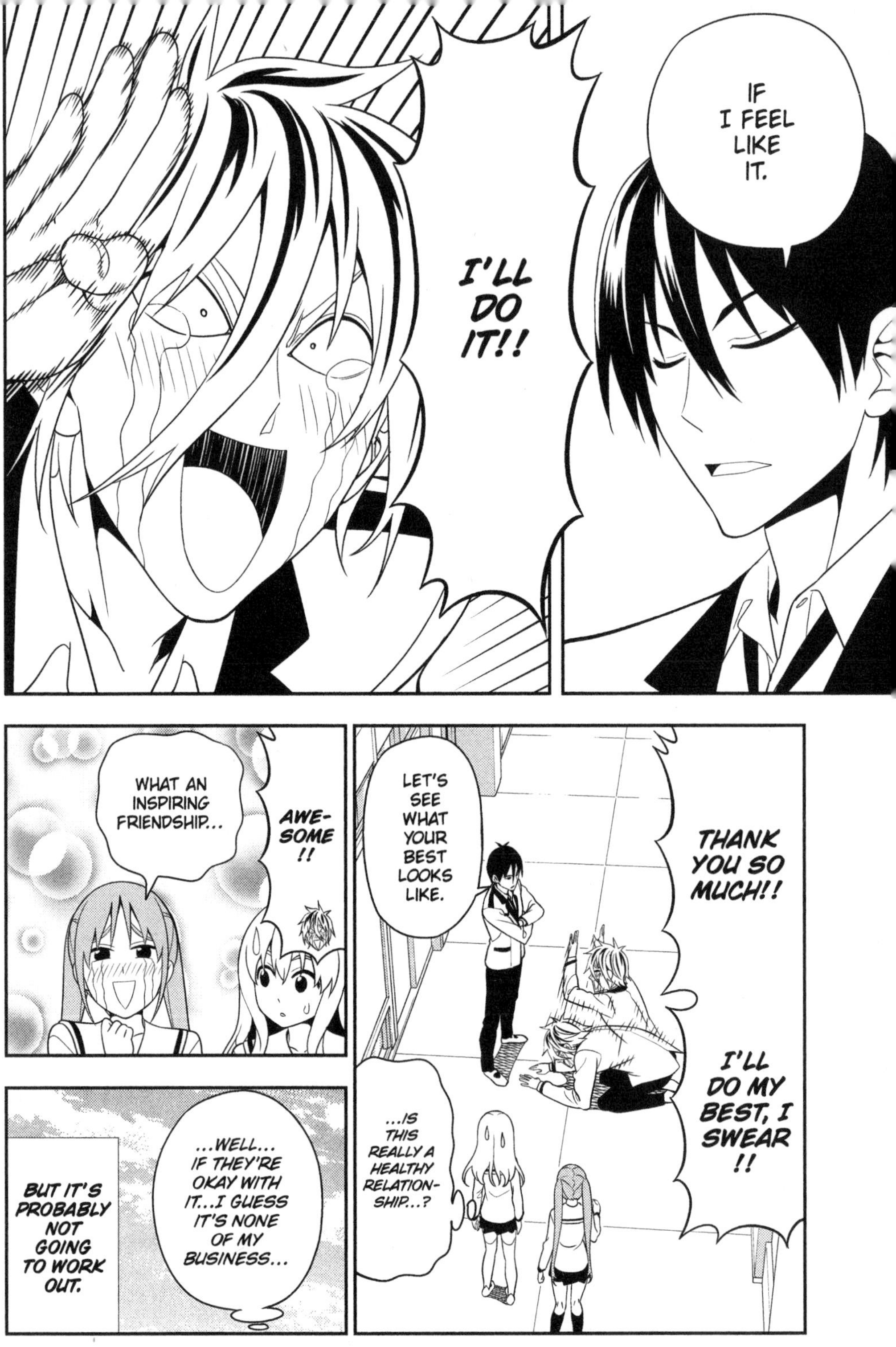
IF I FEEL LIKE IT.
I'LL DO IT!!
THANK YOU SO MUCH!!
I'LL DO MY BEST, I SWEAR!!
LET'S SEE WHAT YOUR BEST LOOKS LIKE.
...IS THIS REALLY A HEALTHY RELATION-SHIP...?
AWE-SOME!!
WHAT AN INSPIRING FRIENDSHIP...
...WELL... IF THEY'RE OKAY WITH IT...I GUESS IT'S NONE OF MY BUSINESS...
BUT IT'S PROBABLY NOT GOING TO WORK OUT.

The Answer is Simple

HUH? I...I MEAN...

...SO WHAT'S SO GREAT ABOUT AKKUN-SAN...?

OH.

THAT'S A LITTLE CREEPY...

E... EVERY-THING...

(See what happens. Let us try)

Aho-Girl

\ˈahôˌgərl\ *Japanese, noun.*
A clueless girl.

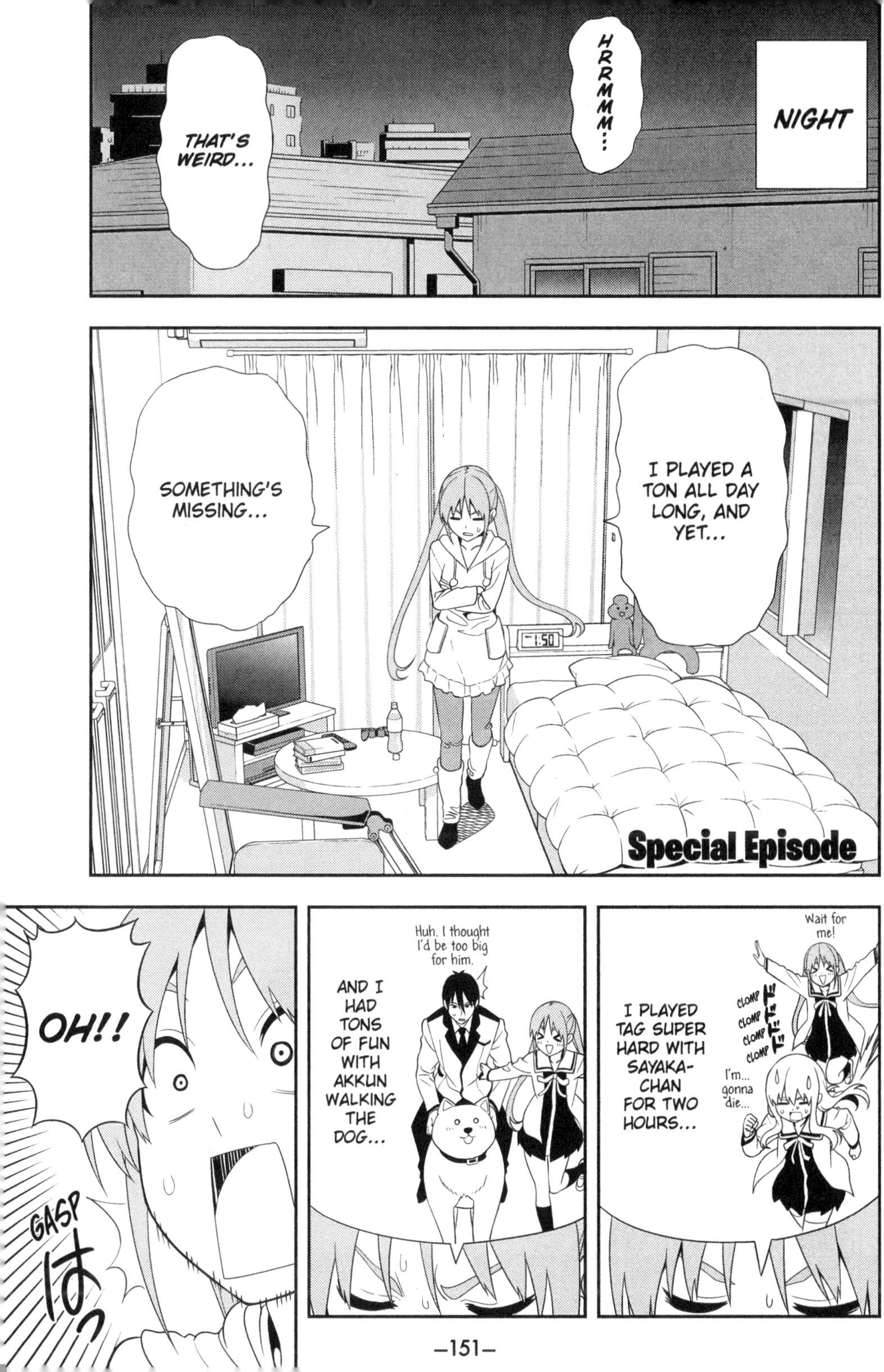
NIGHT
HRRMMM...
THAT'S WEIRD...
I PLAYED A TON ALL DAY LONG, AND YET...
SOMETHING'S MISSING...
Special Episode
Wait for me!
CLOMP CLOMP CLOMP CLOMP
ドドドド
I'm... gonna die...
I PLAYED TAG SUPER HARD WITH SAYAKA-CHAN FOR TWO HOURS...
Huh. I thought I'd be too big for him.
AND I HAD TONS OF FUN WITH AKKUN WALKING THE DOG...
OH!!
GASP
はっ

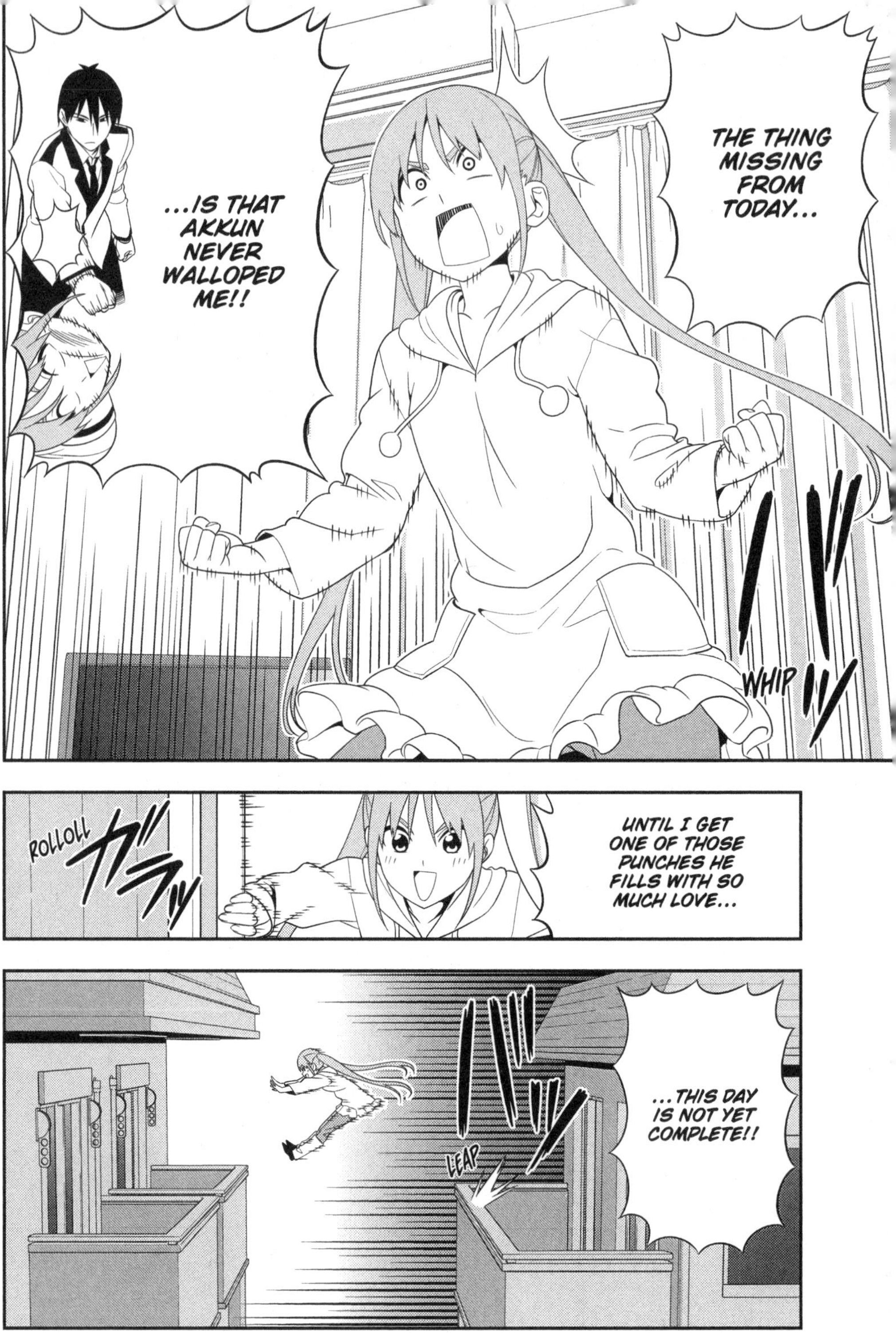
THE THING MISSING FROM TODAY...
...IS THAT AKKUN NEVER WALLOPED ME!!
WHIP
UNTIL I GET ONE OF THOSE PUNCHES HE FILLS WITH SO MUCH LOVE...
ROLLOLL
...THIS DAY IS NOT YET COMPLETE!!
LEAP

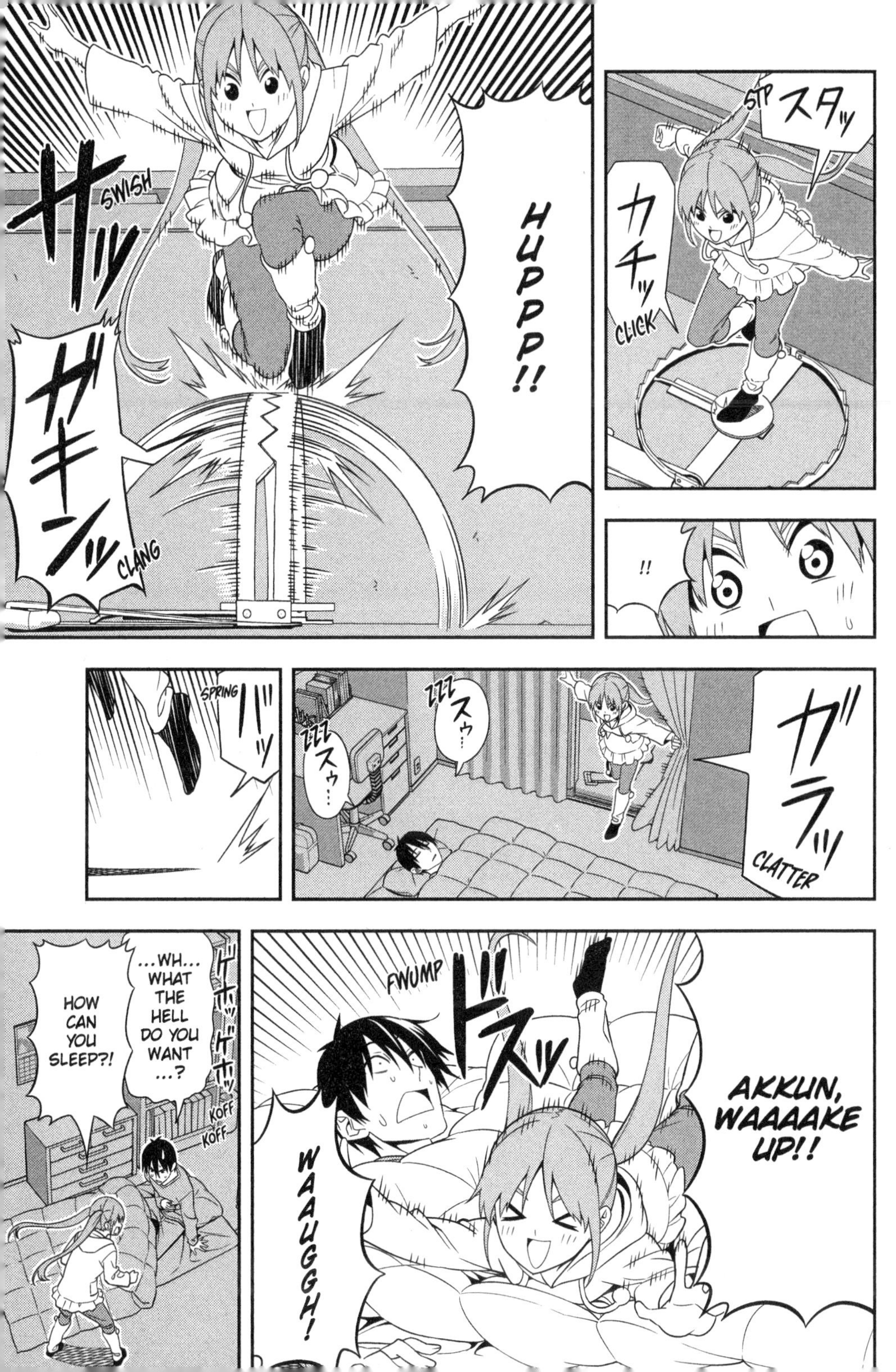

スタッ
STP
カチッ
CLICK
!!
ザッ
SWISH
HUPPPP!!
ガキーンッ
CLANG
ガラッ
CLATTER
ZZZ
スゥ…
ZZZ
スゥ…
バッ
SPRING
AKKUN, WAAAAKE UP!!
ドスッ
FWUMP
WAAUGGH!
ゲホッゲホッ
KOFF
KOFF
...WH... WHAT THE HELL DO YOU WANT ...?
HOW CAN YOU SLEEP?!

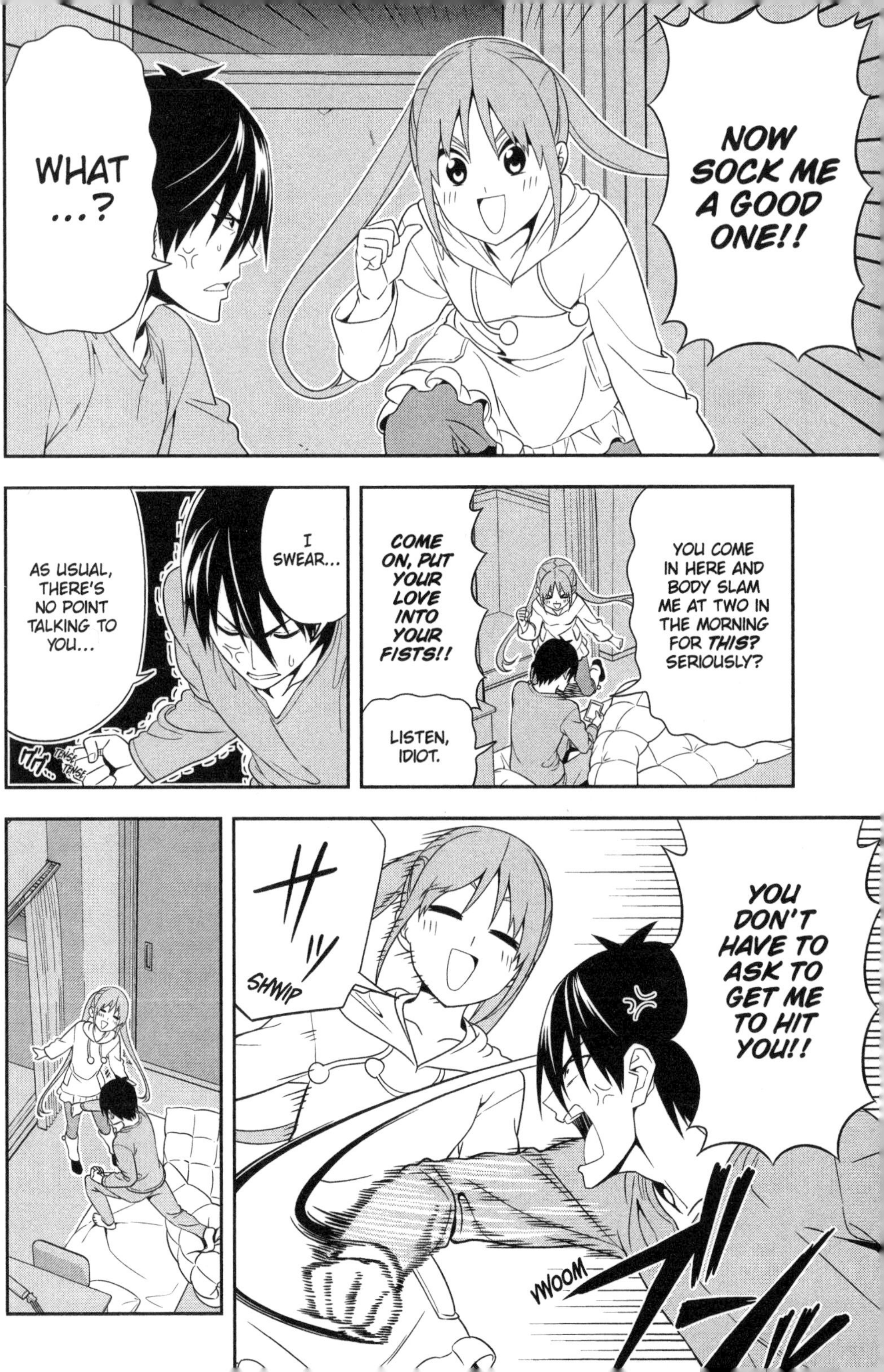
NOW SOCK ME A GOOD ONE!!
WHAT ...?
YOU COME IN HERE AND BODY SLAM ME AT TWO IN THE MORNING FOR THIS? SERIOUSLY?
COME ON, PUT YOUR LOVE INTO YOUR FISTS!!
LISTEN, IDIOT.
I SWEAR...
AS USUAL, THERE'S NO POINT TALKING TO YOU...
TENSE TENSE
YOU DON'T HAVE TO ASK TO GET ME TO HIT YOU!!
SHWIP
VWOOM

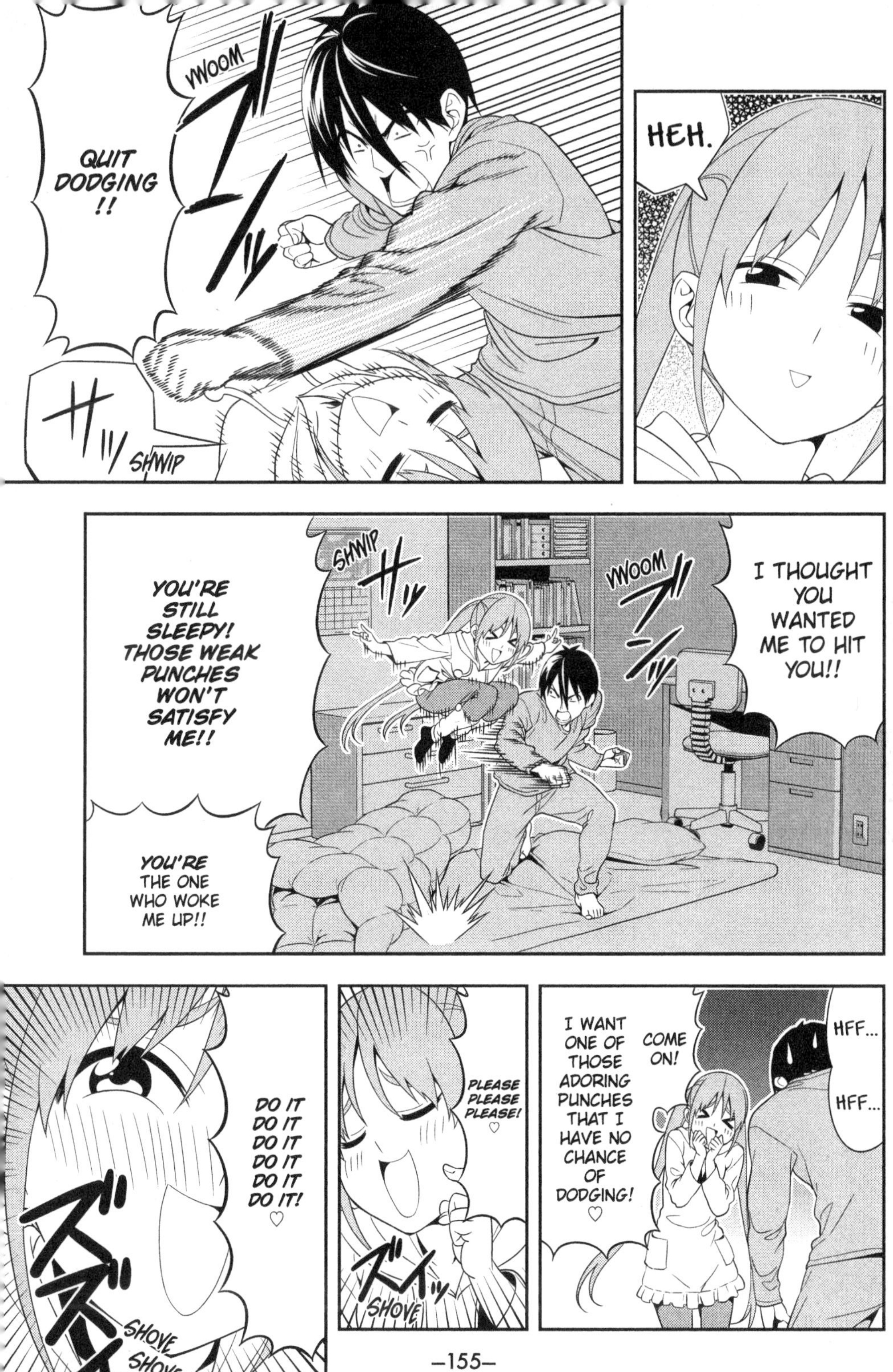
HEH.
VWOOM
QUIT DODGING!!
SHWIP
I THOUGHT YOU WANTED ME TO HIT YOU!!
VWOOM
SHWIP
YOU'RE STILL SLEEPY! THOSE WEAK PUNCHES WON'T SATISFY ME!!
YOU'RE THE ONE WHO WOKE ME UP!!
HFF...
HFF...
COME ON!
I WANT ONE OF THOSE ADORING PUNCHES THAT I HAVE NO CHANCE OF DODGING! ♡
PLEASE PLEASE PLEASE! ♡
SHOVE
DO IT DO IT DO IT DO IT DO IT DO IT! ♡
SHOVE SHOVE

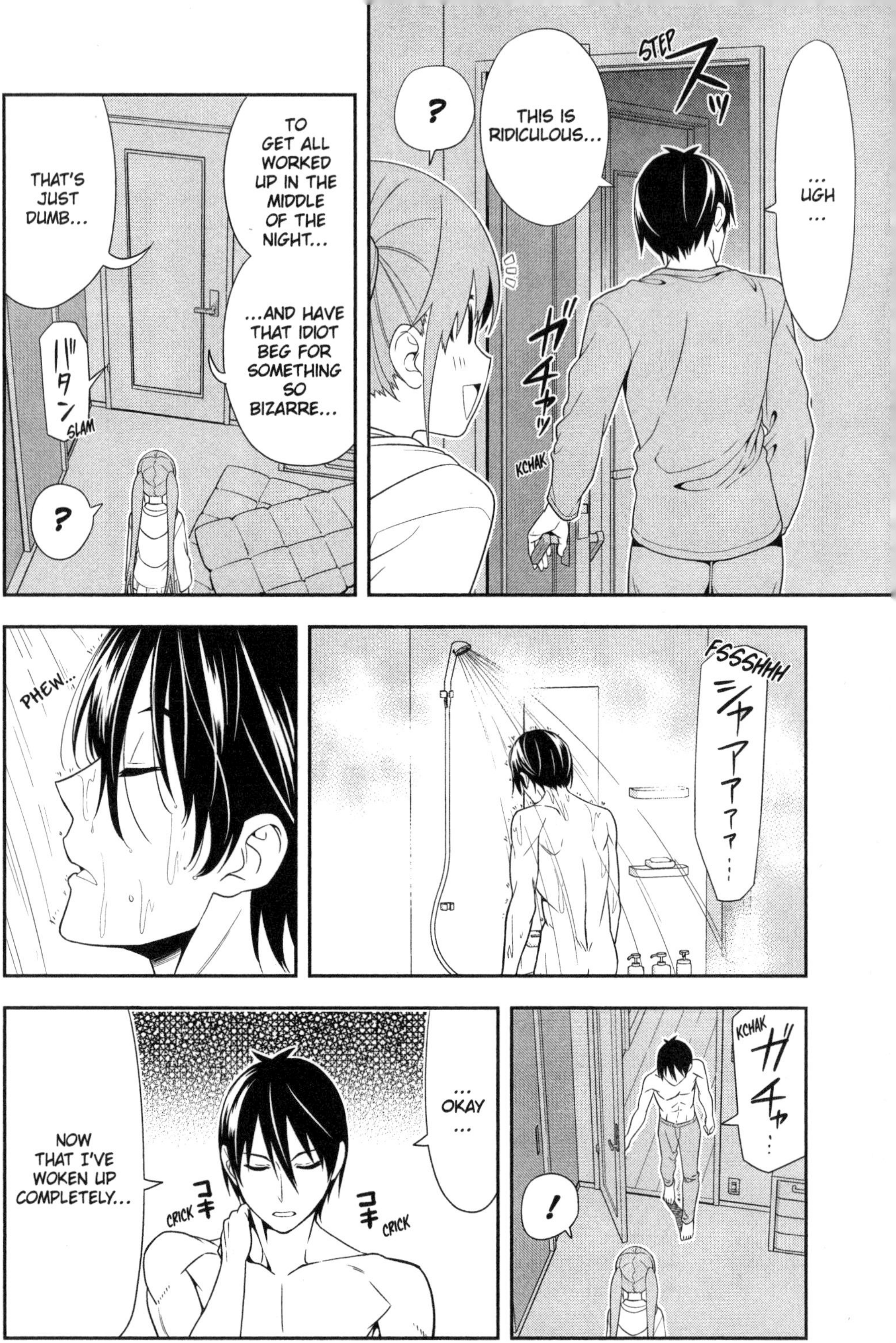
STEP
ズッ
... UGH ...
THIS IS RIDICULOUS...
?
ガチャッ
KCHAK
TO GET ALL WORKED UP IN THE MIDDLE OF THE NIGHT...
...AND HAVE THAT IDIOT BEG FOR SOMETHING SO BIZARRE...
THAT'S JUST DUMB...
バタン
SLAM
?
FSSSHHH
シャアアアア...
PHEW...
KCHAK
ガチャ...
!
... OKAY ...
NOW THAT I'VE WOKEN UP COMPLETELY...
コキ
CRICK
コキ
CRICK

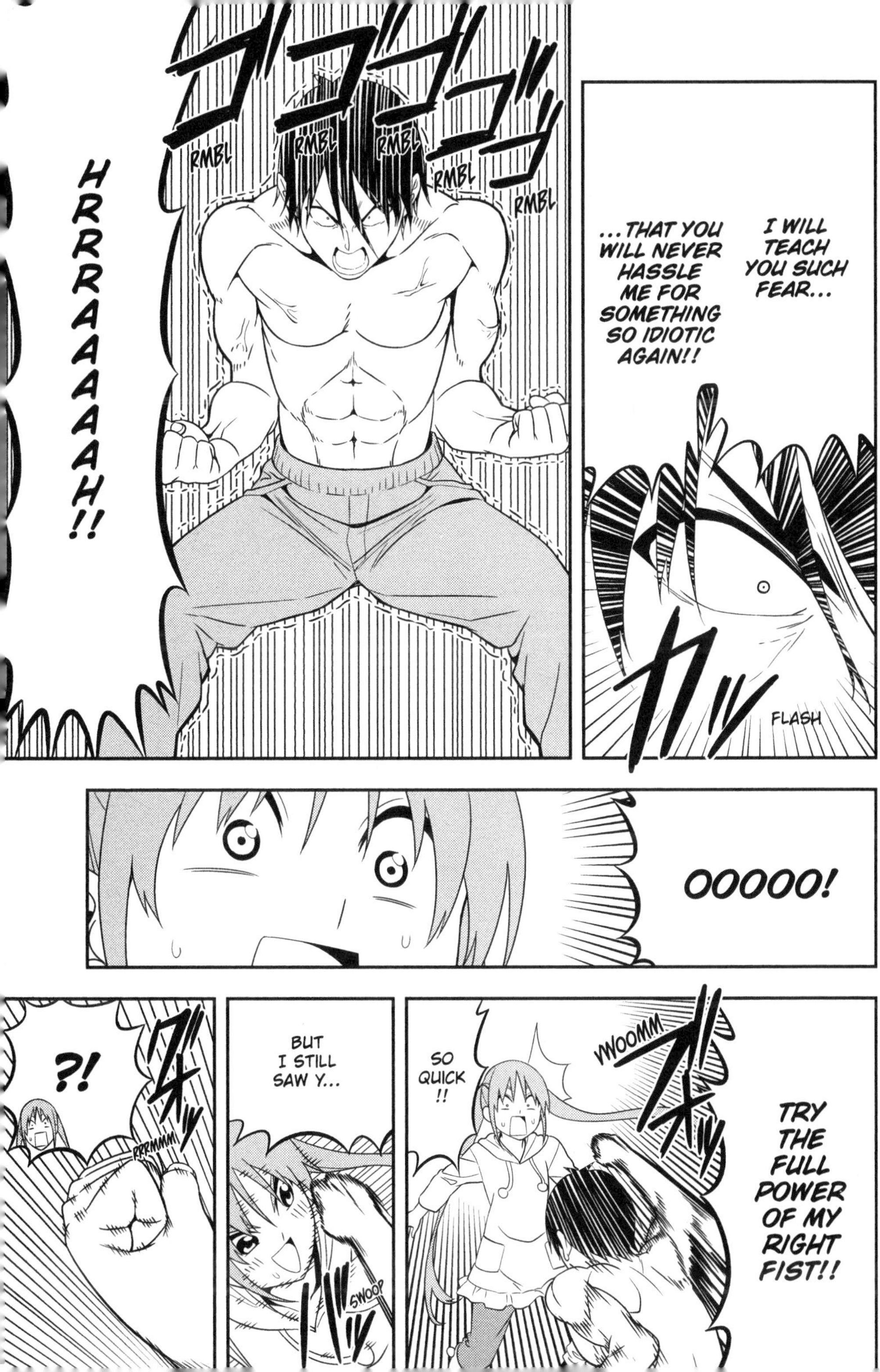
I WILL TEACH YOU SUCH FEAR...
...THAT YOU WILL NEVER HASSLE ME FOR SOMETHING SO IDIOTIC AGAIN!!
FLASH
RMBL RMBL RMBL RMBL RMBL
HRRRAAAAAAAH!!
OOOOO!
TRY THE FULL POWER OF MY RIGHT FIST!!
VWOOMM
SO QUICK!!
BUT I STILL SAW Y...
SWOOP
?!
RRRMMM

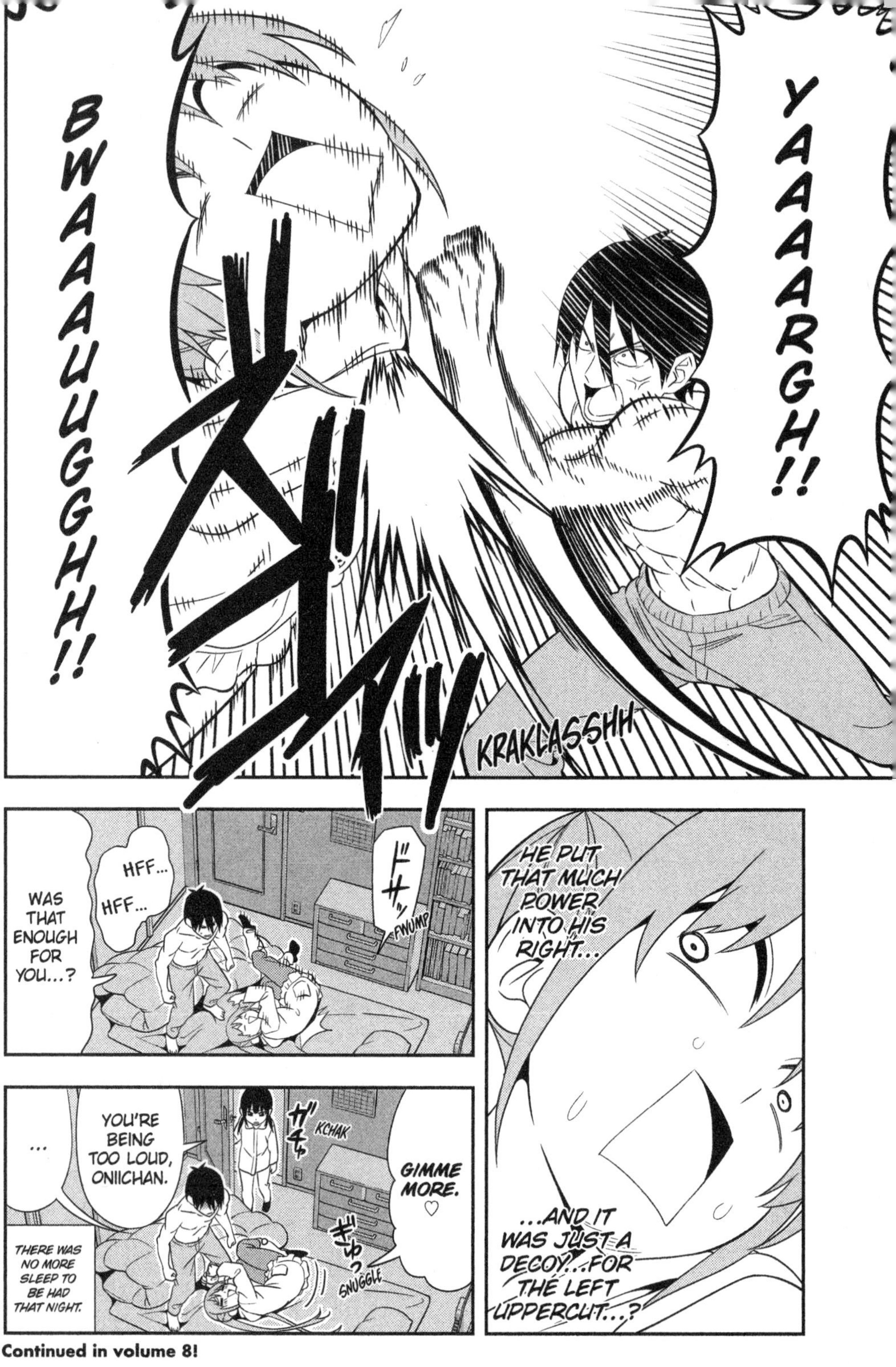
YAAAAARGH!!
BWAAAAUUGGHH!!
KRAKLASSHH
HE PUT THAT MUCH POWER INTO HIS RIGHT...
...AND IT WAS JUST A DECOY... FOR THE LEFT UPPERCUT...?
HFF... HFF...
WAS THAT ENOUGH FOR YOU...?
ドガッ
FWUMP
GIMME MORE. ♡
YOU'RE BEING TOO LOUD, ONIICHAN.
ガチャ
KCHAK
...
ぎゅっ
SNUGGLE
THERE WAS NO MORE SLEEP TO BE HAD THAT NIGHT.

Continued in volume 8!

The Drama of How Hiroyuki Became a Manga-ka 6

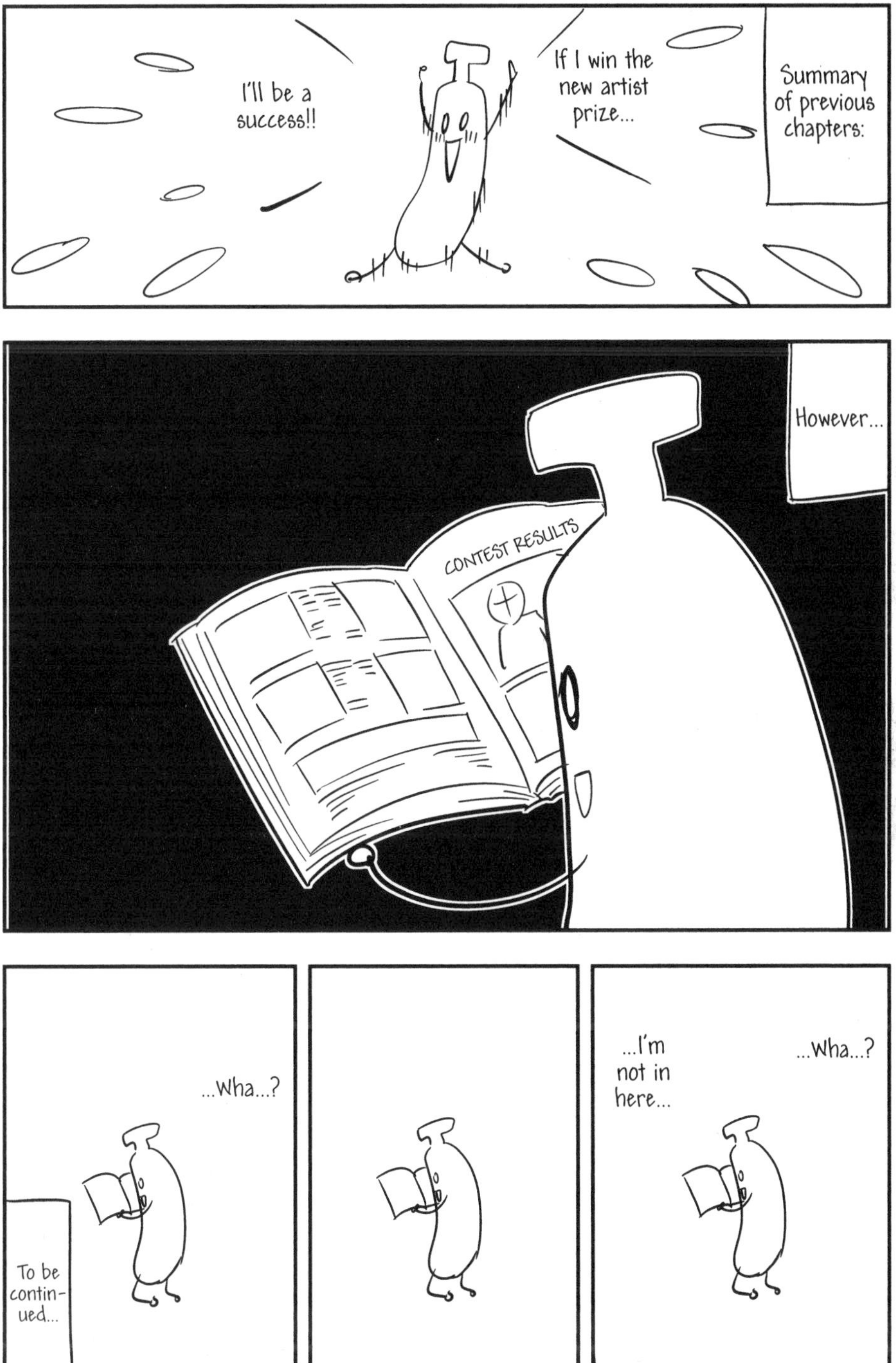
Summary of previous chapters:
If I win the new artist prize...
I'll be a success!!
However...
CONTEST RESULTS
...Wha...?
...I'm not in here...
...Wha...?
To be contin-ued...

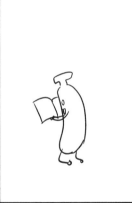

Translation Notes

Page 20
"The battle we refuse to lose is"
This is part of the tagline played on TV Asahi for Japan's national men's soccer team, particularly for World Cup matches. Various stirring clips of the team in action are shown, with the final announcement of the air time and opponent narrated by a resonant male voice saying "The battle we refuse to lose is here."

Page 38
"Look, there—it's"
This comes from a jingle for Circle K Sunkus, a chain of convenience stores in Japan. The jingle is meant to suggest that the stores are conveniently located, everywhere you look.

Page 39
"My boobs got one centimeter bigger"
One centimeter is equivalent to less than half an inch. This is not a very big deal...

Page 59
"*Oneechan*"
Literally "older sister," the term can also be used to address teenage to early 30s-aged women not related to the speaker. The parallel term for men is *oniichan*, "older brother."

Page 61
"Red light, green light"
The original Japanese refers to a game called *daruma-san ga koronda* ("the daruma doll fell over"). The Japanese phrase is ten syllables long, and therefore acts as a way for a child to count to ten during the game. While the "it" person is counting with their eyes closed, the other players may approach, but as soon as they finish—arriving at the "fell over" part of the phrase—everybody has to freeze. In effect, it's similar to Red Light, Green Light, which is what the English edition uses. In the original, Ruri yells out "The daruma doll danced," and "laughed," and "stopped," and "changed" before she runs out of ideas for confusing Yoshiko—this was adapted in this edition as Ruri's shouting of various colors to a similar confusing effect.

Page 79
"College entrance exams"
Whereas U.S. colleges and universities use a variety of metrics such as grade point averages, SAT scores, and AP/IB scores to select students for admission, in Japan, nationally administered standardized tests are used to evaluate all students hoping to enter college in the coming year. These subject-specific tests are given once a year, over the course of two days in January, and are administered simultaneously across the entire country. If a student fails to qualify for the school of their choice, they must wait an entire year to take the tests again and attempt to score higher.

In addition to these national tests, each public college or university may also give its own entrance exam to evaluate students according to its own criteria. Private institutions (which are typically less prestigious than public institutions) tend to rely only on the national tests.

Page 80
"*Oniichan*"
See "*oneechan*" note for page 59.

Page 83
"Absence"
Akkun is studying advanced English vocabulary. The original Japanese gives the words inside quote marks in English, and provides definitions in Japanese.

Page 87
"Todai"
The title of Akkun's vocabulary book indicates that it is targeted for success at one school: The University of Tokyo, the most prestigious institution of higher education in Japan. The Japanese name of the school is *Tokyo Daigaku*, which is commonly abbreviated to "Todai."

Page 100
"He said, at the start of second year"
See note for page 79. The Japanese school year begins in April, and the exams are typically held in January of a student's third year of high school (i.e., three months before graduation).

Page 102
"When will you start?"
This refers to a slogan for a chain of prep schools run by a pop culture figure named Osamu Hayashi, who became a meme for his prep school commercials prioritizing kanji study with the slogan "When will you start? Right now, of course!"

Page 104
"Todai"
See note for page 87.

Page 124
"wat does that even meen? srsly, i just"
This is a reference to an internet meme that arose from a poorly typed post on the ubiquitous 2chan message board, and has been riffed repeatedly into posts with

prestigious.

Page 150

"See what happens. Let us try"

This is a quote from the founder of the beverage company Suntory, Shinjiro Torii. Epitomizing the spirit of experimentation and innovation underlying his company, which was the first-ever European-style wine and whisky distillery in Japan, Torii is quoted as saying "See what happens. Let us try it, and see."

Aho-Girl

\'ahô,gərl\ *Japanese, noun*.
A clueless girl.

a frustrated, childlike incomprehension of not-really-all-that-deep ideas. The line quoted here ends "srsly, i just give up."

Page 135

"'60065' for 'boobs,' of course..."

The original uses a common form of wordplay in Japanese, assigning numbers to replace homophone syllables in words to create a kind of code. Because Japanese has many different pronunciations for each number, the system is quite flexible. The original code is "1104," which Yoshie reads as "*ii oshiri*," or "nice butt." But as anyone who's used a calculator in school knows, English has its own pervy numbers this poor man would have used.

"Now sign it..."

In Japan, few documents are literally "signed" with a person's signature to make them official. Instead, Japanese people use stamps (*hanko*) carved with their names and "put their seal" on a document to make it official. This seal commonly takes the form of the person's name within a box or circle, and is often stamped in red ink.

Page 137

"Now let's use this money he gave me and get some yakiniku!!"

The man gave Yoshie approximately $100, so now she can splurge on a nice meal. Yakiniku literally means "grilled meat," and prototypically uses beef as a main component. However, Japan doesn't have enough land to sustain a large cattle farming industry and must import most of the cattle feed. Instead of dedicating so many resources to cattle farming, Japan mostly imports its beef, which is therefore quite expensive and indulgent.

Page 138

"Last groper"

This refers to an adult video game released in 2001 entitled *Saishuu chikan densha*, or "Last Groper Train." The plot of the game revolves around a conductor's scheme to increase ticket sales on his unfrequented train line by selling special tickets to gropers at exorbitant prices and providing them with a special car where they can molest women. Once the train line makes enough money to stay in business, players then beat the game by cracking down on the gropers again.

Page 147

"Get into a top-three college"

The "top three" Akkun is referring to is spelled out in the Japanese as being Waseda University, Keio University, and Sophia University. These are considered the top three private universities in Japan. However, as noted for page 87, public universities are usually considered more

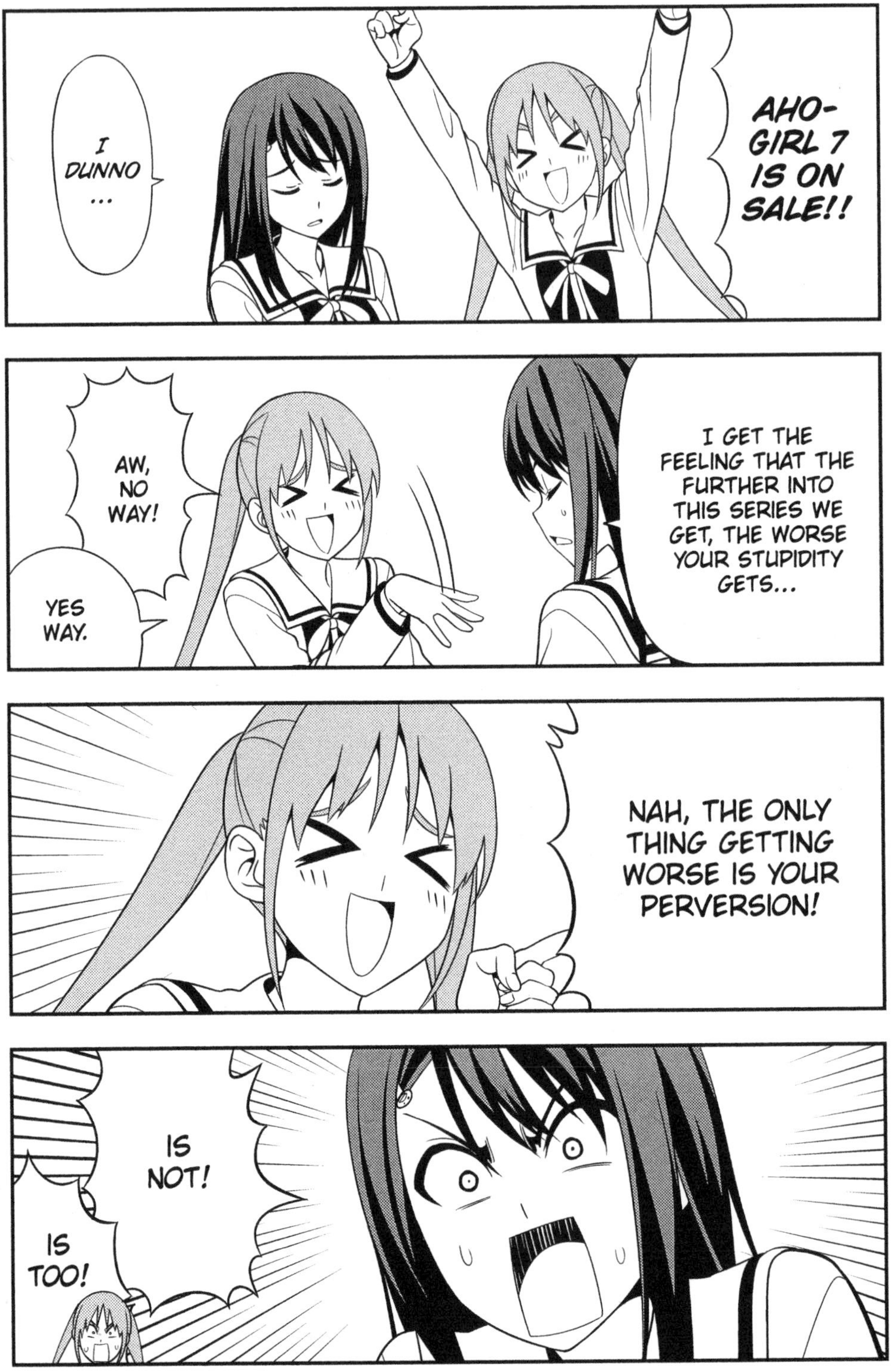

AHO-GIRL 7 IS ON SALE!!
I DUNNO...
I GET THE FEELING THAT THE FURTHER INTO THIS SERIES WE GET, THE WORSE YOUR STUPIDITY GETS...
AW, NO WAY!
YES WAY.
NAH, THE ONLY THING GETTING WORSE IS YOUR PERVERSION!
IS NOT!
IS TOO!

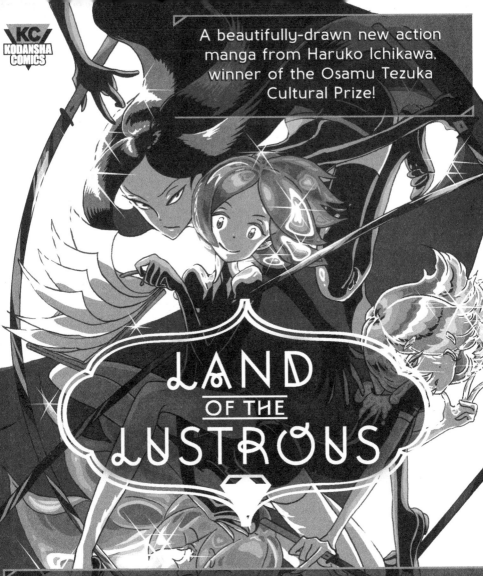

A beautifully-drawn new action manga from Haruko Ichikawa, winner of the Osamu Tezuka Cultural Prize!

LAND OF THE LUSTROUS

In a world inhabited by crystalline life-forms called The Lustrous, every gem must fight for their life against the threat of Lunarians who would turn them into decorations. Phosphophyllite, the most fragile and brittle of gems, longs to join the battle, so when Phos is instead assigned to complete a natural history of their world, it sounds like a dull and pointless task. But this new job brings Phos into contact with Cinnabar, a gem forced to live in isolation. Can Phos's seemingly mundane assignment lead both Phos and Cinnabar to the fulfillment they desire?

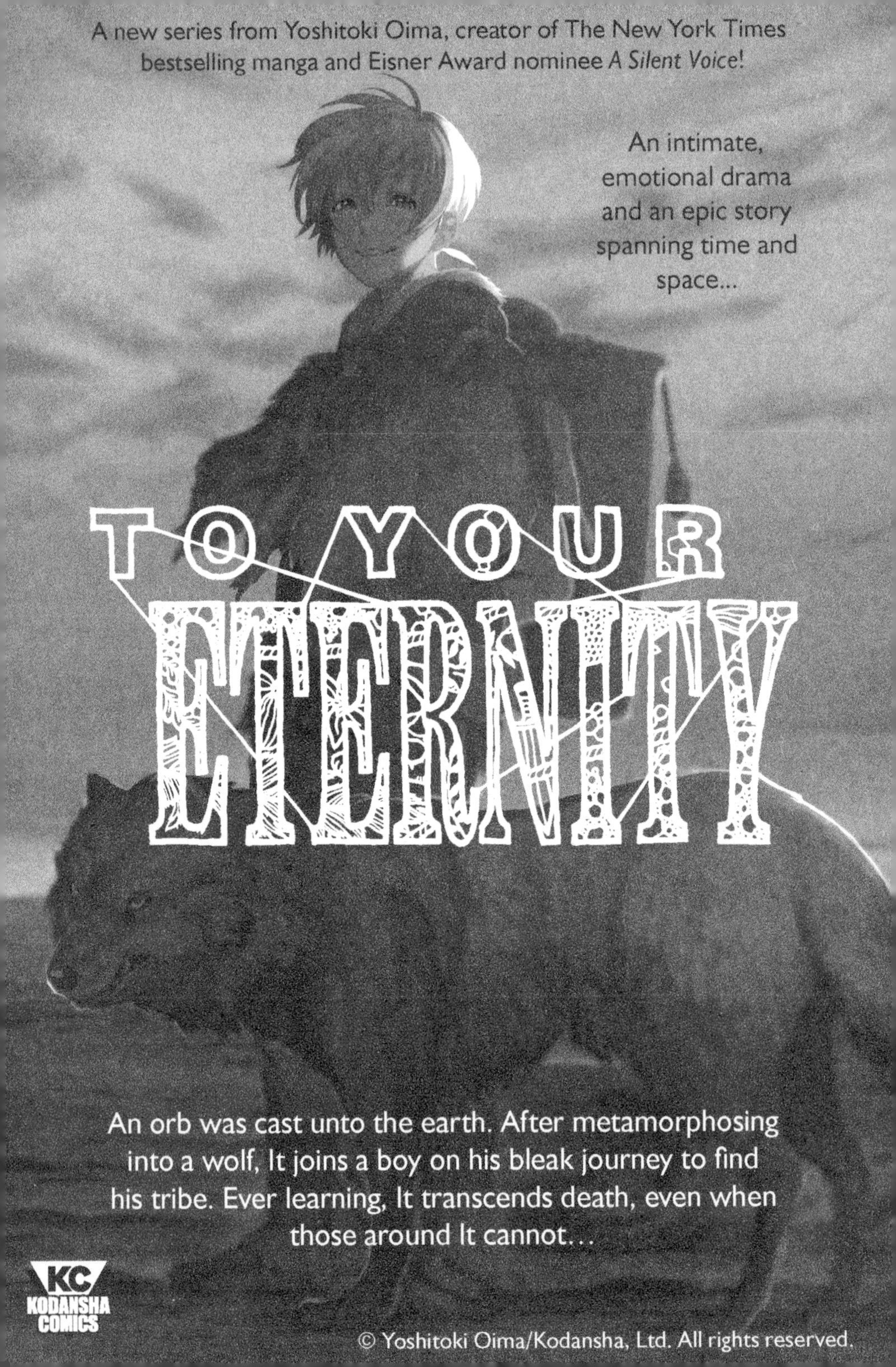
A new series from Yoshitoki Oima, creator of The New York Times bestselling manga and Eisner Award nominee *A Silent Voice*!
An intimate, emotional drama and an epic story spanning time and space...
TO YOUR ETERNITY
An orb was cast unto the earth. After metamorphosing into a wolf, It joins a boy on his bleak journey to find his tribe. Ever learning, It transcends death, even when those around It cannot…
KC KODANSHA COMICS
© Yoshitoki Oima/Kodansha, Ltd. All rights reserved.

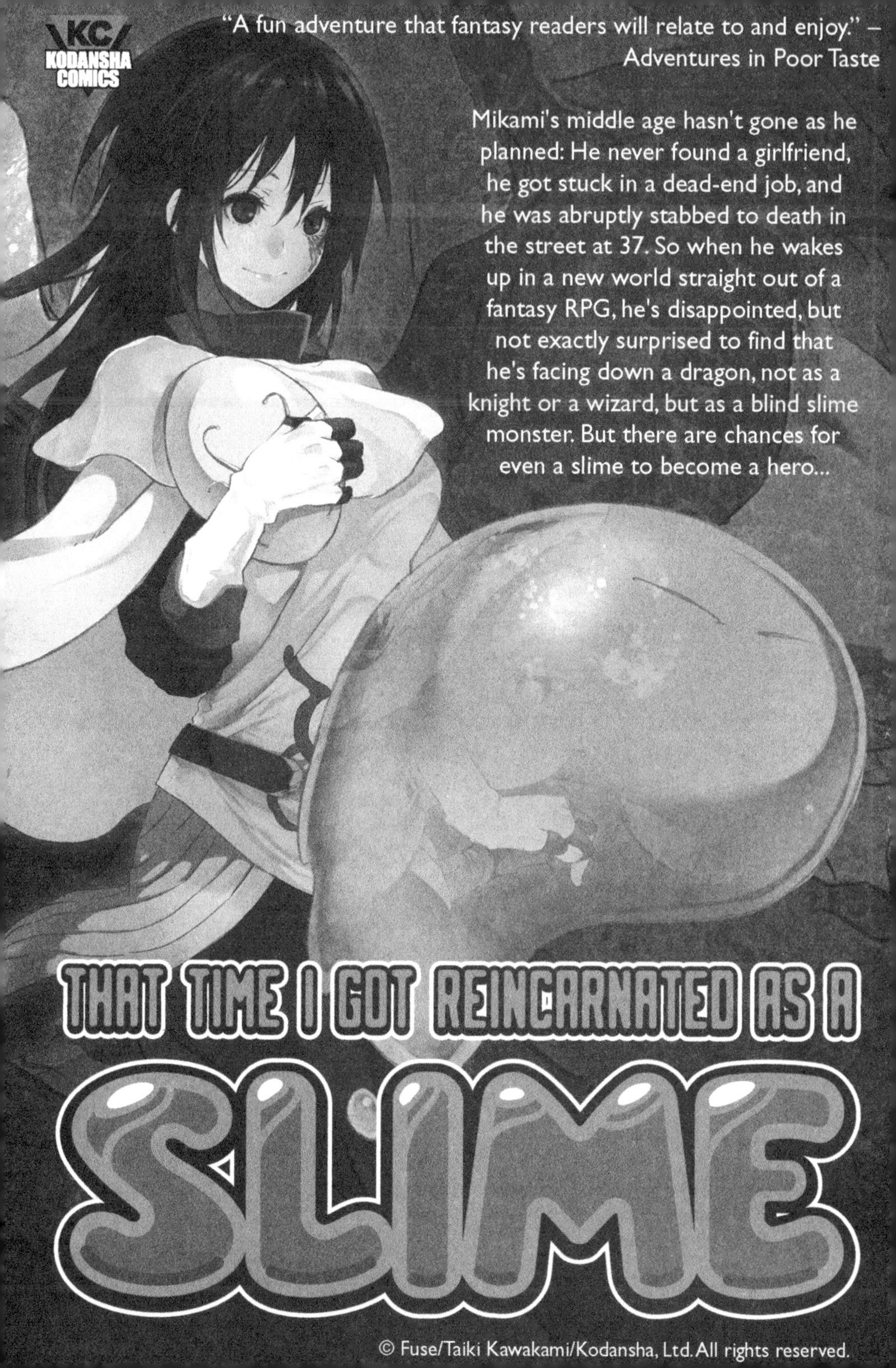
KC
KODANSHA COMICS
"A fun adventure that fantasy readers will relate to and enjoy." – Adventures in Poor Taste
Mikami's middle age hasn't gone as he planned: He never found a girlfriend, he got stuck in a dead-end job, and he was abruptly stabbed to death in the street at 37. So when he wakes up in a new world straight out of a fantasy RPG, he's disappointed, but not exactly surprised to find that he's facing down a dragon, not as a knight or a wizard, but as a blind slime monster. But there are chances for even a slime to become a hero...
THAT TIME I GOT REINCARNATED AS A
SLIME
© Fuse/Taiki Kawakami/Kodansha, Ltd. All rights reserved.

"An emotional and artistic tour de force! We see incredible triumph, and crushing defeat... each panel [is] a thrill!"
—Anitay

"A journey that's instantly compelling."
—Anime News Network

WELCOME TO THE BALLROOM

By Tomo Takeuchi

Feckless high school student Tatara Fujita wants to be good at something—anything. Unfortunately, he's about as average as a slouchy teen can be. The local bullies know this, and make it a habit to hit him up for cash, but all that changes when the debonair Kaname Sengoku sends them packing. Sengoku's not the neighborhood watch, though. He's a professional ballroom dancer. And once Tatara Fujita gets pulled into the world of ballroom, his life will never be the same.

KC
KODANSHA COMICS

The award-winning manga about what happens inside you!

"Far more entertaining than it ought to be... what kid doesn't want to think that every time they sneeze a torpedo shoots out their nose?"
—Anime News Network

Strep throat! Hay fever! Influenza! The world is a dangerous place for a red blood cell just trying to get her deliveries finished. Fortunately, she's not alone...she's got a whole human body's worth of cells ready to help out! The mysterious white blood cells, the buff and brash killer T cells, even the cute little platelets—everyone's got to come together if they want to keep you healthy!

Cells at Work!

By Akane Shimizu

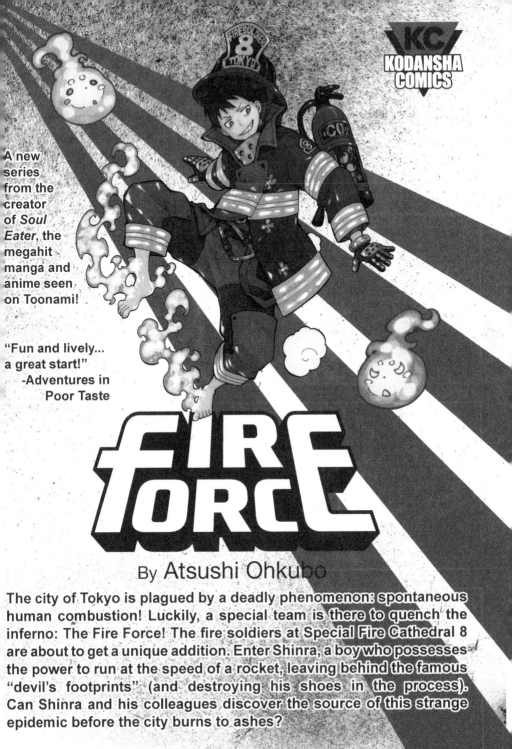

A new
series
from the
creator
of *Soul
Eater*, the
megahit
manga and
anime seen
on Toonami!

"Fun and lively...
a great start!"
-Adventures in
Poor Taste

FIRE FORCE

By Atsushi Ohkubo

The city of Tokyo is plagued by a deadly phenomenon: spontaneous human combustion! Luckily, a special team is there to quench the inferno: The Fire Force! The fire soldiers at Special Fire Cathedral 8 are about to get a unique addition. Enter Shinra, a boy who possesses the power to run at the speed of a rocket, leaving behind the famous "devil's footprints" (and destroying his shoes in the process). Can Shinra and his colleagues discover the source of this strange epidemic before the city burns to ashes?

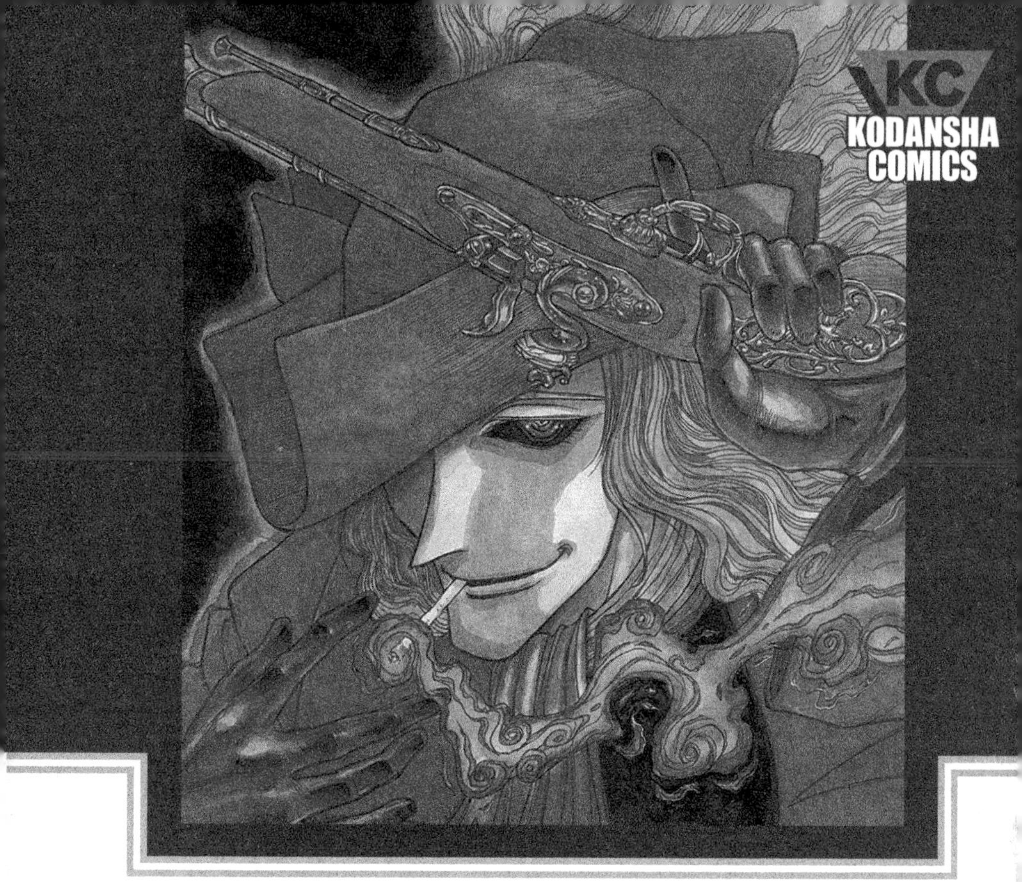
KC
KODANSHA
COMICS

The Black Museum: The Ghost and the Lady

By Kazuhiro Fujita

Deep in Scotland Yard in London sits an evidence room dedicated to the greatest mysteries of British history. In this "Black Museum" sits a misshapen hunk of lead—two bullets fused together—the key to a wartime encounter between Florence Nightingale, the mother of modern nursing, and a supernatural Man in Grey. This story is unknown to most scholars of history, but a special guest of the museum will tell the tale of The Ghost and the Lady...

Praise for Kazuhiro Fujita's *Ushio and Tora*

"A charming revival that combines a classic look with modern depth and pacing... **Essential viewing both for curmudgeons and new fans alike.**" — Anime News Network

"**GREAT!** The first episode of Ushio and Tora captures the essence of '90s anime." — IGN

Japan's most powerful spirit medium delves into the ghost world's greatest mysteries!

Story by Kyo Shirodaira, famed author of mystery fiction and creator of *Spiral*, *Blast of Tempest*, and *The Record of a Fallen Vampire*.

Both touched by spirits called yôkai, Kotoko and Kurô have gained unique superhuman powers. But to gain her powers Kotoko has given up an eye and a leg, and Kurô's personal life is in shambles. So when Kotoko suggests they team up to deal with renegades from the spirit world, Kurô doesn't have many other choices, but Kotoko might just have a few ulterior motives...

IN/SPECTRE

STORY BY **KYO SHIRODAIRA**
ART BY **CHASHIBA KATASE**

HAPPINESS

ハピネス

By Shuzo Oshimi

From the creator of *The Flowers of Evil*

Nothing interesting is happening in Makoto Ozaki's first year of high school. His life is a series of quiet humiliations: low-grade bullies, unreliable friends, and the constant frustration of his adolescent lust. But one night, a pale, thin girl knocks him to the ground in an alley and offers him a choice. Now everything is different. Daylight is searingly bright. Food tastes awful. And worse than anything is the terrible, consuming thirst...

Praise for Shuzo Oshimi's *The Flowers of Evil*

"A shockingly readable story that vividly—one might even say queasily—evokes the fear and confusion of discovering one's own sexuality. Recommended." —The Manga Critic

"A page-turning tale of sordid middle school blackmail." —Otaku USA Magazine

"A stunning new horror manga." —Third Eye Comics

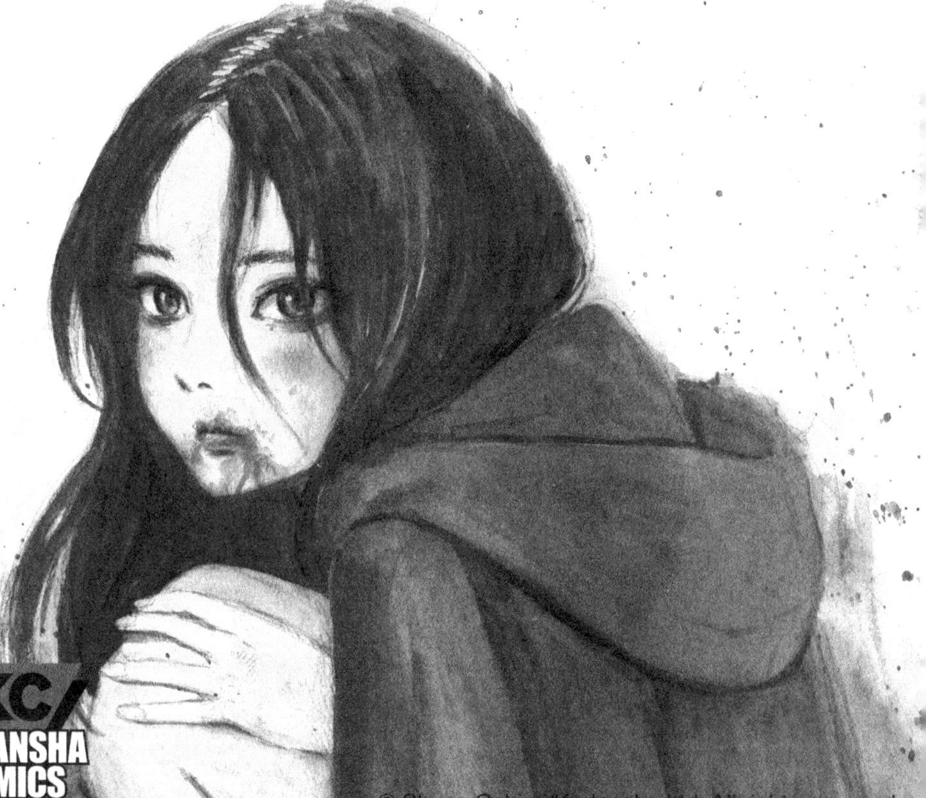

KODANSHA COMICS

Based on the critically acclaimed classic horror manga

The first new *Parasyte* manga in over 20 years!

NEO PARASYTE f

BY ASUMIKO NAKAMURA, EMA TOYAMA, MIKI RINNO, LALAKO KOJIMA, KAORI YUKI, BANKO KUZE, YUUKI OBATA, KASHIO, YUI KUROE, ASIA WATANABE, MIKIMAKI, HIKARU SURUGA, HAJIME SHINJO, RENJURO KINDAICHI, AND YURI NARUSHIMA

A collection of chilling new *Parasyte* stories from Japan's top shojo artists!

Parasites: shape-shifting aliens whose only purpose is to assimilate with and consume the human race... but do these monsters have a different side? A parasite becomes a prince to save his romance-obsessed female host from a dangerous stalker. Another hosts a cooking show, in which the real monsters are revealed. These and 13 more stories, from some of the greatest shojo manga artists alive today, together make up a chilling, funny, and entertaining tribute to one of manga's horror classics!

KC
KODANSHA COMICS

New action series from Hiroyuki Takei, creator of the classic shonen franchise Shaman King!

In medieval Japan, a bell hanging on the collar is a sign that a c has a master. Norachiyo's bell hangs from his katana sheath, but he nonetheless a stray — a ronin. This one-eyed cat samurai travels across dishonest world, cutting through pretense and deception with his blade

By
Hiroyuki Takei

A Kodansha Comics Trade Paperback Original.

Published in the United States by Kodansha Comics, an imprint of Kodansha USA Publishing, LLC, New York.

Publication rights for this English edition arranged through Kodansha Ltd., Tokyo.

First published in Japan in 2016 by Kodansha Ltd., Tokyo, as *Aho Gaaru* volume 7.

ISBN 978-1-63236-611-5

Printed in the United States of America.

www.kodanshacomics.com

9 8 7 6 5 4 3 2 1

Translator: Karen McGillicuddy
Lettering: S. Lee
Editing: Paul Starr
Kodansha Comics edition cover design by Phil Balsman